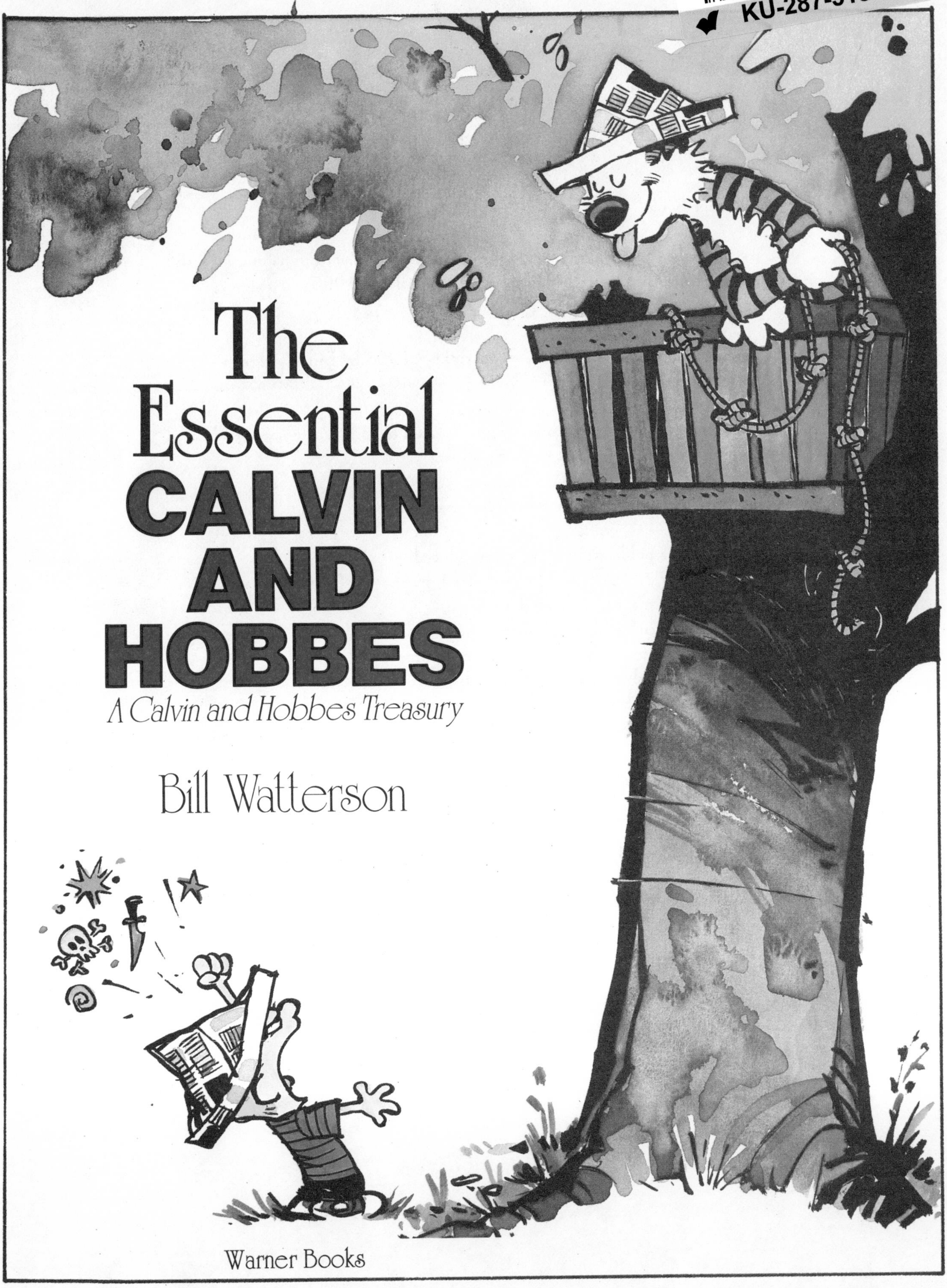

# The Essential CALVIN AND HOBBES

*A Calvin and Hobbes Treasury*

Bill Watterson

Warner Books

A *Warner* Book

First published in the United States by Andrews McMeel Publishing in 1988
First published in Great Britain by Warner Books in 1995
Reprinted 1996, 1997, 1998, 2000

*Calvin and Hobbes* is a cartoon feature created by Bill Watterson, syndicated
internationally by Universal Press Syndicate

The moral right of the author has been asserted

A CIP catalogue record for this book
is available from the British Library

ISBN 0 7515 1274 5

Printed and bound in Great Britain by
The Bath Press, Bath

Warner Books
A Division of
Little, Brown and Company (UK)
Brettenham House
Lancaster Place
London WC2E 7EN

# Foreword

Bill Watterson draws wonderful bedside tables. I admire that. He also draws great water splashes and living room couches and chairs and lamps and yawns and screams, and all the things that make a comic strip fun to look at. I like the thin little arms on Calvin and his shoes that look like dinner rolls.

Drawing in a comic strip is infinitely more important than we may think, for our medium must compete with other entertainments, and if a cartoonist does nothing more than illustrate a joke, he or she is going to lose.

Calvin and Hobbes, however, contains hilarious pictures that cannot be duplicated in other mediums. In short, it is fun to look at, and that is what has made Bill's work such an admirable success.

— CHARLES M. SCHULZ

TO TOM

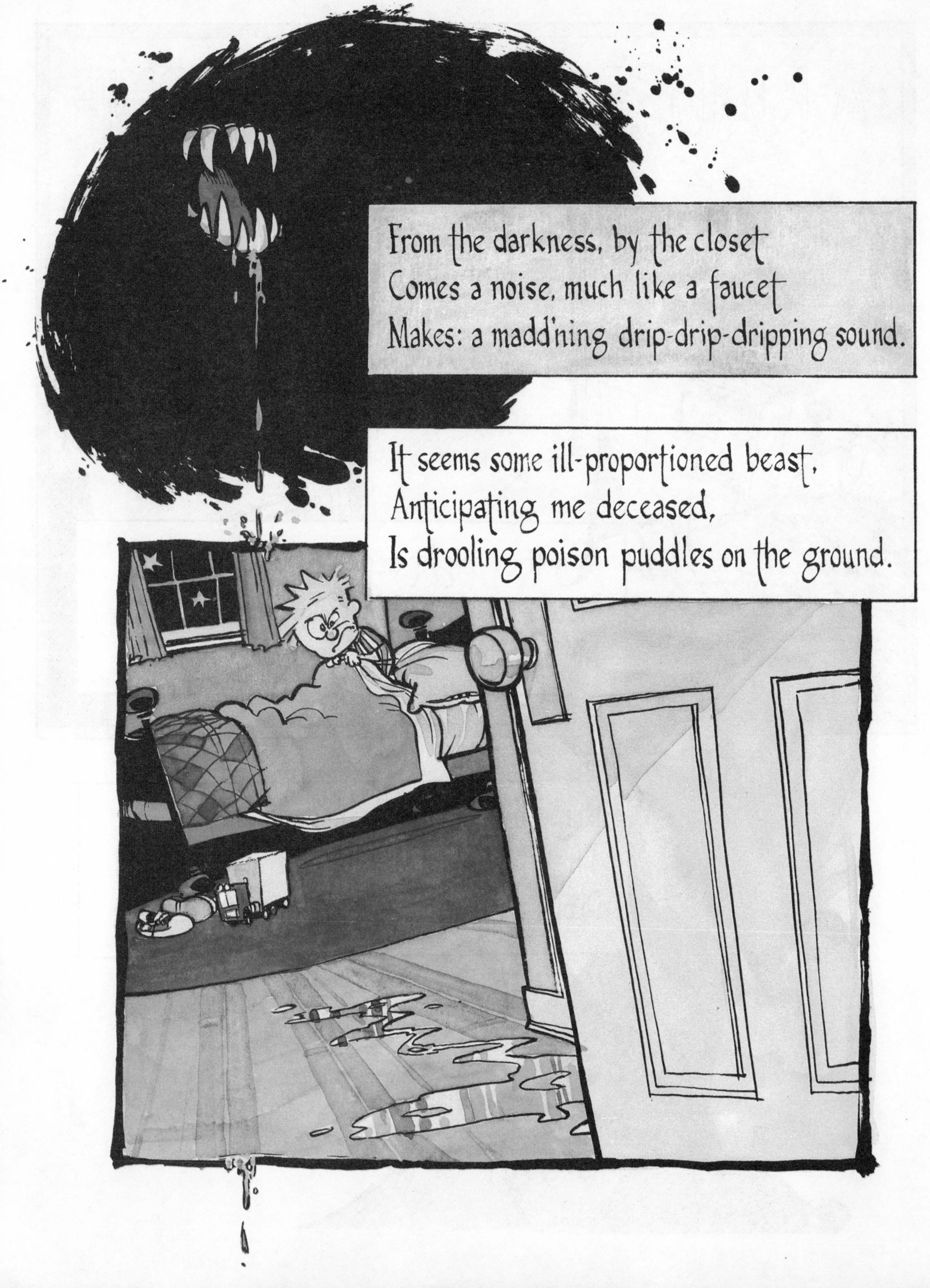
From the darkness, by the closet
Comes a noise, much like a faucet
Makes: a madd'ning drip-drip-dripping sound.
It seems some ill-proportioned beast,
Anticipating me deceased,
Is drooling poison puddles on the ground.

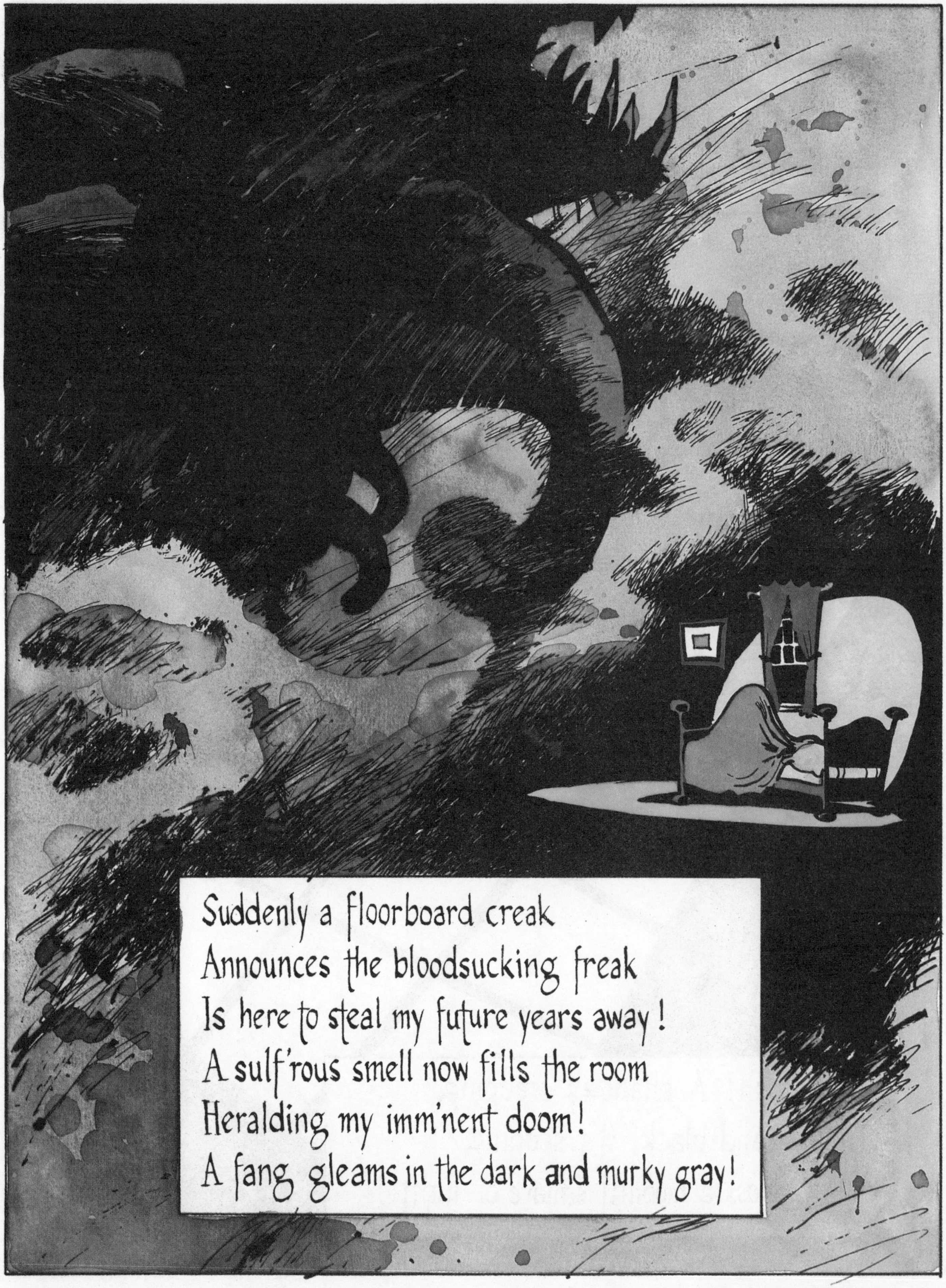
Suddenly a floorboard creak
Announces the bloodsucking freak
Is here to steal my future years away!
A sulf'rous smell now fills the room
Heralding my imm'nent doom!
A fang gleams in the dark and murky gray!

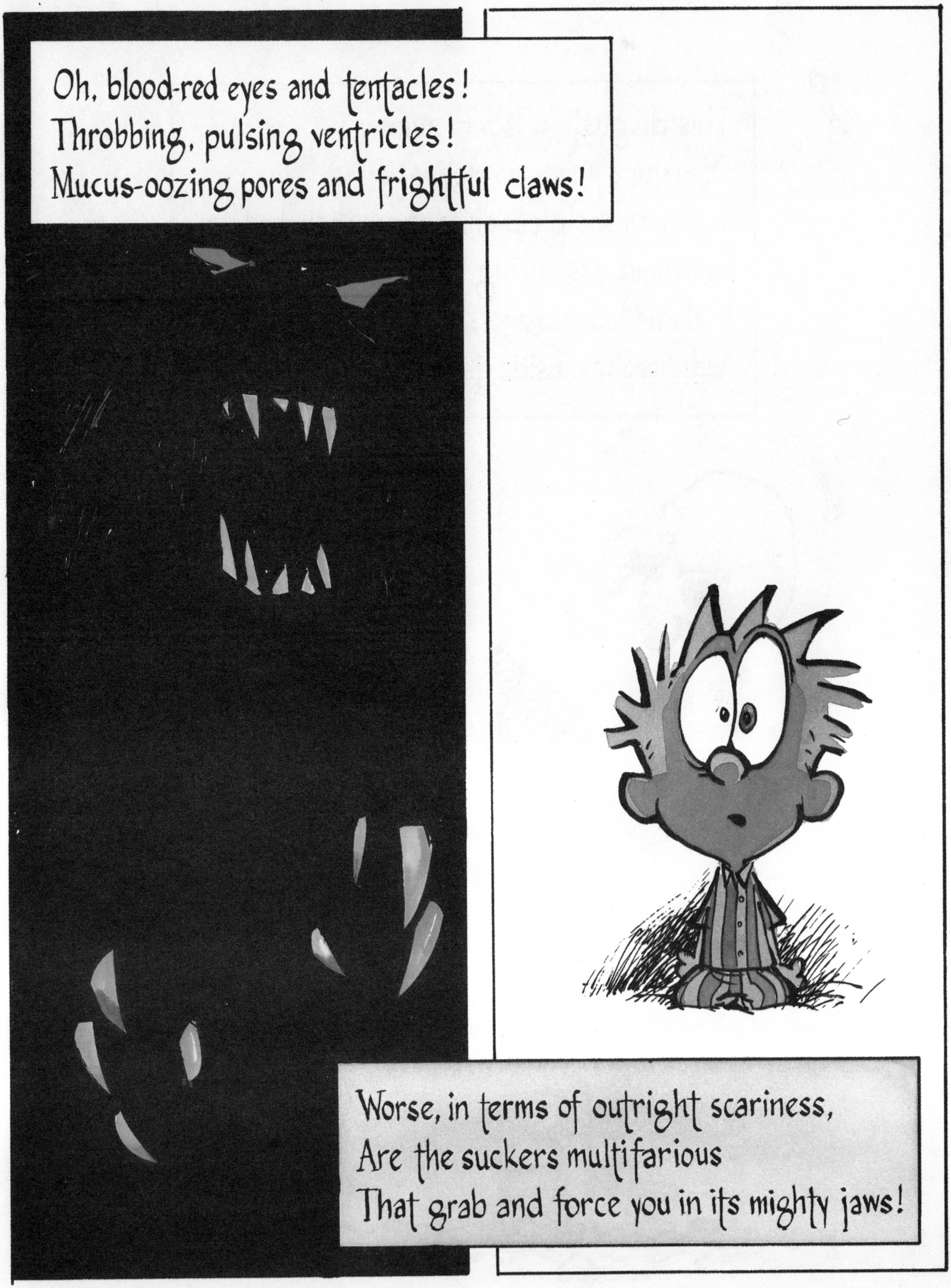
Oh, blood-red eyes and tentacles!
Throbbing, pulsing ventricles!
Mucus-oozing pores and frightful claws!
Worse, in terms of outright scariness,
Are the suckers multifarious
That grab and force you in its mighty jaws!

This disgusting aberration
Of nature needs no motivation
To devour helpless children in their beds.
Relishing despairing moans,
It chews kids up and sucks their bones,
And dissolves inside its mouth their li'l heads!

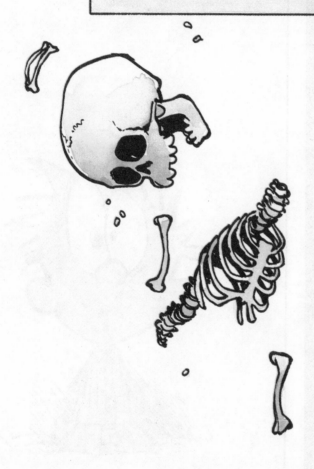

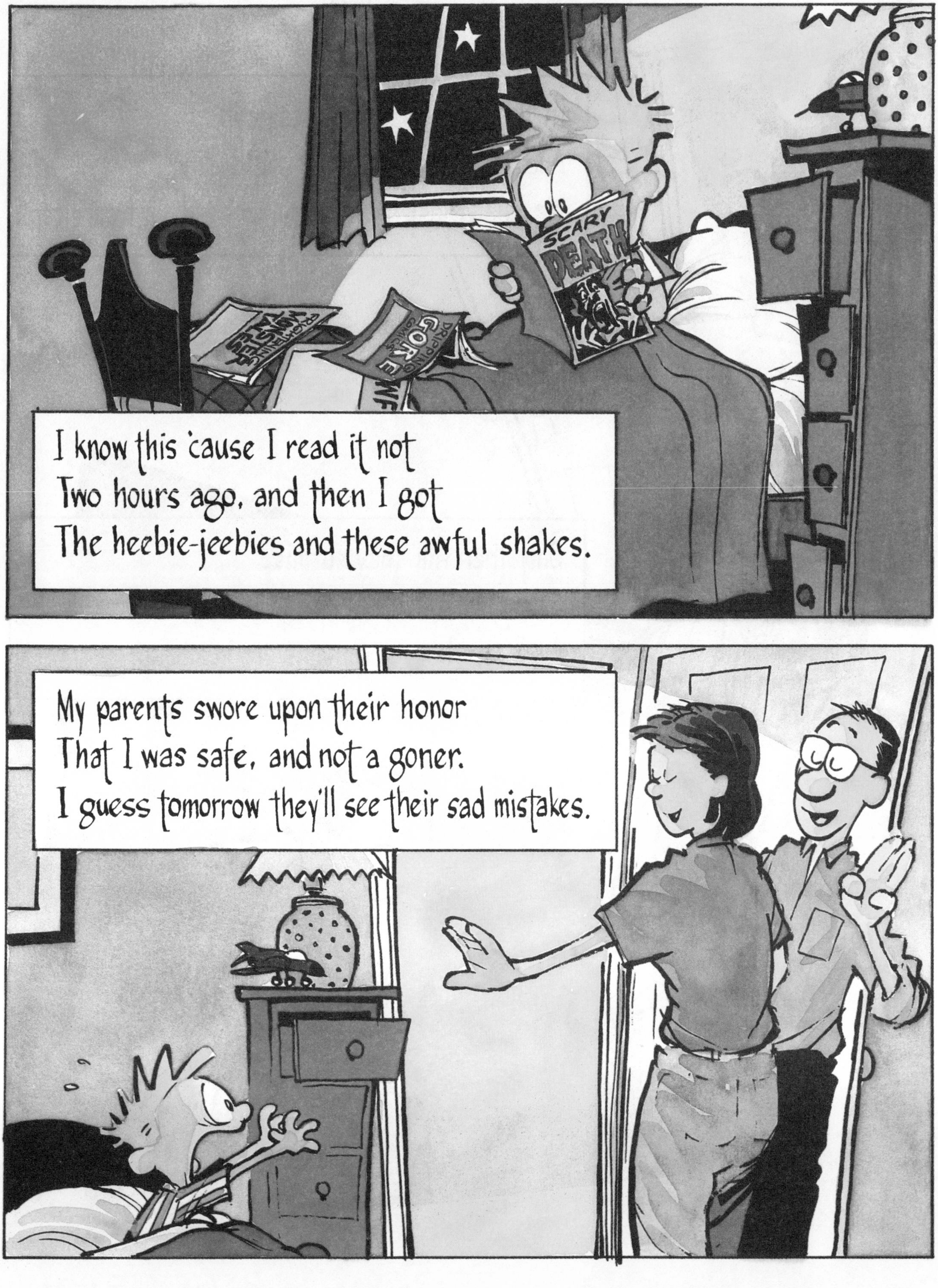
SCARY DEATH
I know this 'cause I read it not
Two hours ago, and then I got
The heebie-jeebies and these awful shakes.
My parents swore upon their honor
That I was safe, and not a goner.
I guess tomorrow they'll see their sad mistakes.

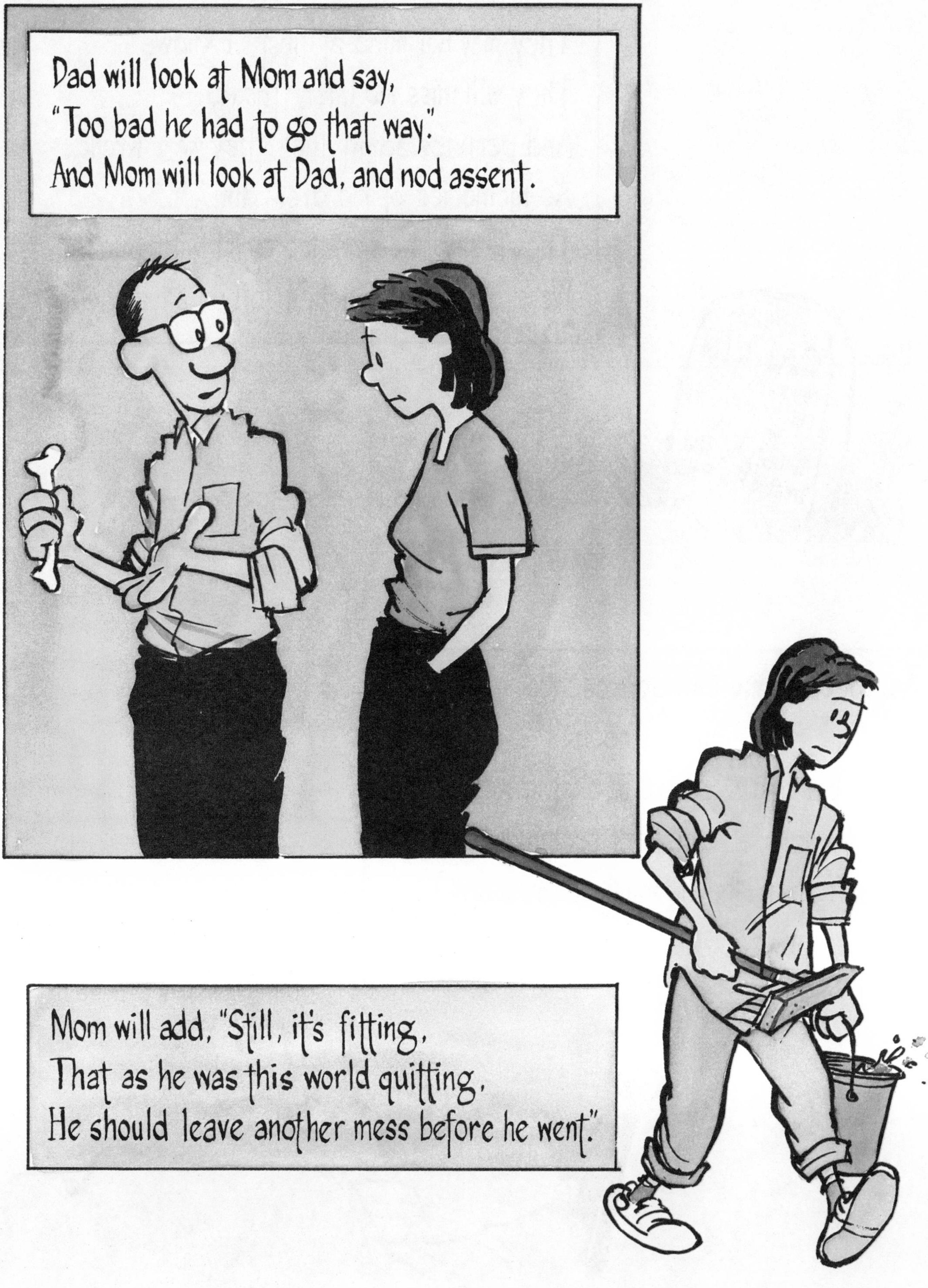
Dad will look at Mom and say,
"Too bad he had to go that way."
And Mom will look at Dad, and nod assent.
Mom will add, "Still, it's fitting,
That as he was this world quitting,
He should leave another mess before he went."

They may not mind at first, I know.
They will miss me later, though,
And perhaps admit that they were wrong.
As memories of me grow dim,
They'll say, "We were too strict with him.
We should have listened to him all along."

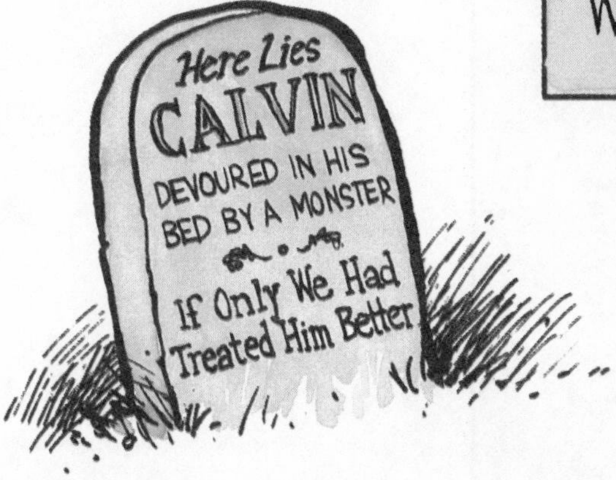
Here Lies
CALVIN
DEVOURED IN HIS
BED BY A MONSTER
If Only We Had
Treated Him Better

As speedily my end approaches,
I bid a final "buenas noches"
To my best friend here in all the world.
Gently snoring, whiskers seeming
To sniff at smells (he must be dreaming),
He lies snuggled in the blankets, curled.

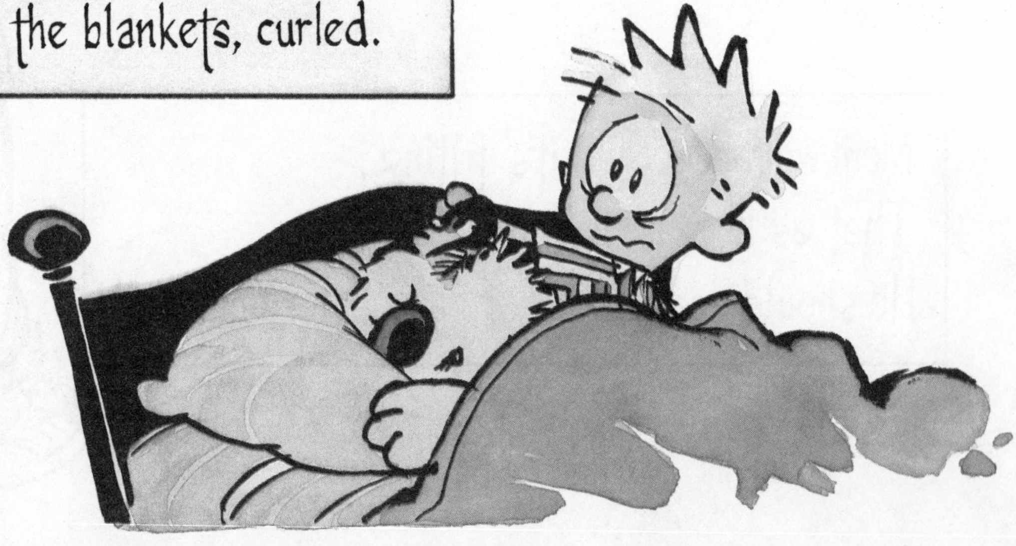

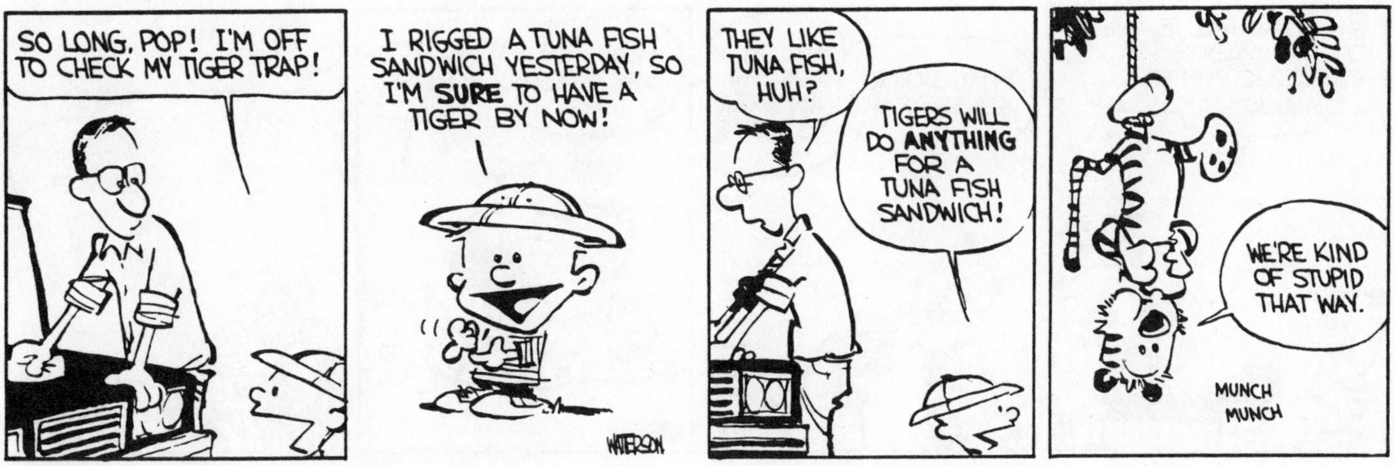
SO LONG, POP! I'M OFF TO CHECK MY TIGER TRAP!
I RIGGED A TUNA FISH SANDWICH YESTERDAY, SO I'M **SURE** TO HAVE A TIGER BY NOW!
WATTERSON
THEY LIKE TUNA FISH, HUH?
TIGERS WILL DO **ANYTHING** FOR A TUNA FISH SANDWICH!
WE'RE KIND OF STUPID THAT WAY.
MUNCH MUNCH

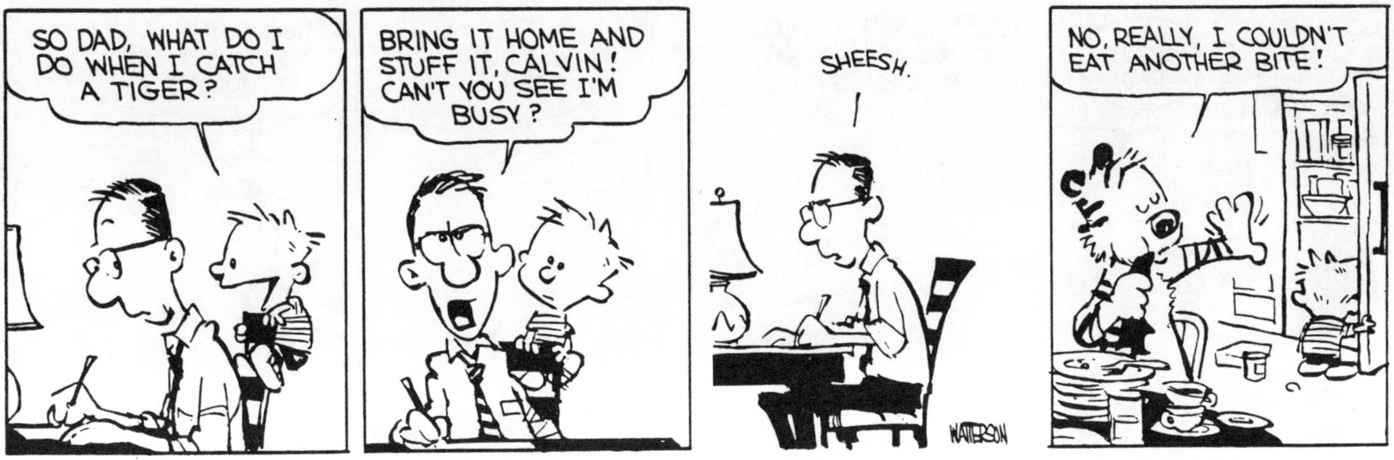
SO DAD, WHAT DO I DO WHEN I CATCH A TIGER?
BRING IT HOME AND STUFF IT, CALVIN! CAN'T YOU SEE I'M BUSY?
SHEESH.
WATTERSON
NO, REALLY, I COULDN'T EAT ANOTHER BITE!

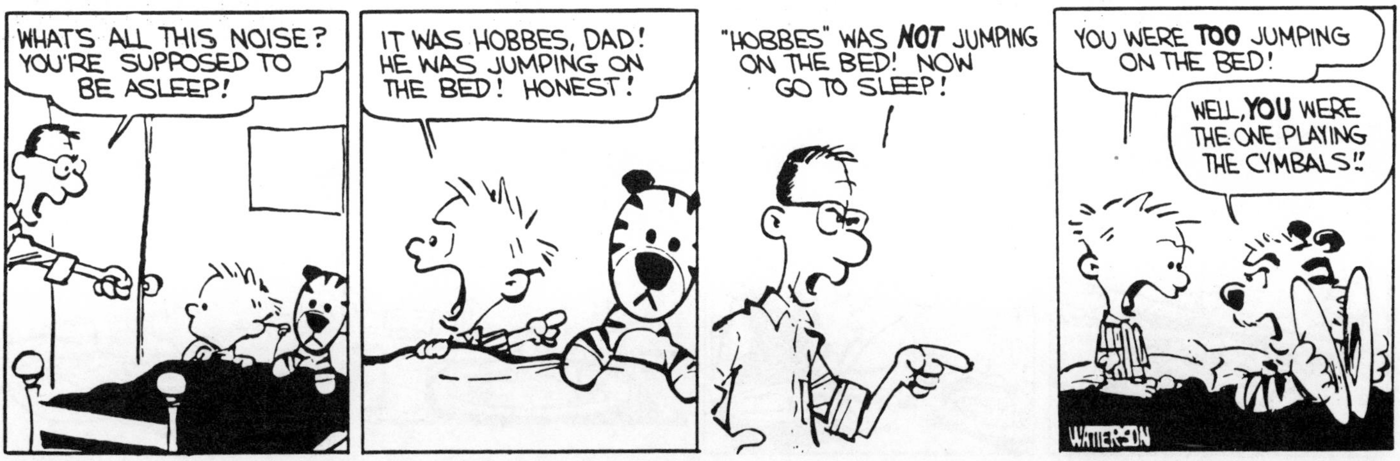
WHAT'S ALL THIS NOISE? YOU'RE SUPPOSED TO BE ASLEEP!
IT WAS HOBBES, DAD! HE WAS JUMPING ON THE BED! HONEST!
"HOBBES" WAS **NOT** JUMPING ON THE BED! NOW GO TO SLEEP!
YOU WERE **TOO** JUMPING ON THE BED!
WELL, **YOU** WERE THE ONE PLAYING THE CYMBALS!!
WATTERSON

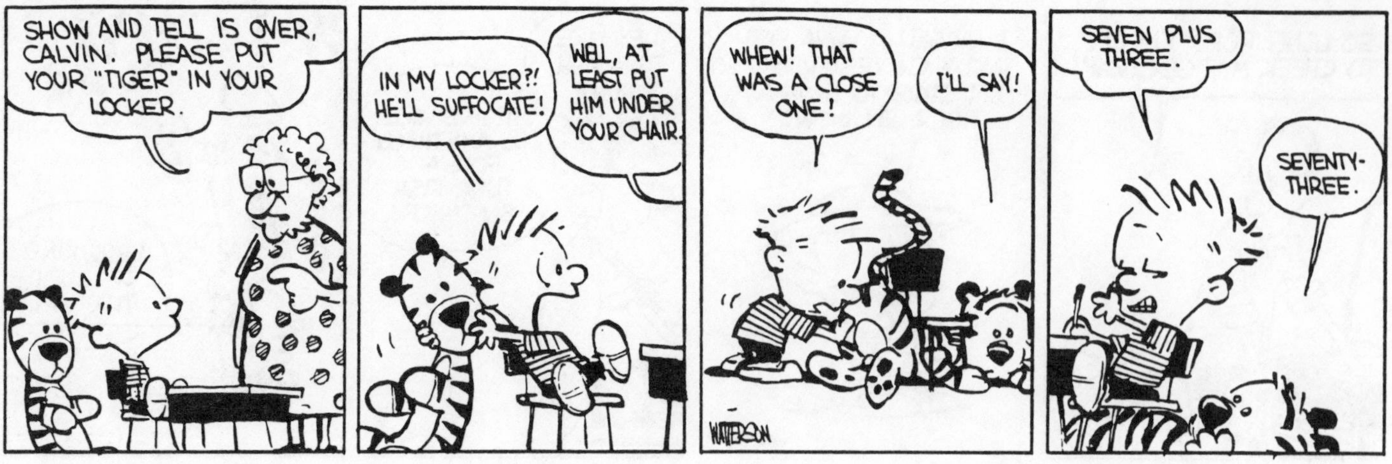
SHOW AND TELL IS OVER, CALVIN. PLEASE PUT YOUR "TIGER" IN YOUR LOCKER.
IN MY LOCKER?! HE'LL SUFFOCATE!
WELL, AT LEAST PUT HIM UNDER YOUR CHAIR.
WHEW! THAT WAS A CLOSE ONE!
I'LL SAY!
SEVEN PLUS THREE.
SEVENTY-THREE.
WATTERSON

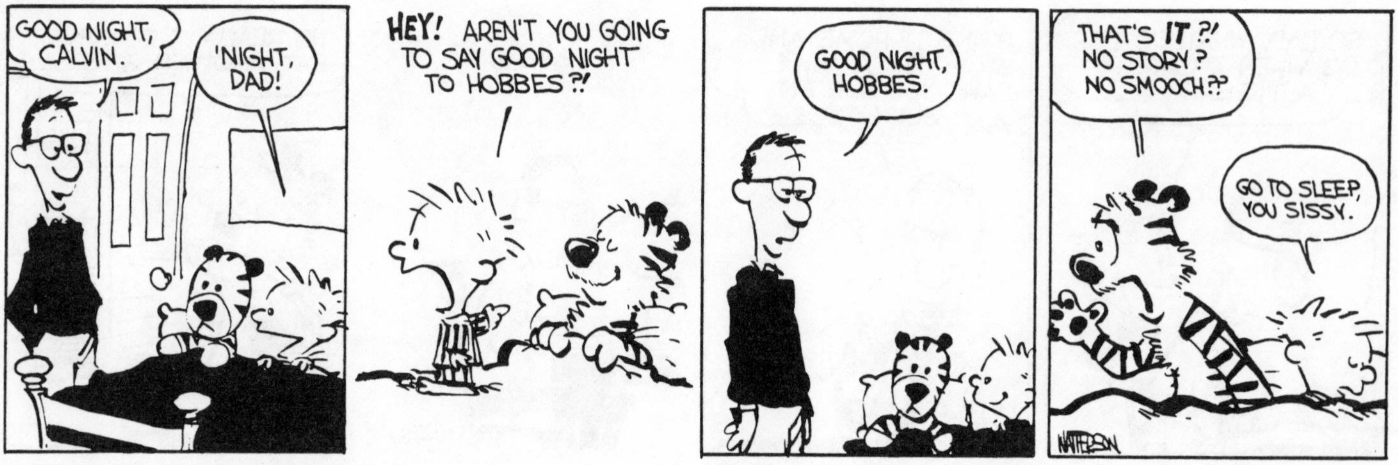
GOOD NIGHT, CALVIN.
'NIGHT, DAD!
HEY! AREN'T YOU GOING TO SAY GOOD NIGHT TO HOBBES?!
GOOD NIGHT, HOBBES.
THAT'S IT?! NO STORY? NO SMOOCH?!?
GO TO SLEEP, YOU SISSY.
WATTERSON

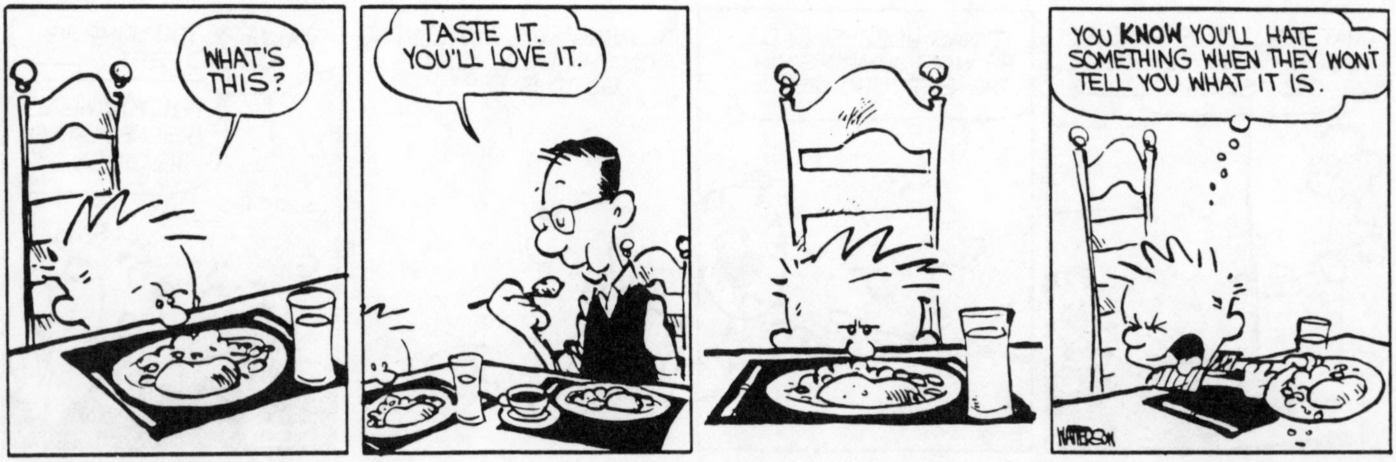
WHAT'S THIS?
TASTE IT. YOU'LL LOVE IT.
YOU KNOW YOU'LL HATE SOMETHING WHEN THEY WON'T TELL YOU WHAT IT IS.
WATTERSON

# Calvin and Hobbes by WATTERSON

OUTRAGE! WHY SHOULD I GO TO BED? I'M NOT TIRED! IT'S ONLY 7:30! THIS IS TYRANNY! I'M!

21

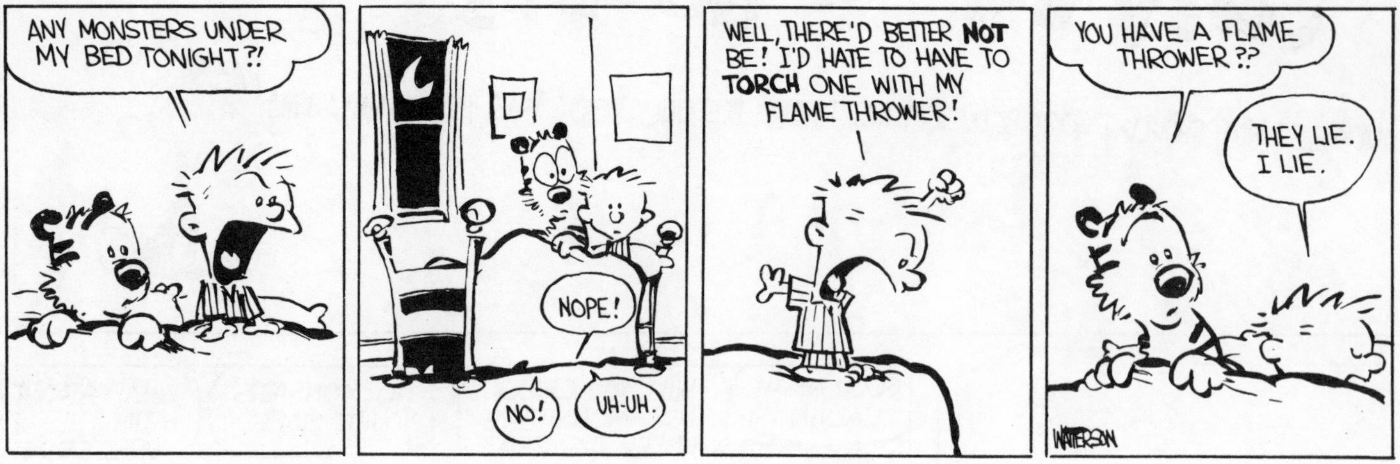
ANY MONSTERS UNDER MY BED TONIGHT?!
NOPE!
NO!
UH-UH.
WELL, THERE'D BETTER **NOT** BE! I'D HATE TO HAVE TO **TORCH** ONE WITH MY FLAME THROWER!
YOU HAVE A FLAME THROWER??
THEY LIE. I LIE.
WATTERSON

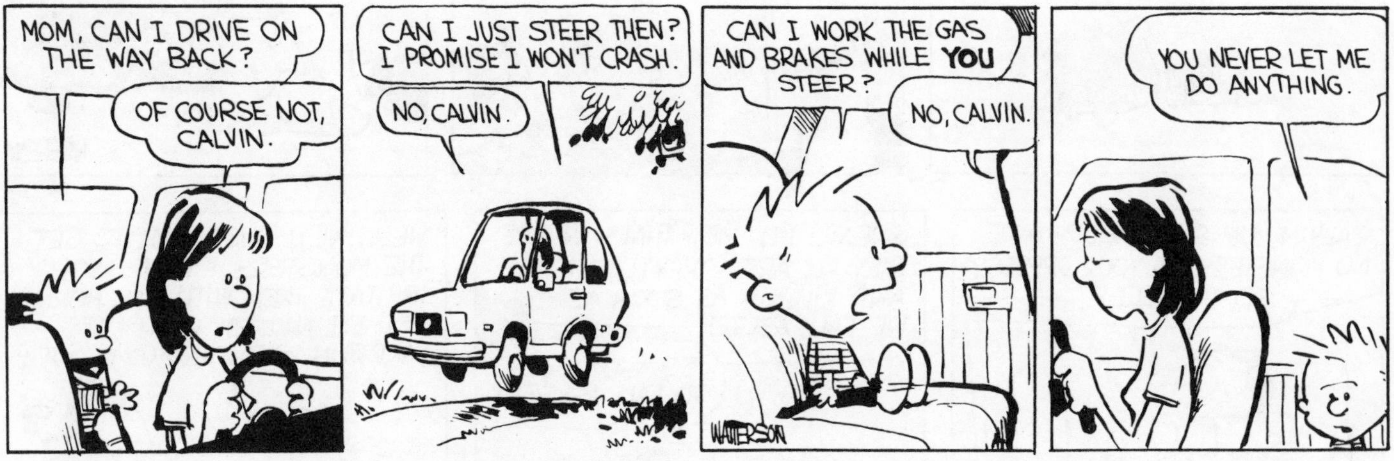
MOM, CAN I DRIVE ON THE WAY BACK?
OF COURSE NOT, CALVIN.
CAN I JUST STEER THEN? I PROMISE I WON'T CRASH.
NO, CALVIN.
CAN I WORK THE GAS AND BRAKES WHILE **YOU** STEER?
NO, CALVIN.
WATTERSON
YOU NEVER LET ME DO ANYTHING.

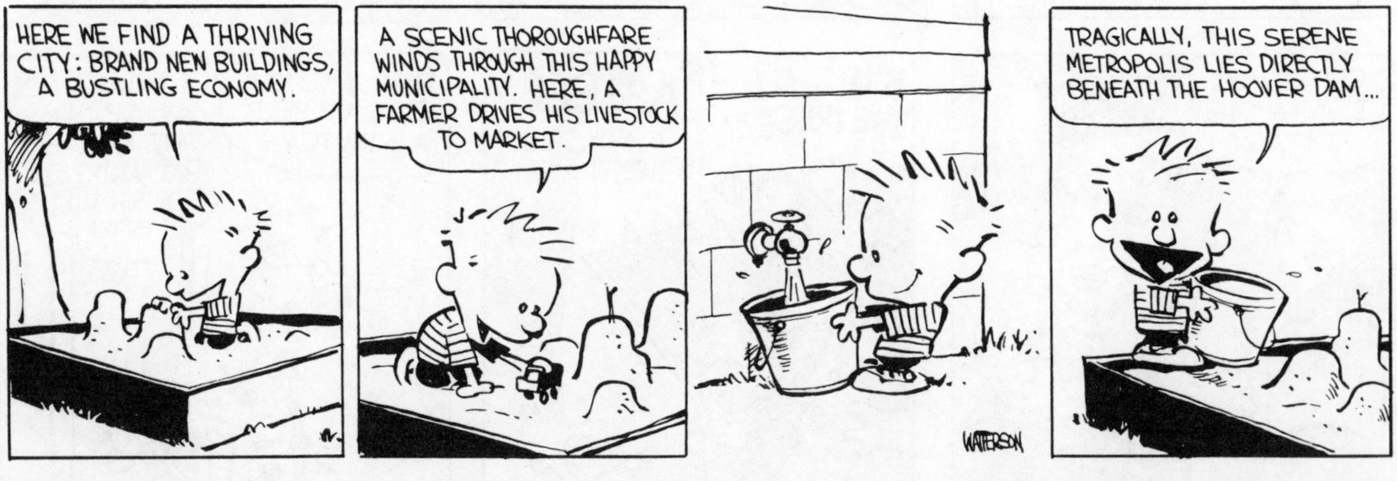
HERE WE FIND A THRIVING CITY: BRAND NEW BUILDINGS, A BUSTLING ECONOMY.
A SCENIC THOROUGHFARE WINDS THROUGH THIS HAPPY MUNICIPALITY. HERE, A FARMER DRIVES HIS LIVESTOCK TO MARKET.
WATTERSON
TRAGICALLY, THIS SERENE METROPOLIS LIES DIRECTLY BENEATH THE HOOVER DAM...

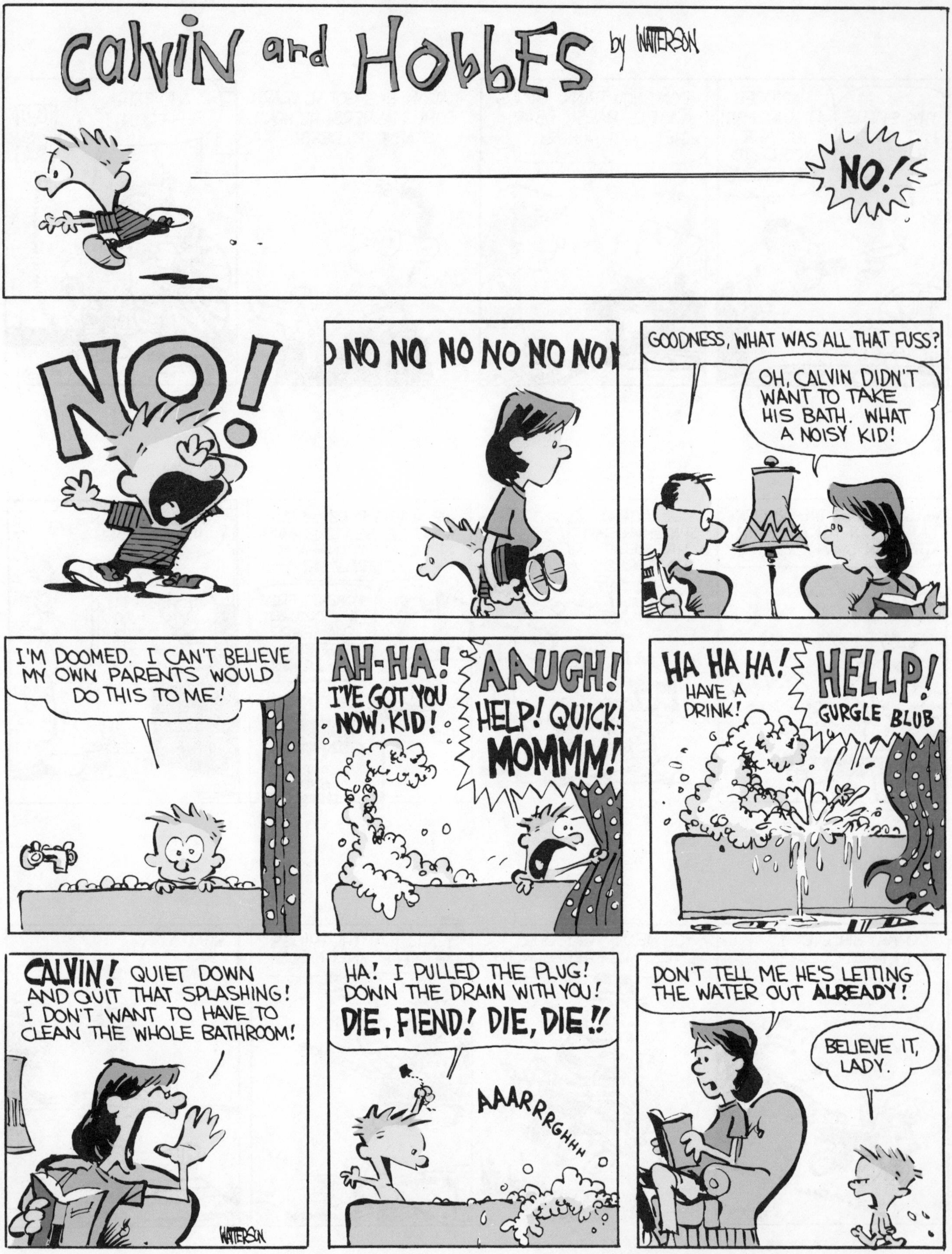
Calvin and Hobbes by WATTERSON
NO!
NO!
NO NO NO NO NO NO
GOODNESS, WHAT WAS ALL THAT FUSS?
OH, CALVIN DIDN'T WANT TO TAKE HIS BATH. WHAT A NOISY KID!
I'M DOOMED. I CAN'T BELIEVE MY OWN PARENTS WOULD DO THIS TO ME!
AH-HA! I'VE GOT YOU NOW, KID!
AAUGH! HELP! QUICK! MOMMM!
HA HA HA! HAVE A DRINK!
HELLP! GURGLE BLUB
CALVIN! QUIET DOWN AND QUIT THAT SPLASHING! I DON'T WANT TO HAVE TO CLEAN THE WHOLE BATHROOM!
WATTERSON
HA! I PULLED THE PLUG! DOWN THE DRAIN WITH YOU! DIE, FIEND! DIE, DIE!!
AAARRRGHHH
DON'T TELL ME HE'S LETTING THE WATER OUT ALREADY!
BELIEVE IT, LADY.

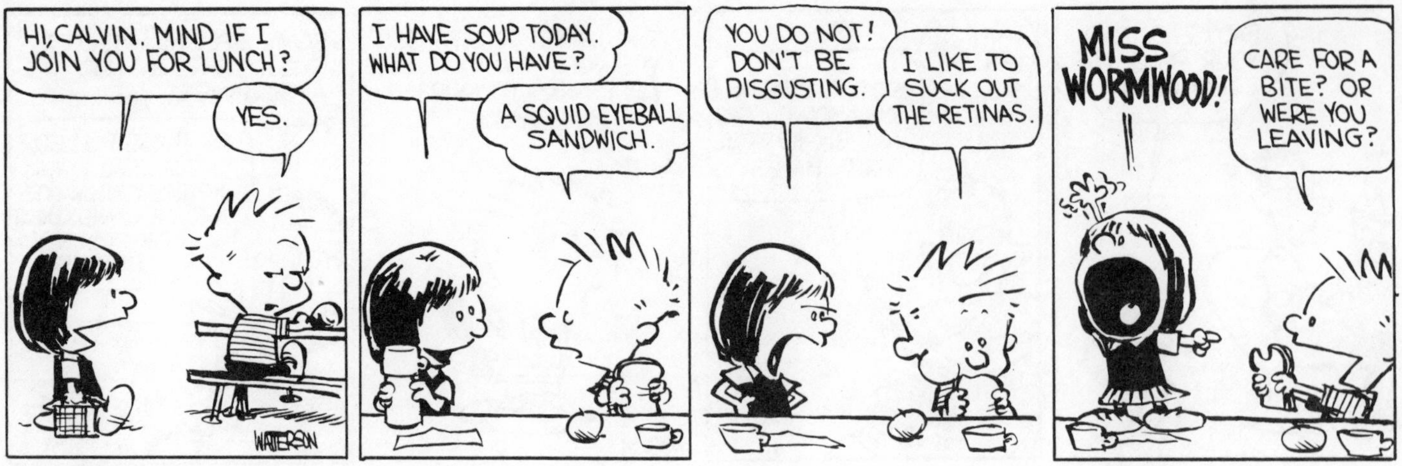
HI, CALVIN. MIND IF I JOIN YOU FOR LUNCH?
YES.
WATTERSON
I HAVE SOUP TODAY. WHAT DO YOU HAVE?
A SQUID EYEBALL SANDWICH.
YOU DO NOT! DON'T BE DISGUSTING.
I LIKE TO SUCK OUT THE RETINAS.
MISS WORMWOOD!
CARE FOR A BITE? OR WERE YOU LEAVING?

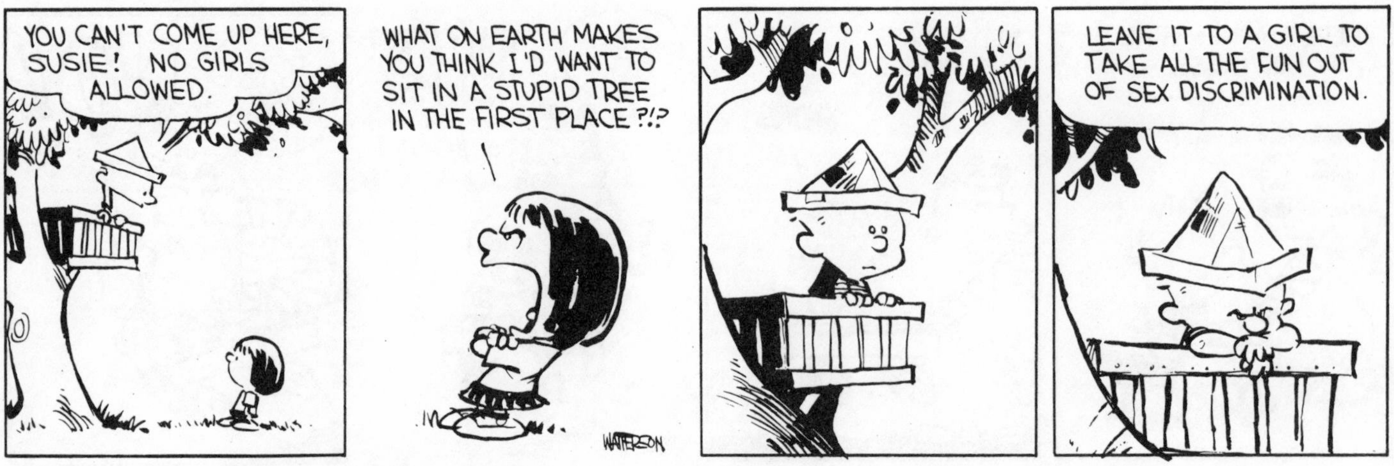
YOU CAN'T COME UP HERE, SUSIE! NO GIRLS ALLOWED.
WHAT ON EARTH MAKES YOU THINK I'D WANT TO SIT IN A STUPID TREE IN THE FIRST PLACE?!?
WATTERSON
LEAVE IT TO A GIRL TO TAKE ALL THE FUN OUT OF SEX DISCRIMINATION.

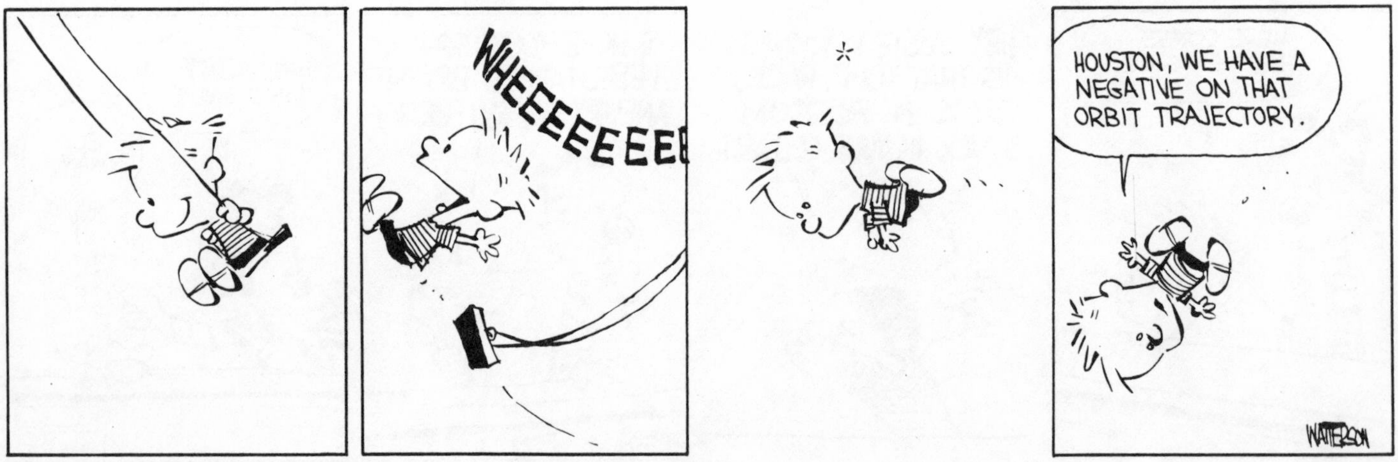
WHEEEEEEEEE
HOUSTON, WE HAVE A NEGATIVE ON THAT ORBIT TRAJECTORY.
WATTERSON

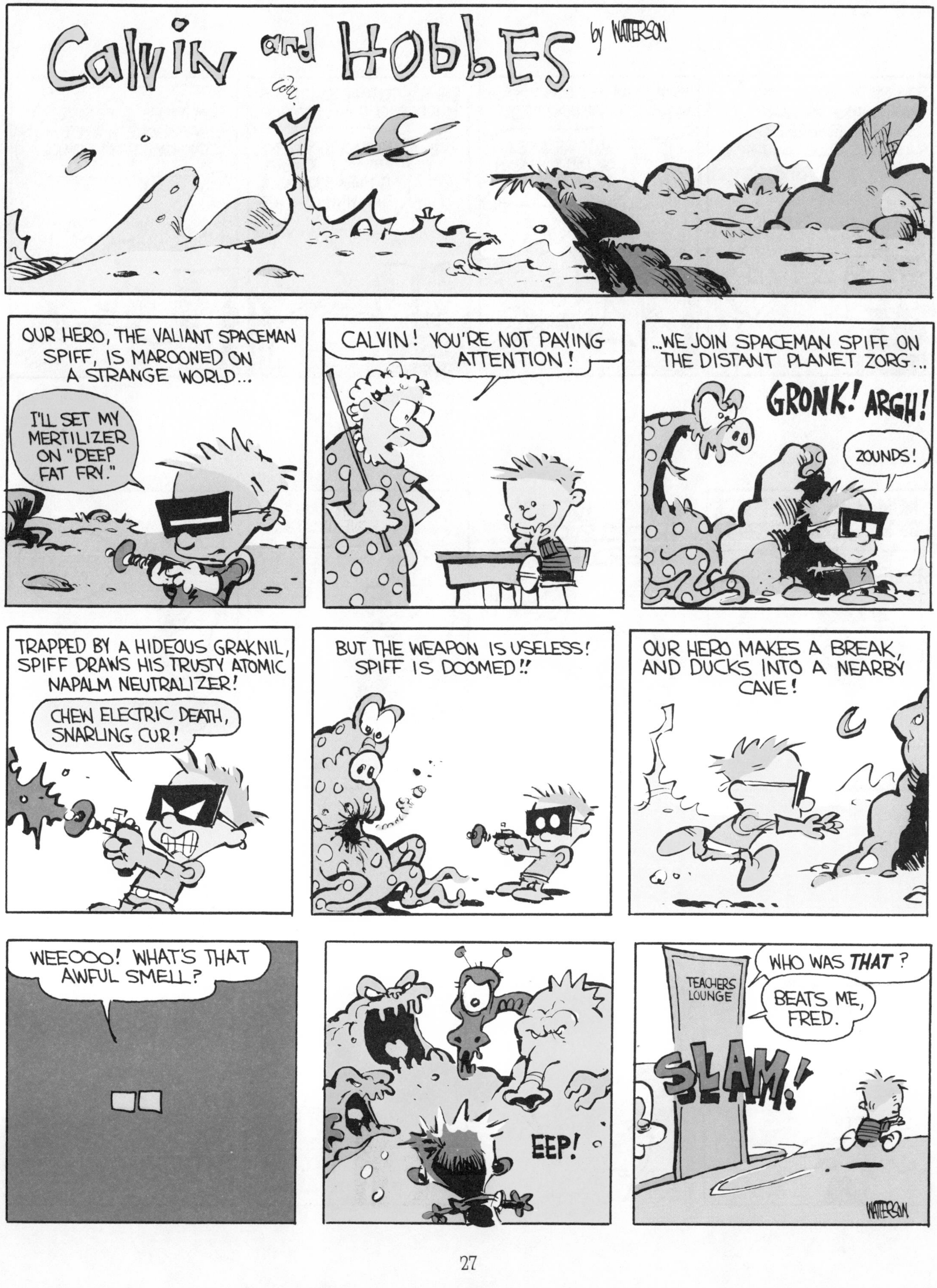
Calvin and Hobbes
by WATTERSON
OUR HERO, THE VALIANT SPACEMAN SPIFF, IS MAROONED ON A STRANGE WORLD...
I'LL SET MY MERTILIZER ON "DEEP FAT FRY."
CALVIN! YOU'RE NOT PAYING ATTENTION!
...WE JOIN SPACEMAN SPIFF ON THE DISTANT PLANET ZORG...
GRONK! ARGH!
ZOUNDS!
TRAPPED BY A HIDEOUS GRAKNIL, SPIFF DRAWS HIS TRUSTY ATOMIC NAPALM NEUTRALIZER!
CHEW ELECTRIC DEATH, SNARLING CUR!
BUT THE WEAPON IS USELESS! SPIFF IS DOOMED!!
OUR HERO MAKES A BREAK, AND DUCKS INTO A NEARBY CAVE!
WEEOOO! WHAT'S THAT AWFUL SMELL?
EEP!
TEACHERS LOUNGE
WHO WAS THAT ?
BEATS ME, FRED.
SLAM!
WATTERSON

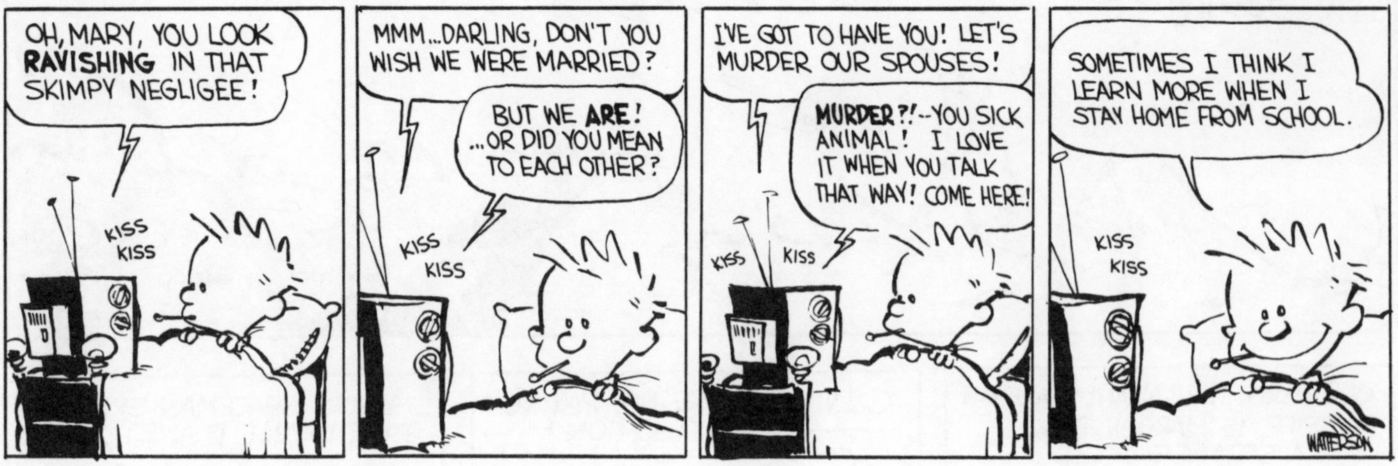
OH, MARY, YOU LOOK **RAVISHING** IN THAT SKIMPY NEGLIGEE!
KISS KISS
MMM...DARLING, DON'T YOU WISH WE WERE MARRIED?
BUT WE **ARE**! ...OR DID YOU MEAN TO EACH OTHER?
KISS KISS
I'VE GOT TO HAVE YOU! LET'S MURDER OUR SPOUSES!
**MURDER**?!--YOU SICK ANIMAL! I LOVE IT WHEN YOU TALK THAT WAY! COME HERE!
KISS KISS
SOMETIMES I THINK I LEARN MORE WHEN I STAY HOME FROM SCHOOL.
KISS KISS
WATTERSON

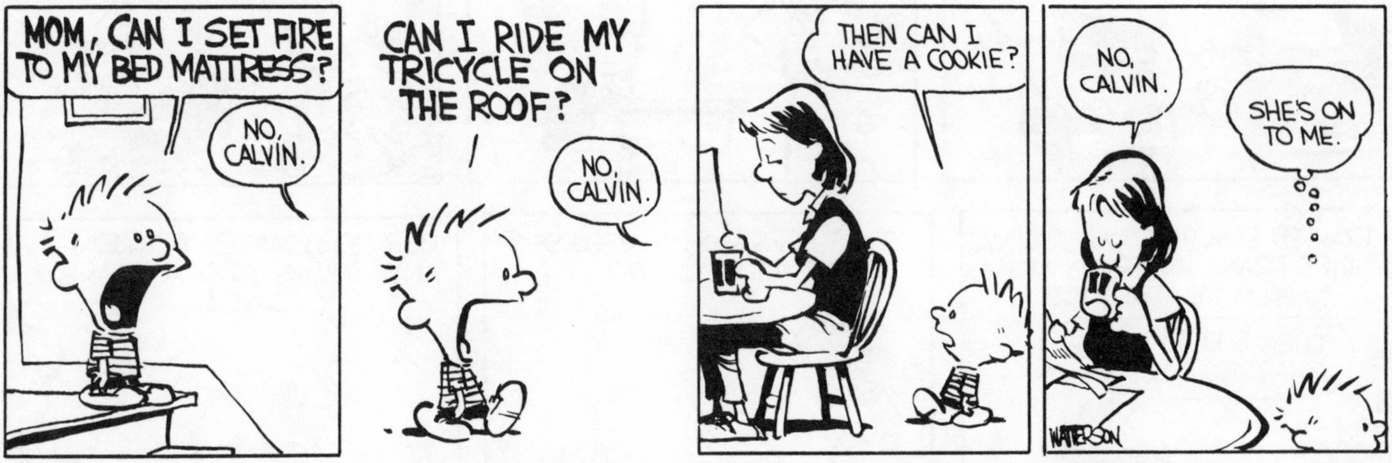
MOM, CAN I SET FIRE TO MY BED MATTRESS?
NO, CALVIN.
CAN I RIDE MY TRICYCLE ON THE ROOF?
NO, CALVIN.
THEN CAN I HAVE A COOKIE?
NO, CALVIN.
SHE'S ON TO ME.
WATTERSON

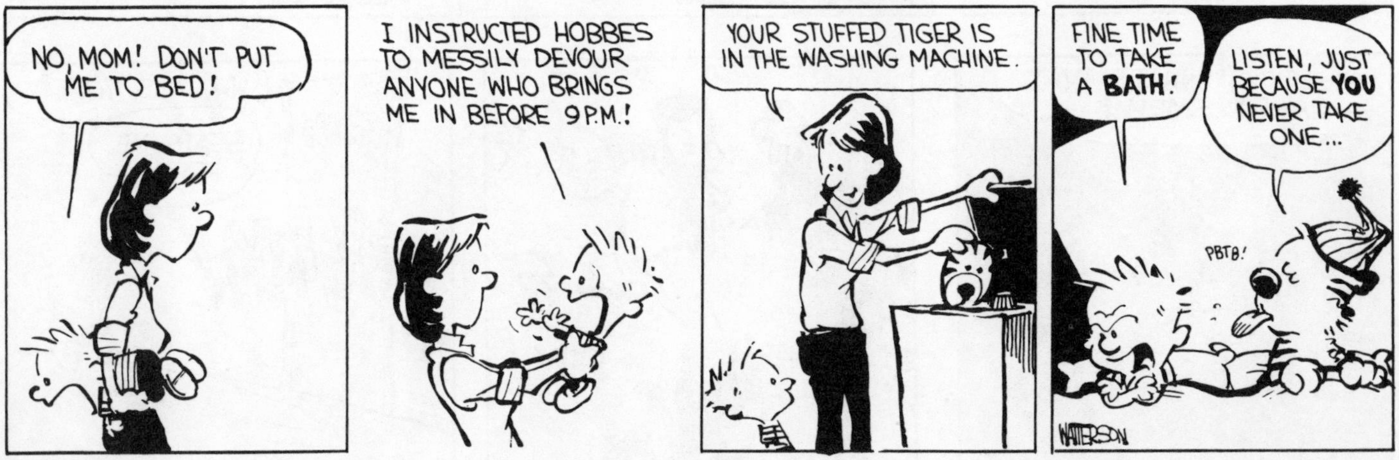
NO, MOM! DON'T PUT ME TO BED!
I INSTRUCTED HOBBES TO MESSILY DEVOUR ANYONE WHO BRINGS ME IN BEFORE 9 P.M.!
YOUR STUFFED TIGER IS IN THE WASHING MACHINE.
FINE TIME TO TAKE A **BATH**!
LISTEN, JUST BECAUSE **YOU** NEVER TAKE ONE...
PBTB!
WATTERSON

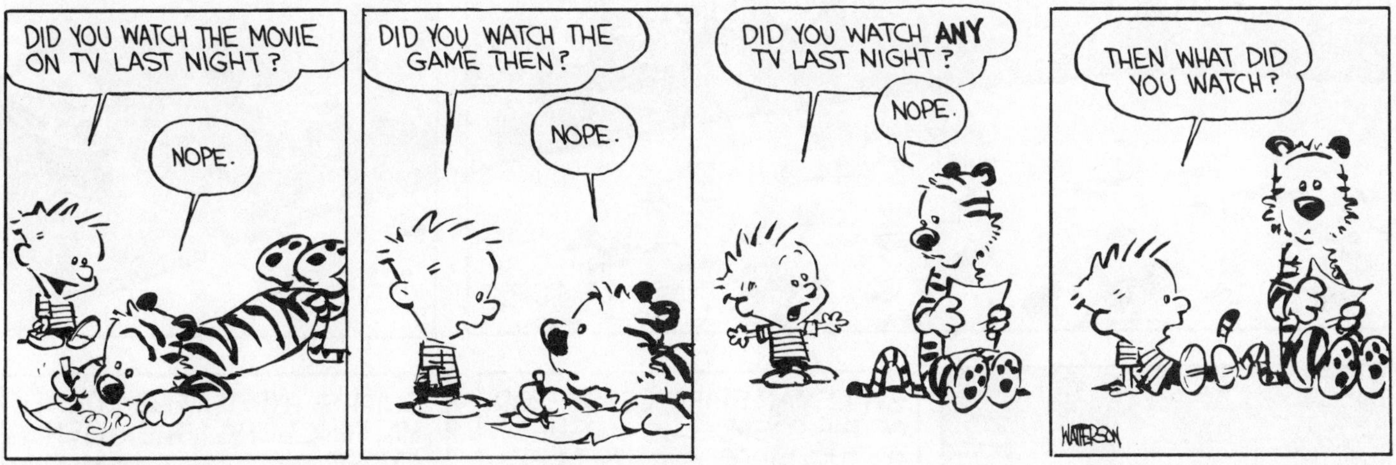
DID YOU WATCH THE MOVIE ON TV LAST NIGHT?
NOPE.
DID YOU WATCH THE GAME THEN?
NOPE.
DID YOU WATCH **ANY** TV LAST NIGHT?
NOPE.
THEN WHAT DID YOU WATCH?
WATTERSON

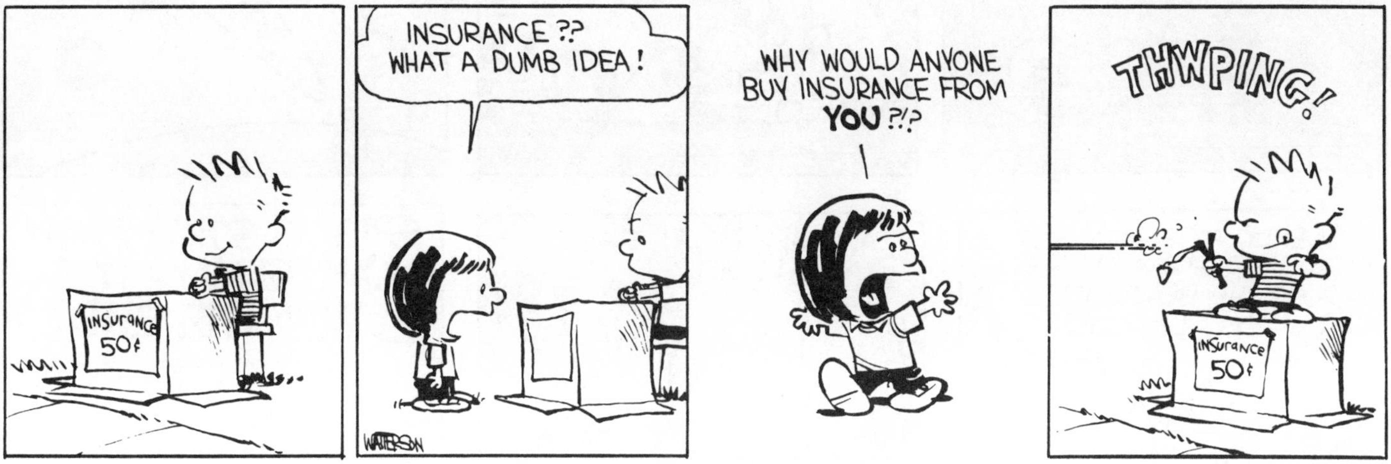
INSURANCE 50¢
INSURANCE ?? WHAT A DUMB IDEA!
WATTERSON
WHY WOULD ANYONE BUY INSURANCE FROM **YOU** ?!?
THWPING!
INSURANCE 50¢

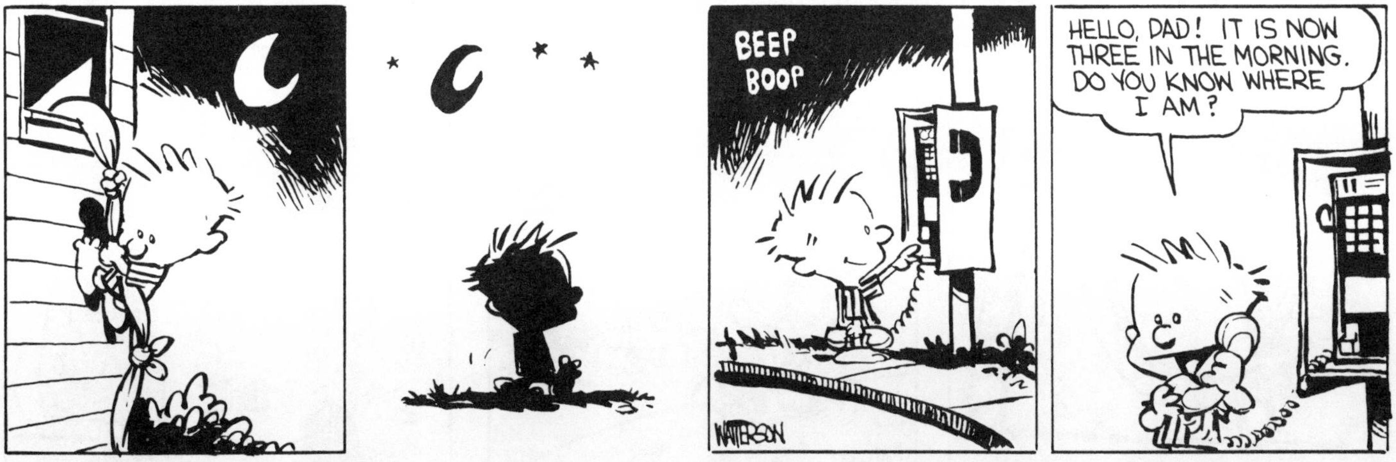
BEEP
BOOP
WATTERSON
HELLO, DAD! IT IS NOW THREE IN THE MORNING. DO YOU KNOW WHERE I AM?

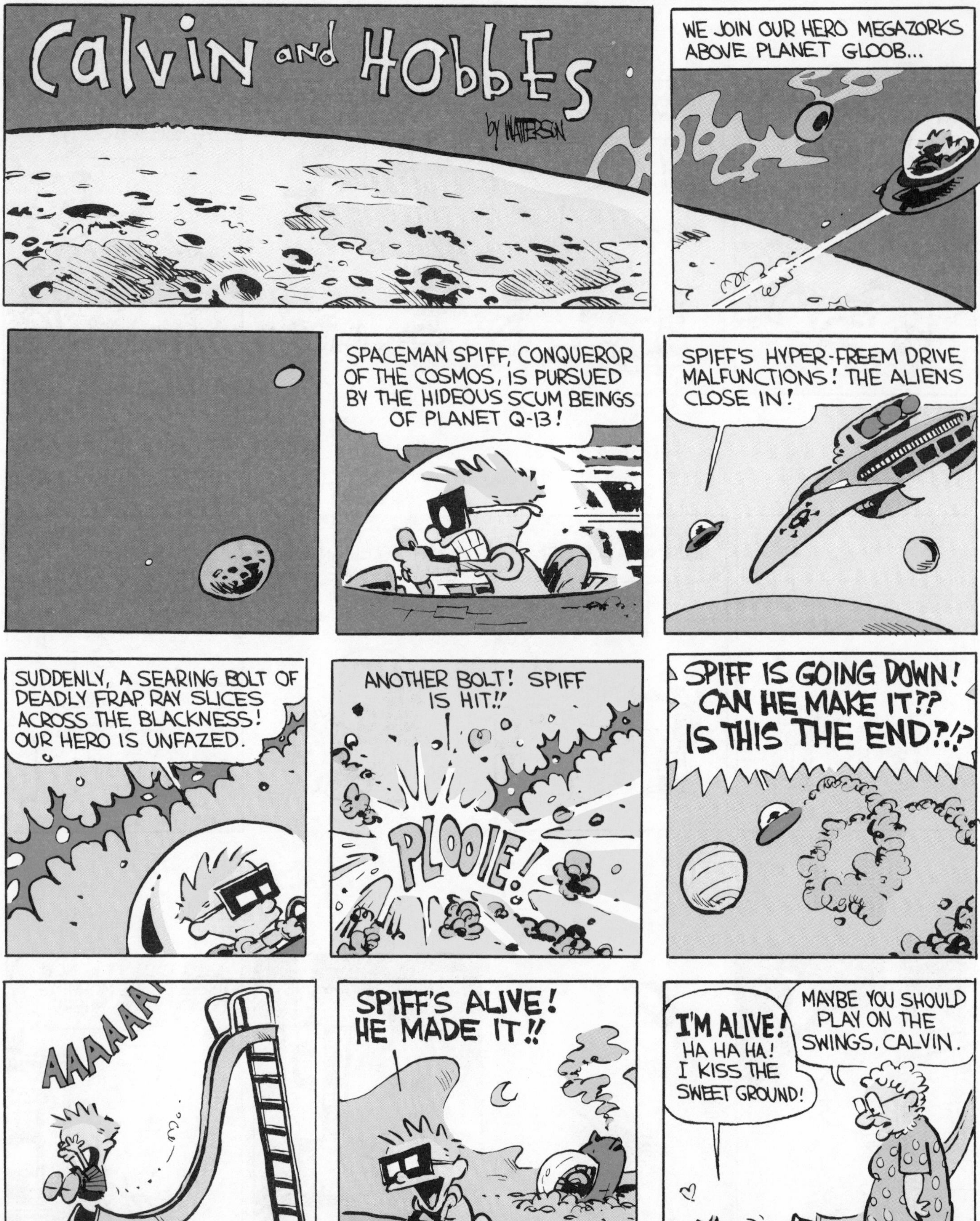
Calvin and HOBBES
by WATTERSON
WE JOIN OUR HERO MEGAZORKS ABOVE PLANET GLOOB...
SPACEMAN SPIFF, CONQUEROR OF THE COSMOS, IS PURSUED BY THE HIDEOUS SCUM BEINGS OF PLANET Q-13!
SPIFF'S HYPER-FREEM DRIVE MALFUNCTIONS! THE ALIENS CLOSE IN!
SUDDENLY, A SEARING BOLT OF DEADLY FRAP RAY SLICES ACROSS THE BLACKNESS! OUR HERO IS UNFAZED.
ANOTHER BOLT! SPIFF IS HIT!!
PLOOIE!
SPIFF IS GOING DOWN! CAN HE MAKE IT?? IS THIS THE END?!?
AAAAAA
SPIFF'S ALIVE! HE MADE IT!!
WATTERSON
I'M ALIVE! HA HA HA! I KISS THE SWEET GROUND!
MAYBE YOU SHOULD PLAY ON THE SWINGS, CALVIN.

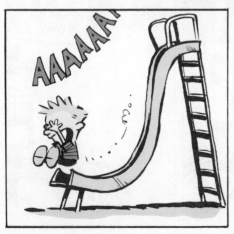

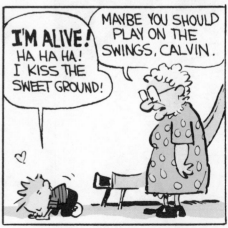

CALVIN, ARE YOU GOING TO TAKE THAT STUFFED TIGER TO SCHOOL AGAIN?

SURE.

DON'T THE KIDS MAKE FUN OF YOU?

TOMMY CHESNUTT DID ONCE, AND NOW NOBODY DOES.

WHY, WHAT HAPPENED TO TOMMY CHESNUTT?

HOBBES ATE HIM!

UGH! HE NEEDED A BATH, TOO...

CALVIN! WHAT'S ALL THIS NOISE?! YOU'RE SUPPOSED TO BE ASLEEP!

MONSTERS UNDER THE BED, DAD! I WAS WHACKING ONE WITH MY BASEBALL BAT!

GOODNESS CALVIN, IT'S JUST YOUR STUFFED TIGER! YOU SHOULD PUT AWAY YOUR TOYS!

SORRY, OL' BUDDY. GOOD THING I MISSED OCCASIONALLY, HUH?

YEAH. LET ME SEE YOUR BAT A MINUTE.

HERE COMES THE SPORTS CAR AT 200 MILES PER HOUR!

HERE COMES A CEMENT TRUCK! LOOK OUT!

AND HERE COMES AN INFLAMMABLE CHEMICAL TRUCK! OH NO!!

THIS OUGHT TO BE GOOD..

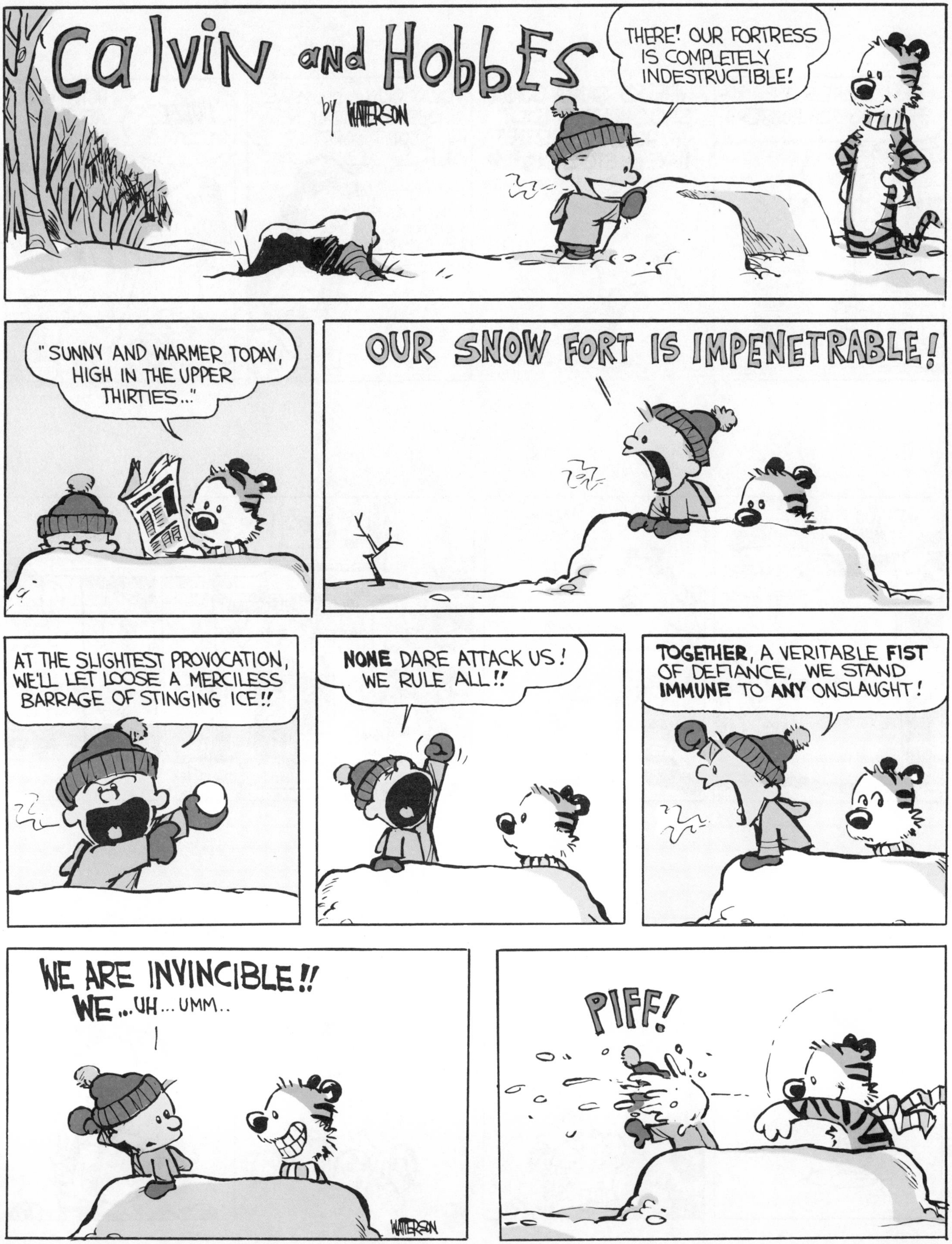

Calvin and Hobbes
by WATTERSON
THERE! OUR FORTRESS IS COMPLETELY INDESTRUCTIBLE!
"SUNNY AND WARMER TODAY, HIGH IN THE UPPER THIRTIES..."
OUR SNOW FORT IS IMPENETRABLE!
AT THE SLIGHTEST PROVOCATION, WE'LL LET LOOSE A MERCILESS BARRAGE OF STINGING ICE!!
NONE DARE ATTACK US! WE RULE ALL!!
TOGETHER, A VERITABLE FIST OF DEFIANCE, WE STAND IMMUNE TO ANY ONSLAUGHT!
WE ARE INVINCIBLE!! WE...UH...UMM..
WATTERSON
PIFF!

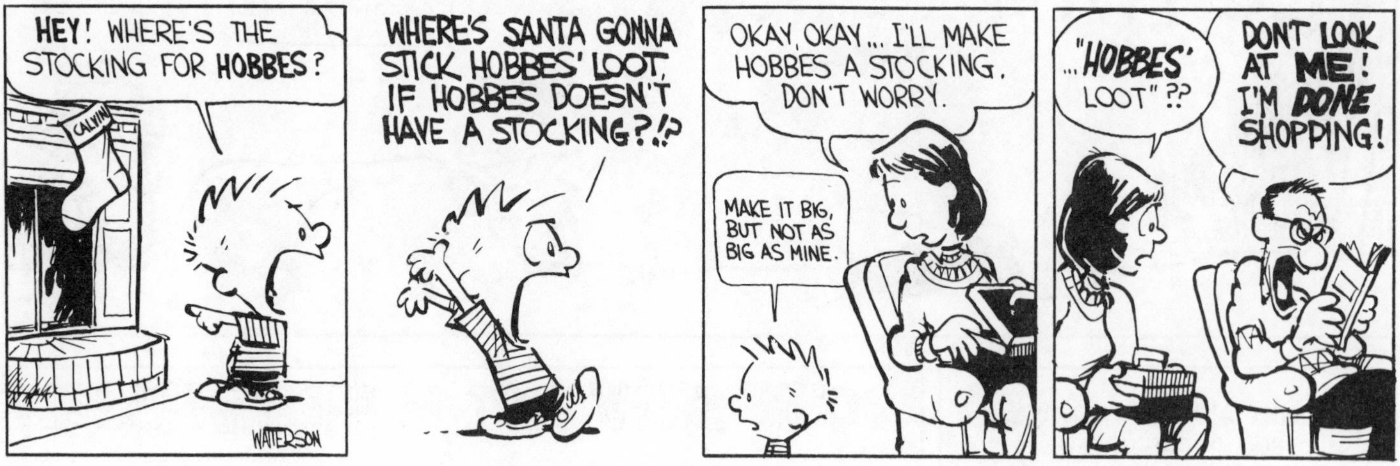
HEY! WHERE'S THE STOCKING FOR HOBBES?
WHERE'S SANTA GONNA STICK HOBBES' LOOT, IF HOBBES DOESN'T HAVE A STOCKING?!?
OKAY, OKAY... I'LL MAKE HOBBES A STOCKING. DON'T WORRY.
MAKE IT BIG, BUT NOT AS BIG AS MINE.
..."HOBBES' LOOT"??
DON'T LOOK AT ME! I'M DONE SHOPPING!
WATTERSON

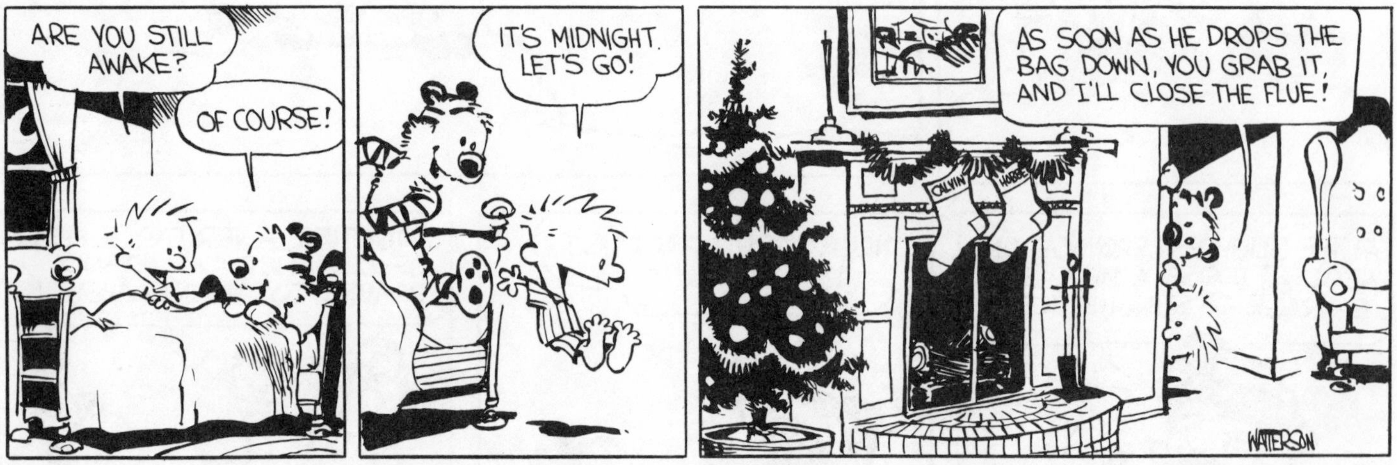
ARE YOU STILL AWAKE?
OF COURSE!
IT'S MIDNIGHT. LET'S GO!
AS SOON AS HE DROPS THE BAG DOWN, YOU GRAB IT, AND I'LL CLOSE THE FLUE!
WATTERSON

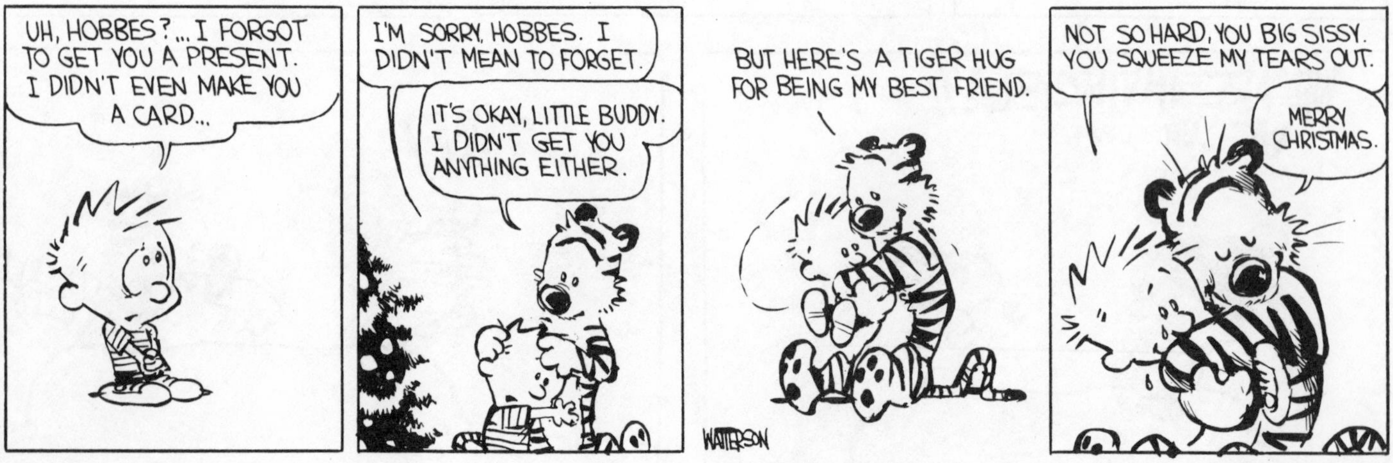
UH, HOBBES?... I FORGOT TO GET YOU A PRESENT. I DIDN'T EVEN MAKE YOU A CARD...
I'M SORRY, HOBBES. I DIDN'T MEAN TO FORGET.
IT'S OKAY, LITTLE BUDDY. I DIDN'T GET YOU ANYTHING EITHER.
BUT HERE'S A TIGER HUG FOR BEING MY BEST FRIEND.
NOT SO HARD, YOU BIG SISSY. YOU SQUEEZE MY TEARS OUT.
MERRY CHRISTMAS.
WATTERSON

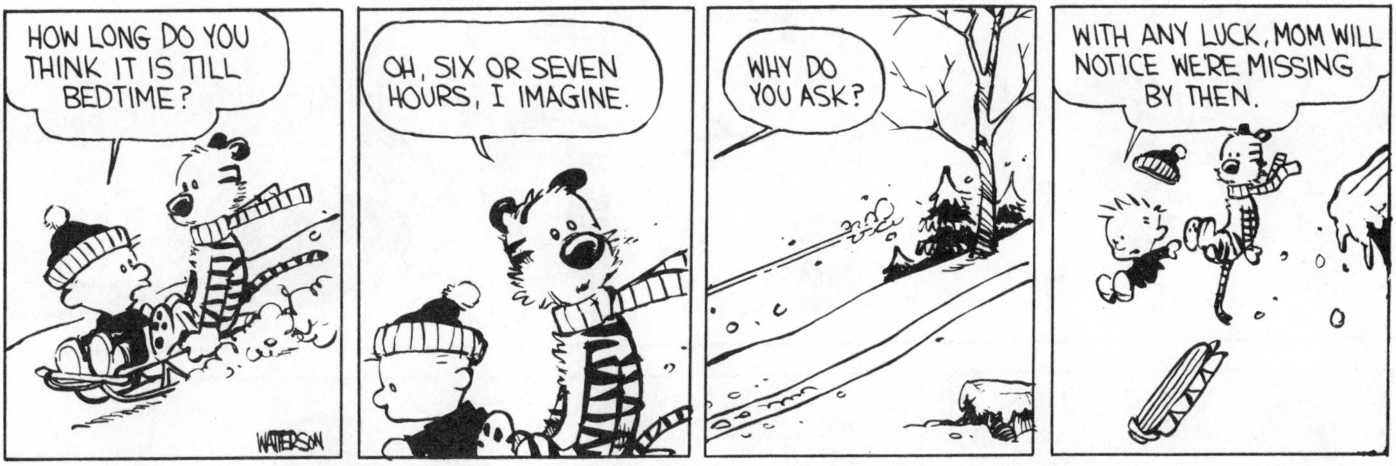
HOW LONG DO YOU THINK IT IS TILL BEDTIME?
OH, SIX OR SEVEN HOURS, I IMAGINE.
WHY DO YOU ASK?
WITH ANY LUCK, MOM WILL NOTICE WE'RE MISSING BY THEN.
WATTERSON

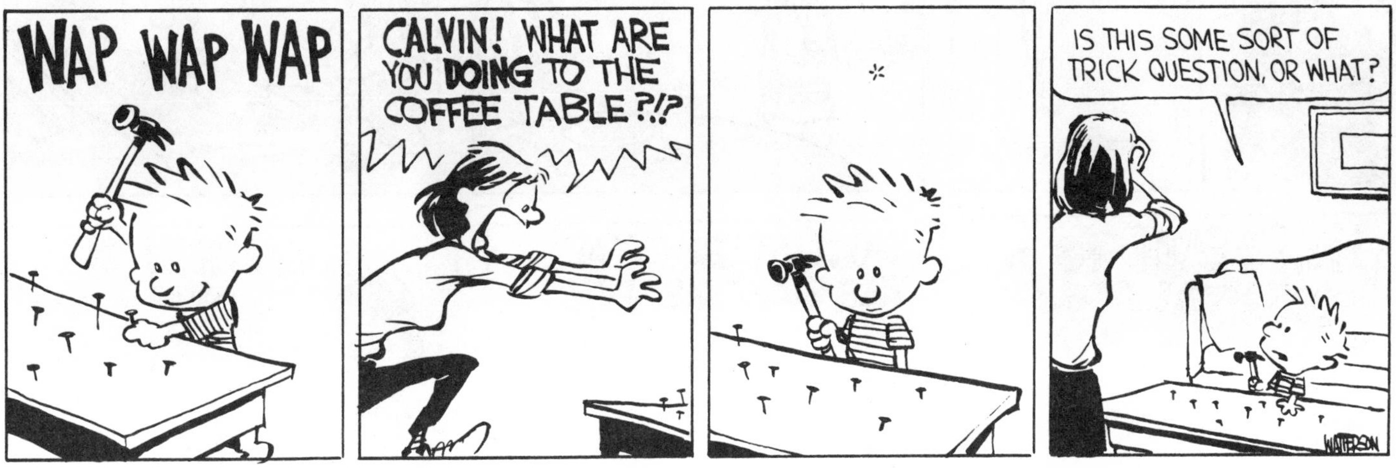
WAP WAP WAP
CALVIN! WHAT ARE YOU DOING TO THE COFFEE TABLE?!?
IS THIS SOME SORT OF TRICK QUESTION, OR WHAT?
WATTERSON

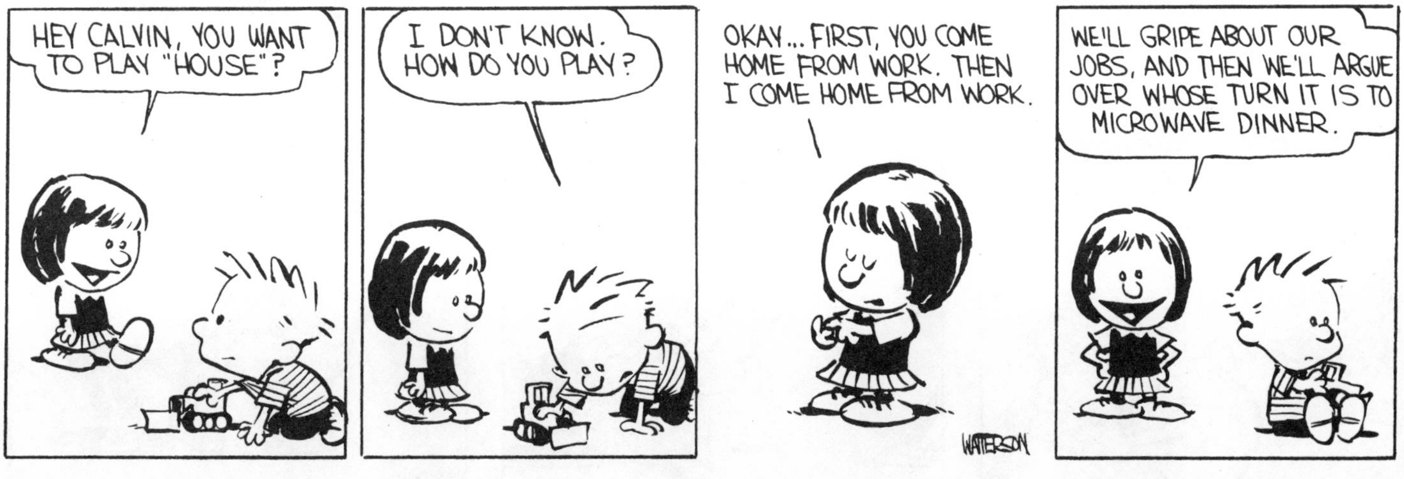
HEY CALVIN, YOU WANT TO PLAY "HOUSE"?
I DON'T KNOW. HOW DO YOU PLAY?
OKAY... FIRST, YOU COME HOME FROM WORK. THEN I COME HOME FROM WORK.
WE'LL GRIPE ABOUT OUR JOBS, AND THEN WE'LL ARGUE OVER WHOSE TURN IT IS TO MICROWAVE DINNER.
WATTERSON

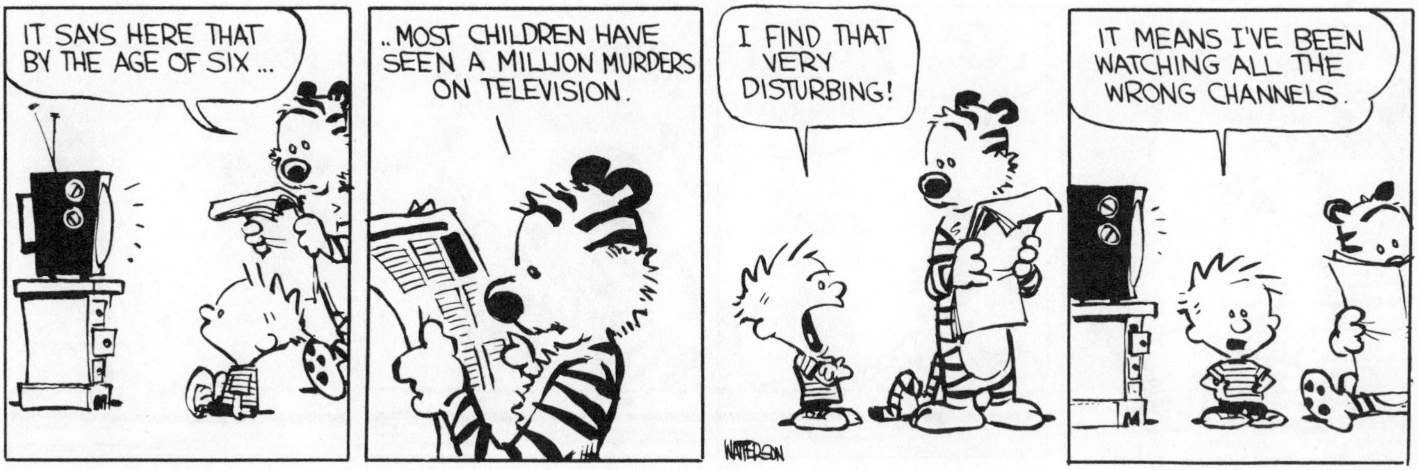
IT SAYS HERE THAT BY THE AGE OF SIX...
..MOST CHILDREN HAVE SEEN A MILLION MURDERS ON TELEVISION.
I FIND THAT VERY DISTURBING!
IT MEANS I'VE BEEN WATCHING ALL THE WRONG CHANNELS.
WATTERSON

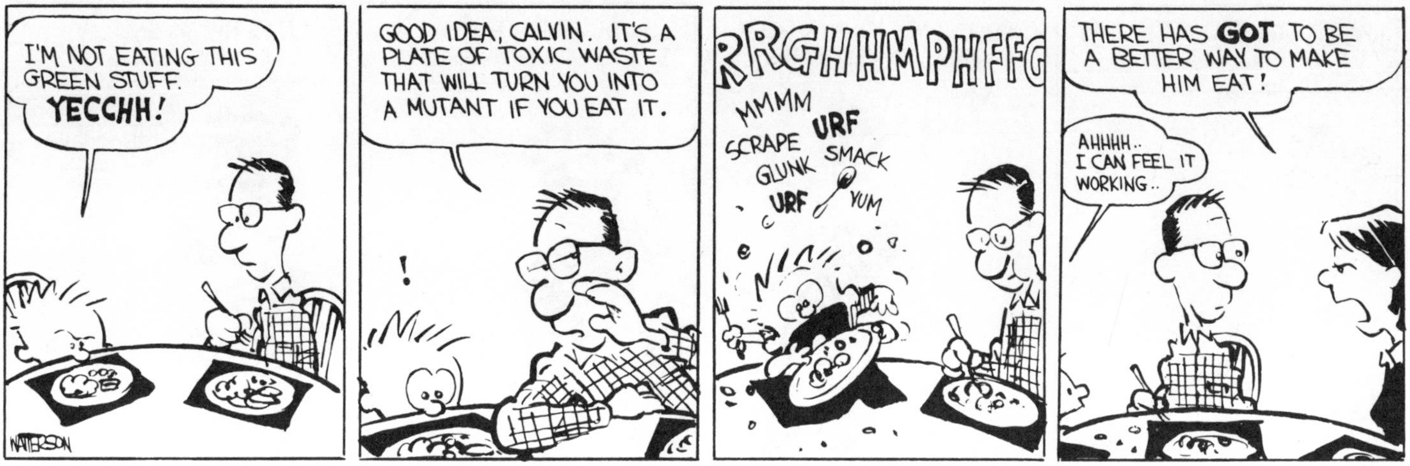
I'M NOT EATING THIS GREEN STUFF. **YECCHH!**
WATTERSON
GOOD IDEA, CALVIN. IT'S A PLATE OF TOXIC WASTE THAT WILL TURN YOU INTO A MUTANT IF YOU EAT IT.
!
RRGHHMPHFFG
MMMM
SCRAPE URF
GLUNK SMACK
URF YUM
THERE HAS **GOT** TO BE A BETTER WAY TO MAKE HIM EAT!
AHHHH.. I CAN FEEL IT WORKING..

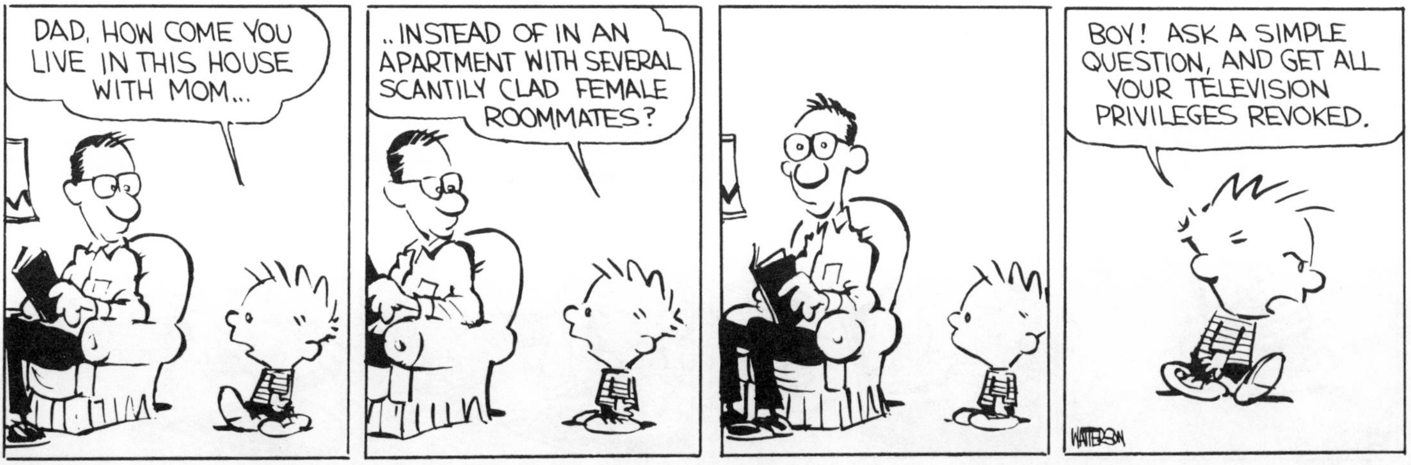
DAD, HOW COME YOU LIVE IN THIS HOUSE WITH MOM...
..INSTEAD OF IN AN APARTMENT WITH SEVERAL SCANTILY CLAD FEMALE ROOMMATES?
BOY! ASK A SIMPLE QUESTION, AND GET ALL YOUR TELEVISION PRIVILEGES REVOKED.
WATTERSON

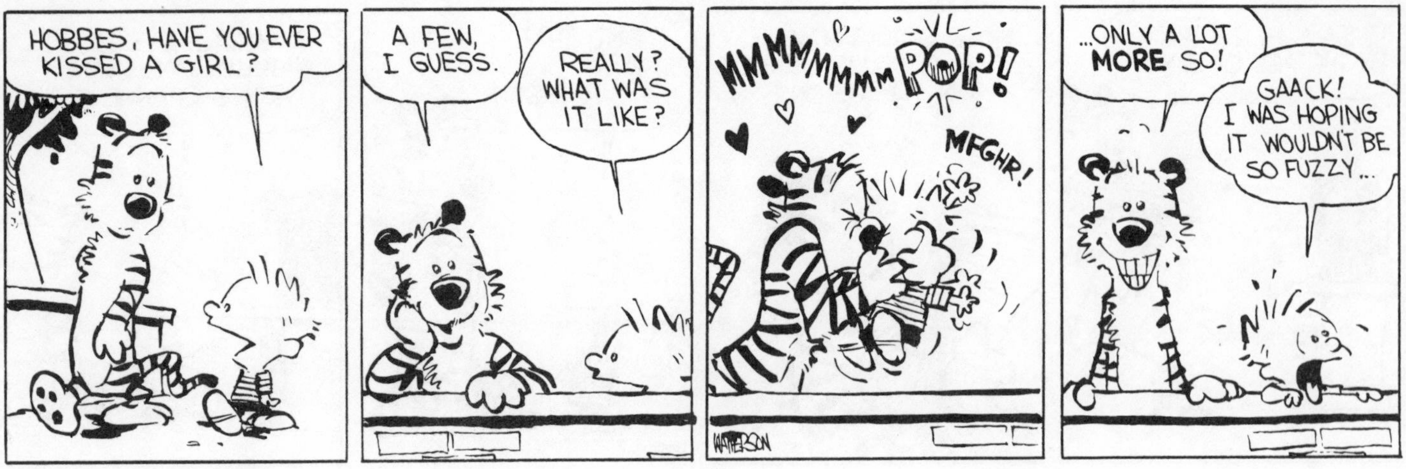
HOBBES, HAVE YOU EVER KISSED A GIRL?
A FEW, I GUESS.
REALLY? WHAT WAS IT LIKE?
MMMMMMMMMMPOP!
MFGHR!
...ONLY A LOT MORE SO!
GAACK! I WAS HOPING IT WOULDN'T BE SO FUZZY...
WATTERSON

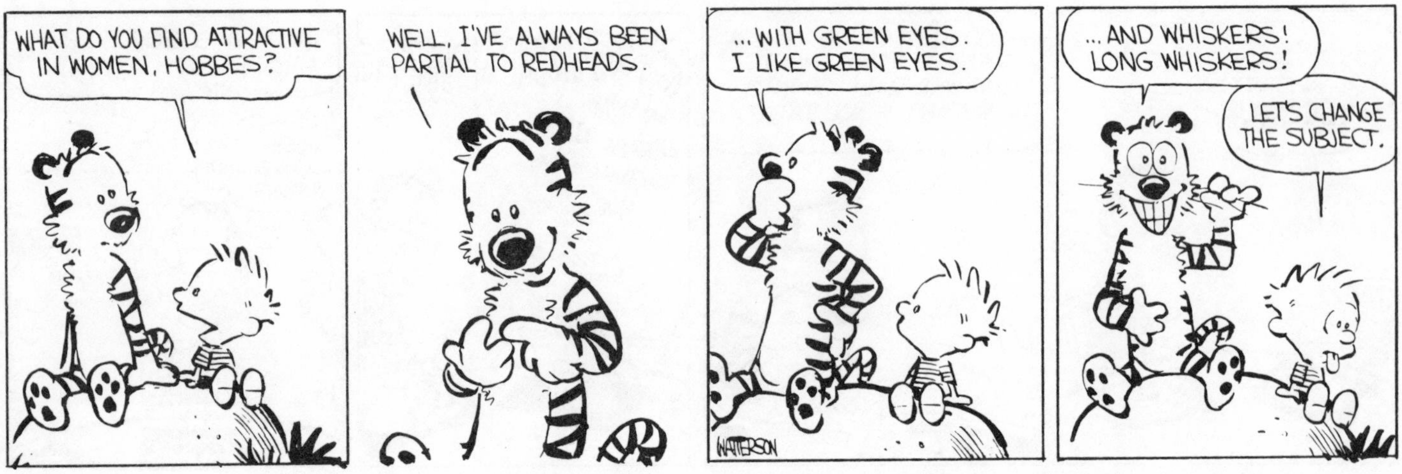
WHAT DO YOU FIND ATTRACTIVE IN WOMEN, HOBBES?
WELL, I'VE ALWAYS BEEN PARTIAL TO REDHEADS.
...WITH GREEN EYES. I LIKE GREEN EYES.
...AND WHISKERS! LONG WHISKERS!
LET'S CHANGE THE SUBJECT.
WATTERSON

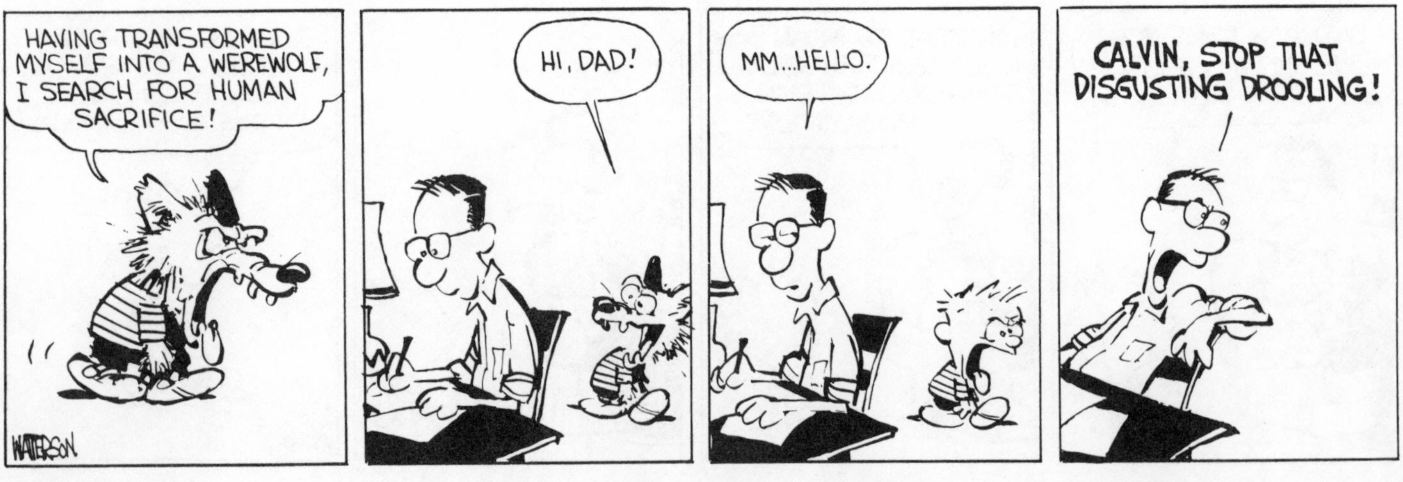
HAVING TRANSFORMED MYSELF INTO A WEREWOLF, I SEARCH FOR HUMAN SACRIFICE!
HI, DAD!
MM...HELLO.
CALVIN, STOP THAT DISGUSTING DROOLING!
WATTERSON

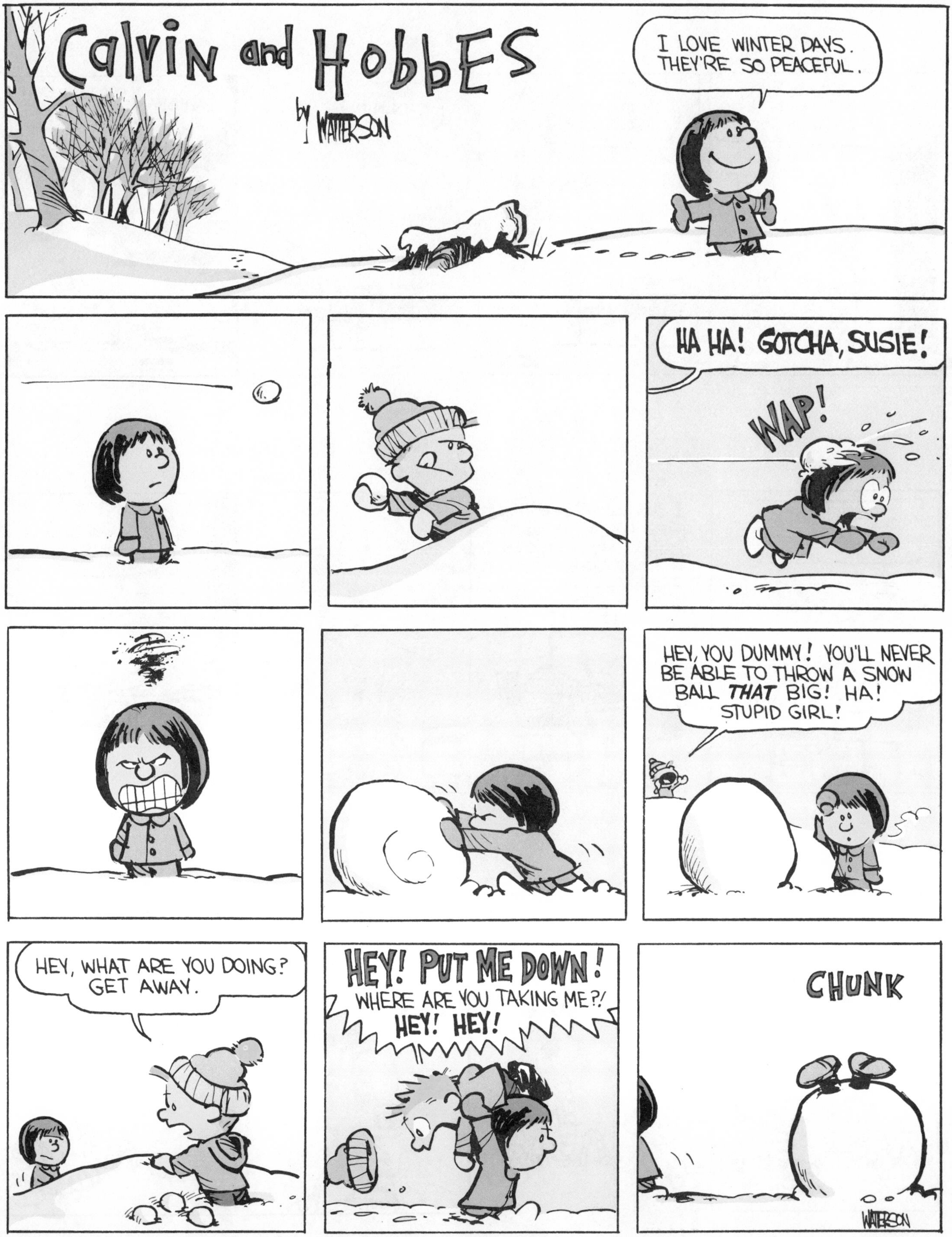
Calvin and Hobbes
by WATTERSON
I LOVE WINTER DAYS. THEY'RE SO PEACEFUL.
HA HA! GOTCHA, SUSIE!
WAP!
HEY, YOU DUMMY! YOU'LL NEVER BE ABLE TO THROW A SNOW BALL THAT BIG! HA! STUPID GIRL!
HEY, WHAT ARE YOU DOING? GET AWAY.
HEY! PUT ME DOWN! WHERE ARE YOU TAKING ME?! HEY! HEY!
CHUNK
WATTERSON

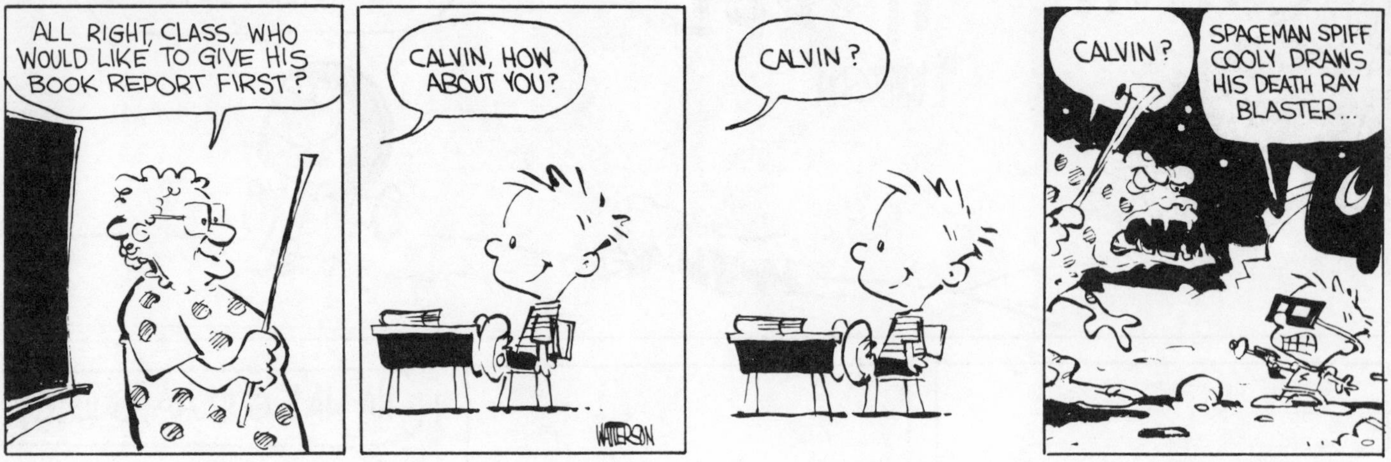
ALL RIGHT, CLASS, WHO WOULD LIKE TO GIVE HIS BOOK REPORT FIRST?
CALVIN, HOW ABOUT YOU?
CALVIN?
CALVIN?
SPACEMAN SPIFF COOLY DRAWS HIS DEATH RAY BLASTER...
WATTERSON

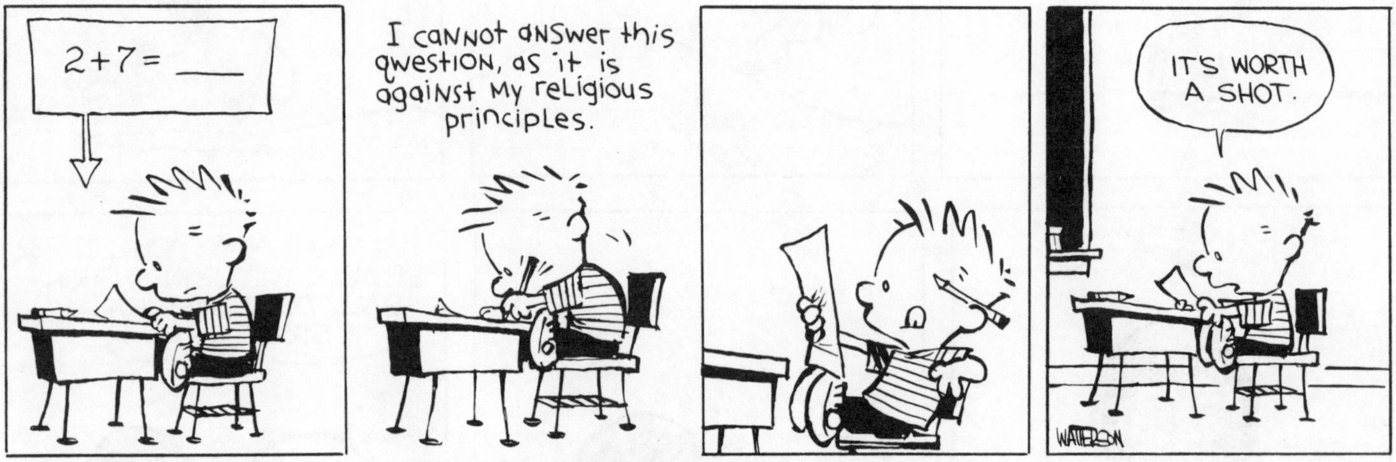
2+7= ____
I cannot answer this qwestion, as it is against my religious principles.
IT'S WORTH A SHOT.
WATTERSON

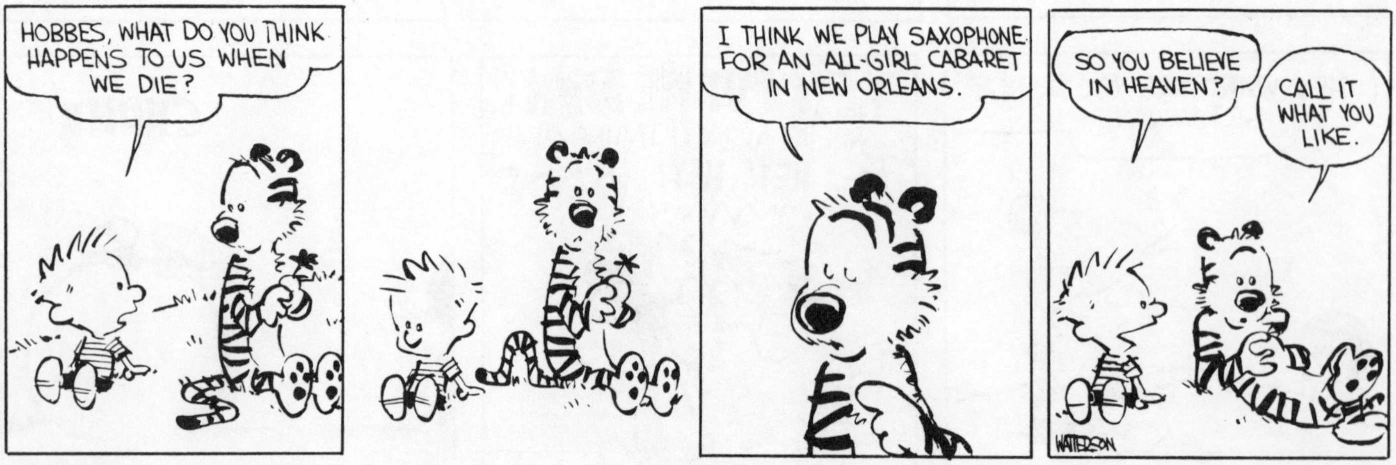
HOBBES, WHAT DO YOU THINK HAPPENS TO US WHEN WE DIE?
I THINK WE PLAY SAXOPHONE FOR AN ALL-GIRL CABARET IN NEW ORLEANS.
SO YOU BELIEVE IN HEAVEN?
CALL IT WHAT YOU LIKE.
WATTERSON

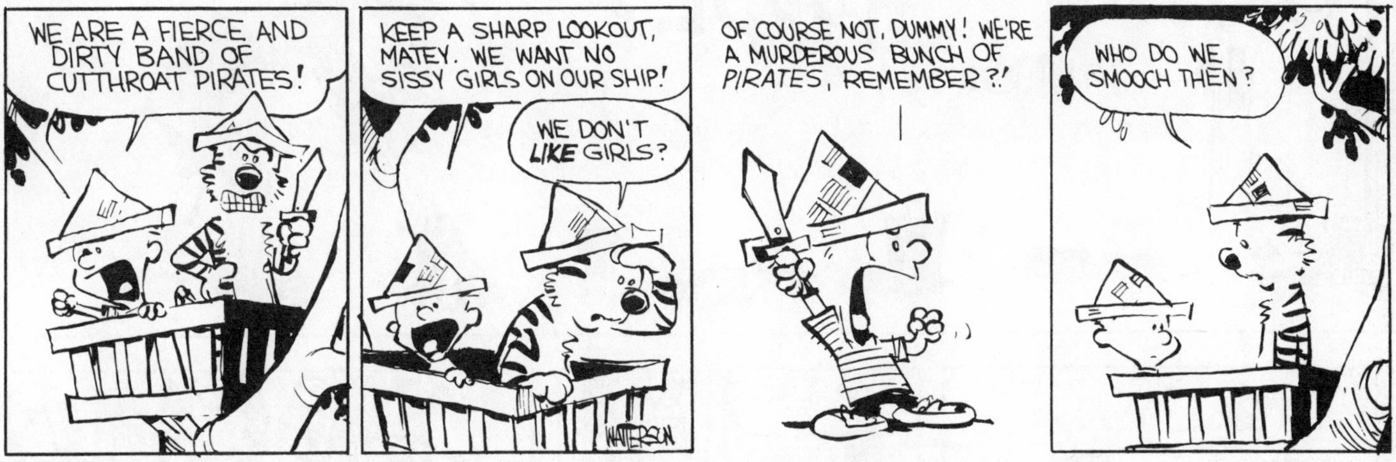
WE ARE A FIERCE AND DIRTY BAND OF CUTTHROAT PIRATES!
KEEP A SHARP LOOKOUT, MATEY. WE WANT NO SISSY GIRLS ON OUR SHIP!
WE DON'T LIKE GIRLS?
OF COURSE NOT, DUMMY! WE'RE A MURDEROUS BUNCH OF PIRATES, REMEMBER?!
WATTERSON
WHO DO WE SMOOCH THEN?

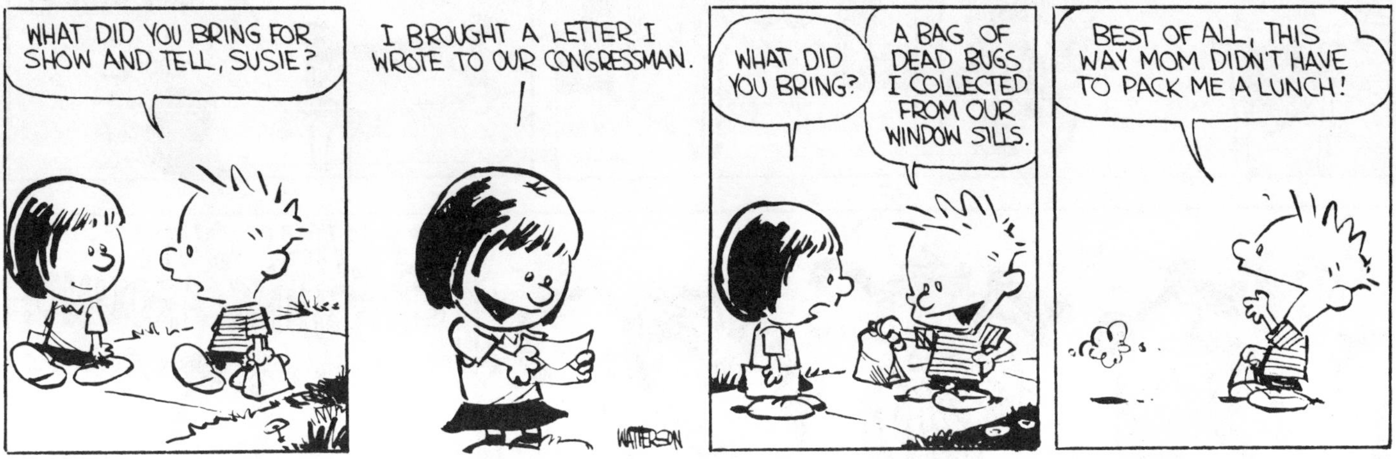
WHAT DID YOU BRING FOR SHOW AND TELL, SUSIE?
I BROUGHT A LETTER I WROTE TO OUR CONGRESSMAN.
WATTERSON
WHAT DID YOU BRING?
A BAG OF DEAD BUGS I COLLECTED FROM OUR WINDOW SILLS.
BEST OF ALL, THIS WAY MOM DIDN'T HAVE TO PACK ME A LUNCH!

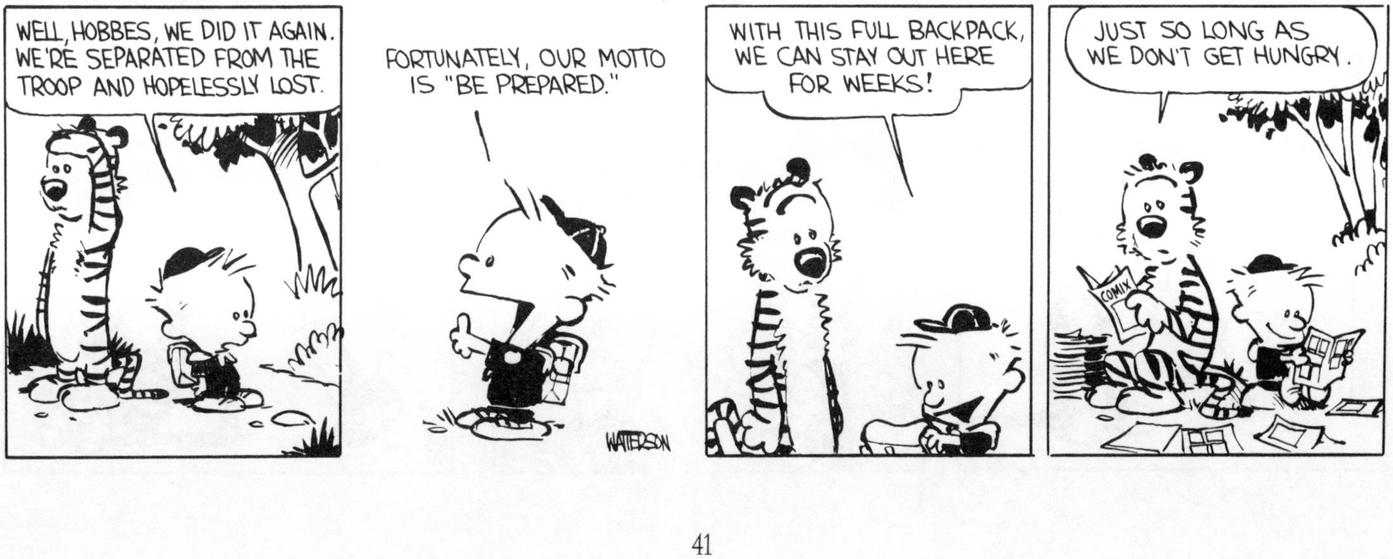
WELL, HOBBES, WE DID IT AGAIN. WE'RE SEPARATED FROM THE TROOP AND HOPELESSLY LOST.
FORTUNATELY, OUR MOTTO IS "BE PREPARED."
WATTERSON
WITH THIS FULL BACKPACK, WE CAN STAY OUT HERE FOR WEEKS!
JUST SO LONG AS WE DON'T GET HUNGRY.
COMIX

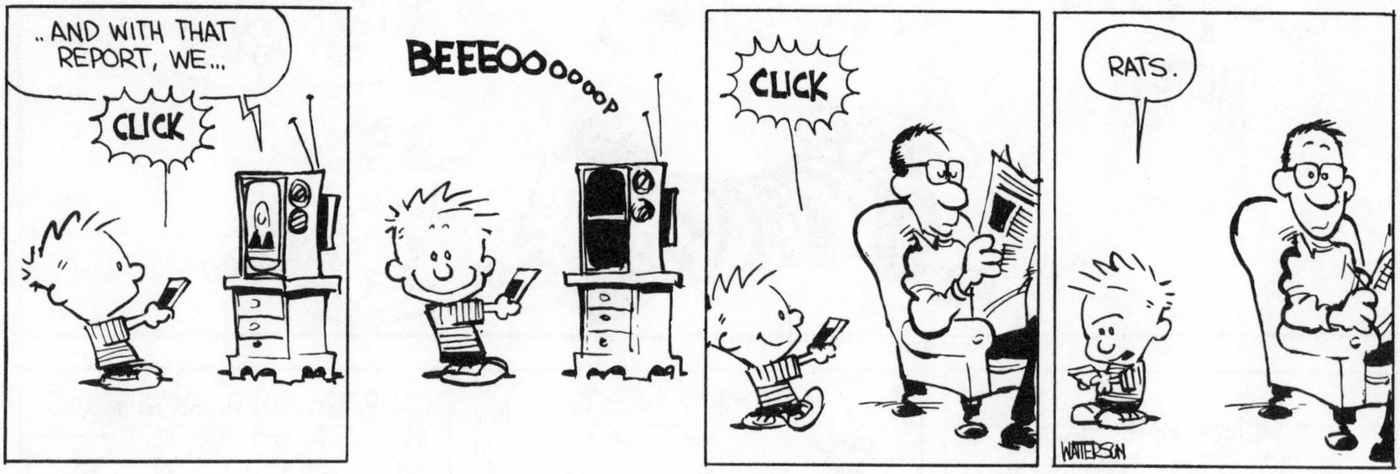

..AND WITH THAT REPORT, WE...
CLICK
BEEEOOooooop
CLICK
RATS.
WATTERSON


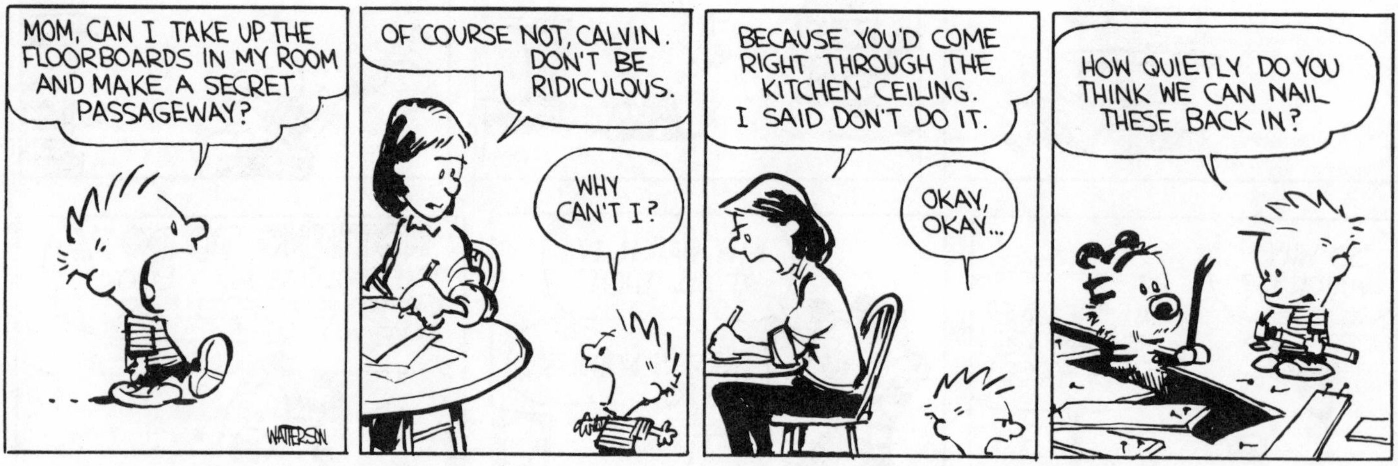

MOM, CAN I TAKE UP THE FLOORBOARDS IN MY ROOM AND MAKE A SECRET PASSAGEWAY?
WATTERSON
OF COURSE NOT, CALVIN. DON'T BE RIDICULOUS.
WHY CAN'T I?
BECAUSE YOU'D COME RIGHT THROUGH THE KITCHEN CEILING. I SAID DON'T DO IT.
OKAY, OKAY...
HOW QUIETLY DO YOU THINK WE CAN NAIL THESE BACK IN?


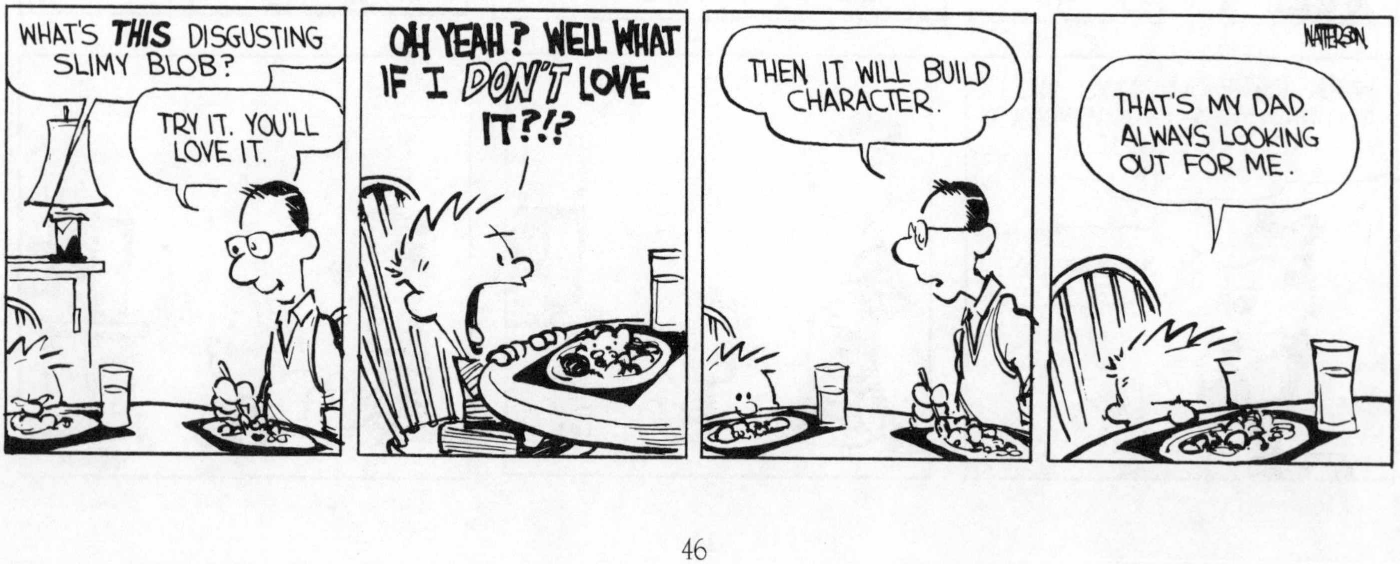

WHAT'S **THIS** DISGUSTING SLIMY BLOB?
TRY IT. YOU'LL LOVE IT.
OH YEAH? WELL WHAT IF I *DON'T* LOVE IT?!?
THEN IT WILL BUILD CHARACTER.
WATTERSON
THAT'S MY DAD. ALWAYS LOOKING OUT FOR ME.

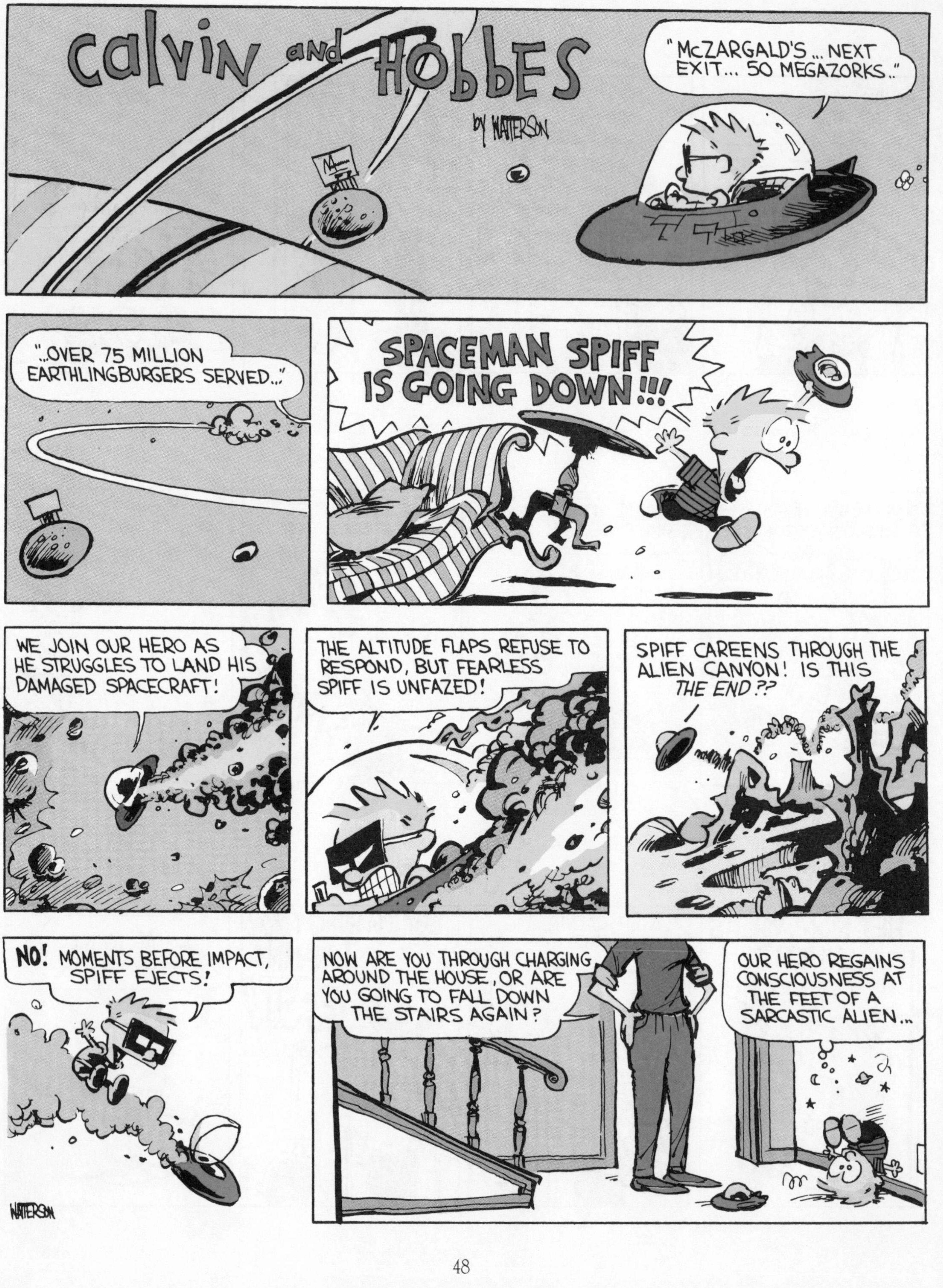
Calvin and Hobbes
by WATTERSON
"McZARGALD'S ... NEXT EXIT... 50 MEGAZORKS.."
"...OVER 75 MILLION EARTHLINGBURGERS SERVED..."
SPACEMAN SPIFF IS GOING DOWN!!!
WE JOIN OUR HERO AS HE STRUGGLES TO LAND HIS DAMAGED SPACECRAFT!
THE ALTITUDE FLAPS REFUSE TO RESPOND, BUT FEARLESS SPIFF IS UNFAZED!
SPIFF CAREENS THROUGH THE ALIEN CANYON! IS THIS THE END??
NO! MOMENTS BEFORE IMPACT, SPIFF EJECTS!
NOW ARE YOU THROUGH CHARGING AROUND THE HOUSE, OR ARE YOU GOING TO FALL DOWN THE STAIRS AGAIN?
OUR HERO REGAINS CONSCIOUSNESS AT THE FEET OF A SARCASTIC ALIEN...
WATTERSON

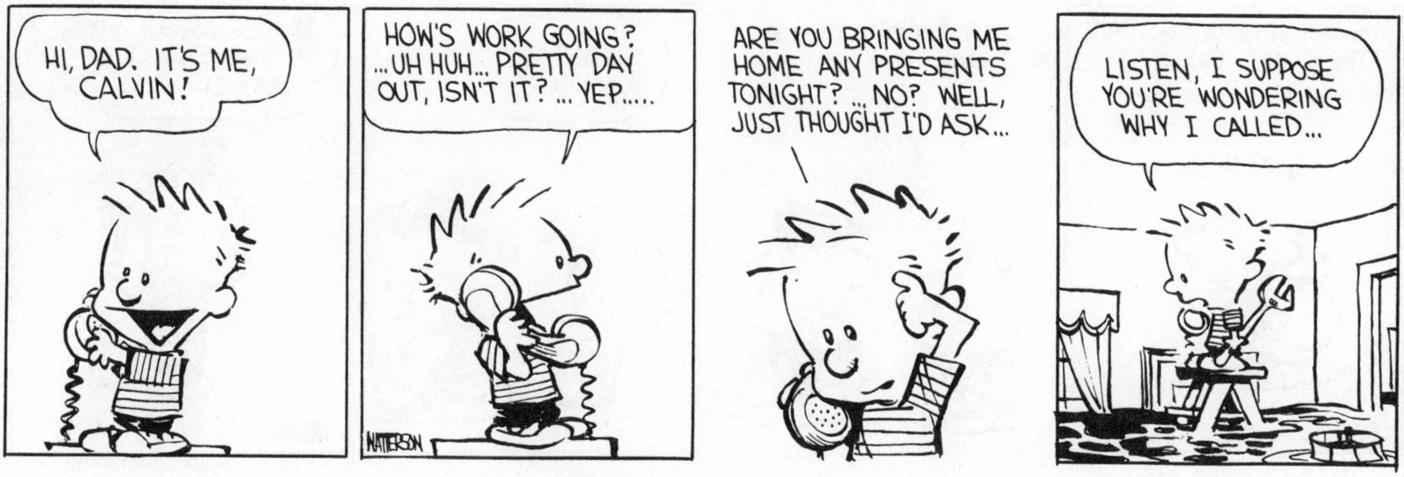
HI, DAD. IT'S ME, CALVIN!
HOW'S WORK GOING? ...UH HUH... PRETTY DAY OUT, ISN'T IT? ... YEP.....
ARE YOU BRINGING ME HOME ANY PRESENTS TONIGHT? ... NO? WELL, JUST THOUGHT I'D ASK...
LISTEN, I SUPPOSE YOU'RE WONDERING WHY I CALLED...

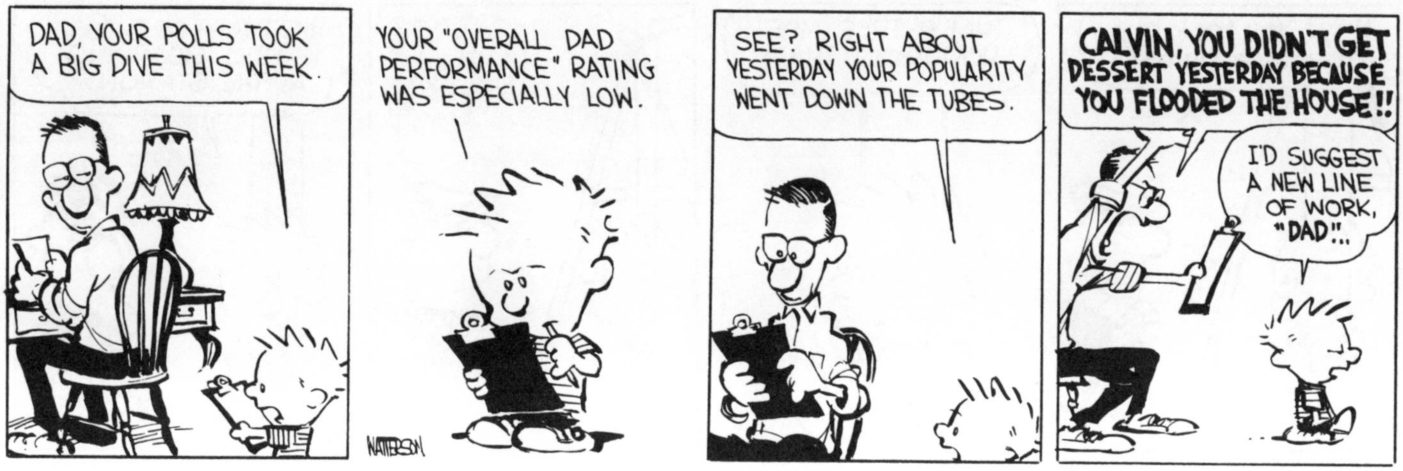
DAD, YOUR POLLS TOOK A BIG DIVE THIS WEEK.
YOUR "OVERALL DAD PERFORMANCE" RATING WAS ESPECIALLY LOW.
SEE? RIGHT ABOUT YESTERDAY YOUR POPULARITY WENT DOWN THE TUBES.
CALVIN, YOU DIDN'T GET DESSERT YESTERDAY BECAUSE YOU FLOODED THE HOUSE!!
I'D SUGGEST A NEW LINE OF WORK, "DAD"!...

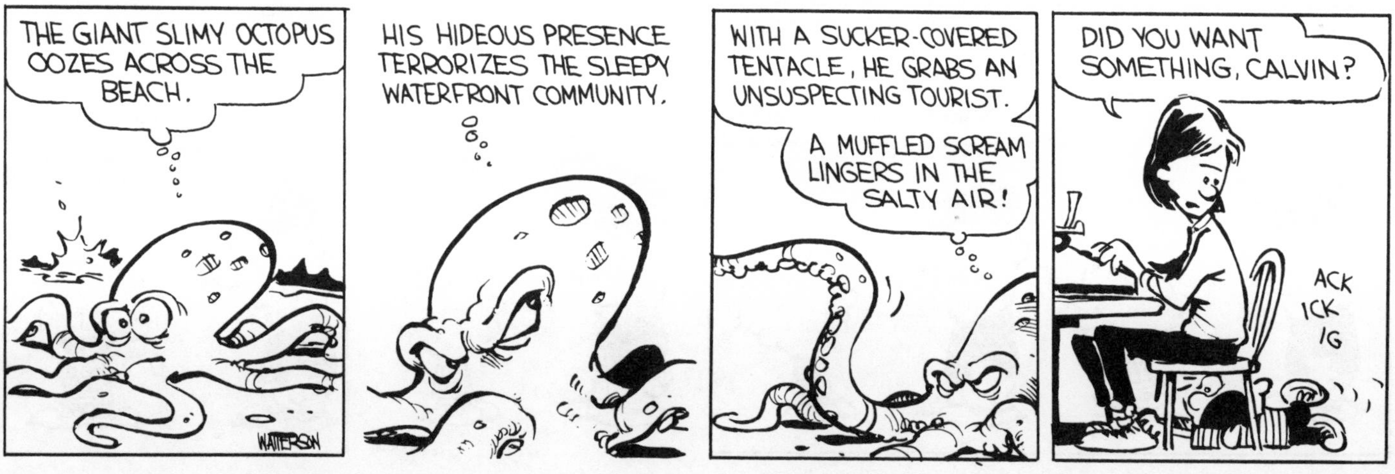
THE GIANT SLIMY OCTOPUS OOZES ACROSS THE BEACH.
HIS HIDEOUS PRESENCE TERRORIZES THE SLEEPY WATERFRONT COMMUNITY.
WITH A SUCKER-COVERED TENTACLE, HE GRABS AN UNSUSPECTING TOURIST.
A MUFFLED SCREAM LINGERS IN THE SALTY AIR!
DID YOU WANT SOMETHING, CALVIN?
ACK
ICK
IG

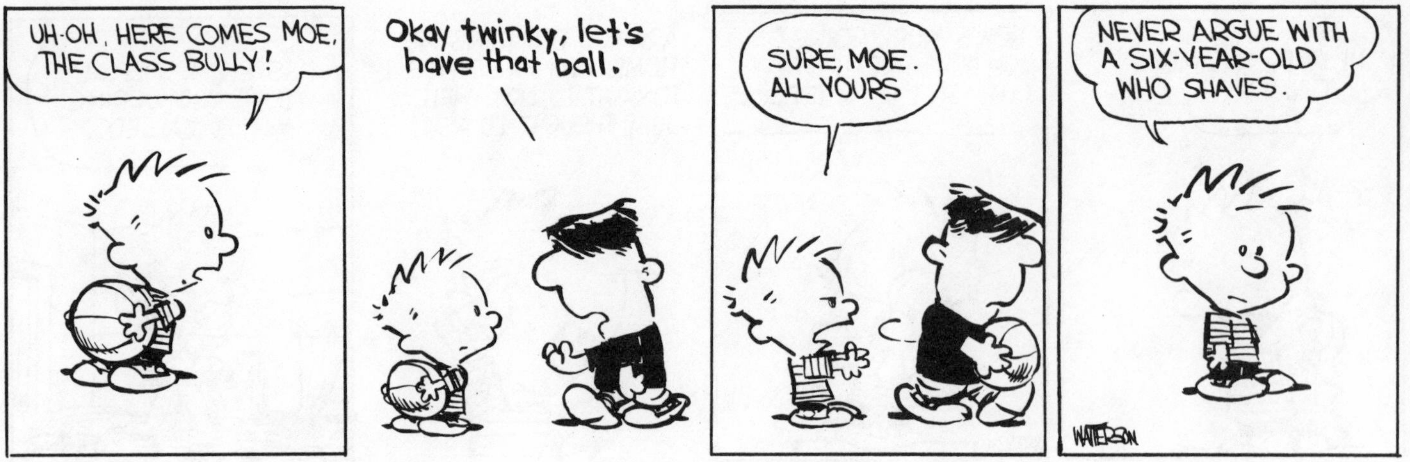
UH-OH, HERE COMES MOE, THE CLASS BULLY!
Okay twinky, let's have that ball.
SURE, MOE. ALL YOURS
NEVER ARGUE WITH A SIX-YEAR-OLD WHO SHAVES.
WATTERSON

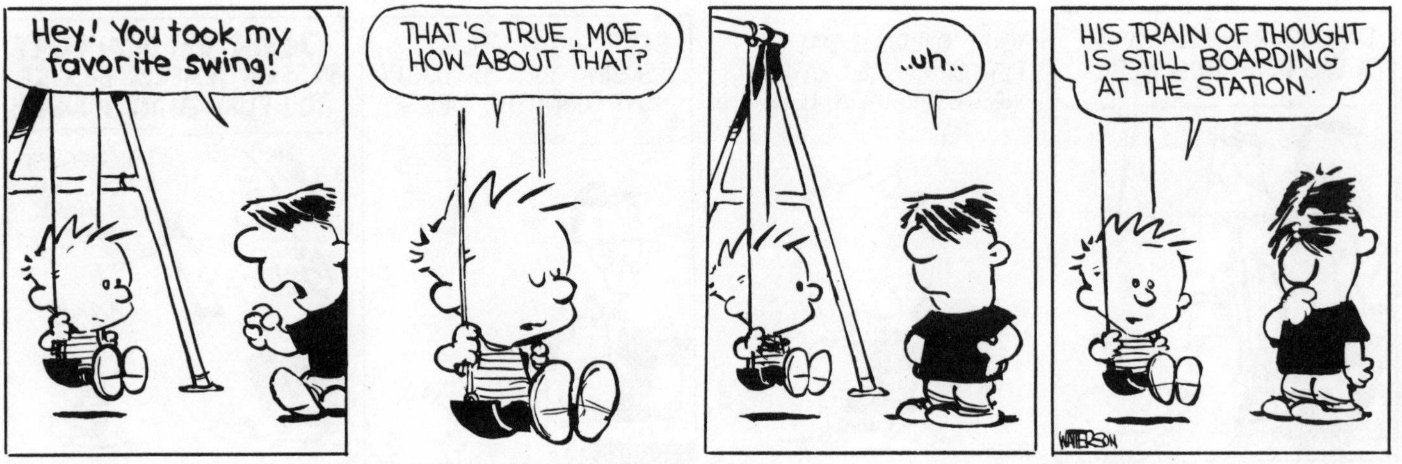
Hey! You took my favorite swing!
THAT'S TRUE, MOE. HOW ABOUT THAT?
..uh..
HIS TRAIN OF THOUGHT IS STILL BOARDING AT THE STATION.
WATTERSON

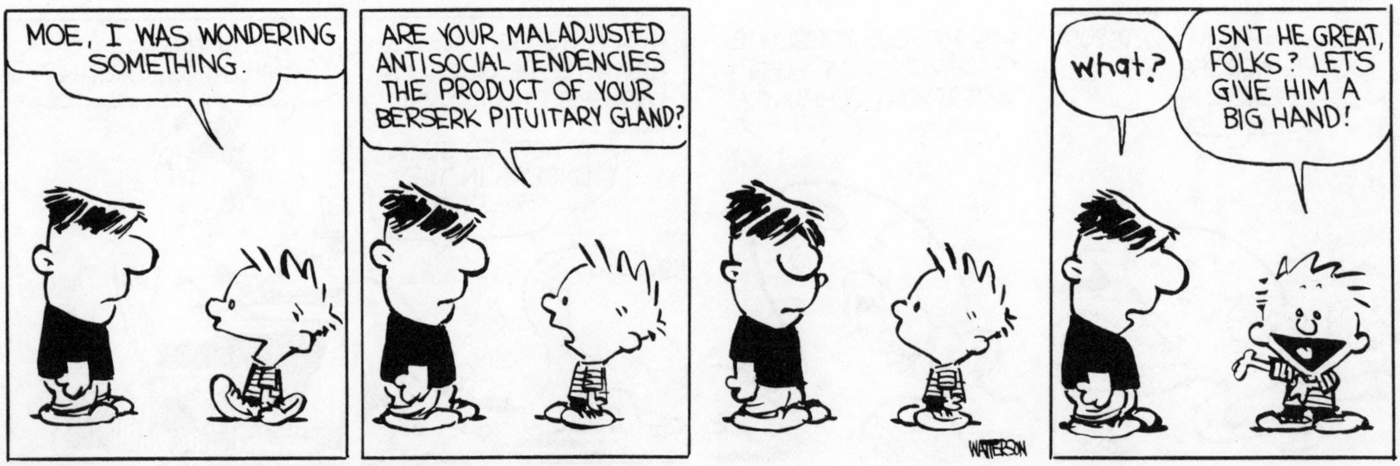
MOE, I WAS WONDERING SOMETHING.
ARE YOUR MALADJUSTED ANTISOCIAL TENDENCIES THE PRODUCT OF YOUR BERSERK PITUITARY GLAND?
WATTERSON
what?
ISN'T HE GREAT, FOLKS? LET'S GIVE HIM A BIG HAND!

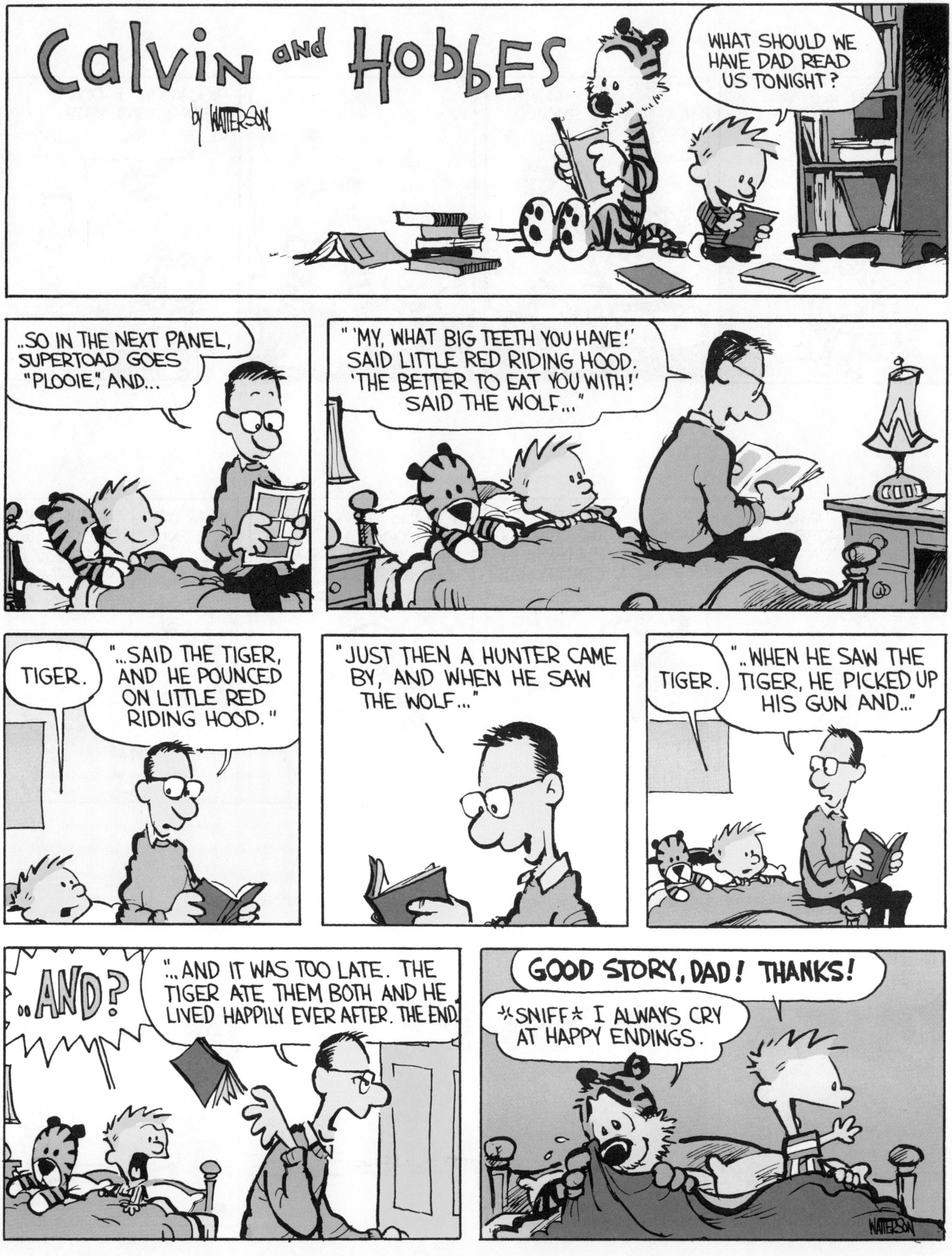
Calvin and Hobbes
by WATTERSON
WHAT SHOULD WE HAVE DAD READ US TONIGHT?
..SO IN THE NEXT PANEL, SUPERTOAD GOES "PLOOIE," AND...
" 'MY, WHAT BIG TEETH YOU HAVE!' SAID LITTLE RED RIDING HOOD. 'THE BETTER TO EAT YOU WITH!' SAID THE WOLF..."
TIGER.
"...SAID THE TIGER, AND HE POUNCED ON LITTLE RED RIDING HOOD."
"JUST THEN A HUNTER CAME BY, AND WHEN HE SAW THE WOLF..."
TIGER.
"..WHEN HE SAW THE TIGER, HE PICKED UP HIS GUN AND..."
..AND?
"...AND IT WAS TOO LATE. THE TIGER ATE THEM BOTH AND HE LIVED HAPPILY EVER AFTER. THE END."
GOOD STORY, DAD! THANKS!
*SNIFF* I ALWAYS CRY AT HAPPY ENDINGS.
WATTERSON

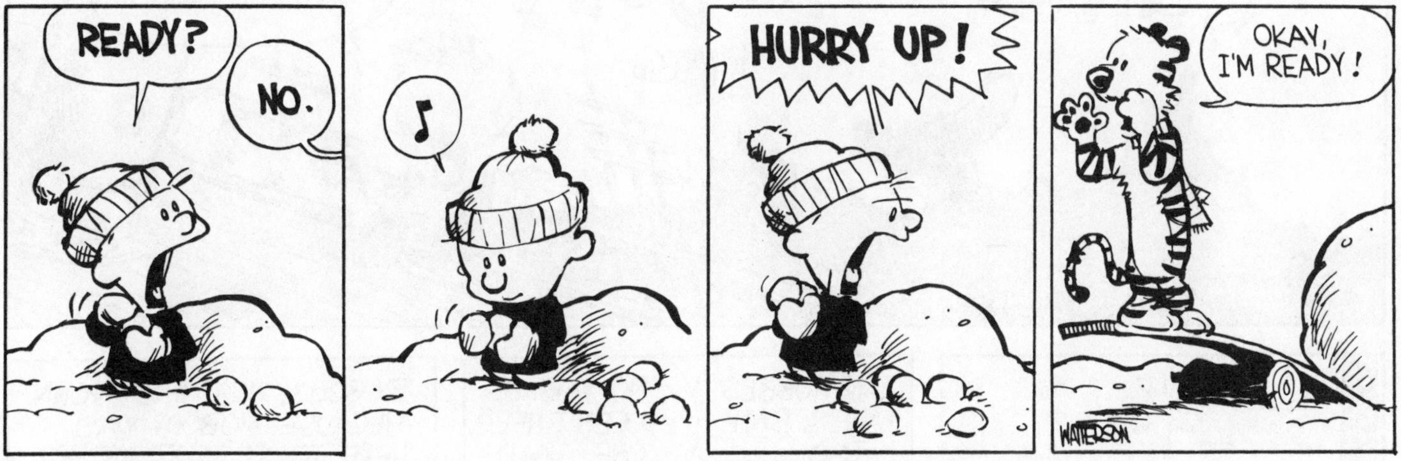
READY?
NO.
♪
HURRY UP!
OKAY, I'M READY!
WATTERSON

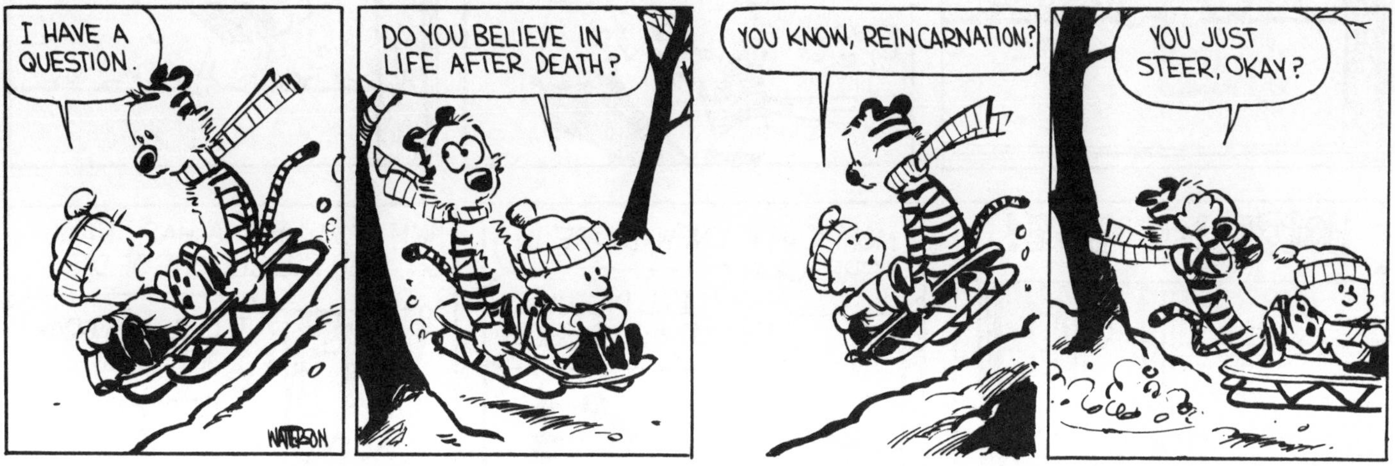
I HAVE A QUESTION.
DO YOU BELIEVE IN LIFE AFTER DEATH?
YOU KNOW, REINCARNATION?
YOU JUST STEER, OKAY?
WATTERSON

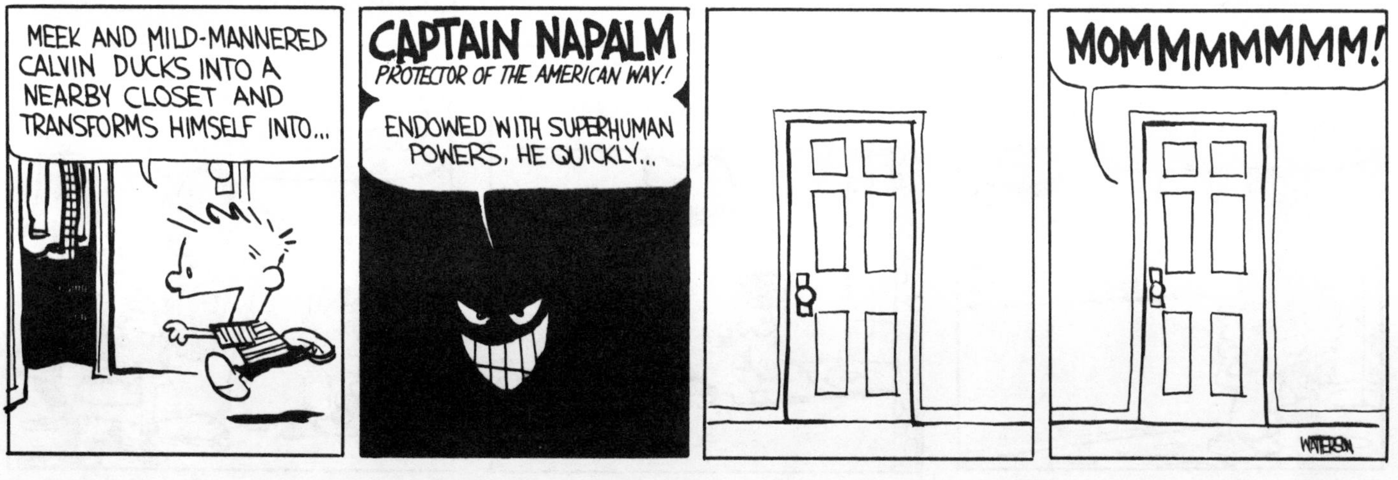
MEEK AND MILD-MANNERED CALVIN DUCKS INTO A NEARBY CLOSET AND TRANSFORMS HIMSELF INTO...
CAPTAIN NAPALM
PROTECTOR OF THE AMERICAN WAY!
ENDOWED WITH SUPERHUMAN POWERS, HE QUICKLY...
MOMMMMMMM!
WATTERSON

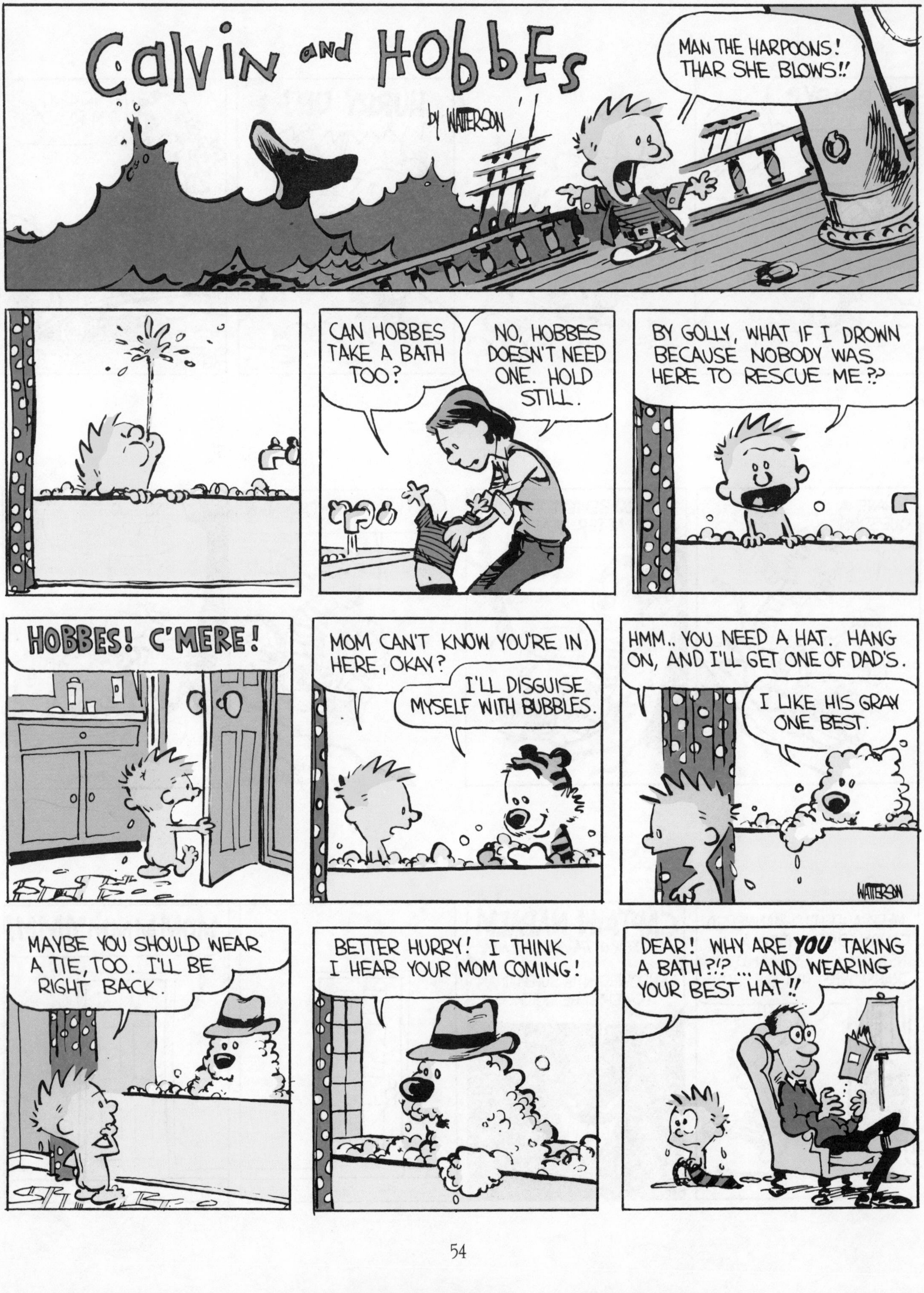
Calvin and Hobbes
by WATTERSON
MAN THE HARPOONS! THAR SHE BLOWS!!
CAN HOBBES TAKE A BATH TOO?
NO, HOBBES DOESN'T NEED ONE. HOLD STILL.
BY GOLLY, WHAT IF I DROWN BECAUSE NOBODY WAS HERE TO RESCUE ME?!?
HOBBES! C'MERE!
MOM CAN'T KNOW YOU'RE IN HERE, OKAY?
I'LL DISGUISE MYSELF WITH BUBBLES.
HMM.. YOU NEED A HAT. HANG ON, AND I'LL GET ONE OF DAD'S.
I LIKE HIS GRAY ONE BEST.
WATTERSON
MAYBE YOU SHOULD WEAR A TIE, TOO. I'LL BE RIGHT BACK.
BETTER HURRY! I THINK I HEAR YOUR MOM COMING!
DEAR! WHY ARE YOU TAKING A BATH?!? ... AND WEARING YOUR BEST HAT!!

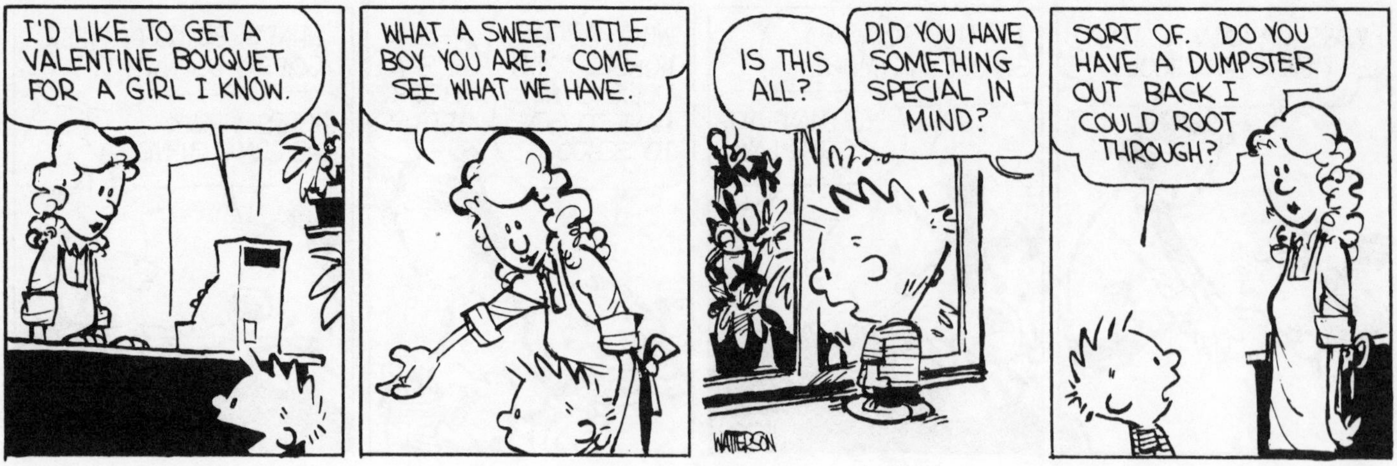
I'D LIKE TO GET A VALENTINE BOUQUET FOR A GIRL I KNOW.
WHAT A SWEET LITTLE BOY YOU ARE! COME SEE WHAT WE HAVE.
IS THIS ALL?
DID YOU HAVE SOMETHING SPECIAL IN MIND?
SORT OF. DO YOU HAVE A DUMPSTER OUT BACK I COULD ROOT THROUGH?
WATTERSON

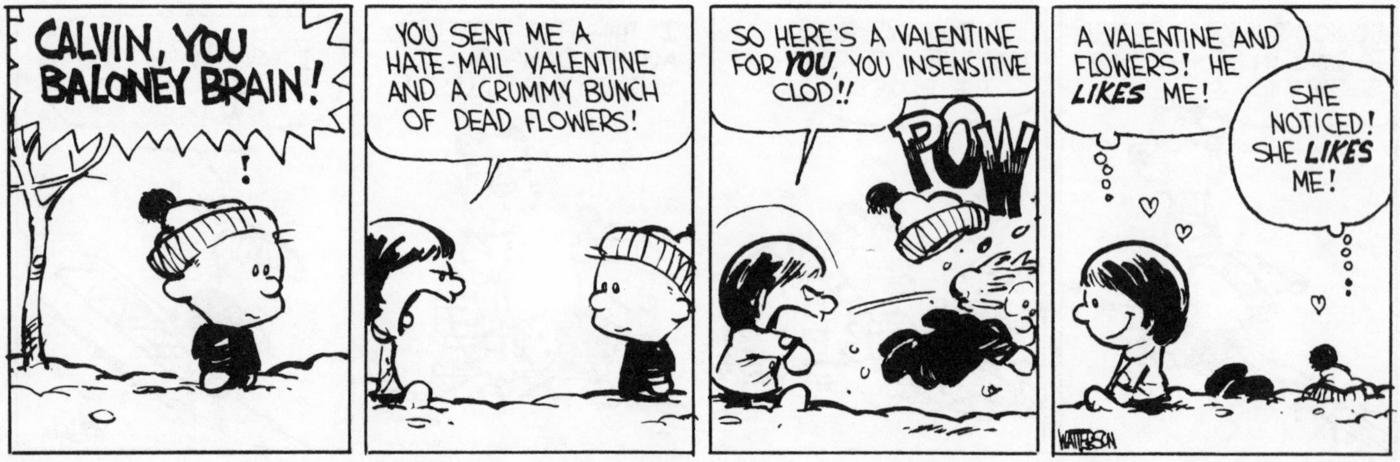
CALVIN, YOU BALONEY BRAIN!
!
YOU SENT ME A HATE-MAIL VALENTINE AND A CRUMMY BUNCH OF DEAD FLOWERS!
SO HERE'S A VALENTINE FOR YOU, YOU INSENSITIVE CLOD!!
POW
A VALENTINE AND FLOWERS! HE LIKES ME!
SHE NOTICED! SHE LIKES ME!
WATTERSON

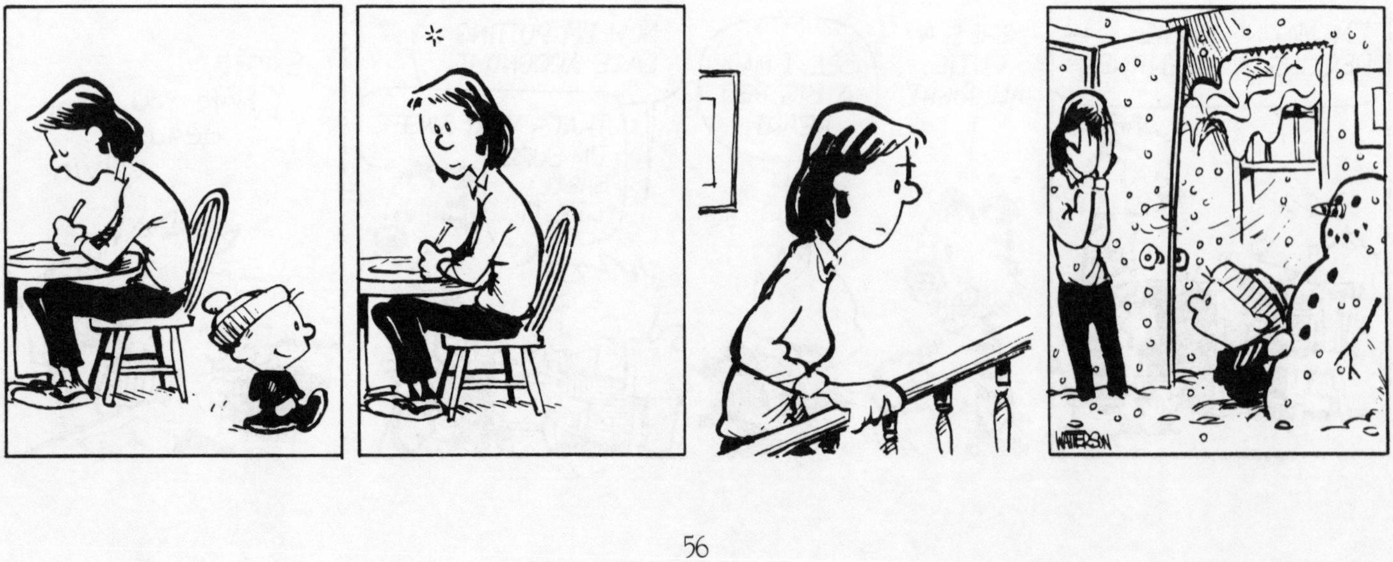
WATTERSON

Hey, Calvin, it's gonna cost you 50 cents to be my friend today.

AND WHAT IF I DON'T *WANT* TO BE YOUR FRIEND TODAY?

Then the janitor scrapes you off the wall with a spatula.

HECK, WHAT'S A LITTLE EXTORTION AMONG FRIENDS?

I GOT THE NEW ALBUM BY SCRAMBLED DEBUTANTE.

ALL THEIR SONGS GLORIFY DEPRAVED VIOLENCE, MINDLESS SEX, AND THE DELIBERATE ABUSE OF DANGEROUS DRUGS.

YOUR MOM'S GOING TO GO INTO CONNIPTIONS WHEN SHE SEES *THIS* LYING AROUND.

WELL I SURE DIDN'T BUY IT FOR THE MUSIC...

MOM, WILL YOU DRIVE ME INTO TOWN?

WHY SHOULD I *DRIVE* YOU, CALVIN? IT'S A PERFECT DAY OUTSIDE!

WHAT DO YOU THINK PEOPLE HAVE *FEET* FOR?

TO WORK THE GAS PEDAL.

I NEED HELP ON MY HOMEWORK. WHAT'S A PRONOUN?

A NOUN THAT LOST ITS AMATEUR STATUS.

MAYBE I CAN GET A POINT FOR ORIGINALITY.

LEAVE YOUR TIGER IN THE CAR, CALVIN.

CAN'T HOBBES COME ALONG, DAD? HE WON'T EAT ANYBODY!

NO, CALVIN. LET'S GO.

WELL, AT LEAST LET ME OPEN THE WINDOW AND GIVE HIM SOME AIR.

SEE IF HE'LL LEAVE THE KEYS, TOO, SO I CAN LISTEN TO THE RADIO.

CALVIN, YOUR MOTHER AND I HAVE DECIDED TO GIVE YOU AN ALLOWANCE.

IT'S IMPORTANT THAT ONE LEARNS THE VALUE OF MONEY.

MONEY! HA HA HA! I'M RICH! I'M RICH! I CAN BUY OFF ANYONE! THE WORLD IS MINE!

POWER! FRIENDS! PRESTIGE!

I BLEW IT AGAIN, DEAR!

I CAN BUY IT ALL! I'M FREE! HA HA HA HA!

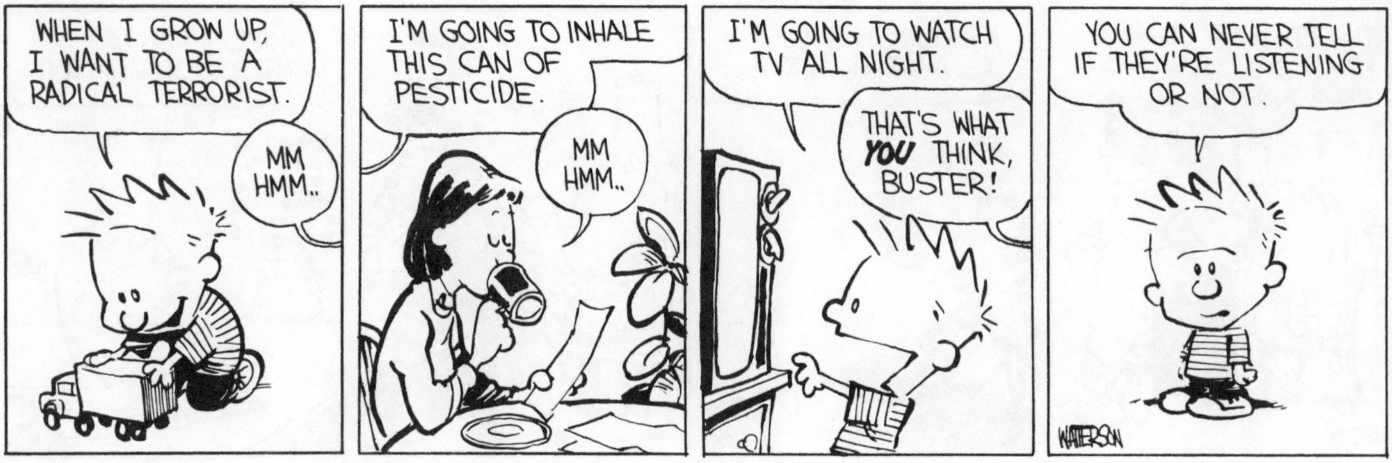
WHEN I GROW UP, I WANT TO BE A RADICAL TERRORIST.
MM HMM..
I'M GOING TO INHALE THIS CAN OF PESTICIDE.
MM HMM..
I'M GOING TO WATCH TV ALL NIGHT.
THAT'S WHAT YOU THINK, BUSTER!
YOU CAN NEVER TELL IF THEY'RE LISTENING OR NOT.
WATTERSON

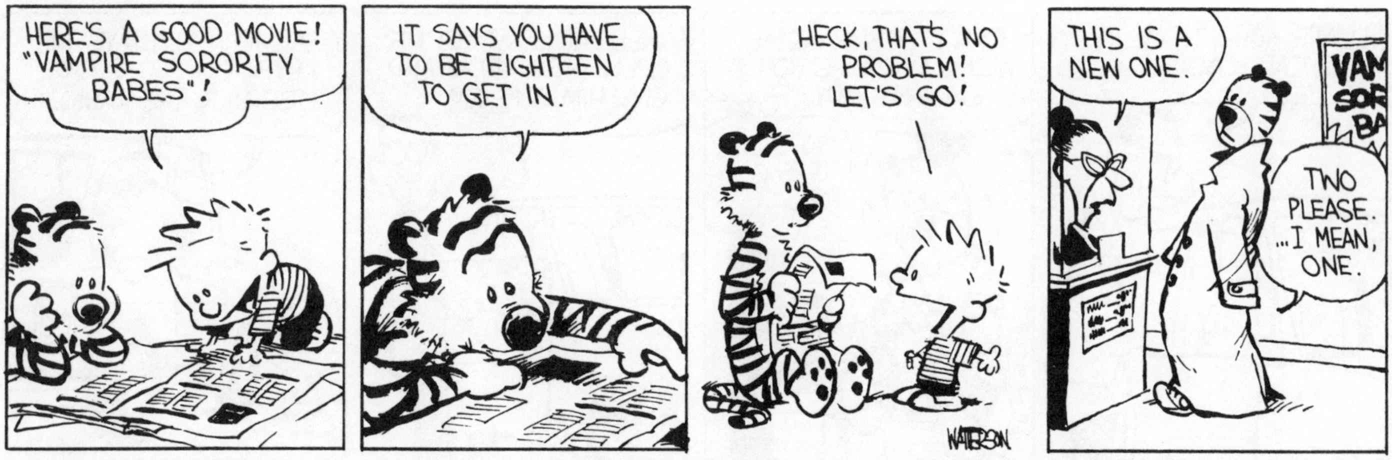
HERE'S A GOOD MOVIE! "VAMPIRE SORORITY BABES"!
IT SAYS YOU HAVE TO BE EIGHTEEN TO GET IN.
HECK, THAT'S NO PROBLEM! LET'S GO!
WATTERSON
THIS IS A NEW ONE.
TWO PLEASE. ...I MEAN, ONE.

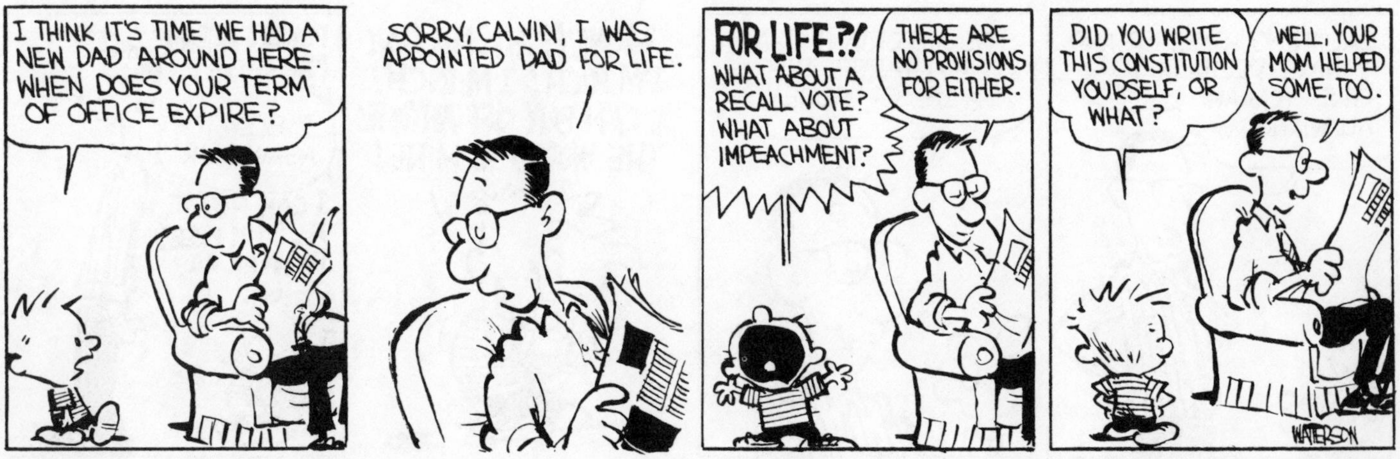
I THINK IT'S TIME WE HAD A NEW DAD AROUND HERE. WHEN DOES YOUR TERM OF OFFICE EXPIRE?
SORRY, CALVIN, I WAS APPOINTED DAD FOR LIFE.
FOR LIFE?! WHAT ABOUT A RECALL VOTE? WHAT ABOUT IMPEACHMENT?
THERE ARE NO PROVISIONS FOR EITHER.
DID YOU WRITE THIS CONSTITUTION YOURSELF, OR WHAT?
WELL, YOUR MOM HELPED SOME, TOO.
WATTERSON

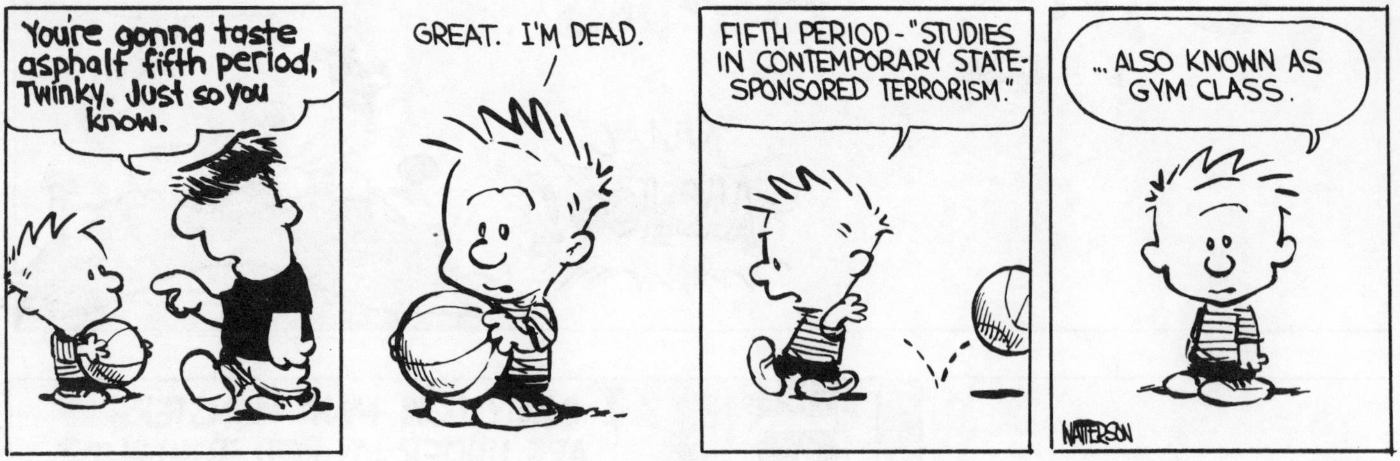
You're gonna taste asphalt fifth period, Twinky. Just so you know.
GREAT. I'M DEAD.
FIFTH PERIOD - "STUDIES IN CONTEMPORARY STATE-SPONSORED TERRORISM."
... ALSO KNOWN AS GYM CLASS.
WATTERSON

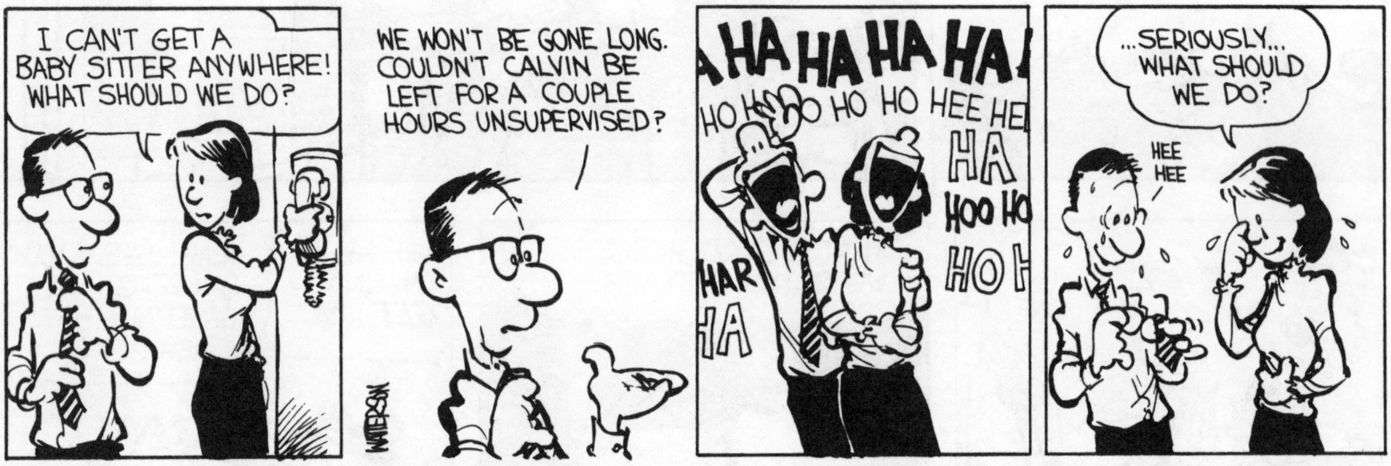
I CAN'T GET A BABY SITTER ANYWHERE! WHAT SHOULD WE DO?
WE WON'T BE GONE LONG. COULDN'T CALVIN BE LEFT FOR A COUPLE HOURS UNSUPERVISED?
WATTERSON
HA HA HA HA HA
HO HO HO HO HO HEE HE
HA
HOO HO
HO H
HAR
HA
...SERIOUSLY... WHAT SHOULD WE DO?
HEE HEE

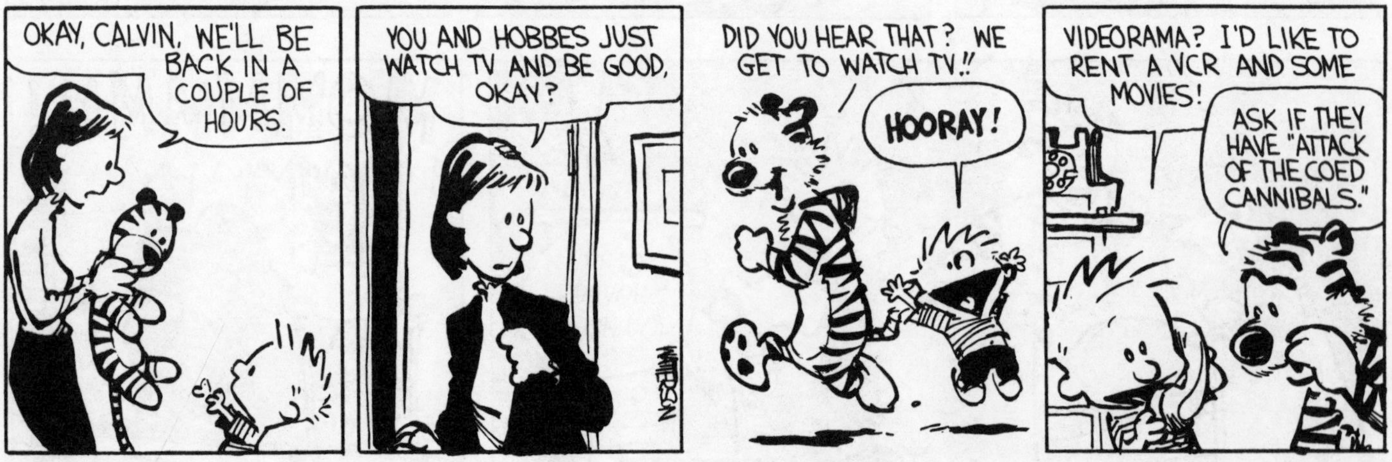
OKAY, CALVIN, WE'LL BE BACK IN A COUPLE OF HOURS.
YOU AND HOBBES JUST WATCH TV AND BE GOOD, OKAY?
WATTERSON
DID YOU HEAR THAT? WE GET TO WATCH TV!!
HOORAY!
VIDEORAMA? I'D LIKE TO RENT A VCR AND SOME MOVIES!
ASK IF THEY HAVE "ATTACK OF THE COED CANNIBALS."

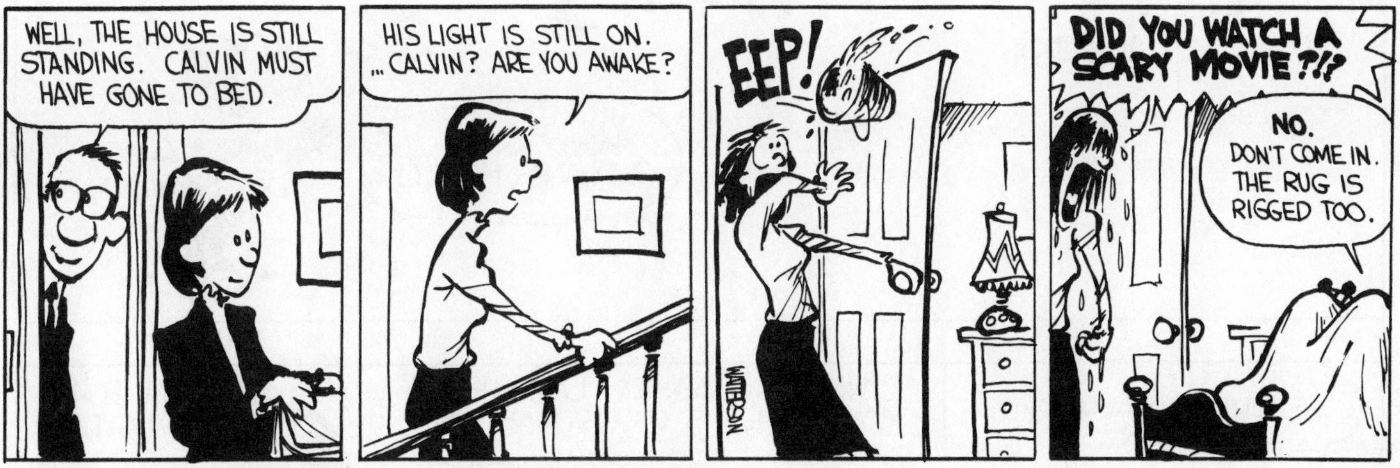
WELL, THE HOUSE IS STILL STANDING. CALVIN MUST HAVE GONE TO BED.
HIS LIGHT IS STILL ON. ... CALVIN? ARE YOU AWAKE?
EEP!
DID YOU WATCH A SCARY MOVIE?!?
NO. DON'T COME IN. THE RUG IS RIGGED TOO.

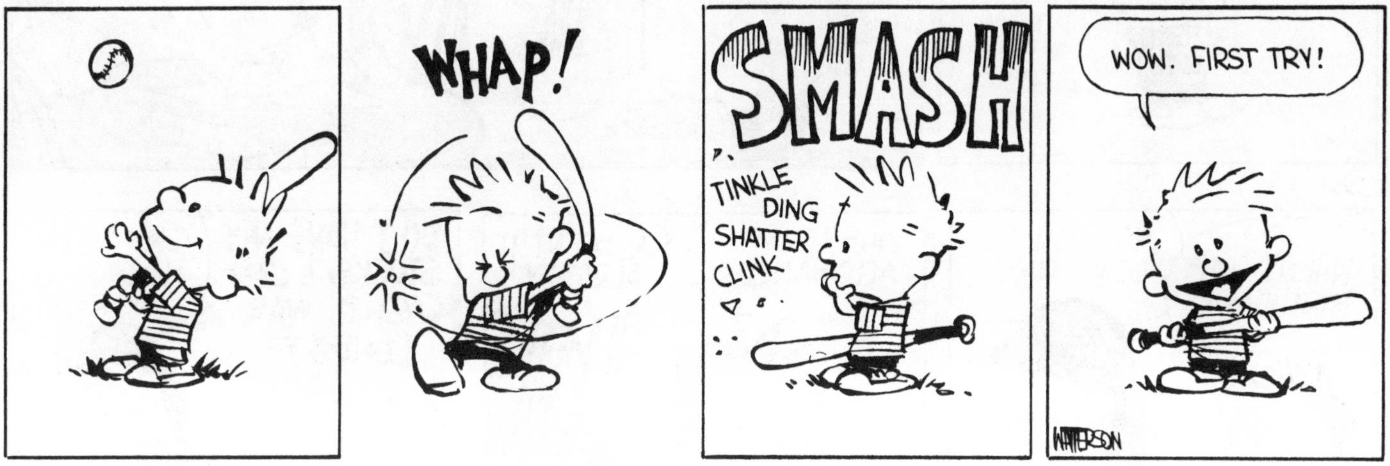
WHAP!
SMASH
TINKLE
DING
SHATTER
CLINK
WOW. FIRST TRY!

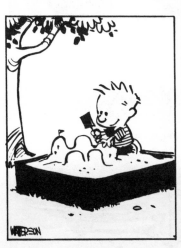

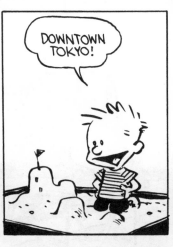

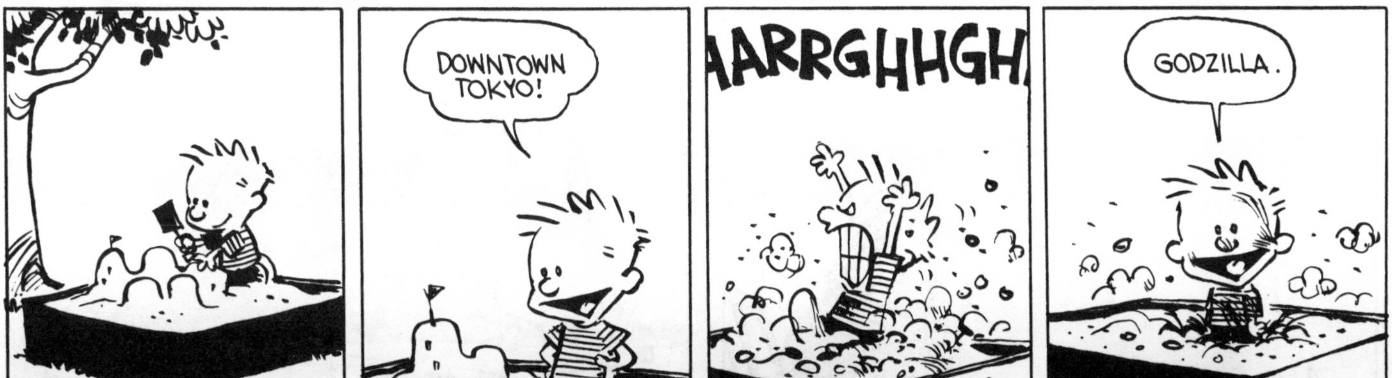
DOWNTOWN TOKYO!
AARRGHHGH
GODZILLA.

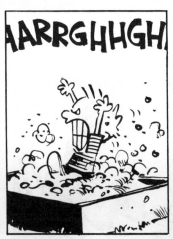

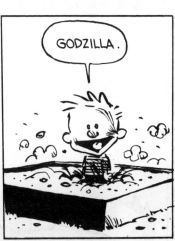

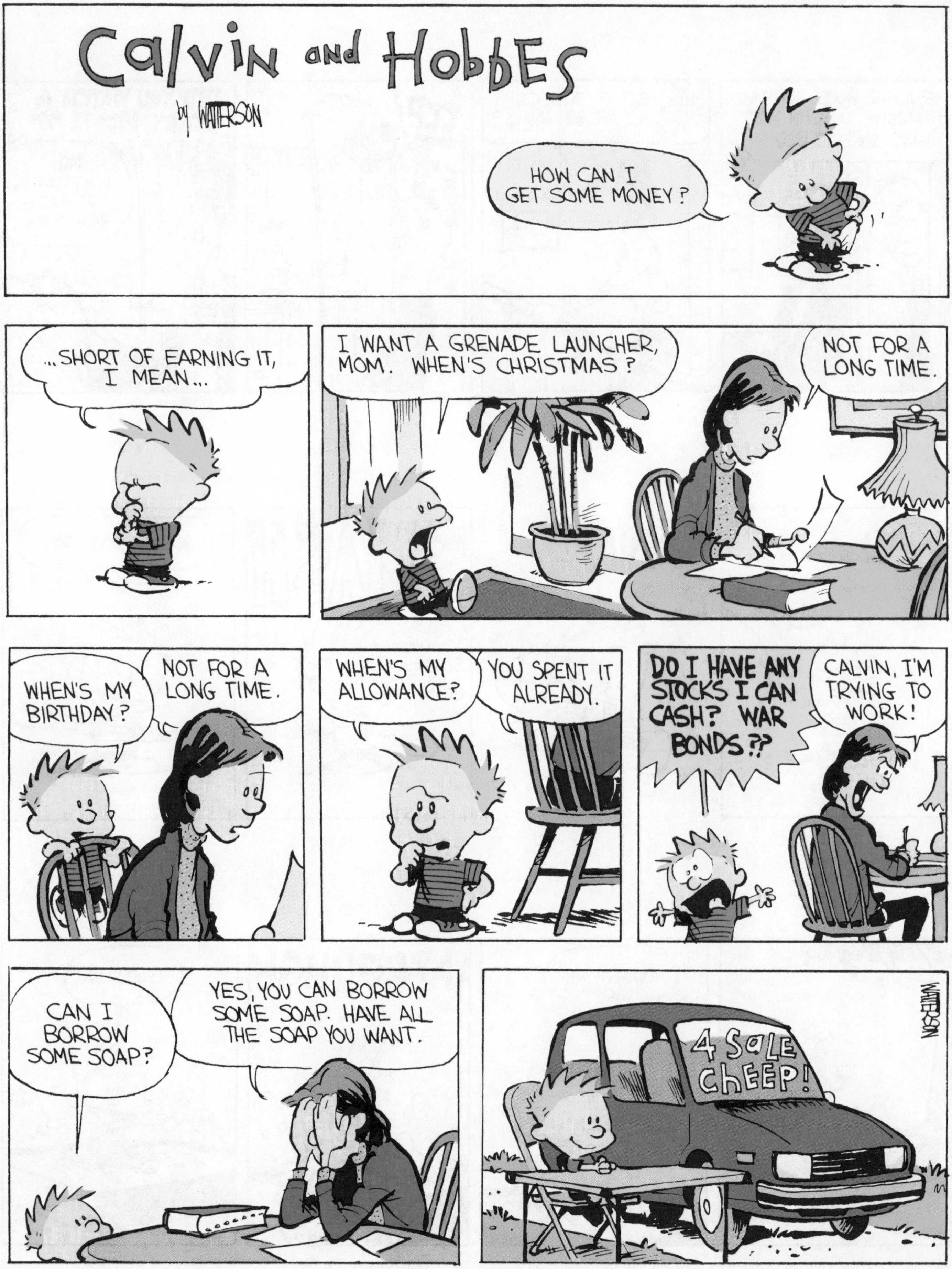
Calvin and Hobbes
by WATTERSON
HOW CAN I GET SOME MONEY?
...SHORT OF EARNING IT, I MEAN...
I WANT A GRENADE LAUNCHER, MOM. WHEN'S CHRISTMAS?
NOT FOR A LONG TIME.
WHEN'S MY BIRTHDAY?
NOT FOR A LONG TIME.
WHEN'S MY ALLOWANCE?
YOU SPENT IT ALREADY.
DO I HAVE ANY STOCKS I CAN CASH? WAR BONDS??
CALVIN, I'M TRYING TO WORK!
CAN I BORROW SOME SOAP?
YES, YOU CAN BORROW SOME SOAP. HAVE ALL THE SOAP YOU WANT.
WATTERSON
4 Sale Cheep!

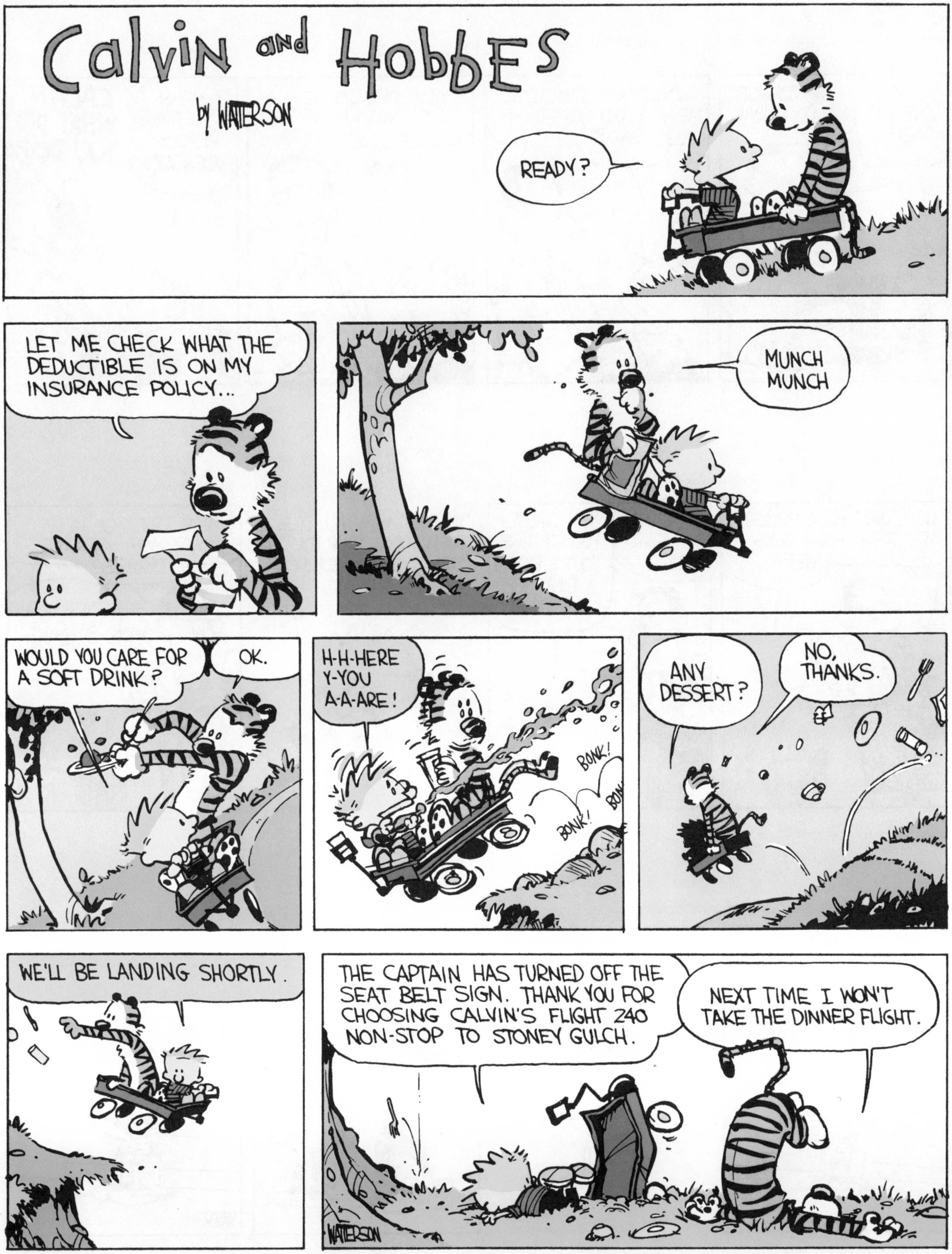
Calvin and Hobbes
by WATTERSON
READY?
LET ME CHECK WHAT THE DEDUCTIBLE IS ON MY INSURANCE POLICY...
MUNCH MUNCH
WOULD YOU CARE FOR A SOFT DRINK?
OK.
H-H-HERE Y-YOU A-A-ARE!
BONK!
BONK!
BONK!
ANY DESSERT?
NO, THANKS.
WE'LL BE LANDING SHORTLY.
THE CAPTAIN HAS TURNED OFF THE SEAT BELT SIGN. THANK YOU FOR CHOOSING CALVIN'S FLIGHT 240 NON-STOP TO STONEY GULCH.
NEXT TIME I WON'T TAKE THE DINNER FLIGHT.
WATTERSON

DO YOU LOVE ME, DAD?

OF COURSE I DO, CALVIN.

WOULD YOU STILL LOVE ME IF I DID SOMETHING BAD?

WELL OF COURSE ... I ... WOULD...

I MEAN SOMETHING REALLY REALLY..

CALVIN, WHAT DID YOU DO?!

WELL, DAD, YOUR POLLS ARE REAL HIGH THIS WEEK.

I'M GLAD TO HEAR THAT.

YEP, THOSE POLLED THINK YOU'RE DOING A FINE JOB AS DAD.

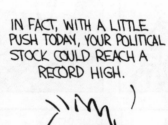

IN FACT, WITH A LITTLE PUSH TODAY, YOUR POLITICAL STOCK COULD REACH A RECORD HIGH.

WATTERSON

NICE TRY. GO HELP YOUR MOM WITH THE DISHES.

OOH DAD! SUICIDE! OOH! OOH!

HERE COMES MOE, THE CLASS BULLY.

HE'S NOT SMART, BUT HE'S STREETWISE.

THAT MEANS HE KNOWS WHAT STREET HE LIVES ON.

WATTERSON

TOLL BOOTH, DAD! YOU CAN'T PUT THE CAR IN UNTIL YOU PAY ME A QUARTER!

WHY SHOULD I PAY YOU TO PUT *MY* CAR IN *MY* GARAGE?

BECAUSE IF YOU DON'T, I'LL PULL THE DOOR DOWN ON THE HOOD AS YOU DRIVE IN!

WHAT A CHEAPSKATE.

A LITTLE LOWER... OK, FINE!

THANKS FOR HELPING ME PUT UP THIS SWING.

WHERE DID YOU EVER FIND THIS GREAT TIRE?

CALVIN! I'VE GOT TO GO TO WORK!!

WHAT'S THAT CEREAL YOU'RE EATING?

IT'S MY NEW FAVORITE, "CHOCOLATE FROSTED SUGAR BOMBS."

HAVE A TASTE.

THANK YOU.

MFFPBTH!! S-SW-SW SWEET!!

ACTUALLY, THEY'RE KINDA BLAND TILL YOU SCOOP SUGAR ON 'EM.

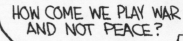

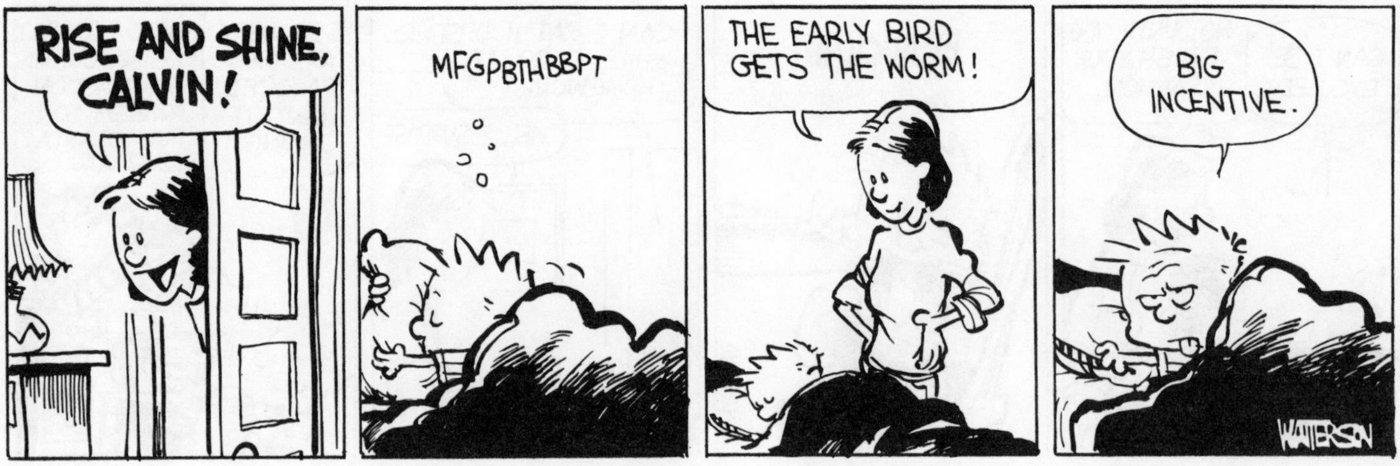
RISE AND SHINE, CALVIN!
MFGPBTHBBPT
THE EARLY BIRD GETS THE WORM!
BIG INCENTIVE.

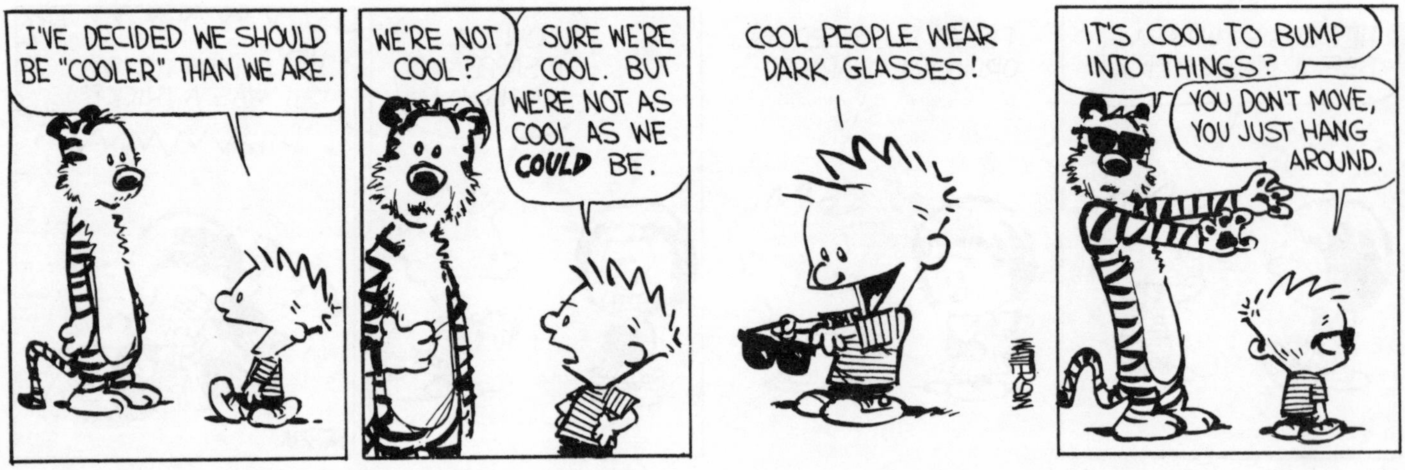
I'VE DECIDED WE SHOULD BE "COOLER" THAN WE ARE.
WE'RE NOT COOL?
SURE WE'RE COOL. BUT WE'RE NOT AS COOL AS WE **COULD** BE.
COOL PEOPLE WEAR DARK GLASSES!
IT'S COOL TO BUMP INTO THINGS?
YOU DON'T MOVE, YOU JUST HANG AROUND.

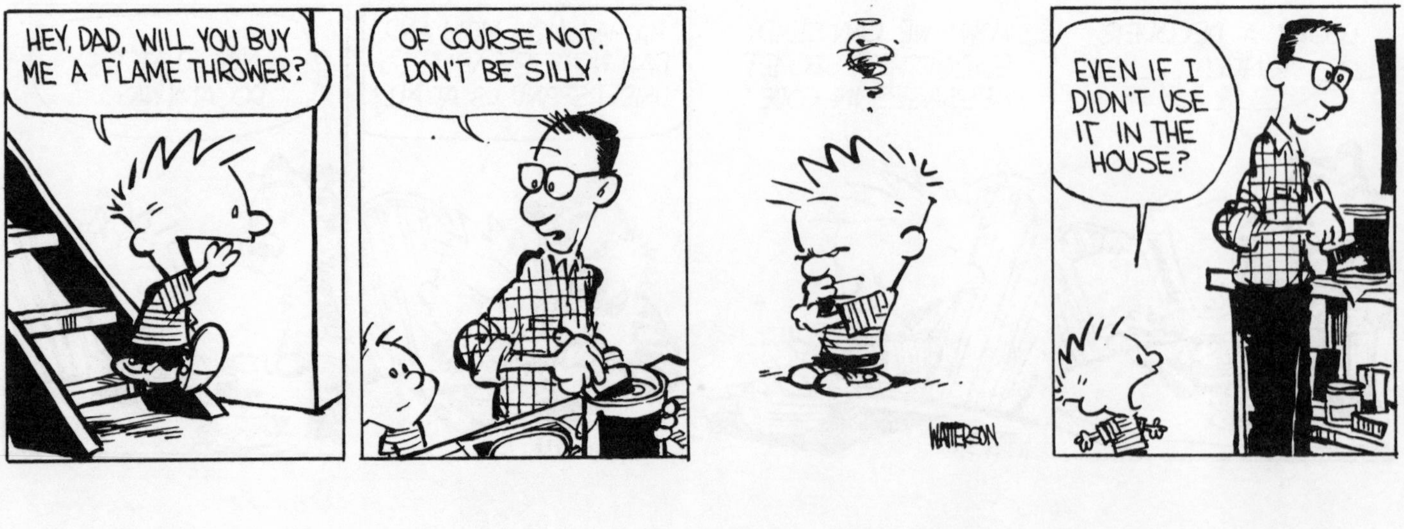
HEY, DAD, WILL YOU BUY ME A FLAME THROWER?
OF COURSE NOT. DON'T BE SILLY.
EVEN IF I DIDN'T USE IT IN THE HOUSE?

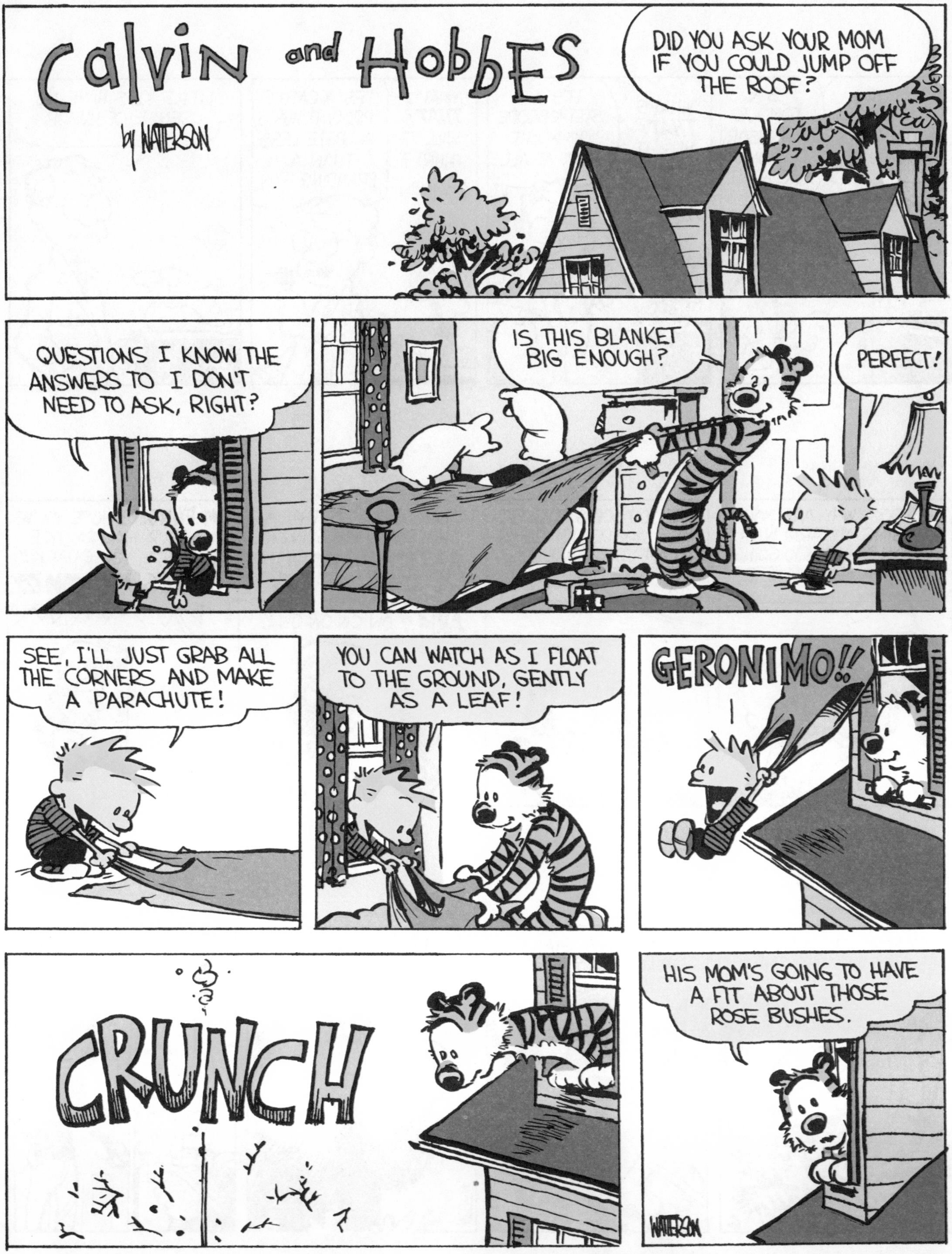
Calvin and Hobbes
by WATTERSON
DID YOU ASK YOUR MOM IF YOU COULD JUMP OFF THE ROOF?
QUESTIONS I KNOW THE ANSWERS TO I DON'T NEED TO ASK, RIGHT?
IS THIS BLANKET BIG ENOUGH?
PERFECT!
SEE, I'LL JUST GRAB ALL THE CORNERS AND MAKE A PARACHUTE!
YOU CAN WATCH AS I FLOAT TO THE GROUND, GENTLY AS A LEAF!
GERONIMO!!
CRUNCH
HIS MOM'S GOING TO HAVE A FIT ABOUT THOSE ROSE BUSHES.
WATTERSON

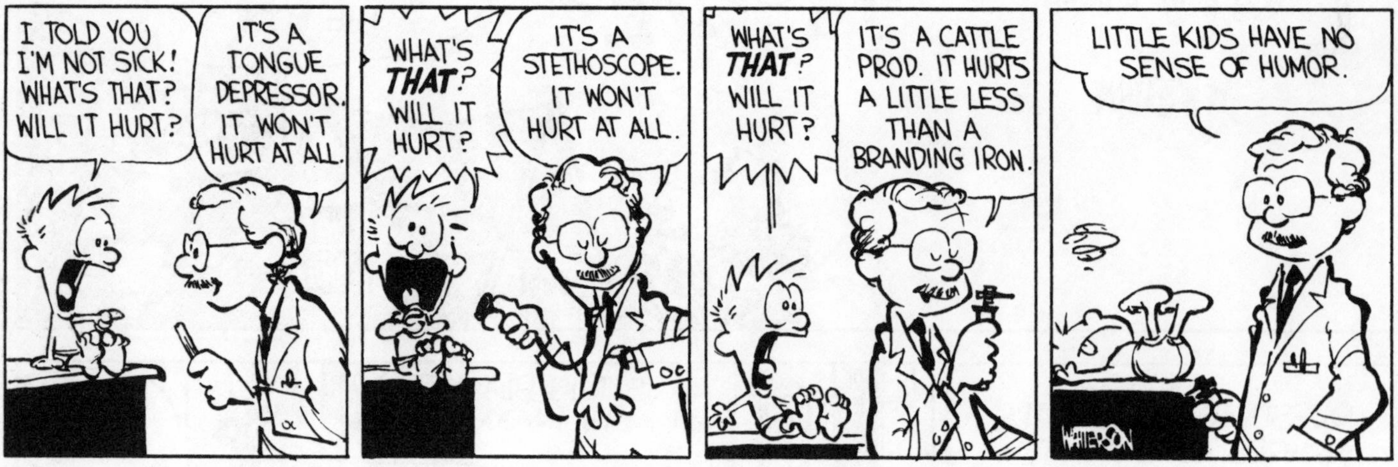
I TOLD YOU I'M NOT SICK! WHAT'S THAT? WILL IT HURT?
IT'S A TONGUE DEPRESSOR. IT WON'T HURT AT ALL.
WHAT'S THAT? WILL IT HURT?
IT'S A STETHOSCOPE. IT WON'T HURT AT ALL.
WHAT'S THAT? WILL IT HURT?
IT'S A CATTLE PROD. IT HURTS A LITTLE LESS THAN A BRANDING IRON.
LITTLE KIDS HAVE NO SENSE OF HUMOR.
WATTERSON

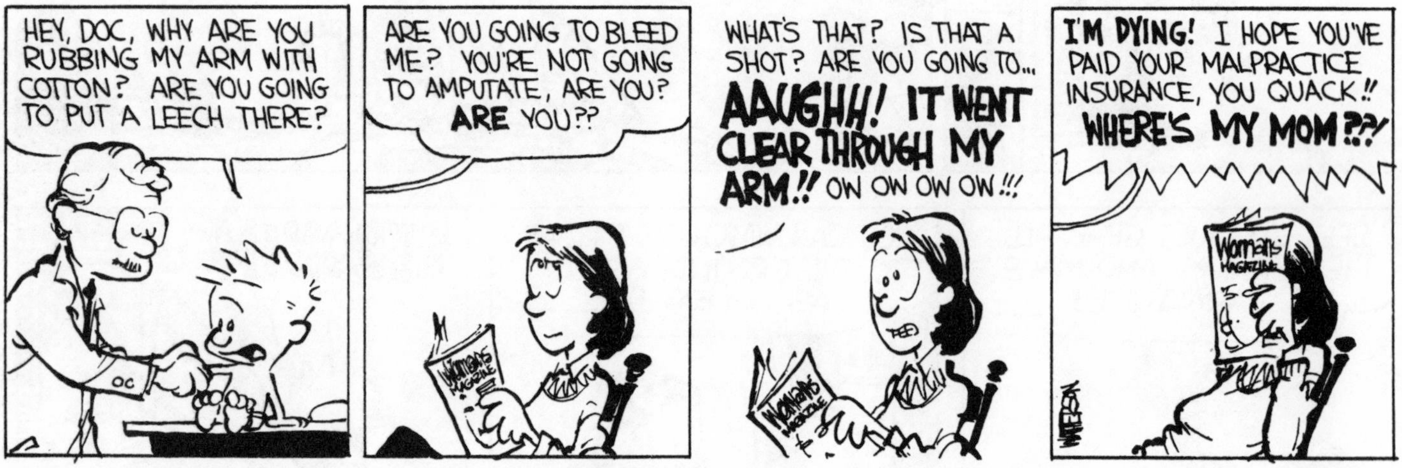
HEY, DOC, WHY ARE YOU RUBBING MY ARM WITH COTTON? ARE YOU GOING TO PUT A LEECH THERE?
ARE YOU GOING TO BLEED ME? YOU'RE NOT GOING TO AMPUTATE, ARE YOU? ARE YOU??
WHAT'S THAT? IS THAT A SHOT? ARE YOU GOING TO... AAUGHH! IT WENT CLEAR THROUGH MY ARM!! OW OW OW OW!!!
I'M DYING! I HOPE YOU'VE PAID YOUR MALPRACTICE INSURANCE, YOU QUACK!! WHERE'S MY MOM??!
WATTERSON

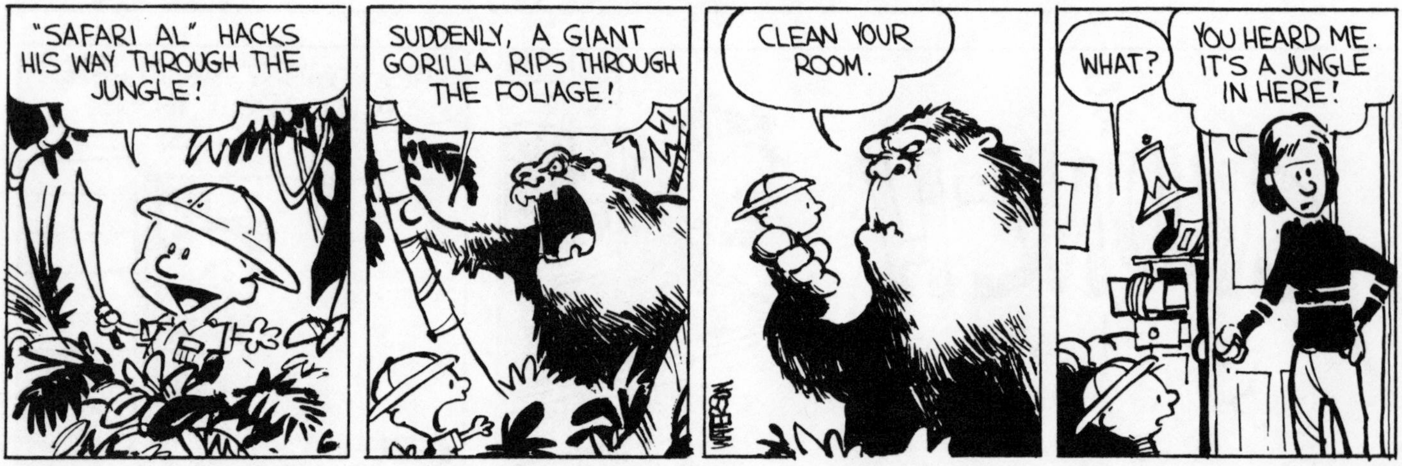
"SAFARI AL" HACKS HIS WAY THROUGH THE JUNGLE!
SUDDENLY, A GIANT GORILLA RIPS THROUGH THE FOLIAGE!
CLEAN YOUR ROOM.
WATTERSON
WHAT?
YOU HEARD ME. IT'S A JUNGLE IN HERE!

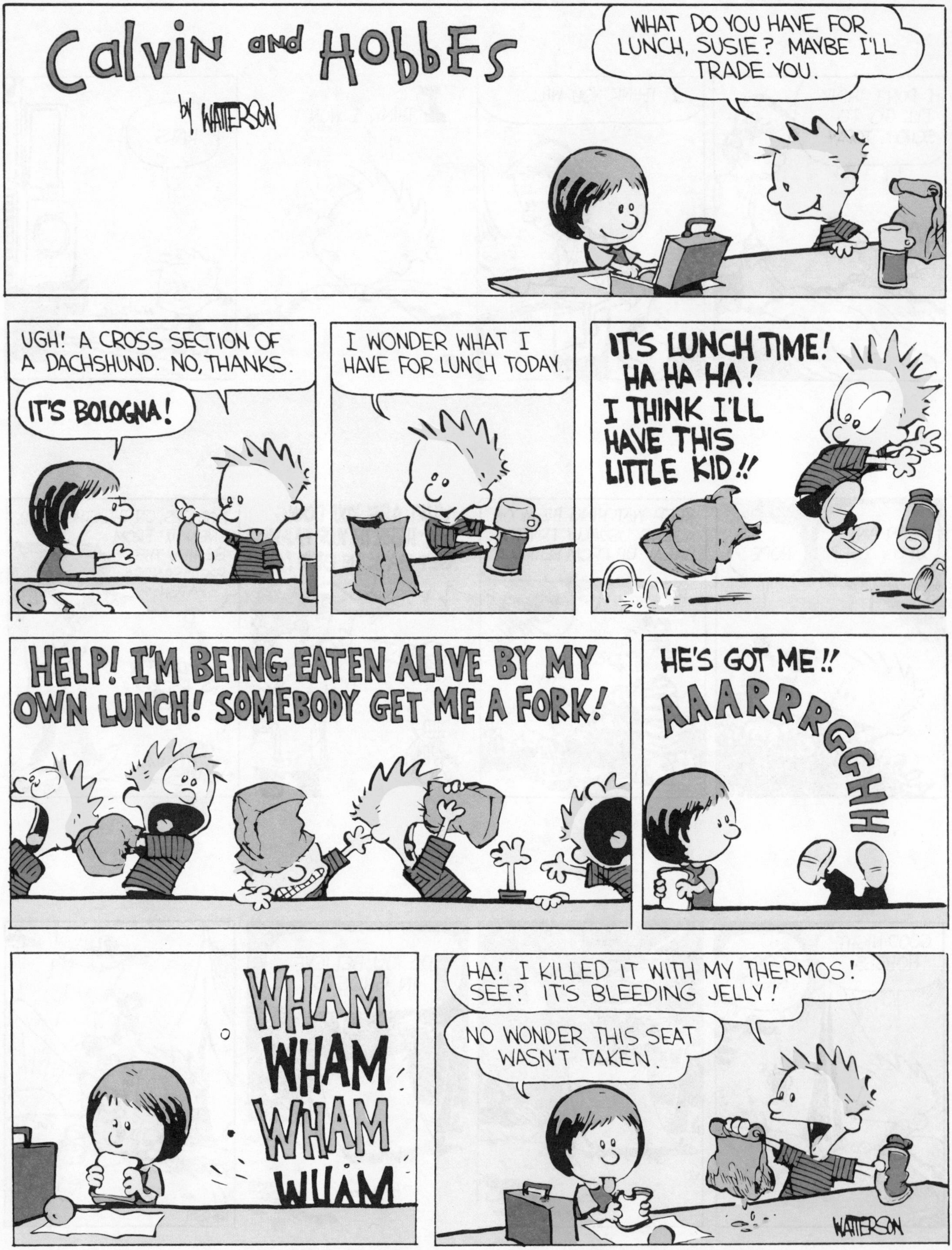

Calvin and HOBBES
by WATTERSON
WHAT DO YOU HAVE FOR LUNCH, SUSIE? MAYBE I'LL TRADE YOU.
UGH! A CROSS SECTION OF A DACHSHUND. NO, THANKS.
IT'S BOLOGNA!
I WONDER WHAT I HAVE FOR LUNCH TODAY.
IT'S LUNCH TIME! HA HA HA! I THINK I'LL HAVE THIS LITTLE KID!!
HELP! I'M BEING EATEN ALIVE BY MY OWN LUNCH! SOMEBODY GET ME A FORK!
HE'S GOT ME!!
AAARRRGGHH
WHAM
WHAM
WHAM
WHAM
HA! I KILLED IT WITH MY THERMOS! SEE? IT'S BLEEDING JELLY!
NO WONDER THIS SEAT WASN'T TAKEN.
WATTERSON

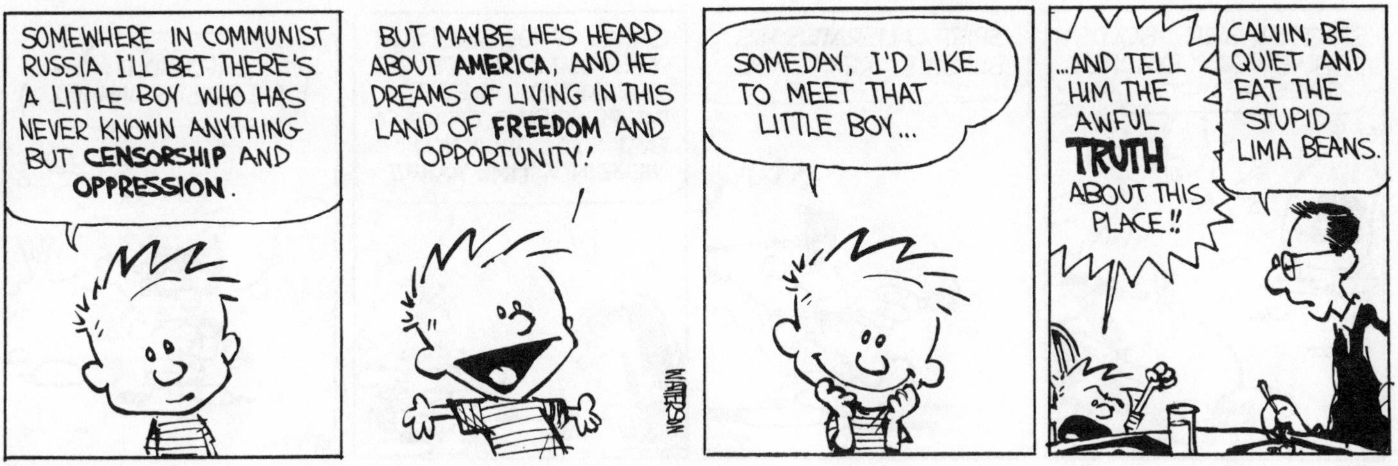
SOMEWHERE IN COMMUNIST RUSSIA I'LL BET THERE'S A LITTLE BOY WHO HAS NEVER KNOWN ANYTHING BUT **CENSORSHIP** AND **OPPRESSION**.
BUT MAYBE HE'S HEARD ABOUT **AMERICA**, AND HE DREAMS OF LIVING IN THIS LAND OF **FREEDOM** AND OPPORTUNITY!
WATTERSON
SOMEDAY, I'D LIKE TO MEET THAT LITTLE BOY...
...AND TELL HIM THE AWFUL **TRUTH** ABOUT THIS PLACE!!
CALVIN, BE QUIET AND EAT THE STUPID LIMA BEANS.

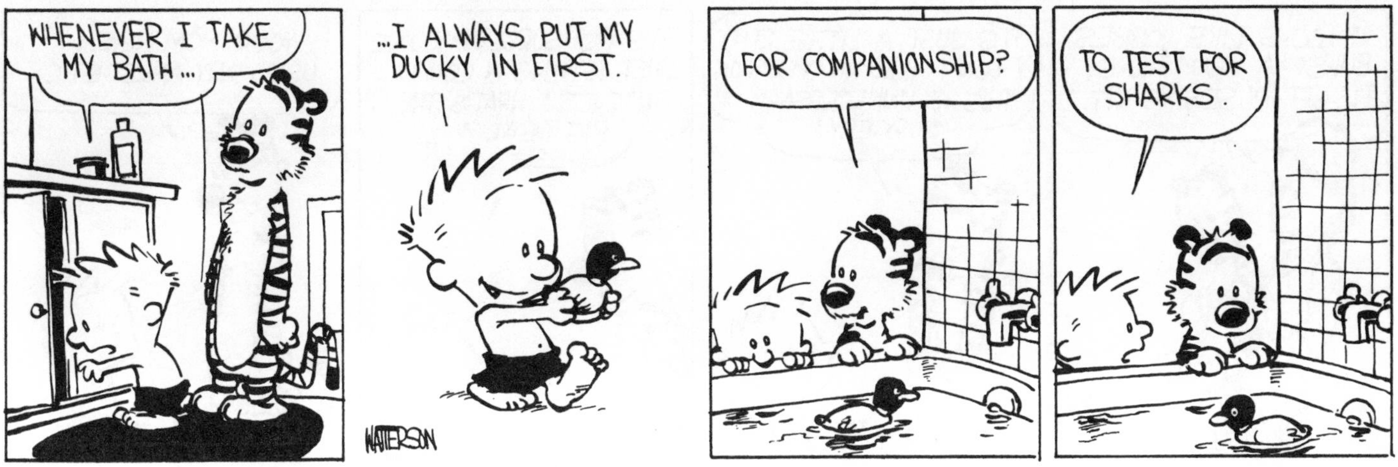
WHENEVER I TAKE MY BATH...
...I ALWAYS PUT MY DUCKY IN FIRST.
WATTERSON
FOR COMPANIONSHIP?
TO TEST FOR SHARKS.

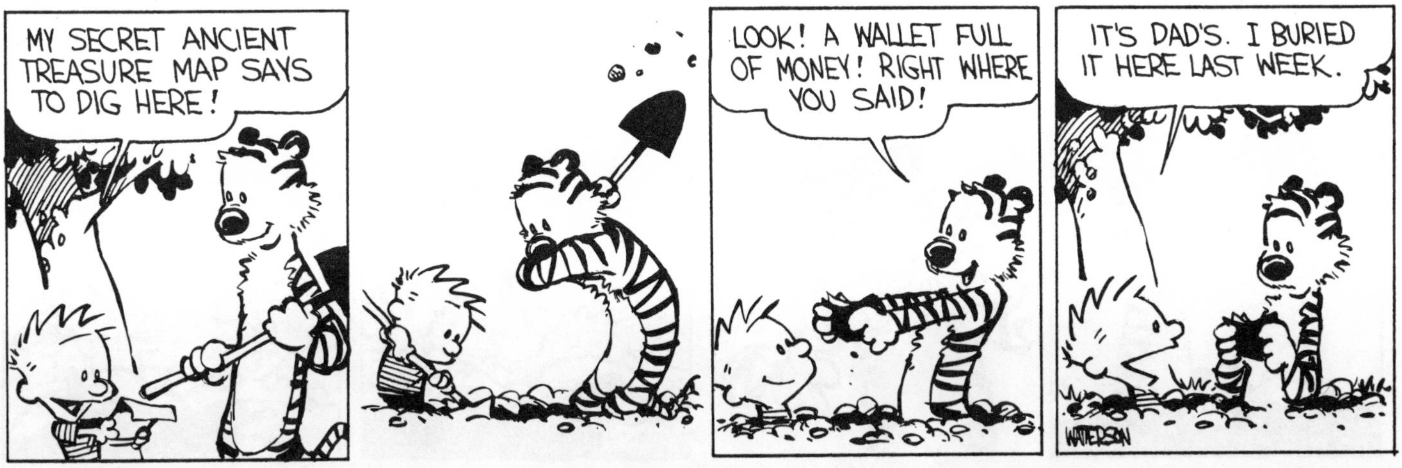
MY SECRET ANCIENT TREASURE MAP SAYS TO DIG HERE!
LOOK! A WALLET FULL OF MONEY! RIGHT WHERE YOU SAID!
IT'S DAD'S. I BURIED IT HERE LAST WEEK.
WATTERSON

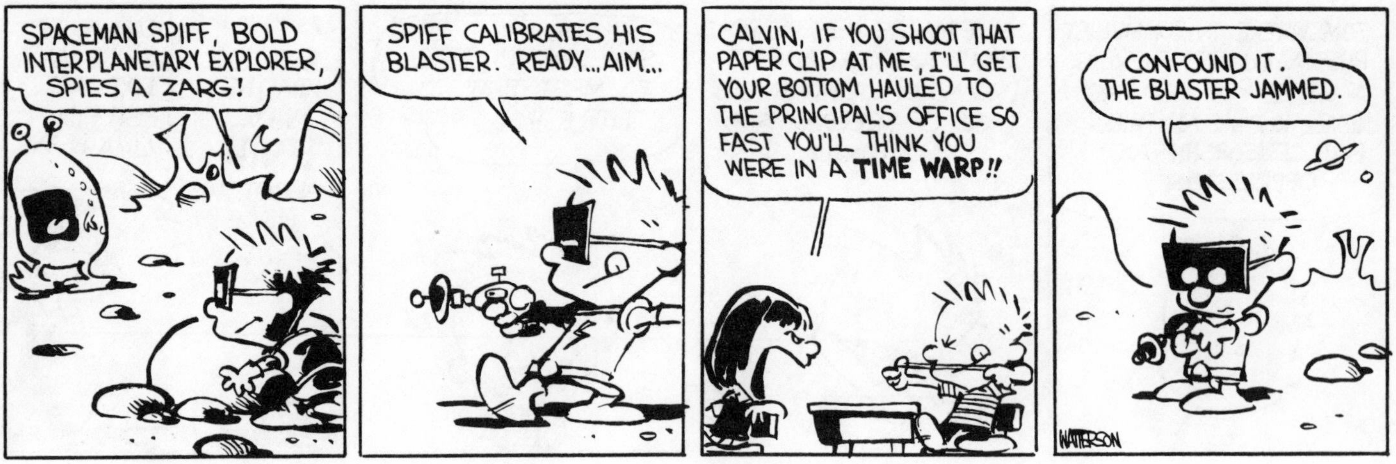
SPACEMAN SPIFF, BOLD INTERPLANETARY EXPLORER, SPIES A ZARG!
SPIFF CALIBRATES HIS BLASTER. READY...AIM...
CALVIN, IF YOU SHOOT THAT PAPER CLIP AT ME, I'LL GET YOUR BOTTOM HAULED TO THE PRINCIPAL'S OFFICE SO FAST YOU'LL THINK YOU WERE IN A **TIME WARP**!!
CONFOUND IT. THE BLASTER JAMMED.
WATTERSON

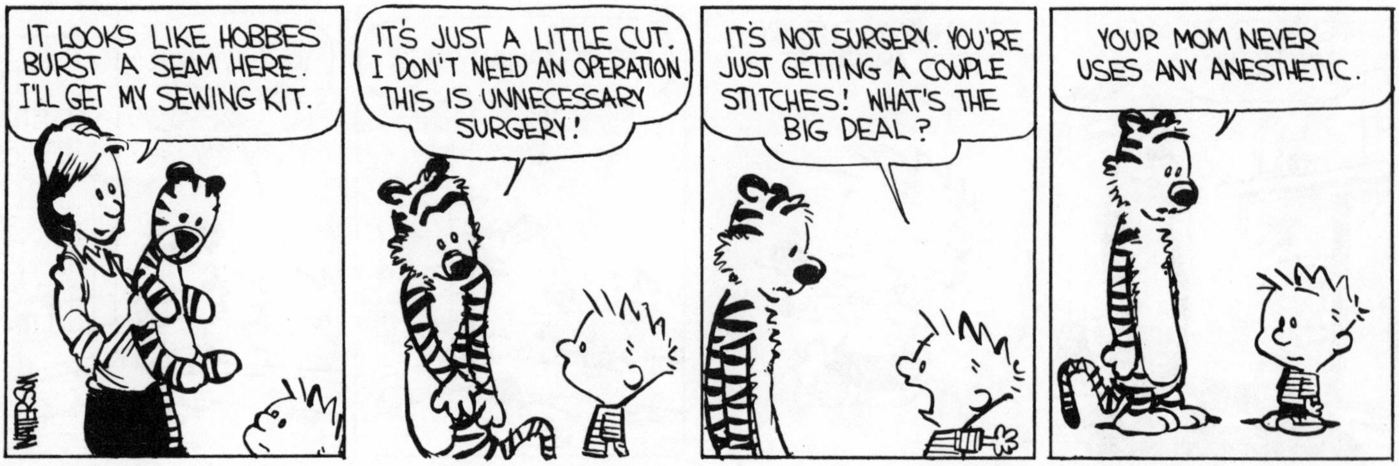
IT LOOKS LIKE HOBBES BURST A SEAM HERE. I'LL GET MY SEWING KIT.
IT'S JUST A LITTLE CUT. I DON'T NEED AN OPERATION. THIS IS UNNECESSARY SURGERY!
IT'S NOT SURGERY. YOU'RE JUST GETTING A COUPLE STITCHES! WHAT'S THE BIG DEAL?
YOUR MOM NEVER USES ANY ANESTHETIC.
WATTERSON

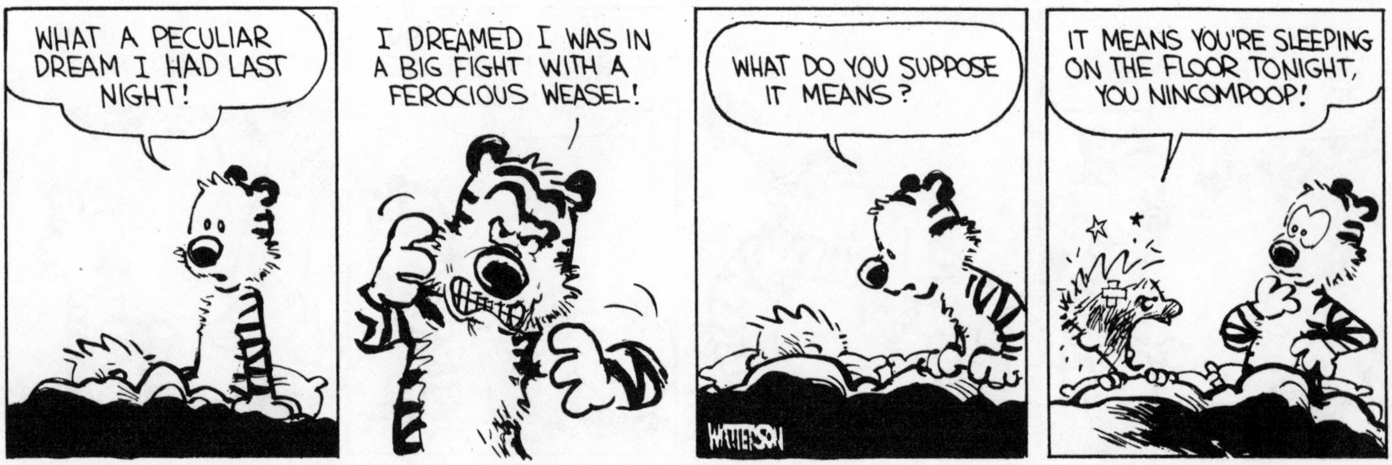
WHAT A PECULIAR DREAM I HAD LAST NIGHT!
I DREAMED I WAS IN A BIG FIGHT WITH A FEROCIOUS WEASEL!
WHAT DO YOU SUPPOSE IT MEANS?
WATTERSON
IT MEANS YOU'RE SLEEPING ON THE FLOOR TONIGHT, YOU NINCOMPOOP!

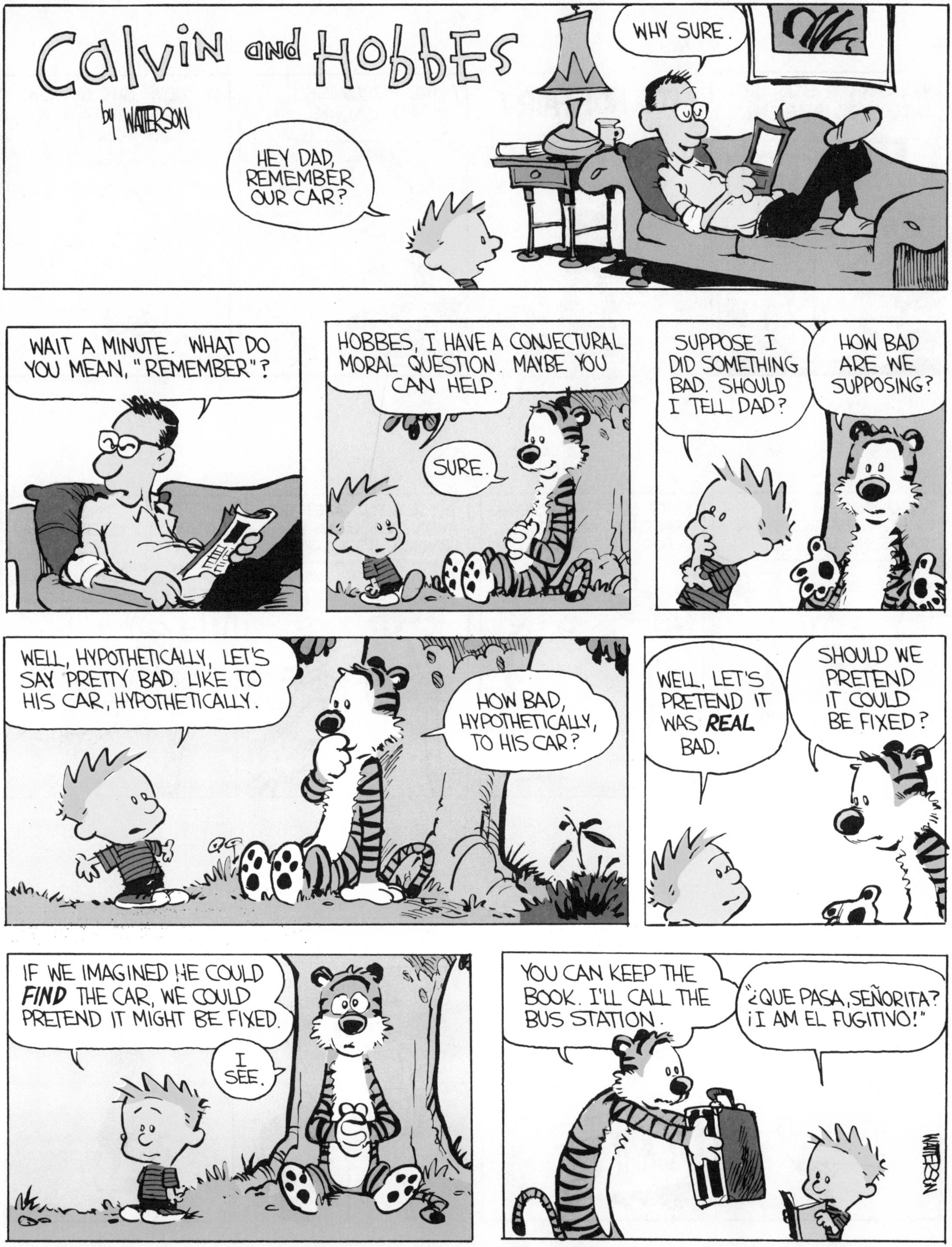
Calvin and Hobbes
by WATTERSON
HEY DAD, REMEMBER OUR CAR?
WHY SURE.
WAIT A MINUTE. WHAT DO YOU MEAN, "REMEMBER"?
HOBBES, I HAVE A CONJECTURAL MORAL QUESTION. MAYBE YOU CAN HELP.
SURE.
SUPPOSE I DID SOMETHING BAD. SHOULD I TELL DAD?
HOW BAD ARE WE SUPPOSING?
WELL, HYPOTHETICALLY, LET'S SAY PRETTY BAD. LIKE TO HIS CAR, HYPOTHETICALLY.
HOW BAD, HYPOTHETICALLY, TO HIS CAR?
WELL, LET'S PRETEND IT WAS **REAL** BAD.
SHOULD WE PRETEND IT COULD BE FIXED?
IF WE IMAGINED HE COULD **FIND** THE CAR, WE COULD PRETEND IT MIGHT BE FIXED.
I SEE.
YOU CAN KEEP THE BOOK. I'LL CALL THE BUS STATION.
"¿QUE PASA, SEÑORITA? ¡I AM EL FUGITIVO!"
WATTERSON

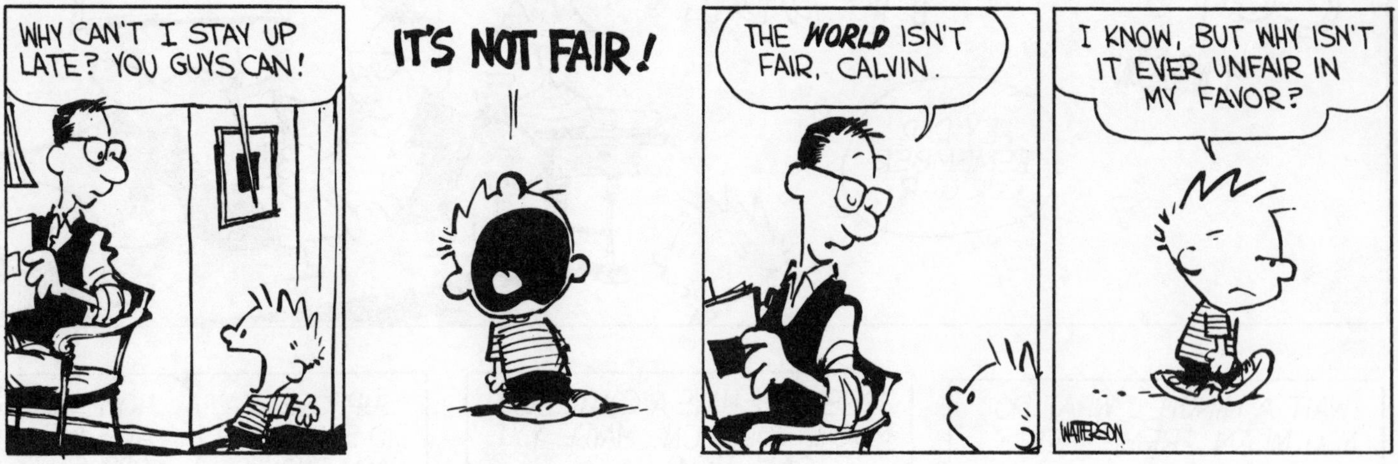
WHY CAN'T I STAY UP LATE? YOU GUYS CAN!
IT'S NOT FAIR!
THE WORLD ISN'T FAIR, CALVIN.
I KNOW, BUT WHY ISN'T IT EVER UNFAIR IN MY FAVOR?

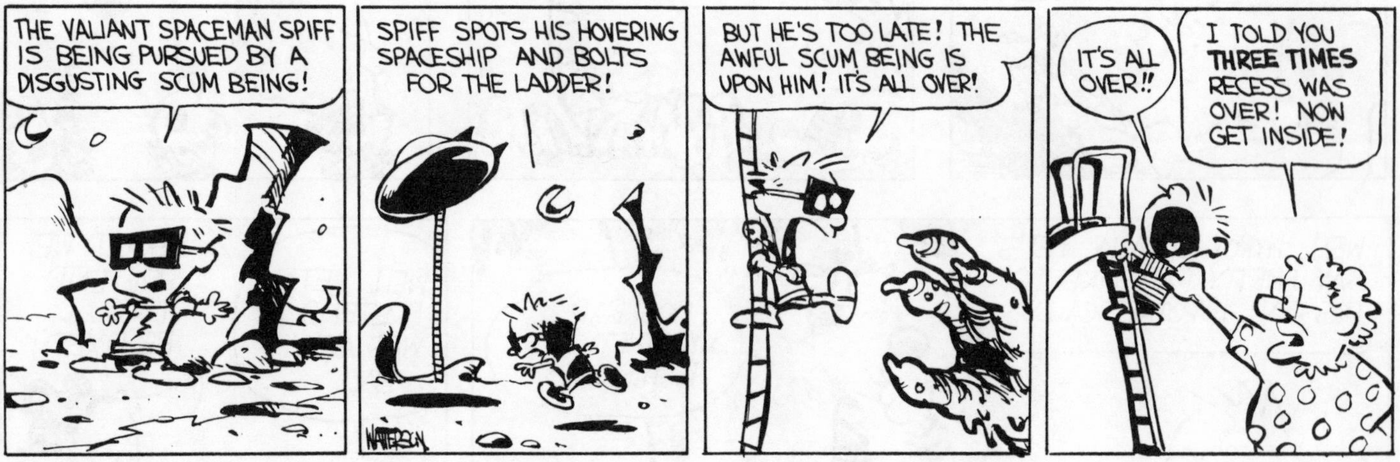
THE VALIANT SPACEMAN SPIFF IS BEING PURSUED BY A DISGUSTING SCUM BEING!
SPIFF SPOTS HIS HOVERING SPACESHIP AND BOLTS FOR THE LADDER!
BUT HE'S TOO LATE! THE AWFUL SCUM BEING IS UPON HIM! IT'S ALL OVER!
IT'S ALL OVER!!
I TOLD YOU THREE TIMES RECESS WAS OVER! NOW GET INSIDE!

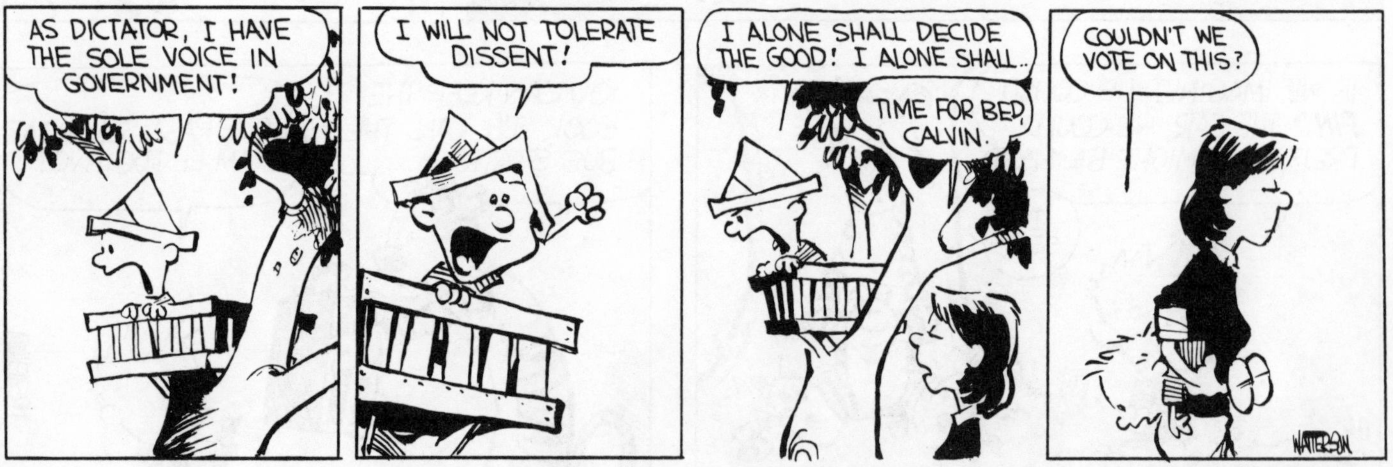
AS DICTATOR, I HAVE THE SOLE VOICE IN GOVERNMENT!
I WILL NOT TOLERATE DISSENT!
I ALONE SHALL DECIDE THE GOOD! I ALONE SHALL...
TIME FOR BED, CALVIN.
COULDN'T WE VOTE ON THIS?

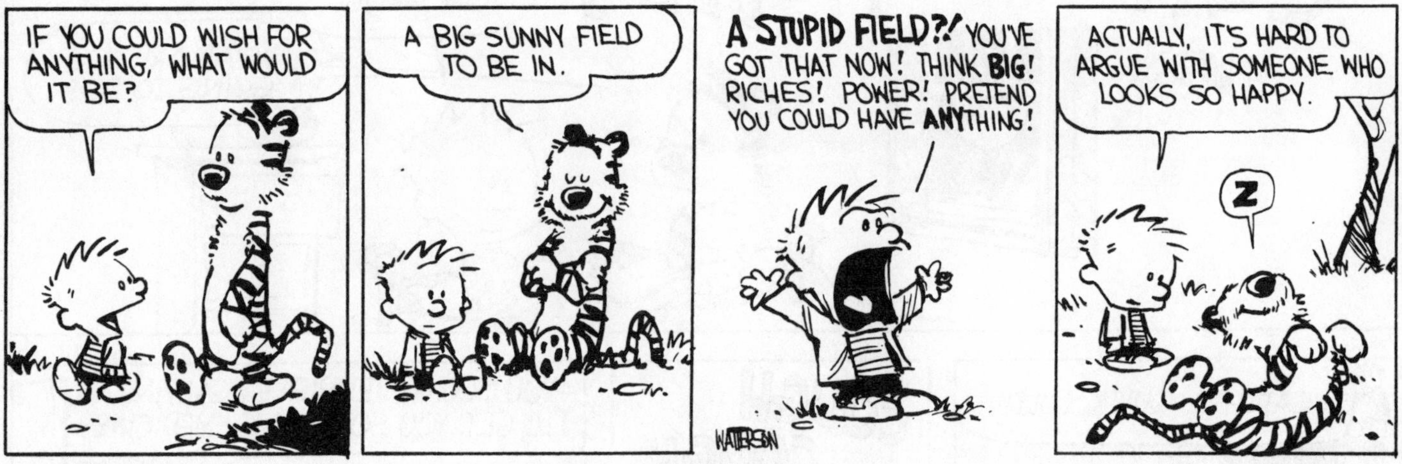
IF YOU COULD WISH FOR ANYTHING, WHAT WOULD IT BE?
A BIG SUNNY FIELD TO BE IN.
A STUPID FIELD?! YOU'VE GOT THAT NOW! THINK BIG! RICHES! POWER! PRETEND YOU COULD HAVE ANYTHING!
WATTERSON
ACTUALLY, IT'S HARD TO ARGUE WITH SOMEONE WHO LOOKS SO HAPPY.
Z

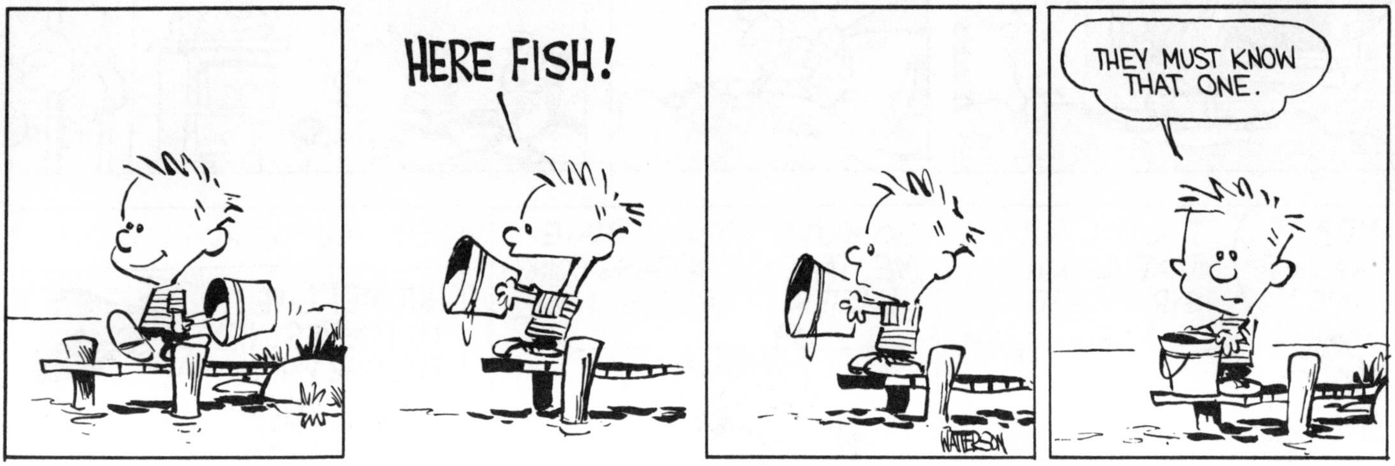
HERE FISH!
WATTERSON
THEY MUST KNOW THAT ONE.

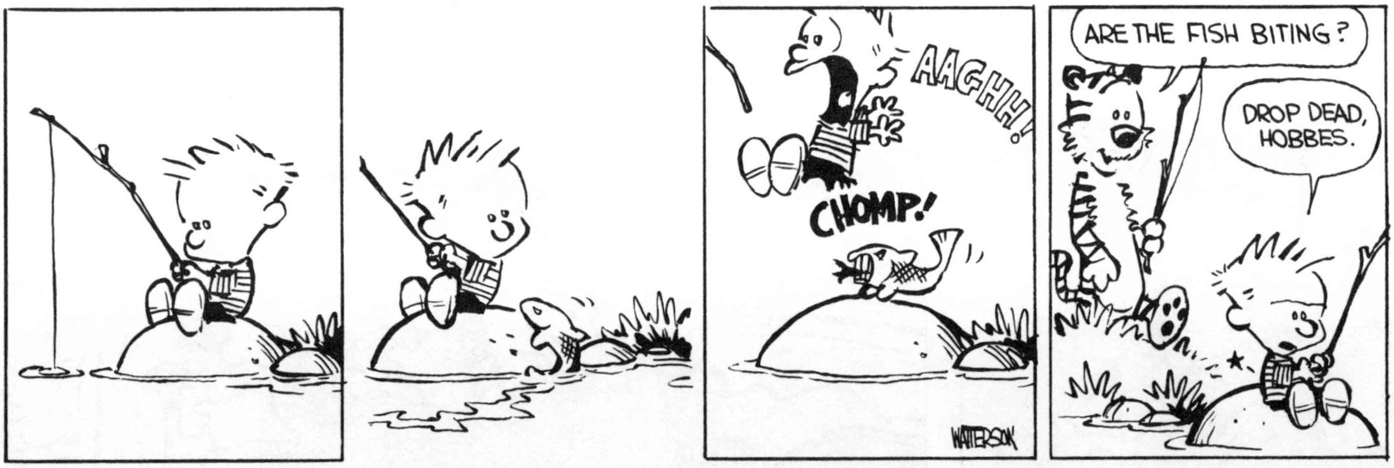
AAGHH!
CHOMP!
WATTERSON
ARE THE FISH BITING?
DROP DEAD, HOBBES.

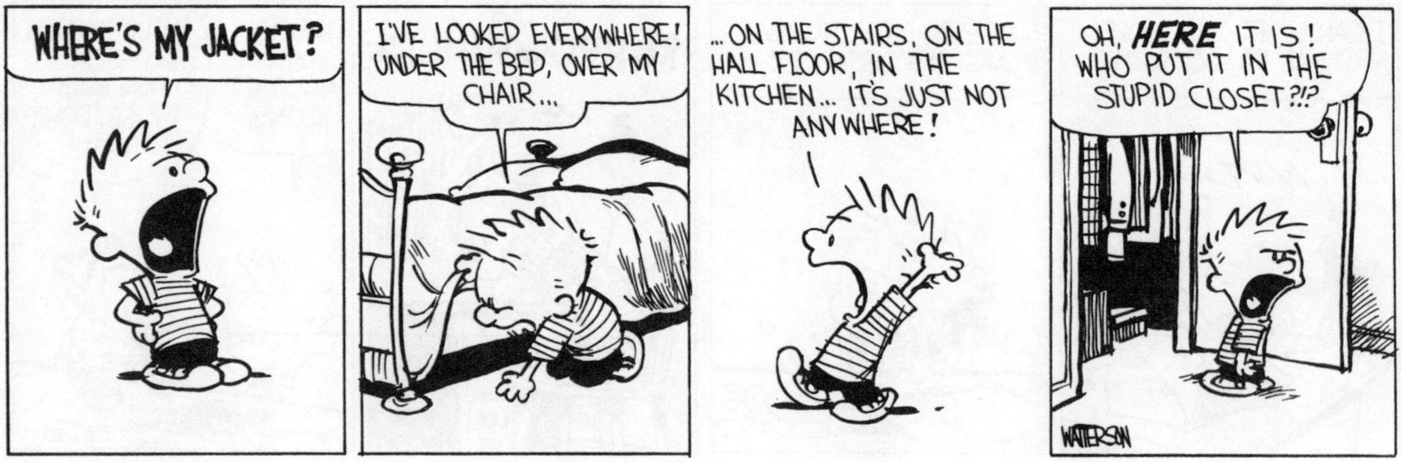
WHERE'S MY JACKET?
I'VE LOOKED EVERYWHERE! UNDER THE BED, OVER MY CHAIR...
...ON THE STAIRS, ON THE HALL FLOOR, IN THE KITCHEN... IT'S JUST NOT ANYWHERE!
OH, HERE IT IS! WHO PUT IT IN THE STUPID CLOSET?!?
WATTERSON

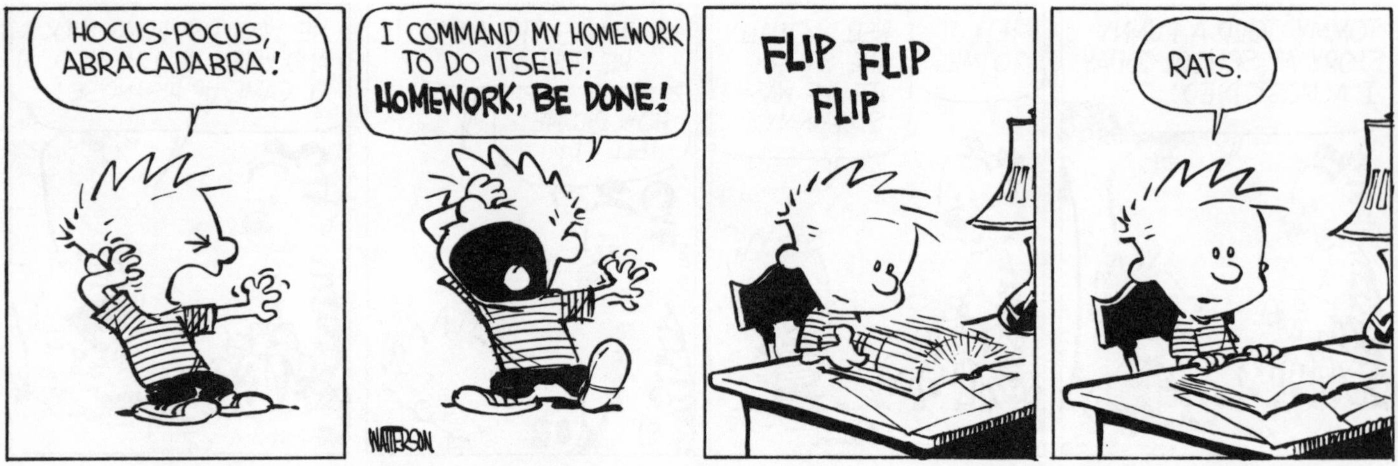
HOCUS-POCUS, ABRACADABRA!
I COMMAND MY HOMEWORK TO DO ITSELF! HOMEWORK, BE DONE!
WATTERSON
FLIP FLIP FLIP
RATS.

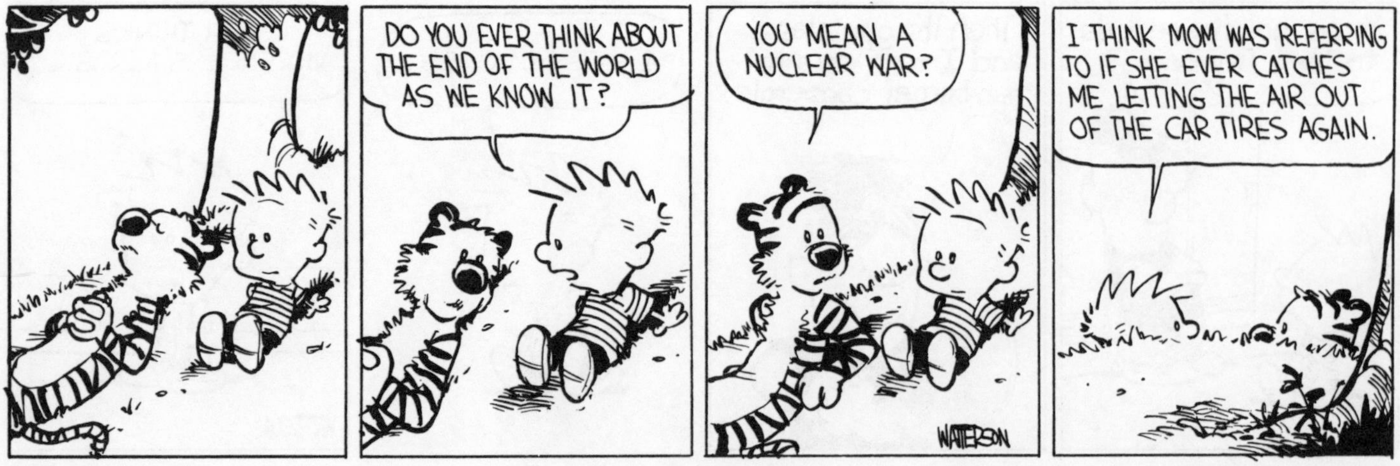
DO YOU EVER THINK ABOUT THE END OF THE WORLD AS WE KNOW IT?
YOU MEAN A NUCLEAR WAR?
WATTERSON
I THINK MOM WAS REFERRING TO IF SHE EVER CATCHES ME LETTING THE AIR OUT OF THE CAR TIRES AGAIN.

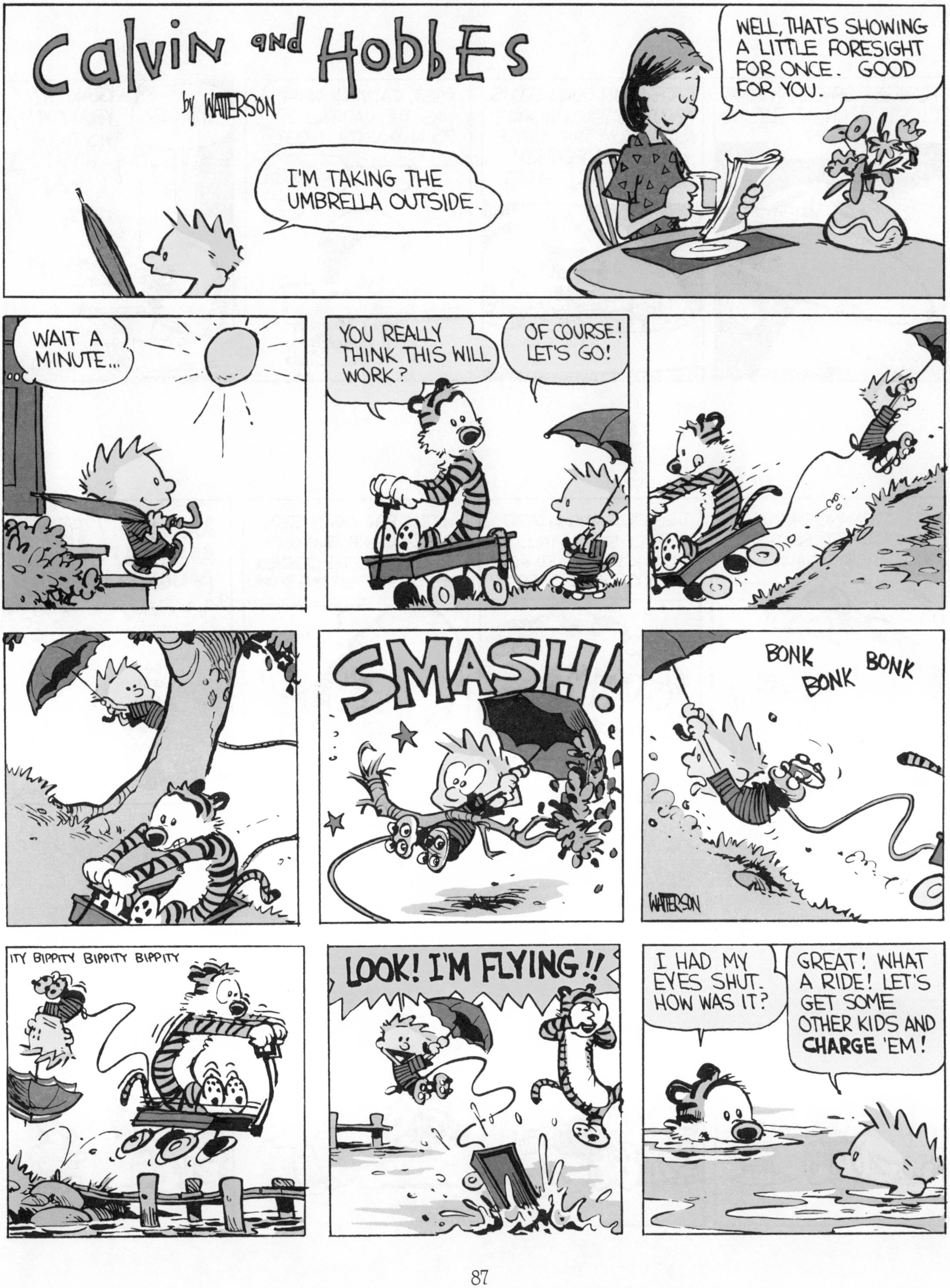
Calvin and Hobbes
by WATTERSON
I'M TAKING THE UMBRELLA OUTSIDE.
WELL, THAT'S SHOWING A LITTLE FORESIGHT FOR ONCE. GOOD FOR YOU.
WAIT A MINUTE...
YOU REALLY THINK THIS WILL WORK?
OF COURSE! LET'S GO!
SMASH!
BONK
BONK
BONK
WATTERSON
ITY BIPPITY BIPPITY BIPPITY
LOOK! I'M FLYING!!
I HAD MY EYES SHUT. HOW WAS IT?
GREAT! WHAT A RIDE! LET'S GET SOME OTHER KIDS AND CHARGE 'EM!

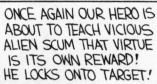

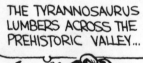

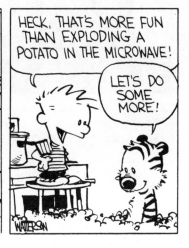

SO THE CONTRACTOR SAYS IT WILL COST ABOUT $200 TO FIX.

OH, THAT DUMB KID!

WELL, IT'S ALL PART OF RAISING A CHILD, RIGHT?

MM.

YOU'RE NOT SORRY WE HAD CALVIN, ARE YOU?

ARE *YOU*?

I ASKED FIRST....BESIDES, IT WASN'T ALL *MY* DECISION.

ALL *I* KNOW IS THAT *I* OFFERED TO BUY US A DACHSHUND, BUT NO, *YOU* SAID...

DO YOU THINK THERE'S A GOD?

WELL *SOME*BODY'S OUT TO GET ME.

SPACEMAN SPIFF CLOSES IN ON THE ALIEN VESSEL!

THE ALIEN, BEING UNNATURALLY STUPID, IS BLISSFULLY IGNORANT OF ITS IMMINENT DOOM!

OUR HERO LOCKS ONTO TARGET AND WARMS UP HIS FRAP-RAY BLASTER!

MISS WORMWOOD!!

ZOUNDS! A GORKON DEATH STATION APPEARS! EVASIVE ACTION!

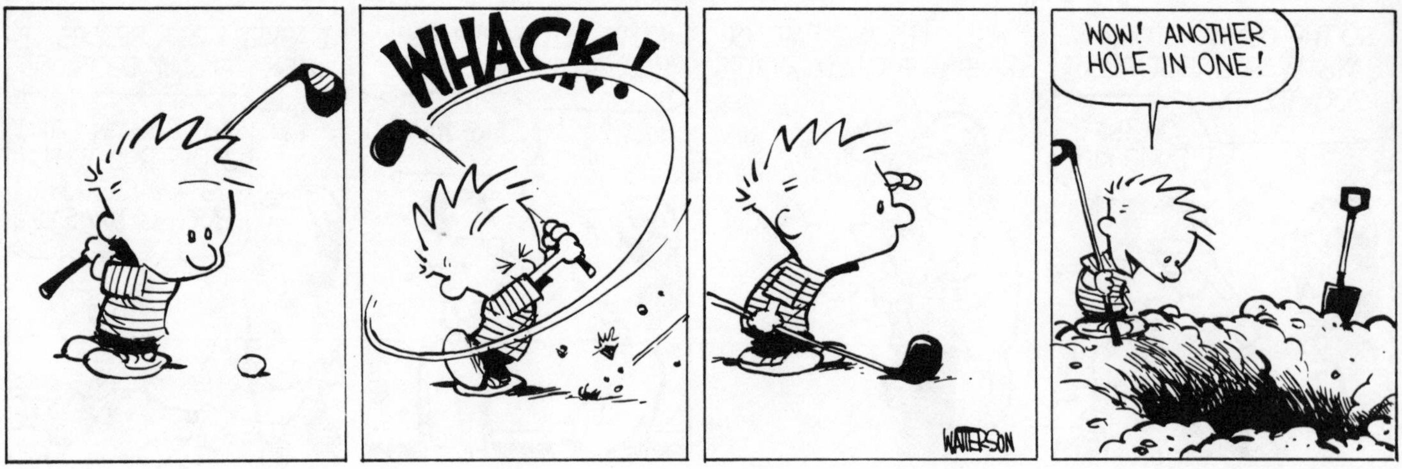
WHACK!
WOW! ANOTHER HOLE IN ONE!
WATTERSON

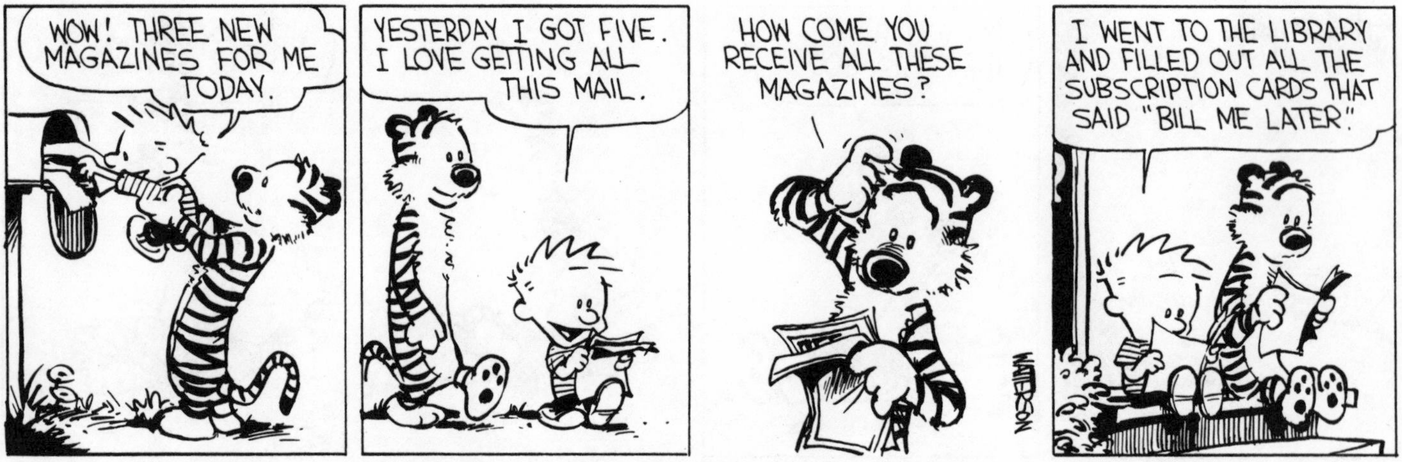
WOW! THREE NEW MAGAZINES FOR ME TODAY.
YESTERDAY I GOT FIVE. I LOVE GETTING ALL THIS MAIL.
HOW COME YOU RECEIVE ALL THESE MAGAZINES?
WATTERSON
I WENT TO THE LIBRARY AND FILLED OUT ALL THE SUBSCRIPTION CARDS THAT SAID "BILL ME LATER".

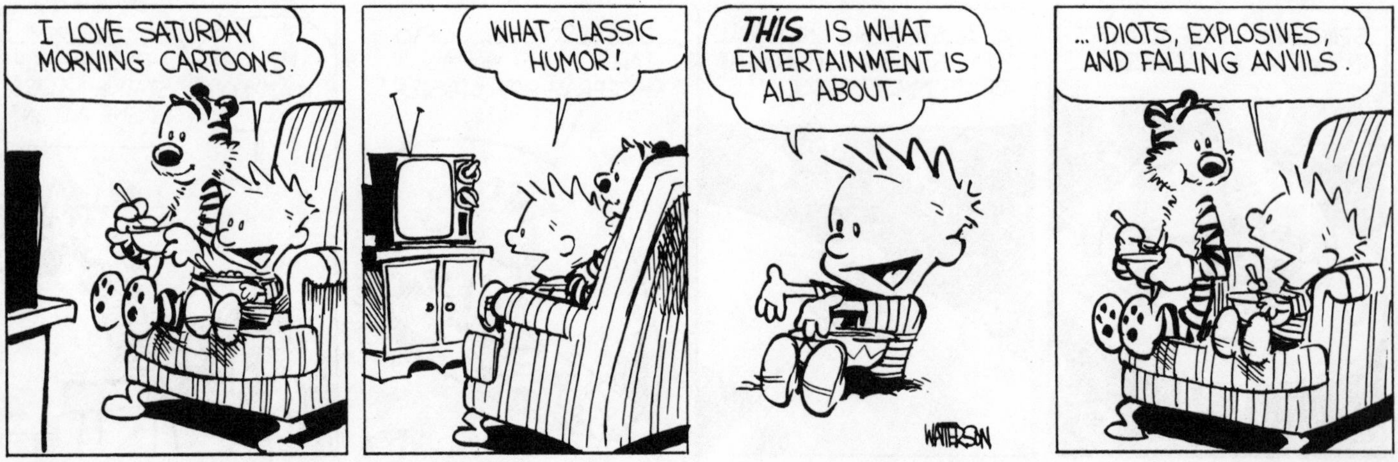
I LOVE SATURDAY MORNING CARTOONS.
WHAT CLASSIC HUMOR!
THIS IS WHAT ENTERTAINMENT IS ALL ABOUT.
WATTERSON
... IDIOTS, EXPLOSIVES, AND FALLING ANVILS.

**Panel 1:** CALVIN, THE HUMAN INSECT, WALKS ACROSS THE DINNER TABLE.

**Panel 2:** WITH PROPORTIONAL INSECT STRENGTH, HE PLACES A GIANT PEA ON THE EDGE OF A SPOON.

**Panel 3:** HE THEN CLIMBS TO THE TOP OF THE OTHER END...

**Panel 4:** ...AND WITH A TINY JUMP... CALVIN, STOP THAT!

**Panel 5:** IN HIS MINUSCULE SIZE, IT TAKES CALVIN, THE HUMAN INSECT, TEN MINUTES TO WALK ACROSS A BOOK'S PAGE!

**Panel 6:** AT THE OTHER END, HE SLOWLY LIFTS THE GIGANTIC SHEET!

**Panel 7:** THEN IT'S ANOTHER TEN-MINUTE JOURNEY BACK, AS HE TURNS IT OVER!

**Panel 8:** GEE, THE KID'S BEEN QUIET FOR ALMOST TWENTY MINUTES. HE'S DOING HIS HOMEWORK.

**Panel 9:** HERE'S A MOVIE WE SHOULD WATCH. WHO'S IN IT?

**Panel 10:** IT SAYS, "JAPANESE CAST."

**Panel 11:** "TWO BIG RUBBERY MONSTERS SLUG IT OUT OVER MAJOR METROPOLITAN CENTERS IN A BATTLE FOR WORLD SUPREMACY."

**Panel 12:** DOESN'T THAT SOUND GREAT? AND PEOPLE SAY THAT FOREIGN FILM IS INACCESSIBLE.

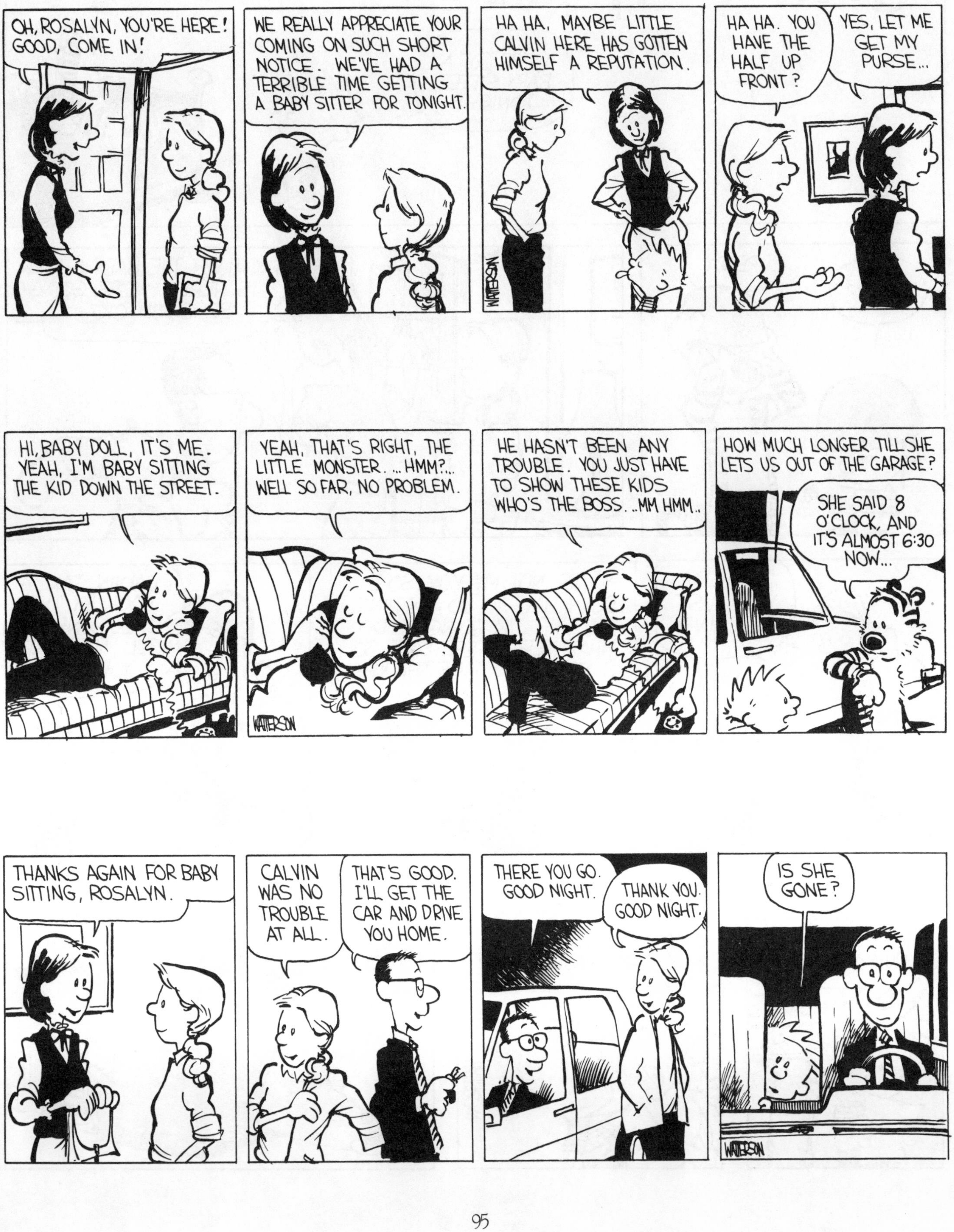
OH, ROSALYN, YOU'RE HERE! GOOD, COME IN!
WE REALLY APPRECIATE YOUR COMING ON SUCH SHORT NOTICE. WE'VE HAD A TERRIBLE TIME GETTING A BABY SITTER FOR TONIGHT.
HA HA. MAYBE LITTLE CALVIN HERE HAS GOTTEN HIMSELF A REPUTATION.
HA HA. YOU HAVE THE HALF UP FRONT?
YES, LET ME GET MY PURSE...
WATTERSON
HI, BABY DOLL, IT'S ME. YEAH, I'M BABY SITTING THE KID DOWN THE STREET.
YEAH, THAT'S RIGHT, THE LITTLE MONSTER. ...HMM?... WELL SO FAR, NO PROBLEM.
HE HASN'T BEEN ANY TROUBLE. YOU JUST HAVE TO SHOW THESE KIDS WHO'S THE BOSS. ..MM HMM..
HOW MUCH LONGER TILL SHE LETS US OUT OF THE GARAGE?
SHE SAID 8 O'CLOCK, AND IT'S ALMOST 6:30 NOW...
WATTERSON
THANKS AGAIN FOR BABY SITTING, ROSALYN.
CALVIN WAS NO TROUBLE AT ALL.
THAT'S GOOD. I'LL GET THE CAR AND DRIVE YOU HOME.
THERE YOU GO. GOOD NIGHT.
THANK YOU. GOOD NIGHT.
IS SHE GONE?
WATTERSON

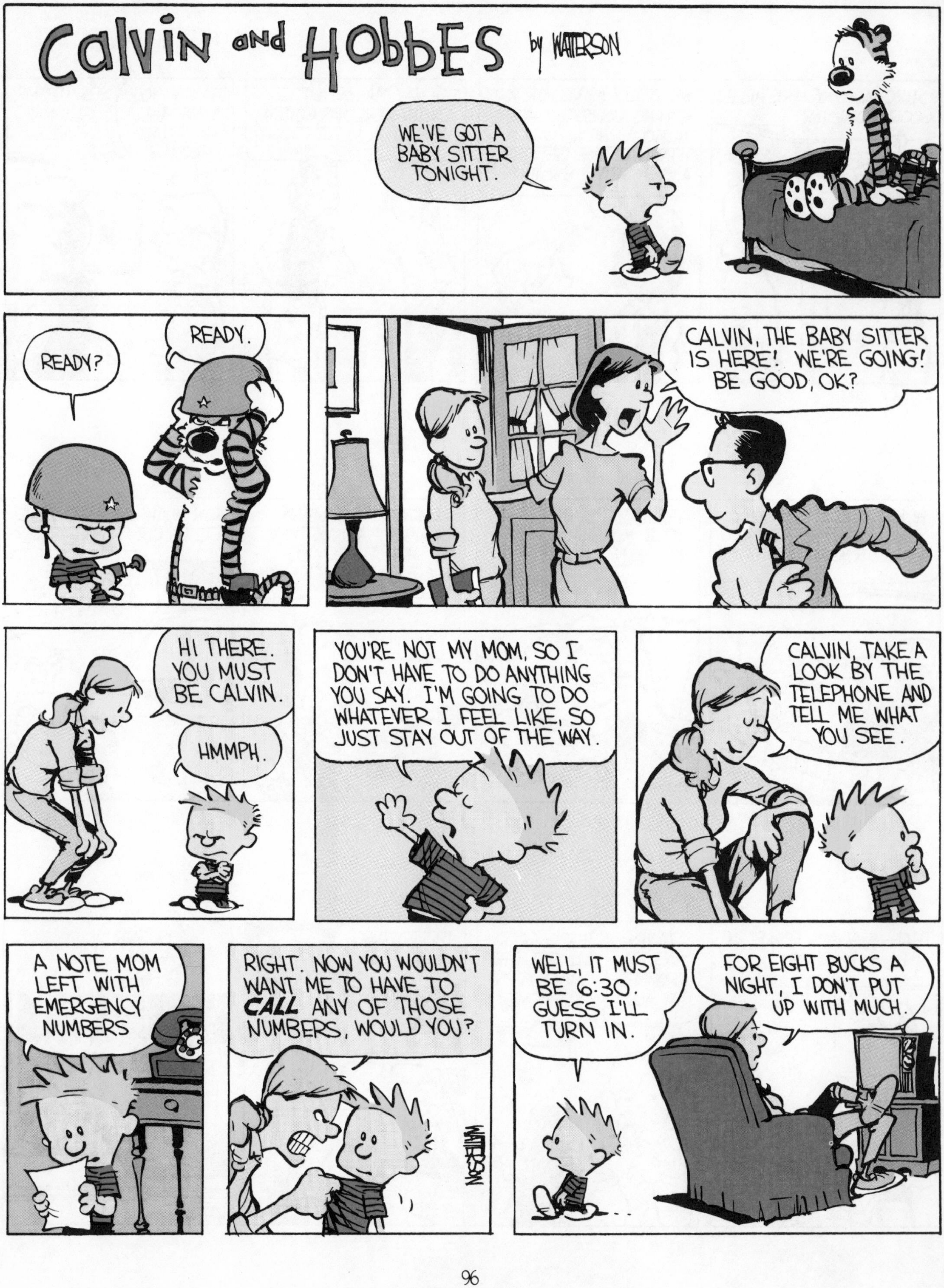
Calvin and HOBBES by WATTERSON
WE'VE GOT A BABY SITTER TONIGHT.
READY?
READY.
CALVIN, THE BABY SITTER IS HERE! WE'RE GOING! BE GOOD, OK?
HI THERE. YOU MUST BE CALVIN.
HMMPH.
YOU'RE NOT MY MOM, SO I DON'T HAVE TO DO ANYTHING YOU SAY. I'M GOING TO DO WHATEVER I FEEL LIKE, SO JUST STAY OUT OF THE WAY.
CALVIN, TAKE A LOOK BY THE TELEPHONE AND TELL ME WHAT YOU SEE.
A NOTE MOM LEFT WITH EMERGENCY NUMBERS
RIGHT. NOW YOU WOULDN'T WANT ME TO HAVE TO CALL ANY OF THOSE NUMBERS, WOULD YOU?
WATTERSON
WELL, IT MUST BE 6:30. GUESS I'LL TURN IN.
FOR EIGHT BUCKS A NIGHT, I DON'T PUT UP WITH MUCH.

WHAT A GREAT NIGHT TO CAMP OUT!

WHERE'S OUR TENT? I THOUGHT THE SCOUTMASTER SAID TO SET THEM UP.

UH OH.

WHEN HE SAID TO PITCH THE TENT, I THREW IT AWAY.

THE BEST PART ABOUT THESE HIKES IS GETTING TO SEE SO MUCH WILDLIFE.

LOOK! A TIGER!

A TIGER?!

DON'T *DO* THAT!

WE'RE SEPARATED FROM THE TROOP AND HOPELESSLY LOST!

LEFT ALONE IN THE UNCOMPROMISING WILD TO SURVIVE BY OUR WITS UNAIDED!

HEY, DUMMY! THE SCOUTMASTER SAYS TO GRAB YOUR STUPID STUFFED TIGER AND GET YOUR REAR IN GEAR!

WE'LL TRY TO LOSE 'EM AGAIN OVER THE NEXT HILL.

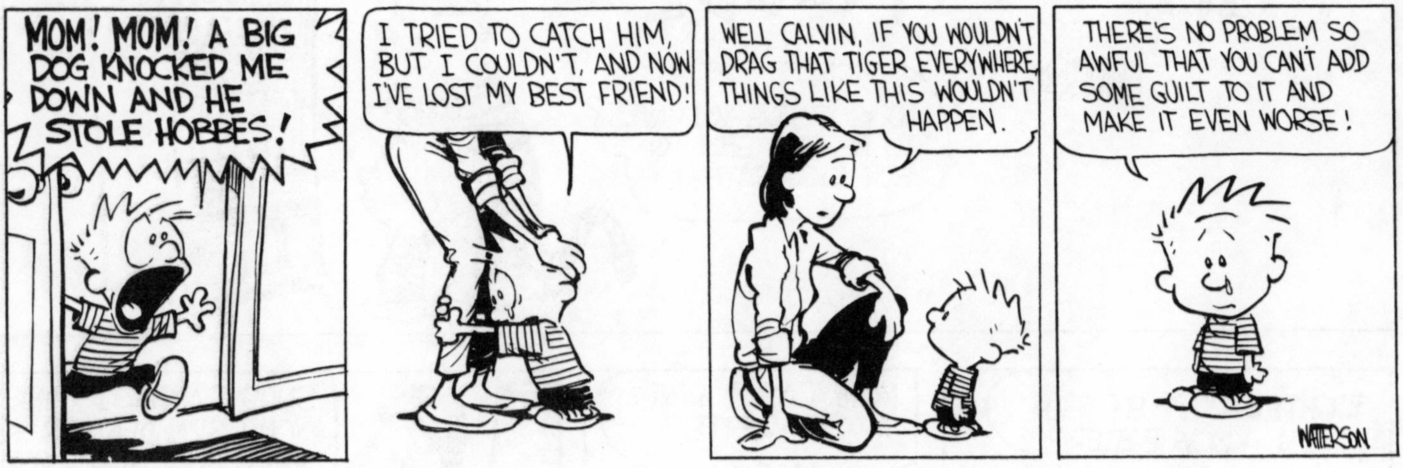
MOM! MOM! A BIG DOG KNOCKED ME DOWN AND HE STOLE HOBBES!
I TRIED TO CATCH HIM, BUT I COULDN'T, AND NOW I'VE LOST MY BEST FRIEND!
WELL CALVIN, IF YOU WOULDN'T DRAG THAT TIGER EVERYWHERE, THINGS LIKE THIS WOULDN'T HAPPEN.
THERE'S NO PROBLEM SO AWFUL THAT YOU CAN'T ADD SOME GUILT TO IT AND MAKE IT EVEN WORSE!
WATTERSON

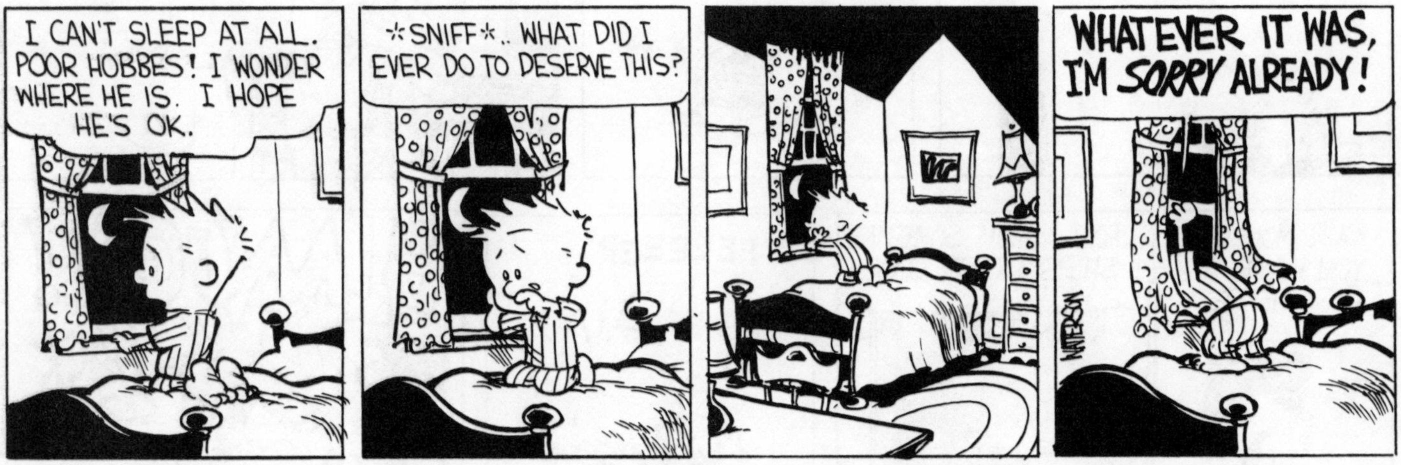
I CAN'T SLEEP AT ALL. POOR HOBBES! I WONDER WHERE HE IS. I HOPE HE'S OK.
*SNIFF*.. WHAT DID I EVER DO TO DESERVE THIS?
WHATEVER IT WAS, I'M SORRY ALREADY!
WATTERSON

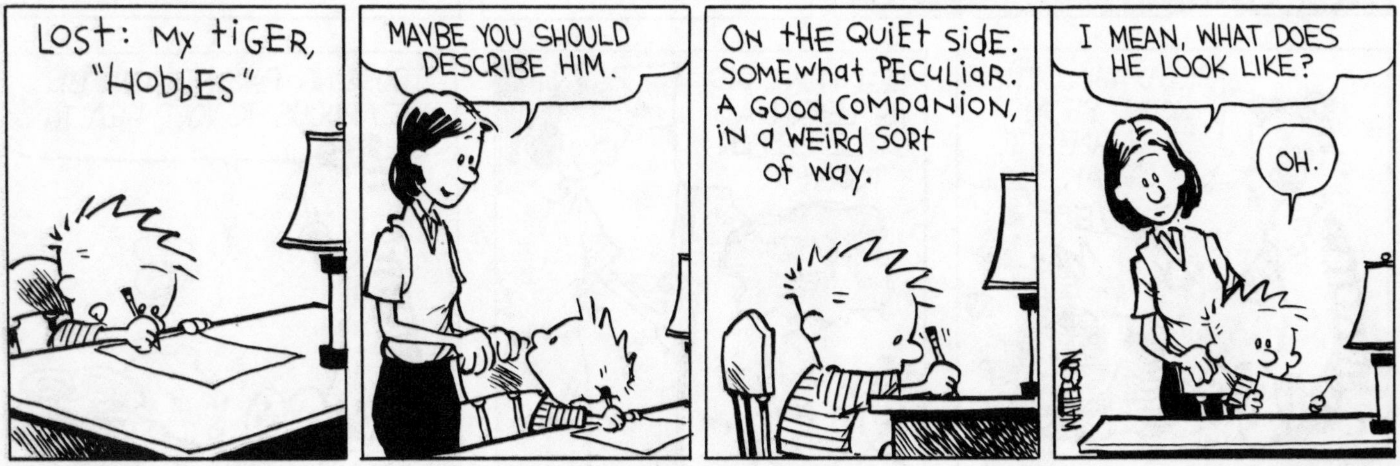
LOST: MY TIGER, "HOBBES"
MAYBE YOU SHOULD DESCRIBE HIM.
ON THE QUIET SIDE. SOMEWHAT PECULIAR. A GOOD COMPANION, IN A WEIRD SORT OF WAY.
WATTERSON
I MEAN, WHAT DOES HE LOOK LIKE?
OH.

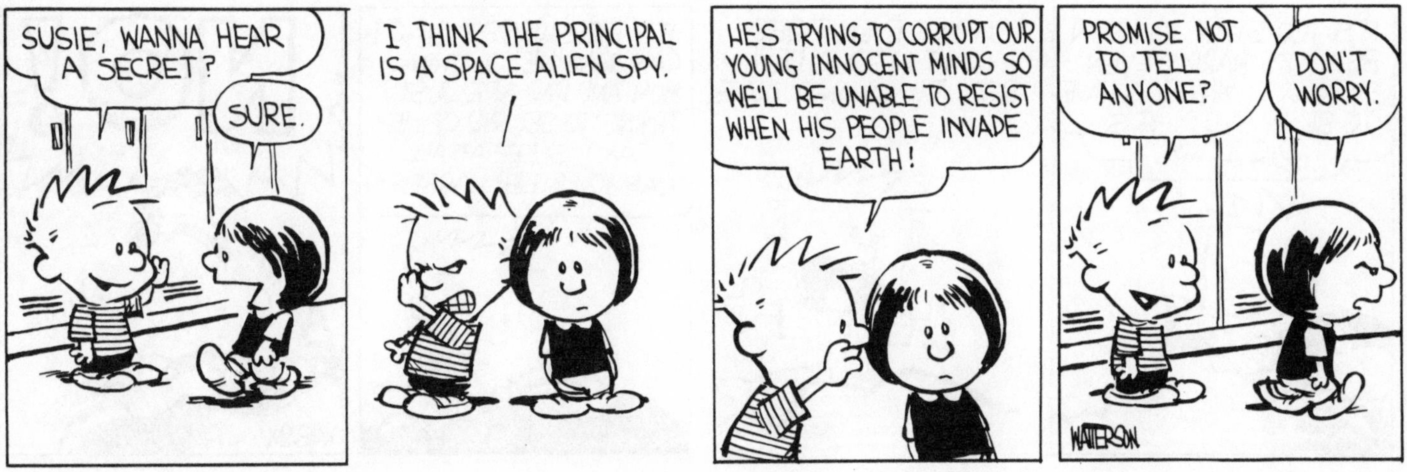
SUSIE, WANNA HEAR A SECRET?
SURE.
I THINK THE PRINCIPAL IS A SPACE ALIEN SPY.
HE'S TRYING TO CORRUPT OUR YOUNG INNOCENT MINDS SO WE'LL BE UNABLE TO RESIST WHEN HIS PEOPLE INVADE EARTH!
PROMISE NOT TO TELL ANYONE?
DON'T WORRY.
WATTERSON

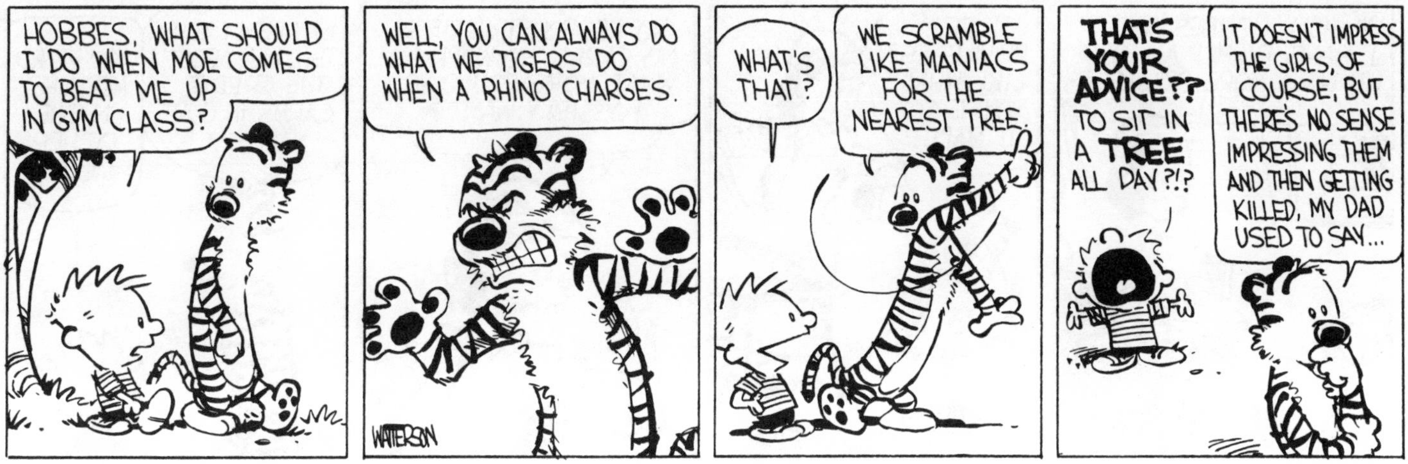
HOBBES, WHAT SHOULD I DO WHEN MOE COMES TO BEAT ME UP IN GYM CLASS?
WATTERSON
WELL, YOU CAN ALWAYS DO WHAT WE TIGERS DO WHEN A RHINO CHARGES.
WHAT'S THAT?
WE SCRAMBLE LIKE MANIACS FOR THE NEAREST TREE.
THAT'S YOUR ADVICE?? TO SIT IN A TREE ALL DAY?!?
IT DOESN'T IMPRESS THE GIRLS, OF COURSE, BUT THERE'S NO SENSE IMPRESSING THEM AND THEN GETTING KILLED, MY DAD USED TO SAY...

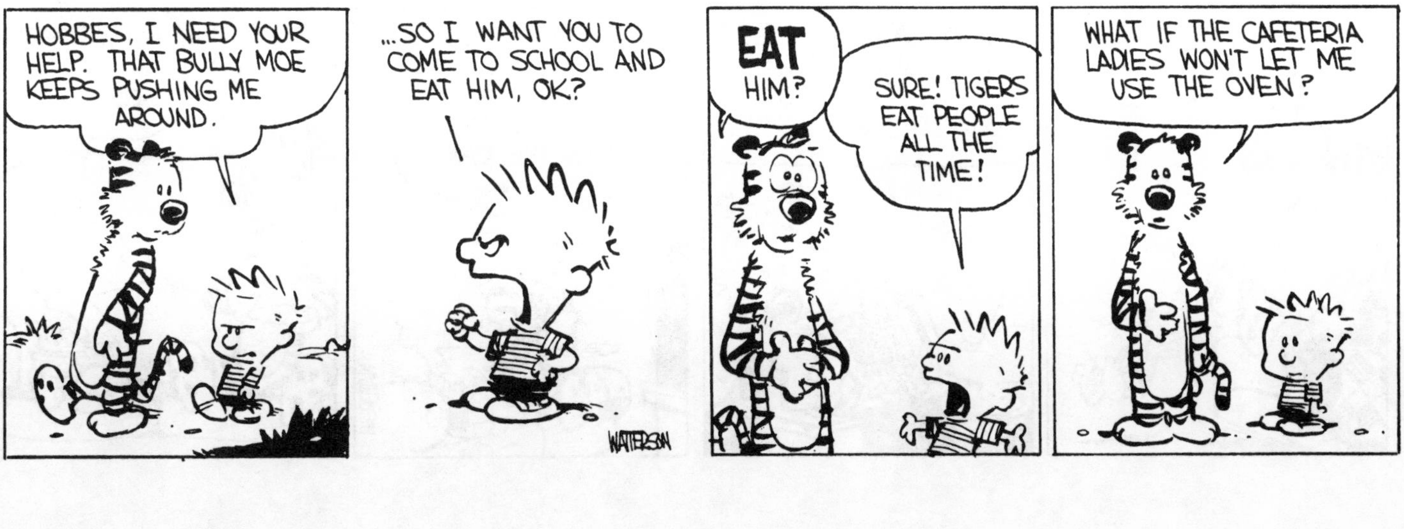
HOBBES, I NEED YOUR HELP. THAT BULLY MOE KEEPS PUSHING ME AROUND.
...SO I WANT YOU TO COME TO SCHOOL AND EAT HIM, OK?
WATTERSON
EAT HIM?
SURE! TIGERS EAT PEOPLE ALL THE TIME!
WHAT IF THE CAFETERIA LADIES WON'T LET ME USE THE OVEN?

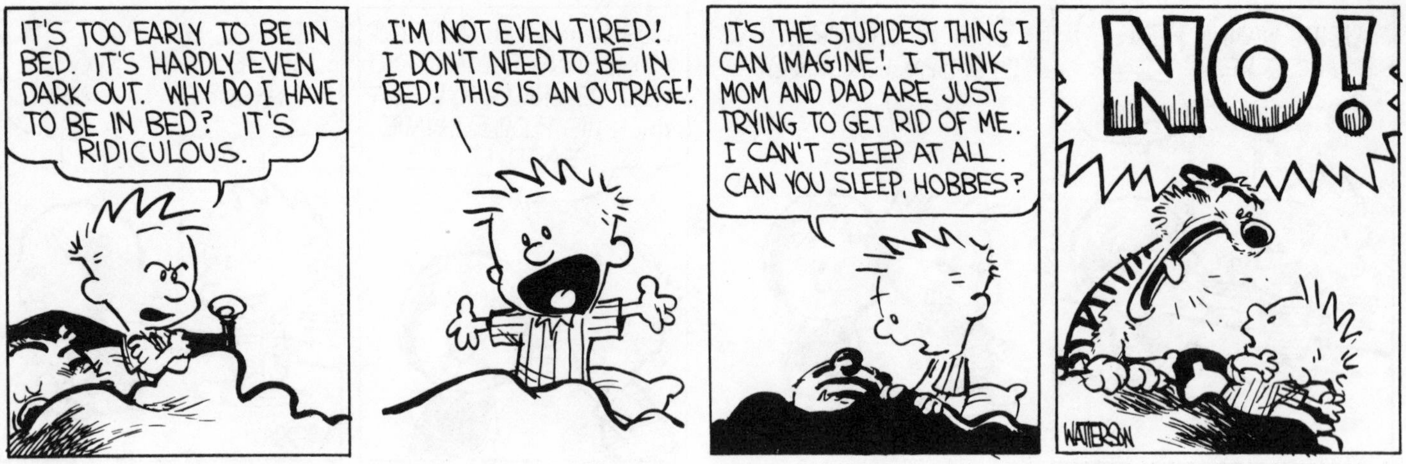
IT'S TOO EARLY TO BE IN BED. IT'S HARDLY EVEN DARK OUT. WHY DO I HAVE TO BE IN BED? IT'S RIDICULOUS.
I'M NOT EVEN TIRED! I DON'T NEED TO BE IN BED! THIS IS AN OUTRAGE!
IT'S THE STUPIDEST THING I CAN IMAGINE! I THINK MOM AND DAD ARE JUST TRYING TO GET RID OF ME. I CAN'T SLEEP AT ALL. CAN YOU SLEEP, HOBBES?
NO!

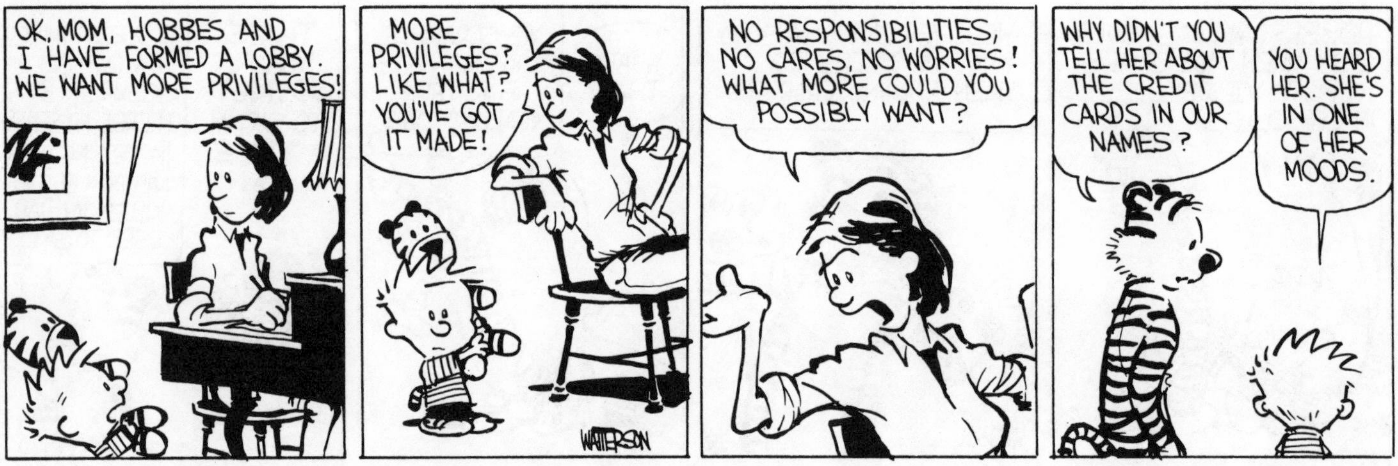
OK, MOM, HOBBES AND I HAVE FORMED A LOBBY. WE WANT MORE PRIVILEGES!
MORE PRIVILEGES? LIKE WHAT? YOU'VE GOT IT MADE!
NO RESPONSIBILITIES, NO CARES, NO WORRIES! WHAT MORE COULD YOU POSSIBLY WANT?
WHY DIDN'T YOU TELL HER ABOUT THE CREDIT CARDS IN OUR NAMES?
YOU HEARD HER. SHE'S IN ONE OF HER MOODS.

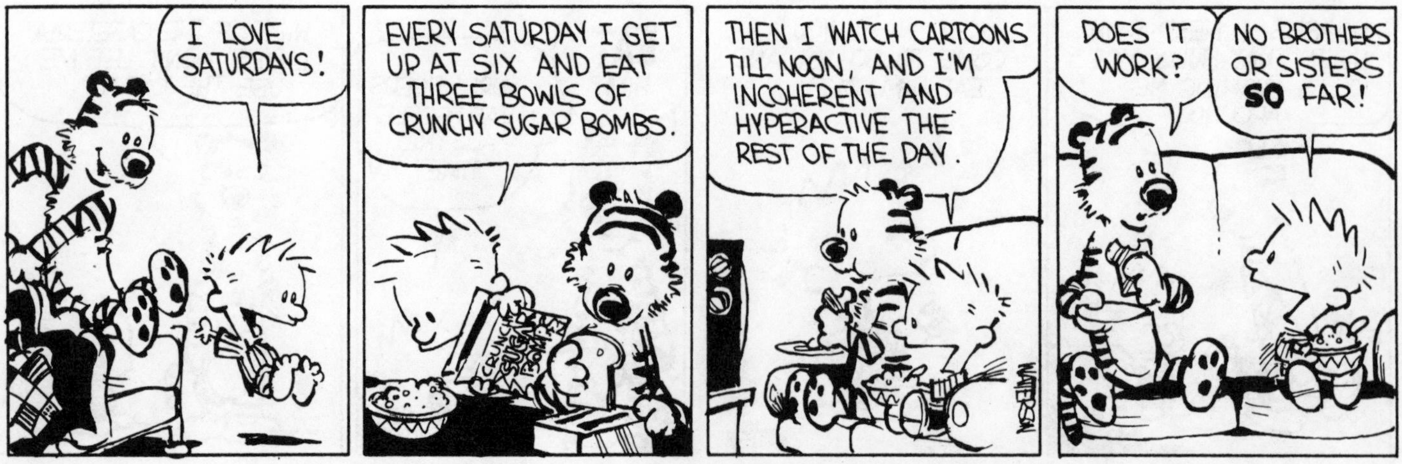
I LOVE SATURDAYS!
EVERY SATURDAY I GET UP AT SIX AND EAT THREE BOWLS OF CRUNCHY SUGAR BOMBS.
THEN I WATCH CARTOONS TILL NOON, AND I'M INCOHERENT AND HYPERACTIVE THE REST OF THE DAY.
DOES IT WORK?
NO BROTHERS OR SISTERS SO FAR!

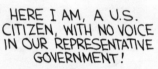

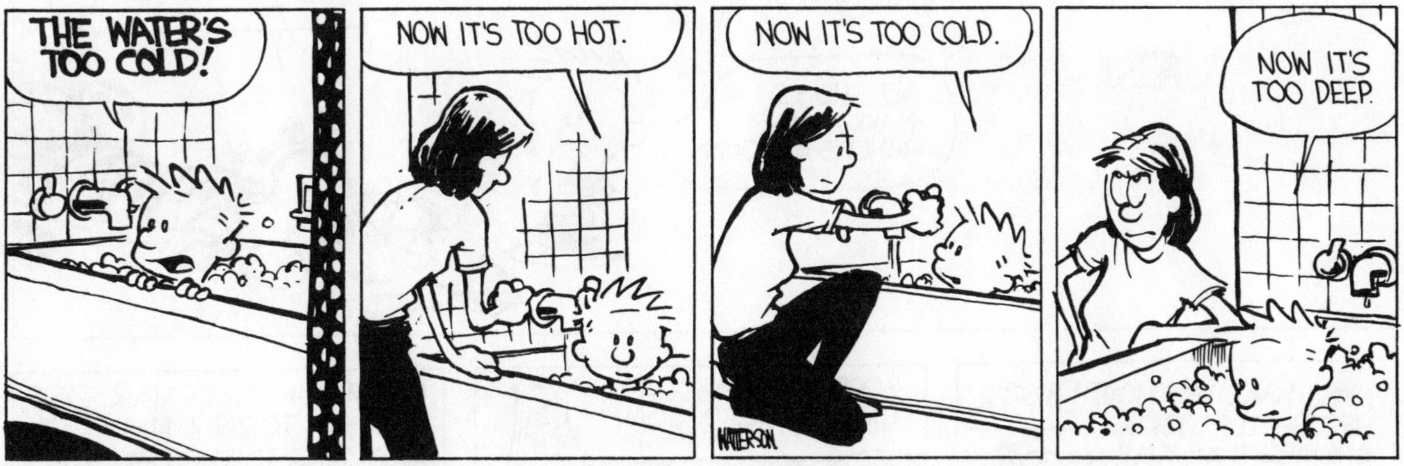
THE WATER'S TOO COLD!
NOW IT'S TOO HOT.
NOW IT'S TOO COLD.
NOW IT'S TOO DEEP.

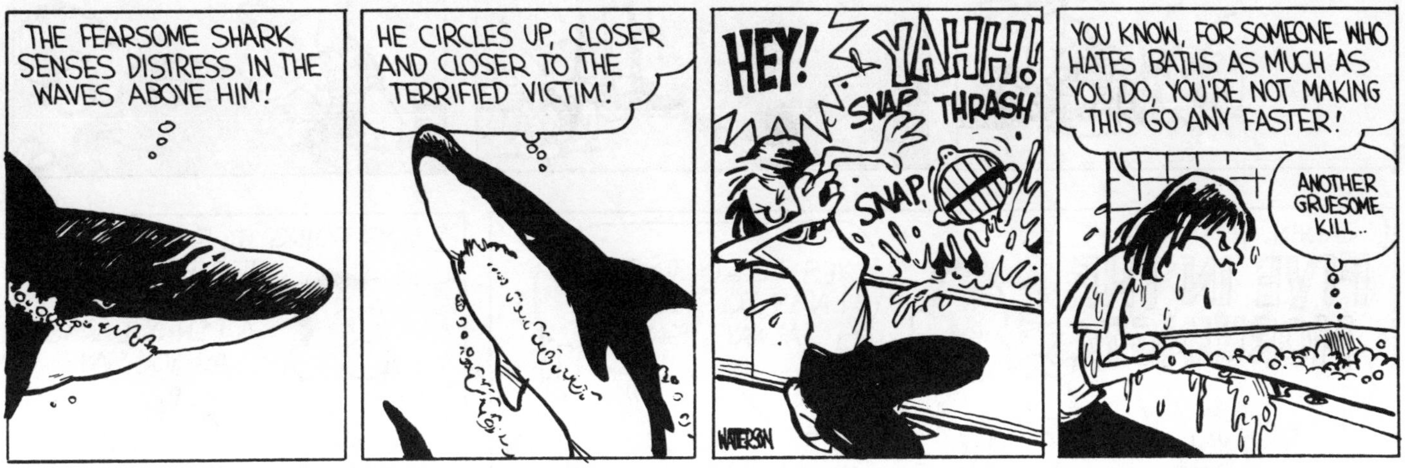
THE FEARSOME SHARK SENSES DISTRESS IN THE WAVES ABOVE HIM!
HE CIRCLES UP, CLOSER AND CLOSER TO THE TERRIFIED VICTIM!
HEY!
YAHH!
SNAP
THRASH
SNAP
YOU KNOW, FOR SOMEONE WHO HATES BATHS AS MUCH AS YOU DO, YOU'RE NOT MAKING THIS GO ANY FASTER!
ANOTHER GRUESOME KILL..

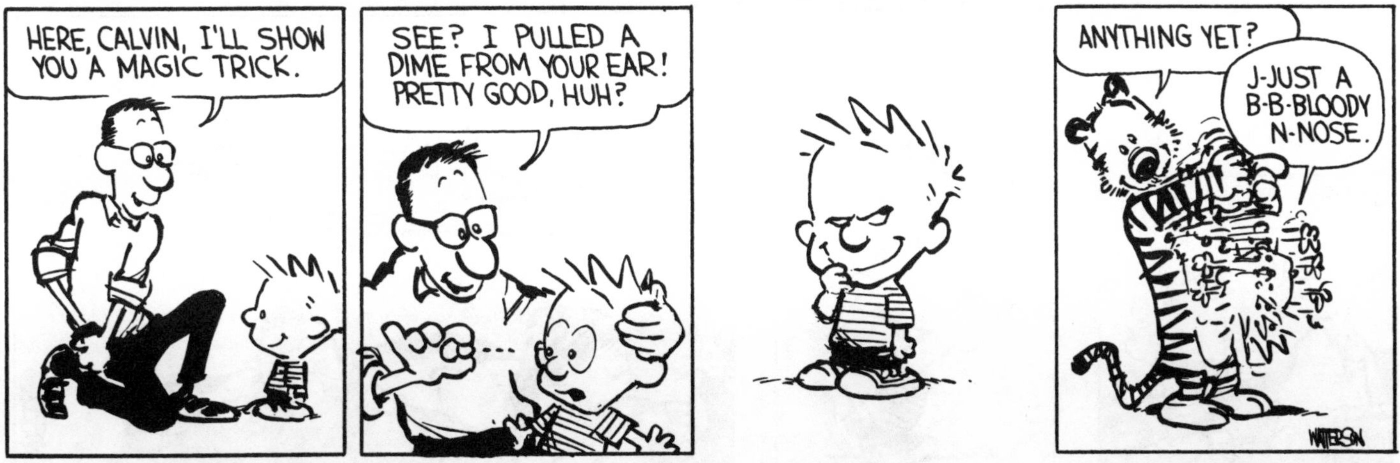
HERE, CALVIN, I'LL SHOW YOU A MAGIC TRICK.
SEE? I PULLED A DIME FROM YOUR EAR! PRETTY GOOD, HUH?
ANYTHING YET?
J-JUST A B-B-BLOODY N-NOSE.

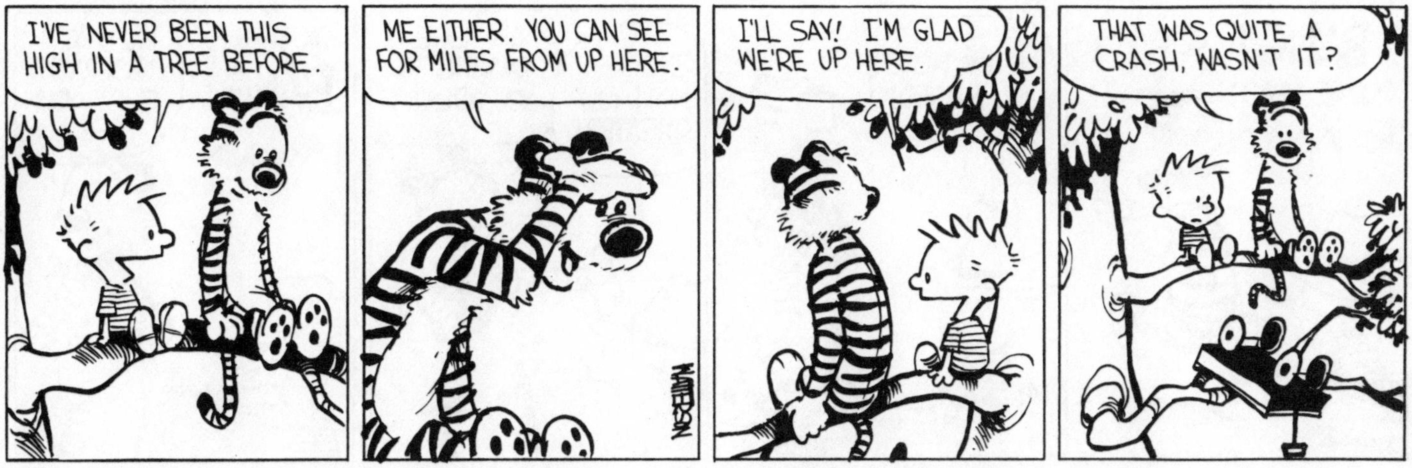
I'VE NEVER BEEN THIS HIGH IN A TREE BEFORE.
ME EITHER. YOU CAN SEE FOR MILES FROM UP HERE.
I'LL SAY! I'M GLAD WE'RE UP HERE.
THAT WAS QUITE A CRASH, WASN'T IT?

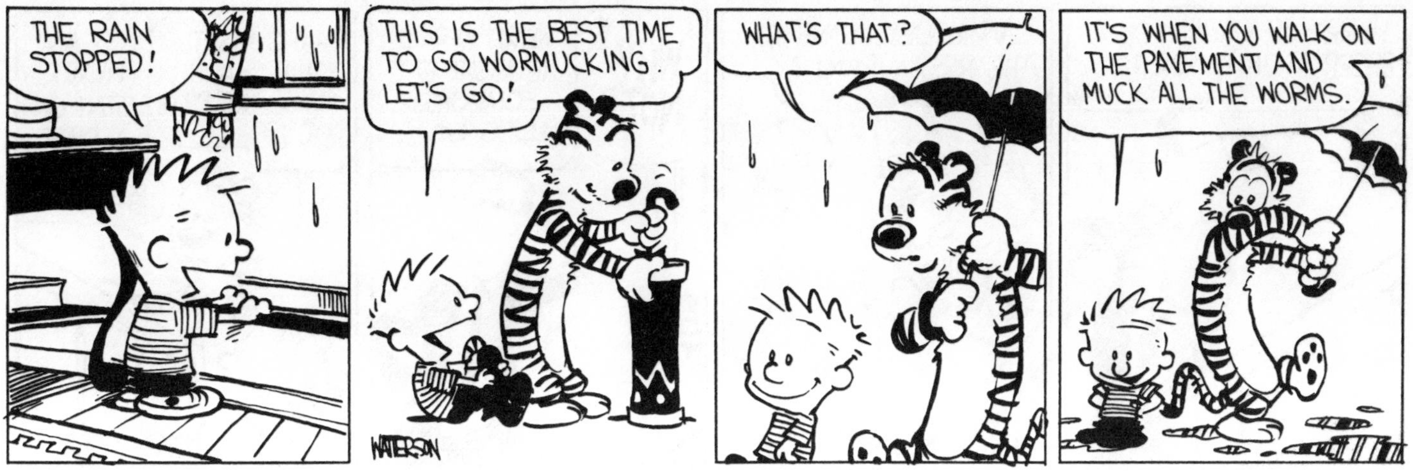
THE RAIN STOPPED!
THIS IS THE BEST TIME TO GO WORMUCKING. LET'S GO!
WHAT'S THAT?
IT'S WHEN YOU WALK ON THE PAVEMENT AND MUCK ALL THE WORMS.

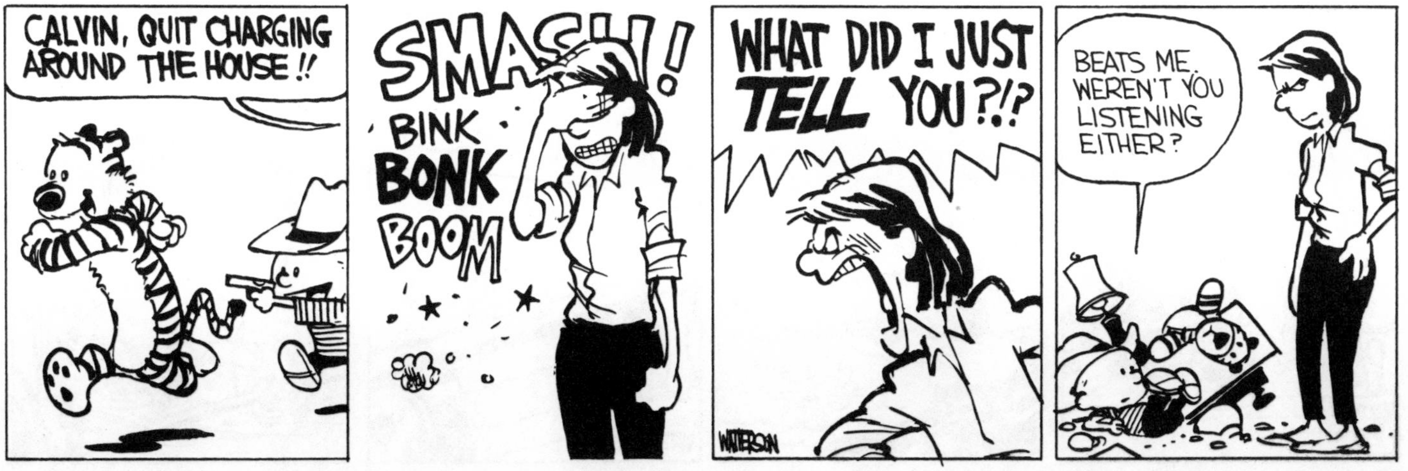
CALVIN, QUIT CHARGING AROUND THE HOUSE!!
SMASH!
BINK
BONK
BOOM
WHAT DID I JUST TELL YOU?!?
BEATS ME. WEREN'T YOU LISTENING EITHER?

110

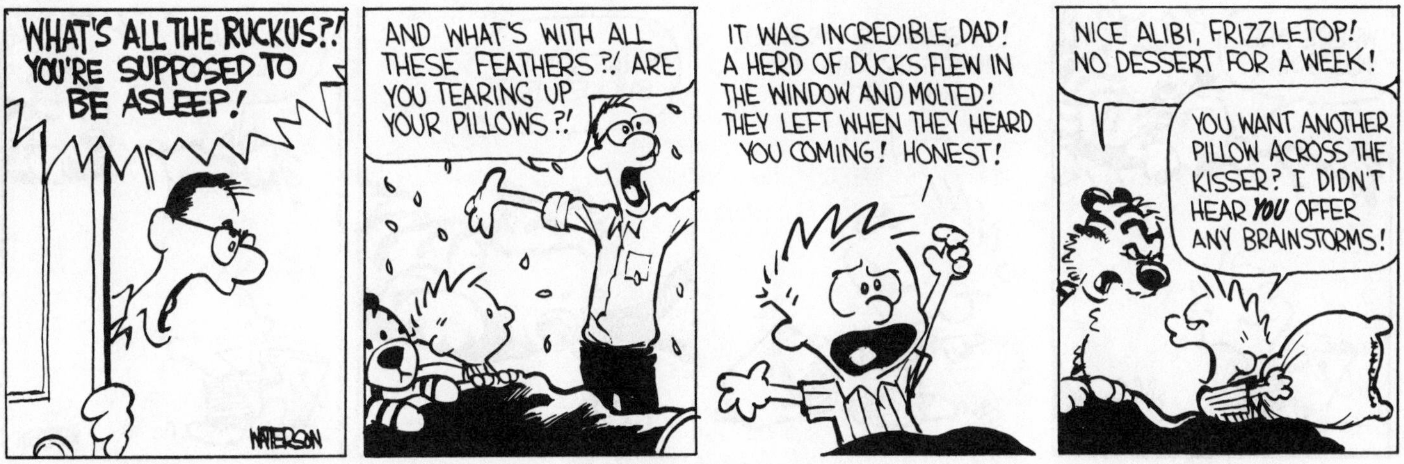
WHAT'S ALL THE RUCKUS?! YOU'RE SUPPOSED TO BE ASLEEP!
AND WHAT'S WITH ALL THESE FEATHERS?! ARE YOU TEARING UP YOUR PILLOWS?!
IT WAS INCREDIBLE, DAD! A HERD OF DUCKS FLEW IN THE WINDOW AND MOLTED! THEY LEFT WHEN THEY HEARD YOU COMING! HONEST!
NICE ALIBI, FRIZZLETOP! NO DESSERT FOR A WEEK!
YOU WANT ANOTHER PILLOW ACROSS THE KISSER? I DIDN'T HEAR YOU OFFER ANY BRAINSTORMS!
WATERSON

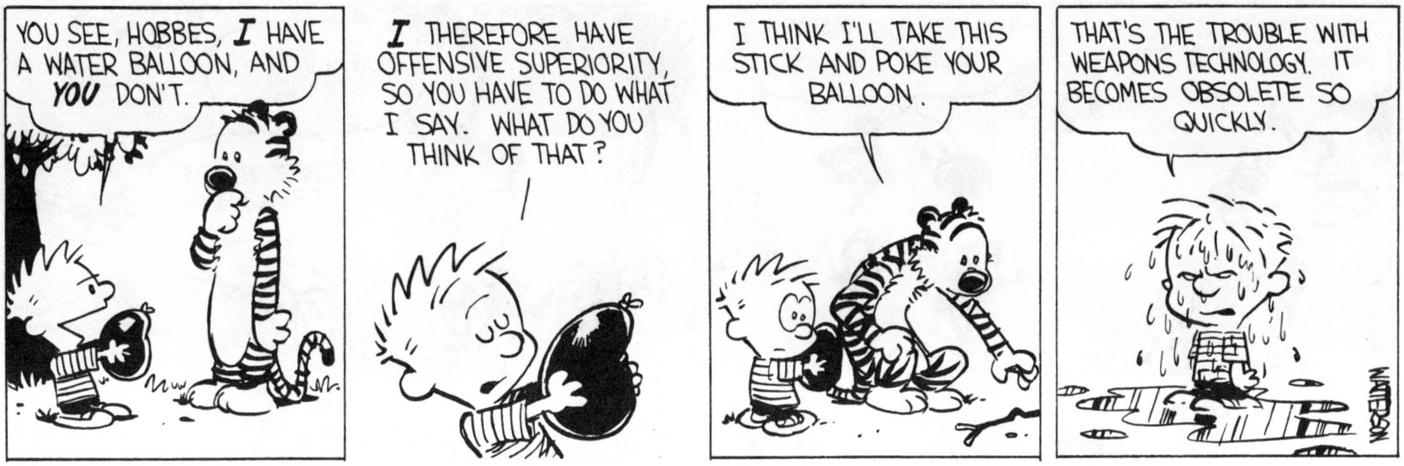
YOU SEE, HOBBES, I HAVE A WATER BALLOON, AND YOU DON'T.
I THEREFORE HAVE OFFENSIVE SUPERIORITY, SO YOU HAVE TO DO WHAT I SAY. WHAT DO YOU THINK OF THAT?
I THINK I'LL TAKE THIS STICK AND POKE YOUR BALLOON.
THAT'S THE TROUBLE WITH WEAPONS TECHNOLOGY. IT BECOMES OBSOLETE SO QUICKLY.
WATERSON

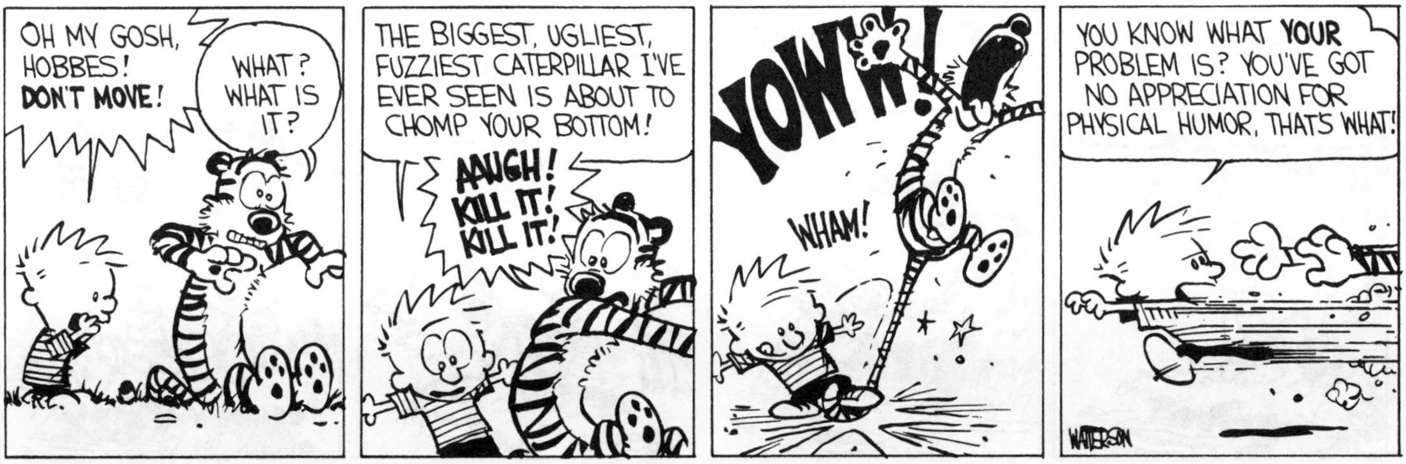
OH MY GOSH, HOBBES! DON'T MOVE!
WHAT? WHAT IS IT?
THE BIGGEST, UGLIEST, FUZZIEST CATERPILLAR I'VE EVER SEEN IS ABOUT TO CHOMP YOUR BOTTOM!
AAUGH! KILL IT! KILL IT!
YOWW!
WHAM!
YOU KNOW WHAT YOUR PROBLEM IS? YOU'VE GOT NO APPRECIATION FOR PHYSICAL HUMOR, THAT'S WHAT!
WATERSON

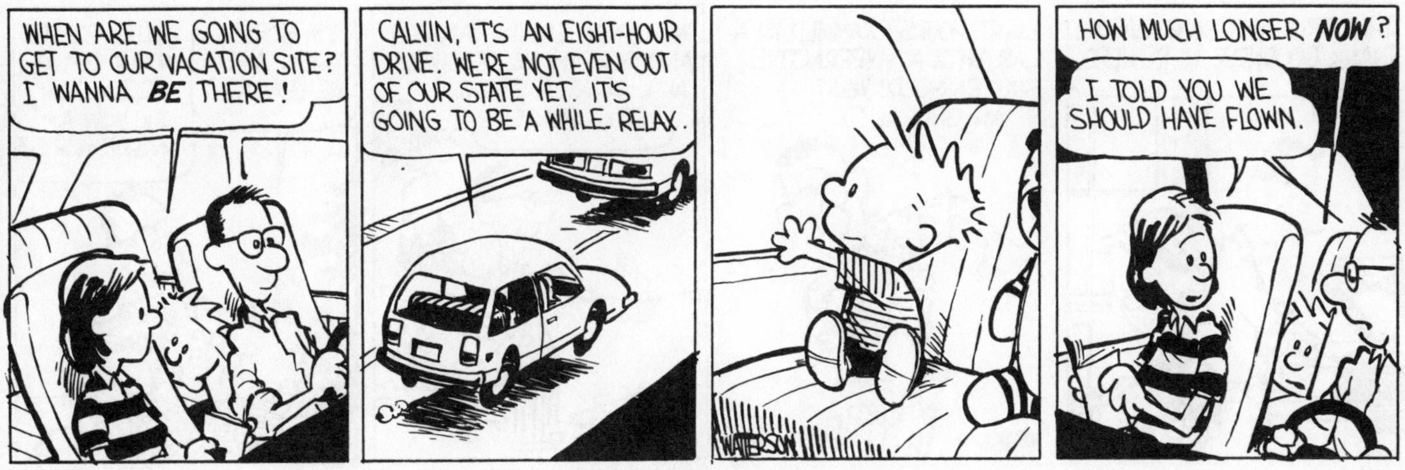
WHEN ARE WE GOING TO GET TO OUR VACATION SITE? I WANNA **BE** THERE!
CALVIN, IT'S AN EIGHT-HOUR DRIVE. WE'RE NOT EVEN OUT OF OUR STATE YET. IT'S GOING TO BE A WHILE. RELAX.
HOW MUCH LONGER **NOW**?
I TOLD YOU WE SHOULD HAVE FLOWN.
WATERSON

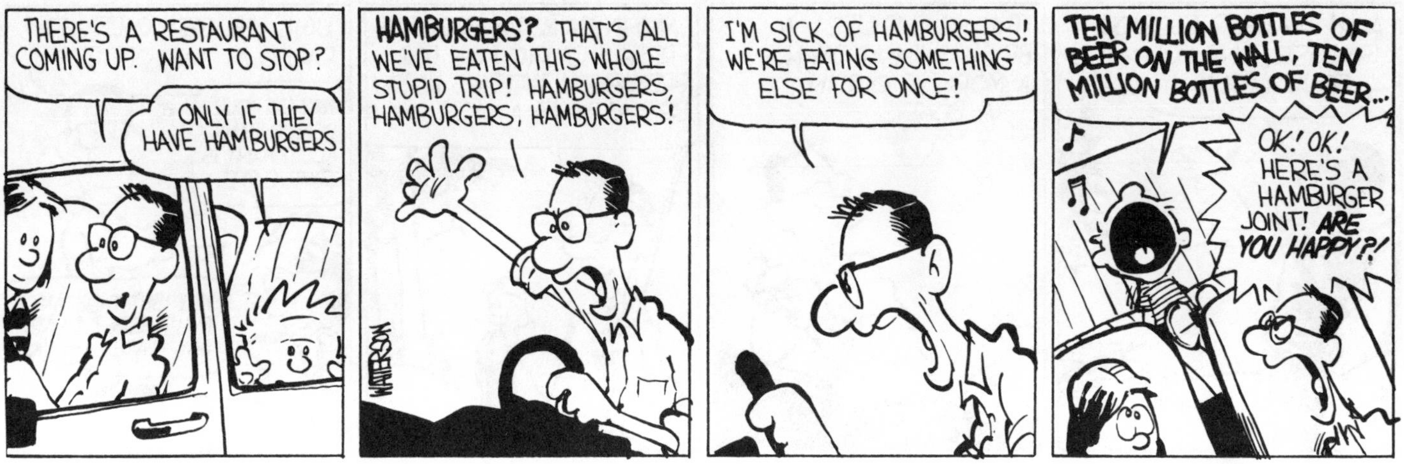
THERE'S A RESTAURANT COMING UP. WANT TO STOP?
ONLY IF THEY HAVE HAMBURGERS.
**HAMBURGERS?** THAT'S ALL WE'VE EATEN THIS WHOLE STUPID TRIP! HAMBURGERS, HAMBURGERS, HAMBURGERS!
I'M SICK OF HAMBURGERS! WE'RE EATING SOMETHING ELSE FOR ONCE!
**TEN MILLION BOTTLES OF BEER ON THE WALL, TEN MILLION BOTTLES OF BEER...**
OK! OK! HERE'S A HAMBURGER JOINT! ***ARE YOU HAPPY?!***
WATERSON

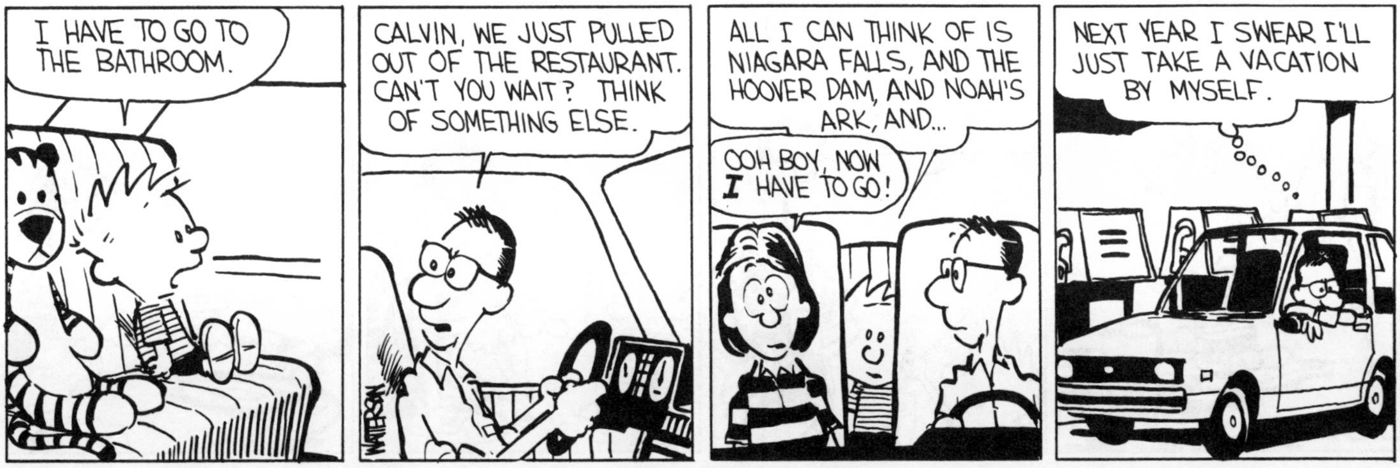
I HAVE TO GO TO THE BATHROOM.
CALVIN, WE JUST PULLED OUT OF THE RESTAURANT. CAN'T YOU WAIT? THINK OF SOMETHING ELSE.
ALL I CAN THINK OF IS NIAGARA FALLS, AND THE HOOVER DAM, AND NOAH'S ARK, AND...
OOH BOY, NOW ***I*** HAVE TO GO!
NEXT YEAR I SWEAR I'LL JUST TAKE A VACATION BY MYSELF.
WATERSON

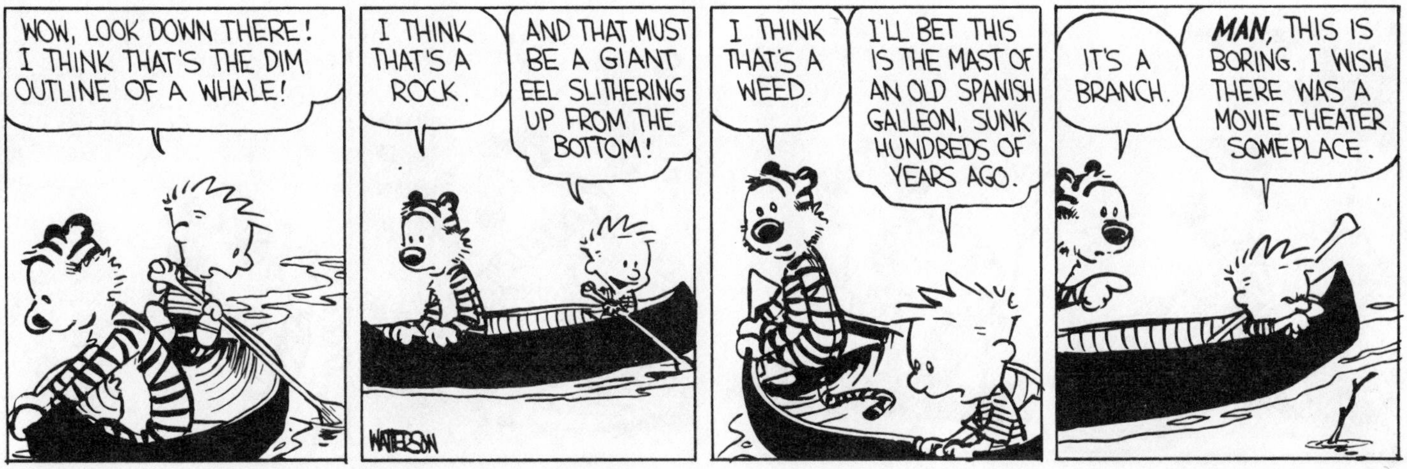
WOW, LOOK DOWN THERE! I THINK THAT'S THE DIM OUTLINE OF A WHALE!
I THINK THAT'S A ROCK.
AND THAT MUST BE A GIANT EEL SLITHERING UP FROM THE BOTTOM!
I THINK THAT'S A WEED.
I'LL BET THIS IS THE MAST OF AN OLD SPANISH GALLEON, SUNK HUNDREDS OF YEARS AGO.
IT'S A BRANCH.
MAN, THIS IS BORING. I WISH THERE WAS A MOVIE THEATER SOMEPLACE.

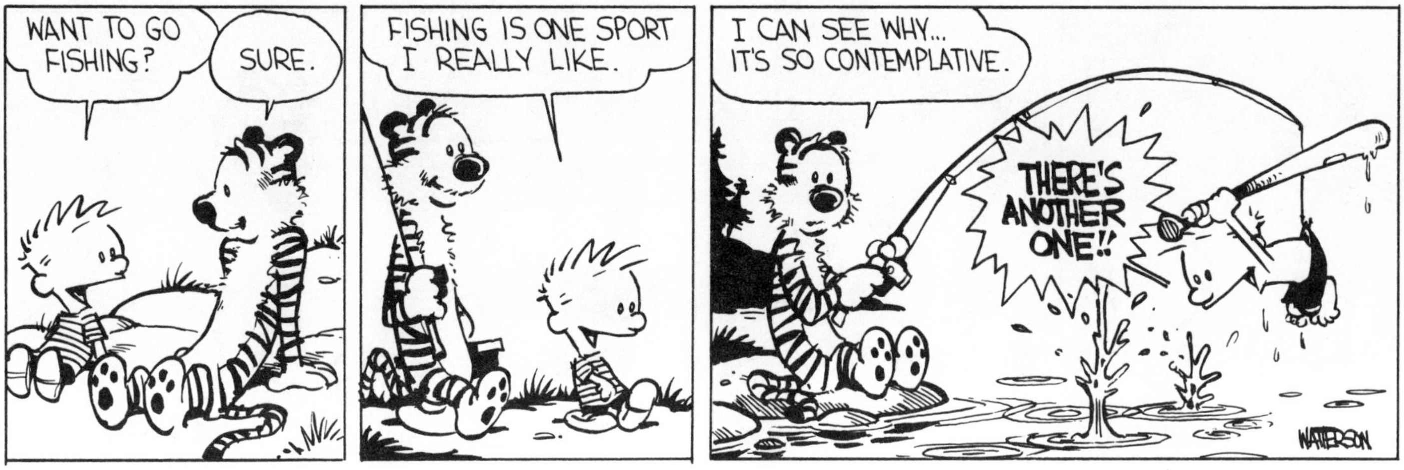
WANT TO GO FISHING?
SURE.
FISHING IS ONE SPORT I REALLY LIKE.
I CAN SEE WHY... IT'S SO CONTEMPLATIVE.
THERE'S ANOTHER ONE!!

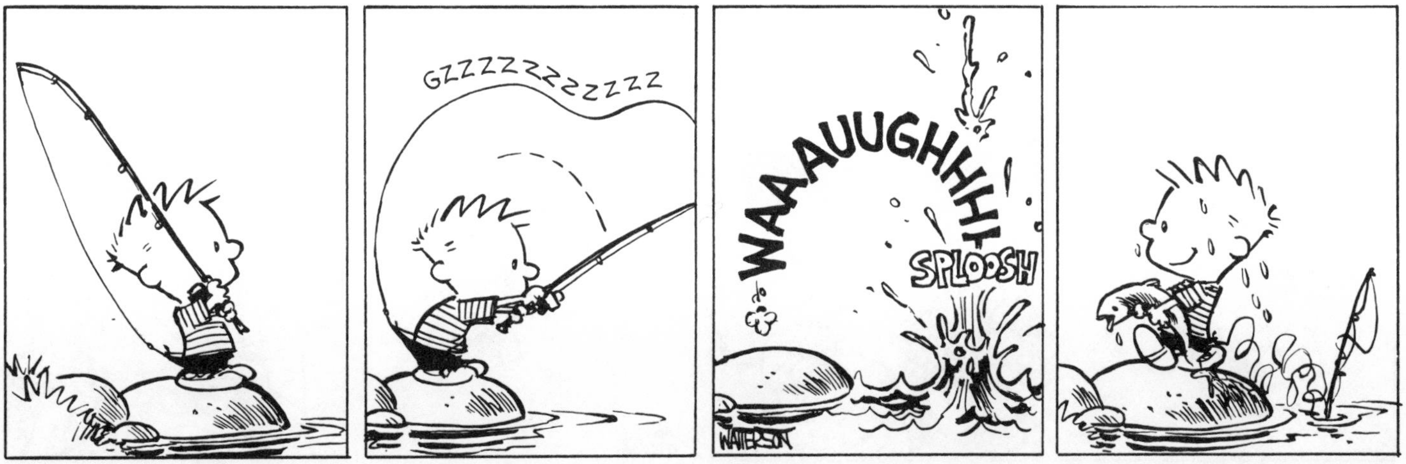
GZZZZZZZZZZZ
WAAAUUGHHHH!
SPLOOSH

STOMP
STOMP
STOMP
STOMP

WHAP
WHAP
WHAP
WHAP

I DON'T *LIKE* FOOD COOKED OUT, DO YOU?

UGH. IT ALL TASTES THE SAME.

CRUNCH CRUNCH

FLOWERS ARE PRETTY STUPID.

SEE, IT'S A BRIGHT, SUNNY DAY OUT, RIGHT?

WELL, WITH THIS WATERING CAN, I CAN MAKE THEM THINK IT'S RAINING.

IT'S FUN TO MESS WITH THEIR MINDS.

THE EXPERIMENT HAS GONE HORRIBLY WRONG! CALVIN HAS MUTATED INTO A GIANT FLY!

HE ZIPS ABOUT IN PARASITIC HUNGER, SEARCHING FOR DECAYING FLESH!

AN UNBEARABLE STENCH FILLS THE AIR. THE HIDEOUS BUG ZEROES IN.

MMM! THIS MAKES ME HUNGRY!

DON'T BE GROSS. JUST TAKE OUT THE GARBAGE LIKE I ASKED YOU, WILL YOU PLEASE?

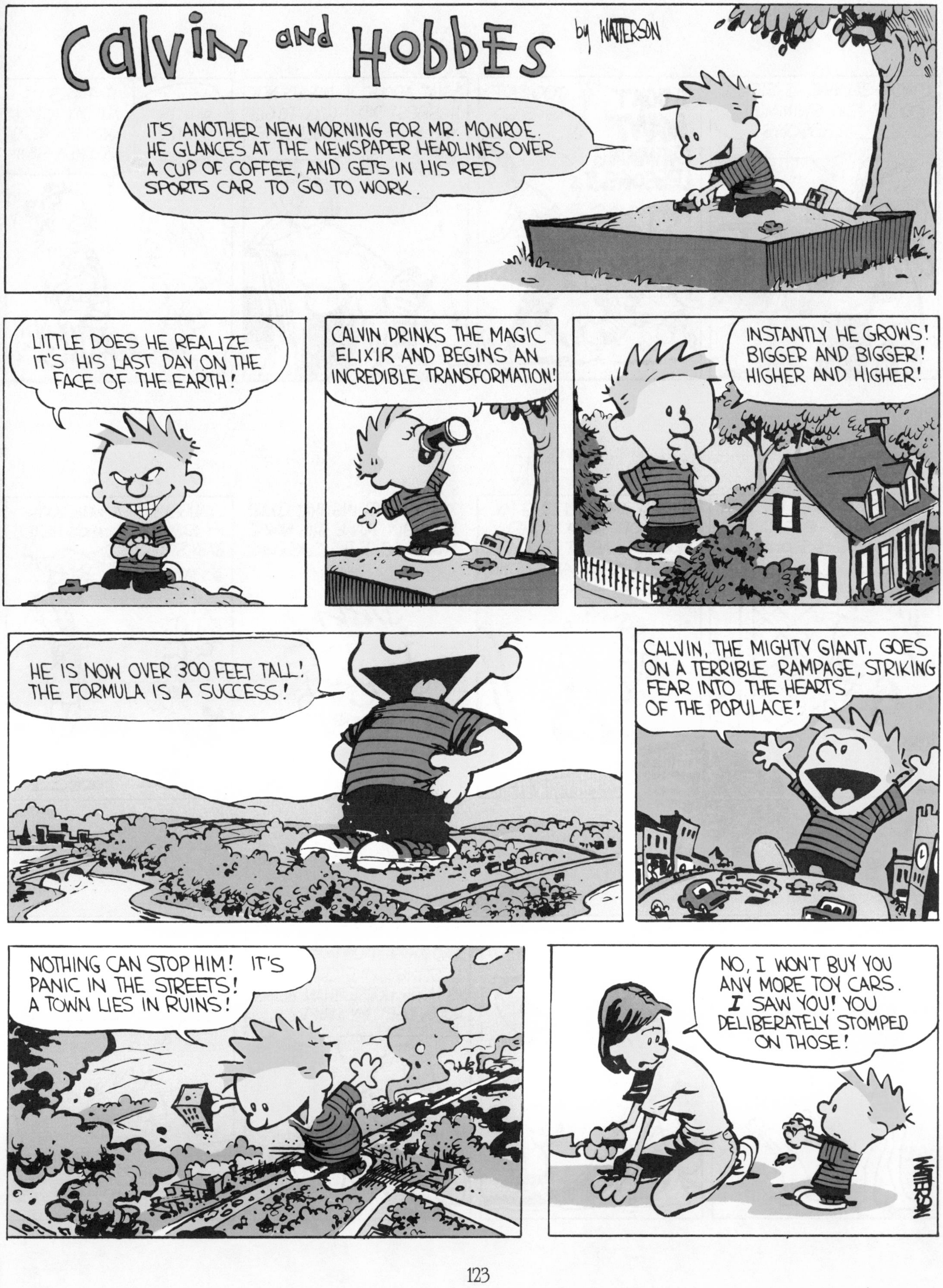
Calvin and HOBBES
by WATTERSON
IT'S ANOTHER NEW MORNING FOR MR. MONROE. HE GLANCES AT THE NEWSPAPER HEADLINES OVER A CUP OF COFFEE, AND GETS IN HIS RED SPORTS CAR TO GO TO WORK.
LITTLE DOES HE REALIZE IT'S HIS LAST DAY ON THE FACE OF THE EARTH!
CALVIN DRINKS THE MAGIC ELIXIR AND BEGINS AN INCREDIBLE TRANSFORMATION!
INSTANTLY HE GROWS! BIGGER AND BIGGER! HIGHER AND HIGHER!
HE IS NOW OVER 300 FEET TALL! THE FORMULA IS A SUCCESS!
CALVIN, THE MIGHTY GIANT, GOES ON A TERRIBLE RAMPAGE, STRIKING FEAR INTO THE HEARTS OF THE POPULACE!
NOTHING CAN STOP HIM! IT'S PANIC IN THE STREETS! A TOWN LIES IN RUINS!
NO, I WON'T BUY YOU ANY MORE TOY CARS. I SAW YOU! YOU DELIBERATELY STOMPED ON THOSE!
WATTERSON

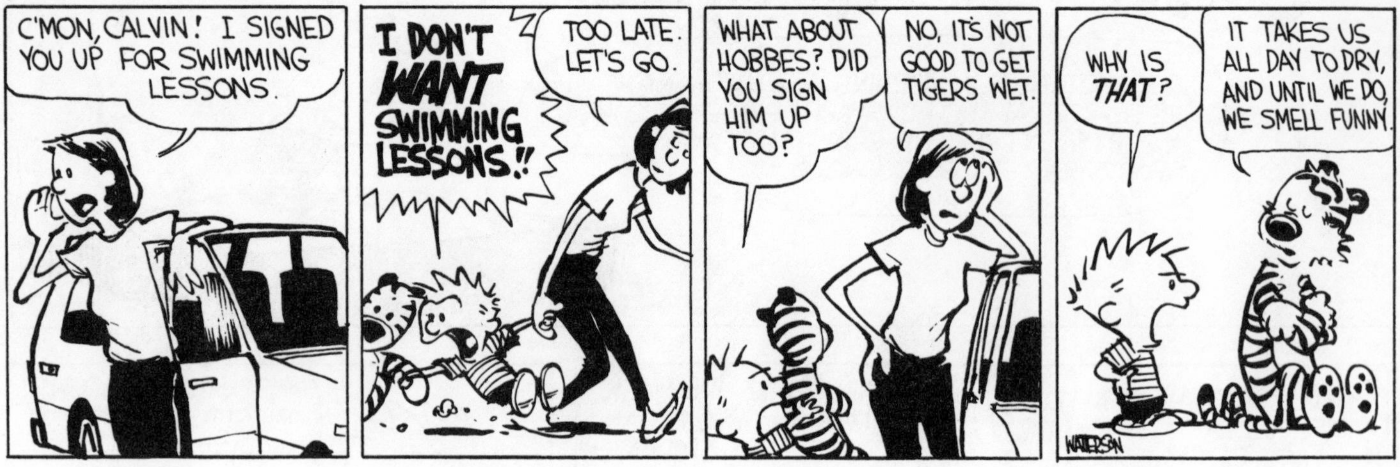
C'MON, CALVIN! I SIGNED YOU UP FOR SWIMMING LESSONS.
I DON'T WANT SWIMMING LESSONS!!
TOO LATE. LET'S GO.
WHAT ABOUT HOBBES? DID YOU SIGN HIM UP TOO?
NO, IT'S NOT GOOD TO GET TIGERS WET.
WHY IS THAT?
IT TAKES US ALL DAY TO DRY, AND UNTIL WE DO, WE SMELL FUNNY.
WATTERSON

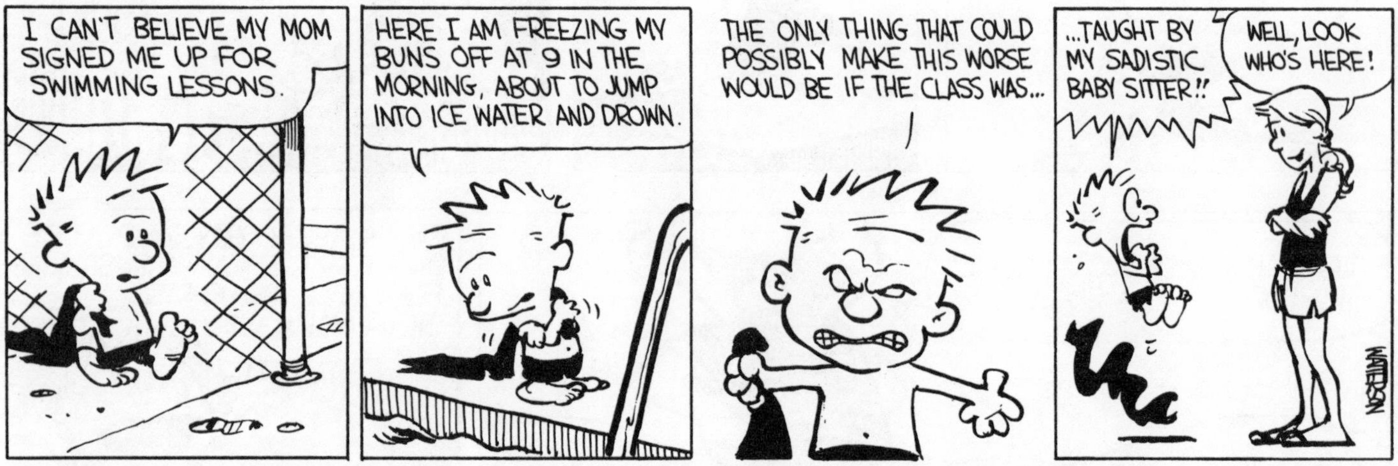
I CAN'T BELIEVE MY MOM SIGNED ME UP FOR SWIMMING LESSONS.
HERE I AM FREEZING MY BUNS OFF AT 9 IN THE MORNING, ABOUT TO JUMP INTO ICE WATER AND DROWN.
THE ONLY THING THAT COULD POSSIBLY MAKE THIS WORSE WOULD BE IF THE CLASS WAS...
...TAUGHT BY MY SADISTIC BABY SITTER!!
WELL, LOOK WHO'S HERE!
WATTERSON

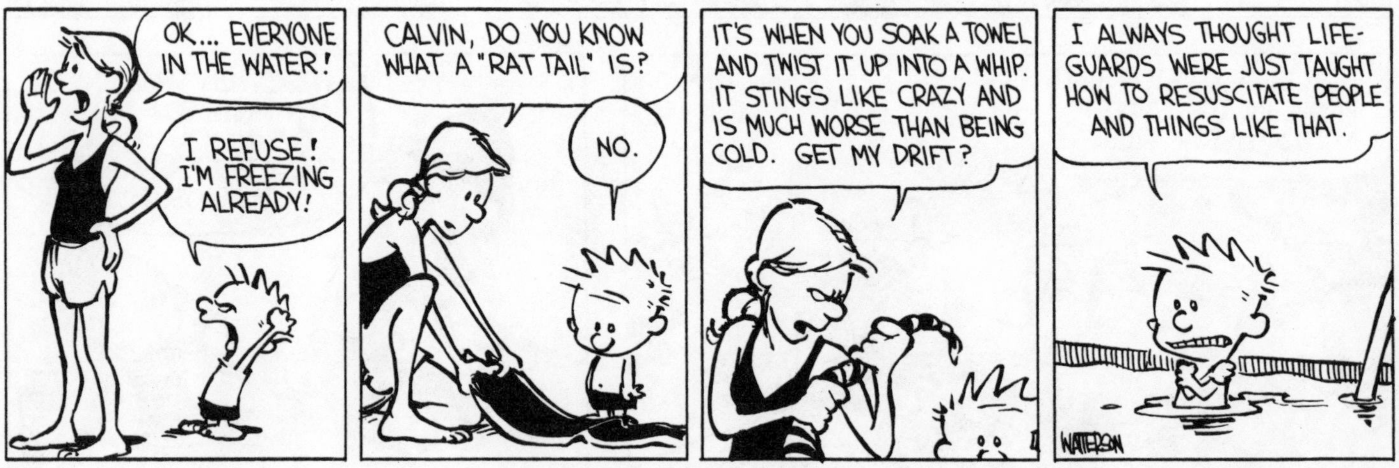
OK... EVERYONE IN THE WATER!
I REFUSE! I'M FREEZING ALREADY!
CALVIN, DO YOU KNOW WHAT A "RAT TAIL" IS?
NO.
IT'S WHEN YOU SOAK A TOWEL AND TWIST IT UP INTO A WHIP. IT STINGS LIKE CRAZY AND IS MUCH WORSE THAN BEING COLD. GET MY DRIFT?
I ALWAYS THOUGHT LIFE-GUARDS WERE JUST TAUGHT HOW TO RESUSCITATE PEOPLE AND THINGS LIKE THAT.
WATTERSON

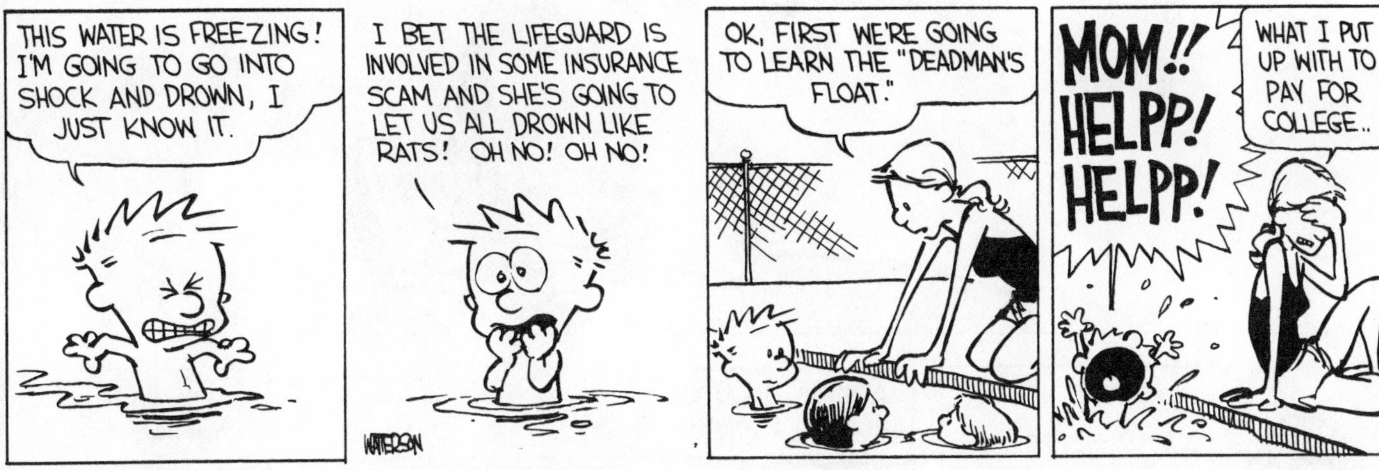
THIS WATER IS FREEZING! I'M GOING TO GO INTO SHOCK AND DROWN, I JUST KNOW IT.
I BET THE LIFEGUARD IS INVOLVED IN SOME INSURANCE SCAM AND SHE'S GOING TO LET US ALL DROWN LIKE RATS! OH NO! OH NO!
OK, FIRST WE'RE GOING TO LEARN THE "DEADMAN'S FLOAT."
MOM!! HELPP! HELPP!
WHAT I PUT UP WITH TO PAY FOR COLLEGE..

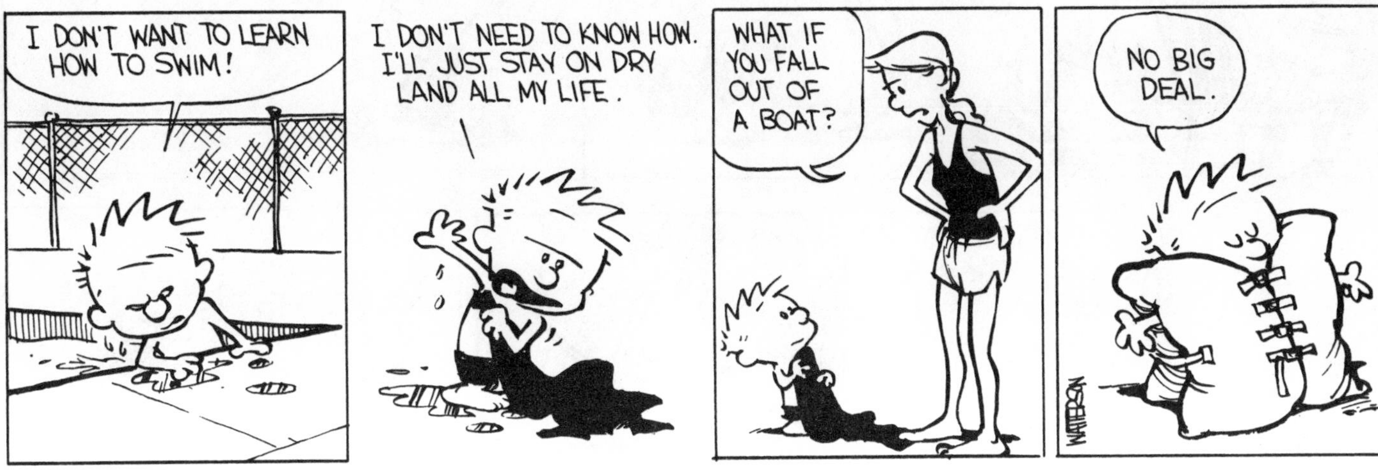
I DON'T WANT TO LEARN HOW TO SWIM!
I DON'T NEED TO KNOW HOW. I'LL JUST STAY ON DRY LAND ALL MY LIFE.
WHAT IF YOU FALL OUT OF A BOAT?
NO BIG DEAL.

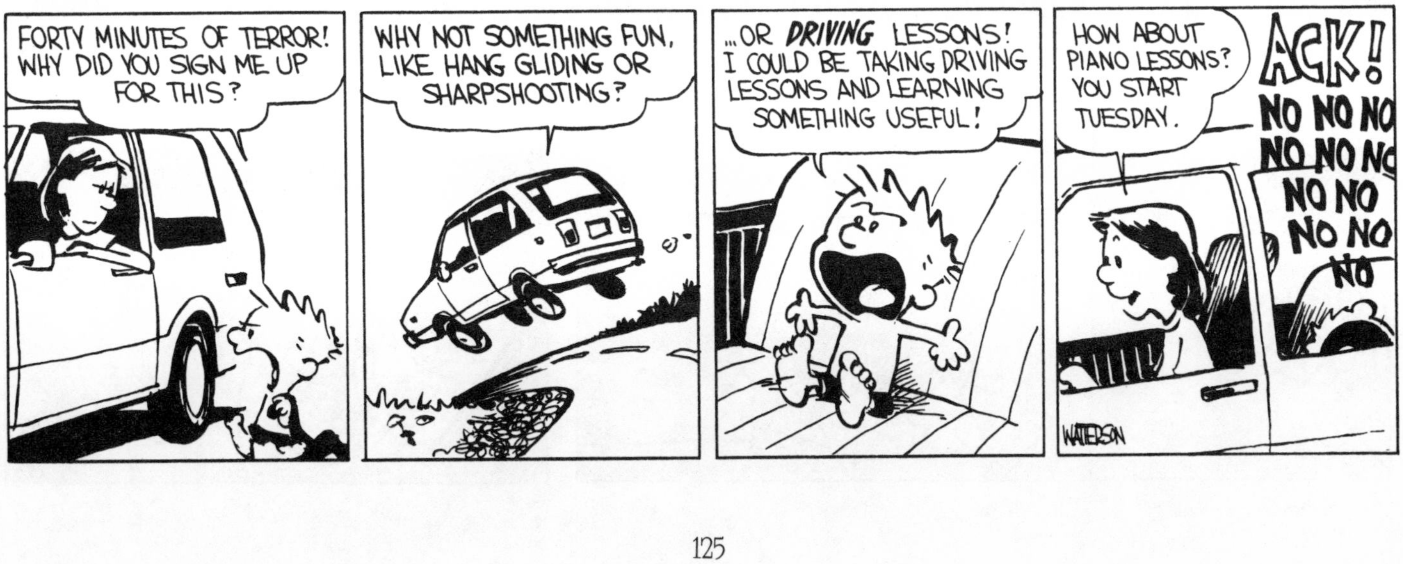
FORTY MINUTES OF TERROR! WHY DID YOU SIGN ME UP FOR THIS?
WHY NOT SOMETHING FUN, LIKE HANG GLIDING OR SHARPSHOOTING?
...OR DRIVING LESSONS! I COULD BE TAKING DRIVING LESSONS AND LEARNING SOMETHING USEFUL!
HOW ABOUT PIANO LESSONS? YOU START TUESDAY.
ACK! NO NO NO NO NO NO NO NO NO NO NO

**Calvin and Hobbes** by WATTERSON

HEY, MOM, ARE YOU NERVOUS?

NO. ... WHY?

CALVIN, GO OUTSIDE AND QUIT BUGGING ME!

CALVIN THE BUG BUZZES OFF!

FLYING LOW OVER THE GRASS, HE SEARCHES FOR DEAD MEAT!

UP AND OVER THE FLOWERS, DARTING THIS WAY AND THAT!

OH NO! HE'S CAUGHT IN A SPIDER WEB!

THRASHING ABOUT IN A DESPERATE BID FOR FREEDOM, HE ONLY BECOMES MORE ENTANGLED! SOON THE SPIDER WILL SUCK OUT HIS INNARDS! HELP!

I WAS GOING TO JOIN YOU IN THE HAMMOCK, BUT I THINK I'LL FORGET IT.

HI, CALVIN, WHAT ARE YOU DOING?

BIG IMPORTANT SECRET THINGS! GO AWAY! GET LOST!

ALL RIGHT, DANDELION HEAD! WHO CARES WHAT YOU DO ANYWAY!

*WE'RE* DOING GREAT THINGS. *WE'RE* HAVING *FUN*!

I THOUGHT WE WERE BORED OUT OF OUR SKULLS.

OH HUSH. YOU DON'T KNOW ANYTHING.

THAT STUPID CALVIN. HE'S SO MEAN.

ALL I TRY TO DO IS BE FRIENDS, AND HE TREATS ME LIKE I'M NOBODY.

WELL, WHO NEEDS JERKS LIKE HIM ANYWAY? I DON'T NEED HIM FOR A FRIEND. I CAN HAVE FUN BY MYSELF!

POOP.

SUSIE, HOBBES THOUGHT I WAS RUDE, SO I'M SORRY, AND YOU CAN COME PLAY WITH US IF YOU WANT.

THANKS, CALVIN. THAT'S REALLY NICE OF YOU.

OK, WE'LL PLAY HOUSE NOW. I'LL BE THE HIGH-POWERED EXECUTIVE WIFE, THE TIGER HERE CAN BE MY UNEMPLOYED, HOUSEKEEPING HUSBAND, AND YOU CAN BE OUR BRATTY AND BRAINLESS KID IN A DAY CARE CENTER.

THIS WAS *YOUR* IDEA, PEA BRAIN.

DON'T YOU TALK TO YOUR FATHER THAT WAY!

I'M OFF TO WALL STREET. DON'T WAIT UP.

THE ALIENS ARE GAINING ON OUR HERO! IN A SURPRISE MOVE, SPACEMAN SPIFF SHIFTS INTO REVERSE!

THE ALIENS ROAR AHEAD! SPIFF SHIFTS BACK INTO FORWARD, AND PURSUES THE ALIENS!

...BUT THE ALIENS HAVE TURNED AROUND AND ARE HEADED STRAIGHT FOR OUR HERO! SPIFF SHIFTS INTO REVERSE!

I'M GETTING SICK.

WHACK!

???

TELL ME THIS ISN'T A SPITBALL!!

HOBBES, QUICK! HOW DO I STOP?!?

STEER INTO A GRAVEL DRIVEWAY AND FALL DOWN!

SKRUNCH!

THAT WAS ONLY A SUGGESTION.

LOOK AT THAT THING IN THE DIRT! IT MUST BE A FOSSIL!

I WONDER WHAT PECULIAR ANIMAL *THIS* WAS.

BUT IT'S NOT A BONE. IT MUST BE SOME PRIMITIVE HUNTING WEAPON OR EATING UTENSIL FOR CAVE MEN.

MAYBE IT HAD SOME RELIGIOUS FUNCTION.

THIS EXPLAINS WHY YOUR CLOTHES STAY ON THE FLOOR.

MAKING A SIGN?

I'M DECLARING THE CREEK BACK IN THE WOODS "CALVIN'S CREEK."

WHEN YOU DISCOVER SOMETHING, YOU'RE ALLOWED TO NAME IT AND PUT UP A SIGN.

BUT SUPPOSE YOU DIDN'T DISCOVER THAT CREEK.

OF COURSE I DID! NOBODY *ELSE* HAS A SIGN THERE, RIGHT?

CAN HOBBES AND I GO PLAY IN THE RAIN, MOM?

NO.

WHY NOT?

YOU'LL GET SOAKED.

WHAT'S WRONG WITH THAT?

YOU COULD CATCH PNEUMONIA, RUN UP A TERRIBLE HOSPITAL BILL, LINGER A FEW MONTHS, AND DIE.

I ALWAYS FORGET. IF YOU ASK A MOM, YOU GET A WORST-CASE SCENARIO.

I HAD NO IDEA THESE LITTLE SHOWERS WERE SO *DANGEROUS.*

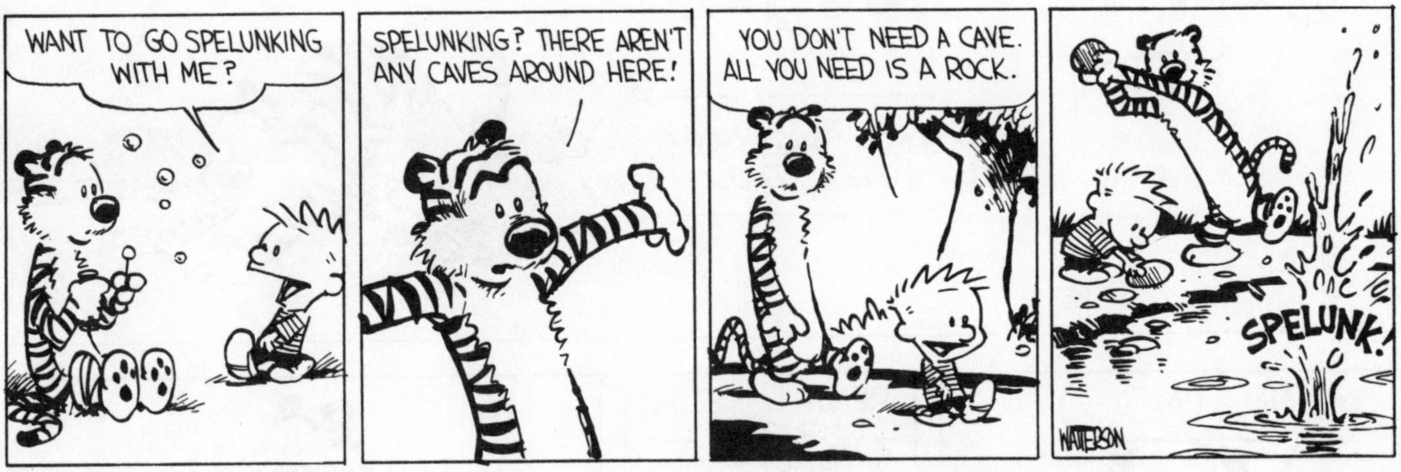
WANT TO GO SPELUNKING WITH ME?
SPELUNKING? THERE AREN'T ANY CAVES AROUND HERE!
YOU DON'T NEED A CAVE. ALL YOU NEED IS A ROCK.
SPELUNK!
WATTERSON

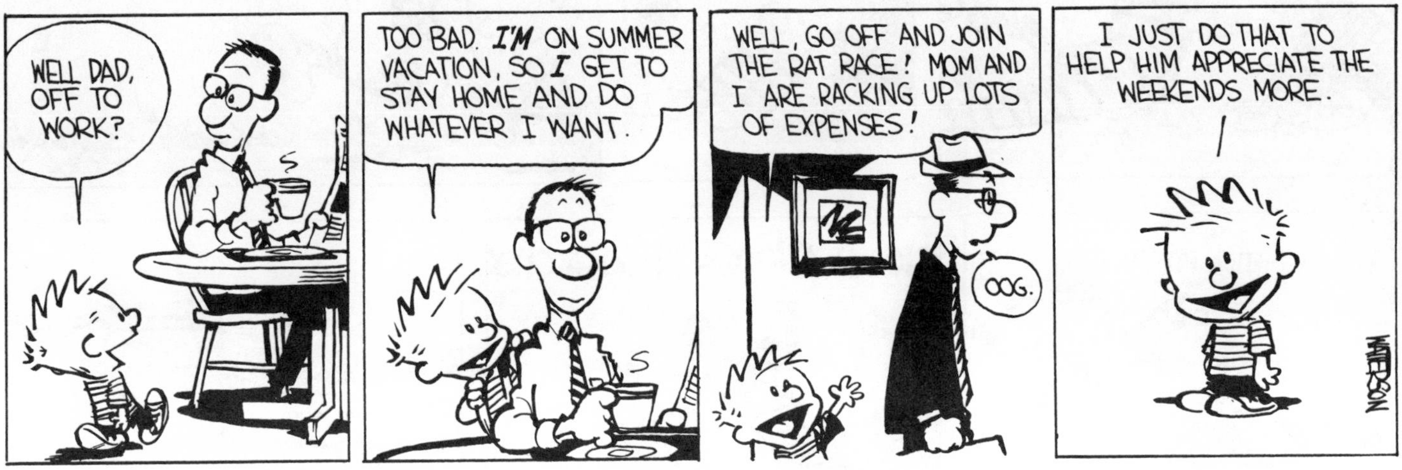
WELL DAD, OFF TO WORK?
TOO BAD. *I'M* ON SUMMER VACATION, SO *I* GET TO STAY HOME AND DO WHATEVER I WANT.
WELL, GO OFF AND JOIN THE RAT RACE! MOM AND I ARE RACKING UP LOTS OF EXPENSES!
OOG.
I JUST DO THAT TO HELP HIM APPRECIATE THE WEEKENDS MORE.
WATTERSON

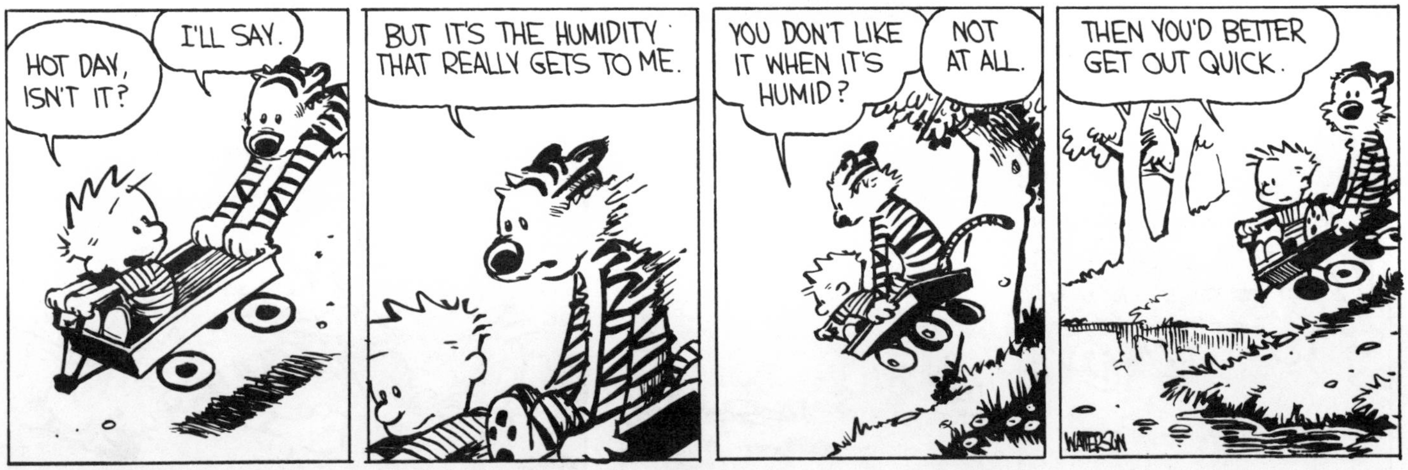
HOT DAY, ISN'T IT?
I'LL SAY.
BUT IT'S THE HUMIDITY THAT REALLY GETS TO ME.
YOU DON'T LIKE IT WHEN IT'S HUMID?
NOT AT ALL.
THEN YOU'D BETTER GET OUT QUICK.
WATTERSON

HERE COMES SUSIE.

HA! WON'T SHE BE HORRIFIED TO SEE HOW OUR FACES HAVE TRAGICALLY FROZEN!

HI, SUSIE.

HI, CALVIN.

WHAT DID YOU DO, GET YOUR HEAD STUCK IN THE BLENDER? IT'S AN IMPROVEMENT.

ARE THE COALS HOT?

YES, THEY'RE VERY HOT. I'M JUST ABOUT TO PUT ON THE HAMBURGERS.

BEFORE YOU DO, COULD YOU TOSS IN THE CAN OF LIGHTER FLUID AND MAKE A GIANT FIREBALL?

I'VE GOT THE MOST BORING DAD IN THE WORLD.

WITH THESE SNORKELS, WE CAN STAY UNDER WATER INDEFINITELY.

JUST THINK OF ALL THE FISH WE'LL BE ABLE TO SEE!

WE CAN COLLECT SHELLS!

LET'S GO!

WELL SO FAR, THIS HAS BEEN A MAJOR DISAPPOINTMENT

137

# Calvin and Hobbes

by WATTERSON

WANNA TOSS THE OL' PIGSKIN AROUND?

HECK NO.

PHOOEY.

THE CENTER SNAPS THE BALL!

THE QUARTERBACK LOOKS FOR AN OPENING!

THE DEFENSE DISINTEGRATES BENEATH THE COMING ONSLAUGHT! THE QUARTERBACK JUMPS AND DODGES!

HOBBES BREAKS CLEAR!

CALVIN PASSES!

AN AMAZING CATCH! HOBBES IS AT THE 30... THE 20... THE 10...

...BUT HE'S TACKLED FROM BEHIND AND LATERALS TO CALVIN SO *HE* CAN MAKE THE TOUCHDOWN!

BUT CALVIN FUMBLES THE BALL AND HOBBES RECOVERS IT!

BUT A PENALTY IS CALLED ON THE PLAY AND HOBBES IS SENT TO THE BENCH!

HOBBES DEFECTS TO THE OTHER TEAM AND IS GREETED WITH ENTHUSIASTIC CHEERS! THE CROWD GOES WILD!

CALVIN PREPARES TO CRIPPLE THE TRAITOR WITH AN ILLEGAL FACE MASK PULL!

HOBBES DEFIES HIM BY POURING OUT HIS MOUTH GUARD ONTO CALVIN'S HELMET!

BOY, YOU CAN SEE WHY FOOTBALL IS SUCH A VIOLENT GAME!

HOBBES' TEAM GAINS A YARD! ALL THE CHEERLEADERS COME OUT FOR SMOOCHES!!

WATTERSON

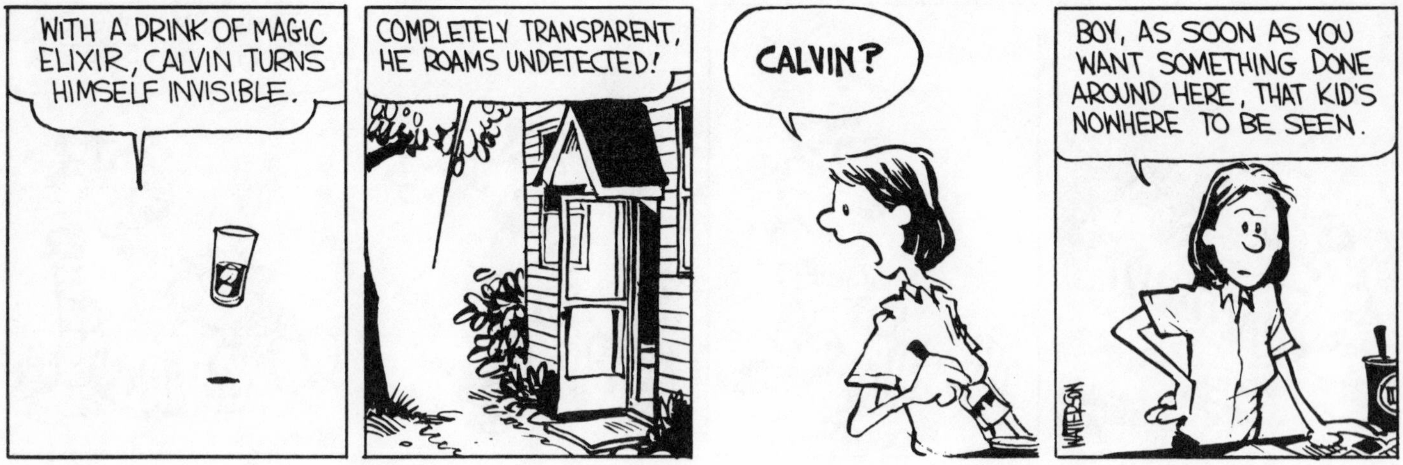
WITH A DRINK OF MAGIC ELIXIR, CALVIN TURNS HIMSELF INVISIBLE.
COMPLETELY TRANSPARENT, HE ROAMS UNDETECTED!
CALVIN?
BOY, AS SOON AS YOU WANT SOMETHING DONE AROUND HERE, THAT KID'S NOWHERE TO BE SEEN.

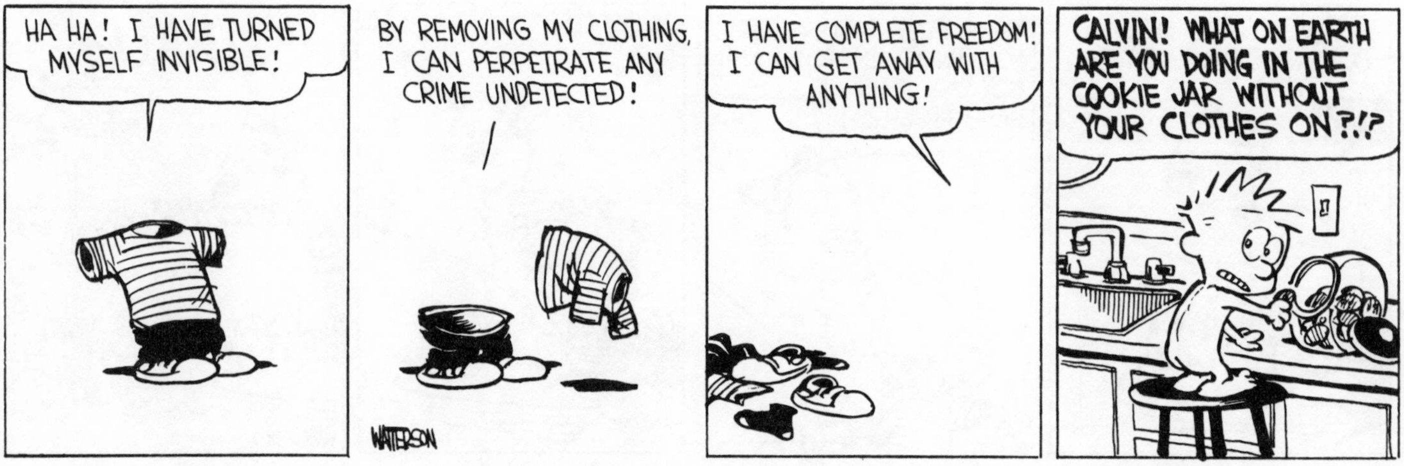
HA HA! I HAVE TURNED MYSELF INVISIBLE!
BY REMOVING MY CLOTHING, I CAN PERPETRATE ANY CRIME UNDETECTED!
I HAVE COMPLETE FREEDOM! I CAN GET AWAY WITH ANYTHING!
CALVIN! WHAT ON EARTH ARE YOU DOING IN THE COOKIE JAR WITHOUT YOUR CLOTHES ON?!?

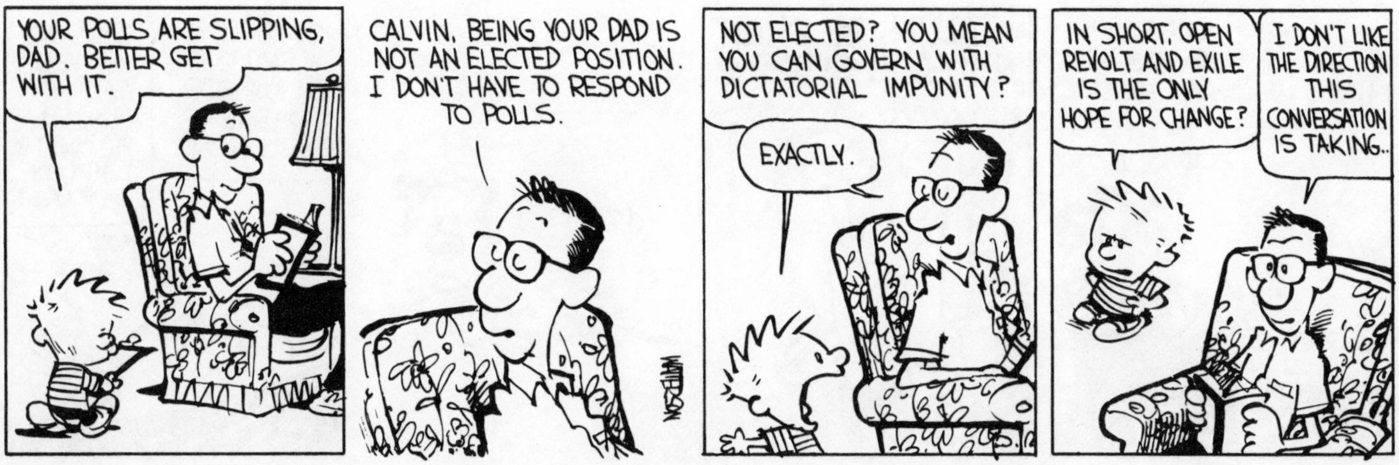
YOUR POLLS ARE SLIPPING, DAD. BETTER GET WITH IT.
CALVIN, BEING YOUR DAD IS NOT AN ELECTED POSITION. I DON'T HAVE TO RESPOND TO POLLS.
NOT ELECTED? YOU MEAN YOU CAN GOVERN WITH DICTATORIAL IMPUNITY?
EXACTLY.
IN SHORT, OPEN REVOLT AND EXILE IS THE ONLY HOPE FOR CHANGE?
I DON'T LIKE THE DIRECTION THIS CONVERSATION IS TAKING..

# Calvin and Hobbes
## by Watterson

GRAVITY IS ARBITRARY!

CALVIN WAKES UP ONE DAY TO FIND HE IS IMMUNE TO THE FORCE OF GRAVITY.

HE HANGS ON TO THE GROUND FOR DEAR LIFE, BUT HIS GRIP IS WEAKENING!

HE CAN'T HOLD ON! HE... HE **LETS GO!**

AAAAAA

HIGHER AND HIGHER, AS UPWARD HE FALLS!

ONLY BY GRABBING THE TAIL FIN OF A PASSING JET DOES CALVIN SAVE HIMSELF FROM BEING HURLED OUT INTO SPACE!

WATTERSON

NO, NO, LET HIM FINISH. THIS IS VERY INTERESTING. SO AFTER YOU LANDED IN PHOENIX, WHAT HAPPENED?

WELL, I DON'T CARE. I'M NOT SEWING VELCRO ON THE OUTSIDE OF ALL HIS CLOTHES.

WELL, ABOUT THEN MY GRAVITY CAME BACK, SO I...

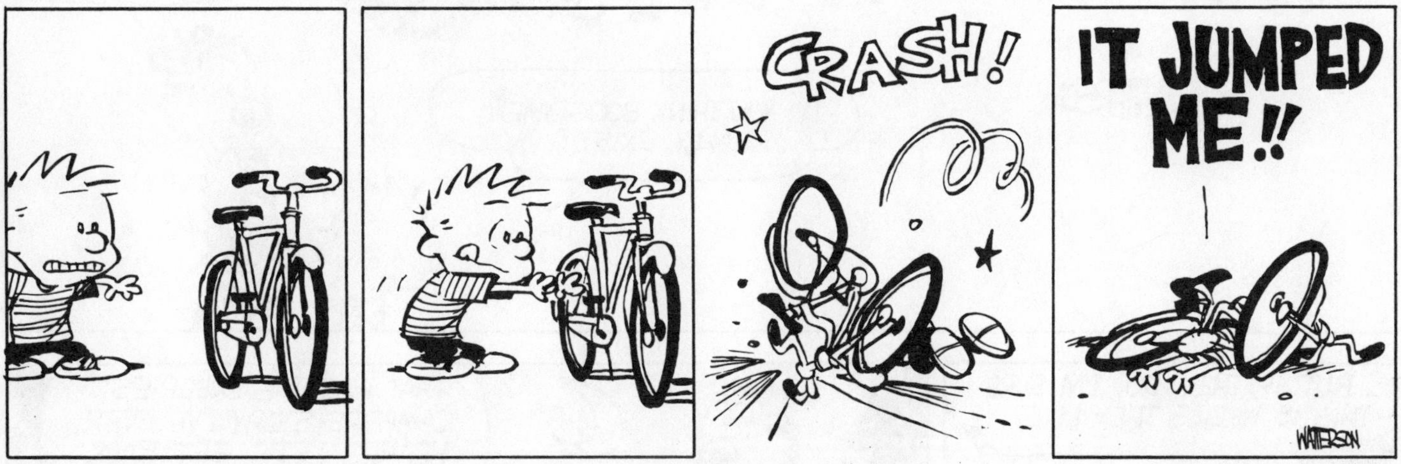
CRASH!
IT JUMPED ME!!

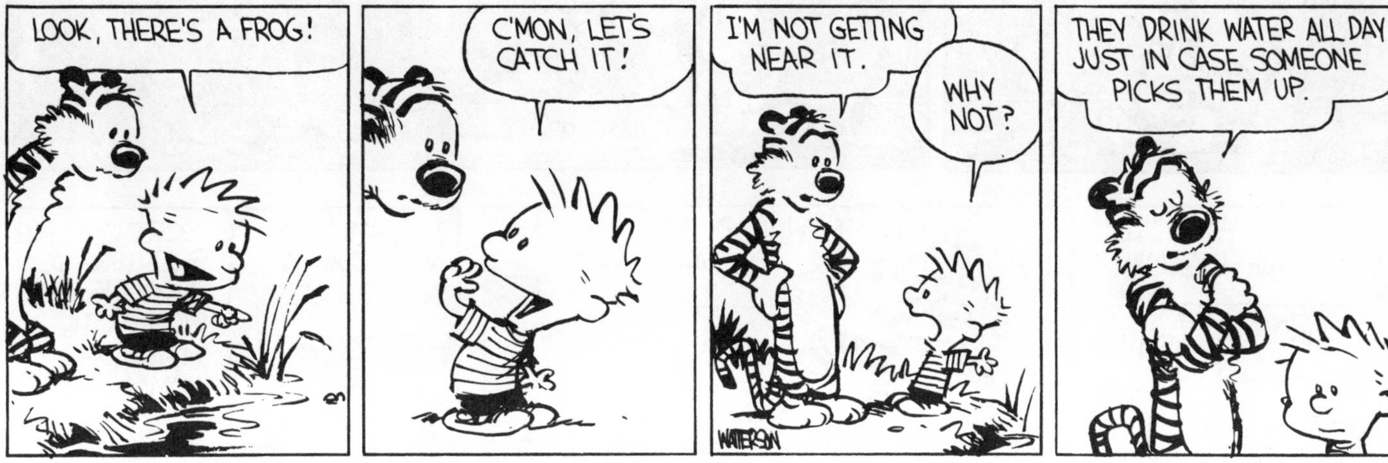
LOOK, THERE'S A FROG!
C'MON, LET'S CATCH IT!
I'M NOT GETTING NEAR IT.
WHY NOT?
THEY DRINK WATER ALL DAY JUST IN CASE SOMEONE PICKS THEM UP.

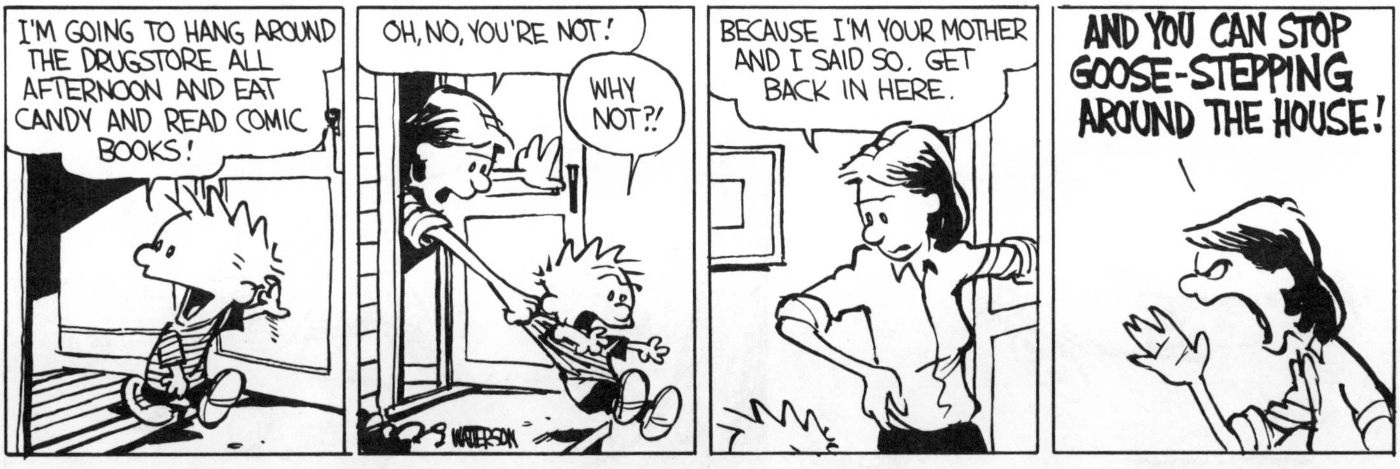
I'M GOING TO HANG AROUND THE DRUGSTORE ALL AFTERNOON AND EAT CANDY AND READ COMIC BOOKS!
OH, NO, YOU'RE NOT!
WHY NOT?!
BECAUSE I'M YOUR MOTHER AND I SAID SO. GET BACK IN HERE.
AND YOU CAN STOP GOOSE-STEPPING AROUND THE HOUSE!

HEY, MOM, CAN WE GO OUT FOR PIZZA TONIGHT?

NO, WE HAD PIZZA LAST NIGHT, AND BESIDES, IT'S TOO EXPENSIVE TO EAT OUT ALL THE TIME.

OH, YOU'D RATHER BLOW THE EVENING COOKING AND WASHING DISHES THAN SPEND A FEW BUCKS?

IT SEEMS LIKE WE GO OUT FOR PIZZA A LOT THESE DAYS.

IF YOU'D RATHER FIX A DISH OF CEREAL AT HOME, BE MY GUEST.

HOBBES WANTS TRIPLE ANCHOVIES.

CALVIN AND HIS TRUSTY NAVIGATOR HOBBES ROAR DOWN THE RESIDENTIAL ROAD AT 90 MPH!

HOBBES PUTS ON THE TURN SIGNAL.

FASTER AND FASTER THEY GO! A BUSLOAD OF SCHOOLCHILDREN DIVES FROM THE SIDEWALK!

HOBBES PUTS ON THE WINDSHIELD WIPERS.

THE POLICE ARE AFTER THEM! CALVIN CRAWLS DOWN TO PUT IN THE CLUTCH AND SHIFT!

HOBBES STEERS AND BLOWS THE HORN!

ALL RIGHT, I'M BACK ALREADY! CAN'T I EVEN RUN AN ERRAND WITHOUT YOU BLOWING THE HORN ACROSS THE PARKING LOT?!

IT WAS HOBBES, MOM. NOT ME.

SEE ANY UFOs?

NOT YET.

WELL, KEEP YOUR EYES PEELED. THEY'RE BOUND TO LAND HERE SOONER OR LATER.

WHAT WILL WE DO WHEN THEY COME?

SEE IF WE CAN SELL MOM AND DAD INTO SLAVERY FOR A STAR CRUISER.

SPACEMAN SPIFF IS HIT! HE'S GOING DOWN!

FORTUNATELY, OUR HERO ALWAYS BUCKLES UP!

THE FEARLESS SPACEMAN SPIFF HAS CRASHED ON A DISTANT WORLD!

THE PLANET'S ATMOSPHERE IS THICK WITH NOXIOUS FUMES AND GASES! OUR HERO CAN HARDLY BREATHE.

SPIFF MUST FIND HELP QUICKLY... BUT IS THERE ANY LIFE ON THIS HOSTILE WORLD?

HIS QUESTION IS ANSWERED WHEN A HIDEOUS BLOB OF GELATINOUS MUCK OOZES OUT OF A CREVICE TOWARD HIM!

SPIFF'S BLASTER IS USELESS AGAINST THE SLIME!

OUR HERO TRIES TO ESCAPE, BUT THE SUFFOCATING STENCH ENVELOPS HIM! WHAT A DISGUSTING FATE!

※YECHHH※ I SURE WISH I'D *BROUGHT* MY LUNCH TODAY!

THAT'S GROSS, CALVIN! IF YOU DON'T LIKE THE CAFETERIA'S TAPIOCA, JUST LEAVE IT ALONE!

I HAVE A HYPOTHETICAL QUESTION. SUPPOSE A KID AT SCHOOL CALLED ME A NASTY NAME...

...SHOULD I KICK HIM REAL HARD IN THE SHINS?

NO, I DON'T THINK VIOLENCE WOULD BE JUSTIFIED.

HERE'S ANOTHER HYPOTHETICAL QUESTION. WHAT IF I ALREADY DID?

I'VE DECIDED TO GROW A BEARD, MOM.

A *LONG* BEARD. LIKE THE GUYS IN ZZ TOP.

THAT'S NICE, CALVIN. YOU GO AHEAD AND DO THAT.

I THOUGHT SHE'D PUT UP MORE OF A FUSS THAN THAT.

HOW ABOUT THESE PANTS, MOM? CAN I GET THESE?

GOOD HEAVENS, LOOK AT THE PRICE! *I* DON'T HAVE PANTS THAT COST THIS MUCH!

AND YOU'LL GROW RIGHT OUT OF THESE! HONESTLY, WHY WOULD ANY KID NEED DESIGNER CLOTHES??

"BABES."

BABES, MOM. I GOTTA LOOK COOL.

**Pay up, Squirt.**

**FORGET IT, MOE. I'M NOT GIVING YOU MONEY.**

**IN FACT, I DON'T EVEN HAVE ANY.**

**Gee, that's too bad.**

**OH WAIT, YES, I DO! HERE.**

**FOR A KID WITH A MONOSYLLABIC VOCABULARY, HE'S AWFULLY PERSUASIVE.**

---

**OK, HOBBES, HERE'S THE PLAN TO PUT MOE OUT OF COMMISSION.**

**YOU COME TO SCHOOL WITH ME, AND WHEN MOE COMES TO STEAL MY MONEY, YOU JUMP OUT AND EAT HIM!**

**EAT HIM?? I COULDN'T DO THAT!**

**SURE YOU COULD! WHAT'S WRONG WITH THAT?!**

**FAT KIDS ARE HIGH IN CHOLESTEROL.**

**WELL, JUST CHEW HIM UP AND SPIT HIM OUT, I DON'T CARE!!**

---

**IF THAT BULLY IS EXTORTING MONEY, I'M GOING TO CALL THE SCHOOL AND PUT AN END TO IT.**

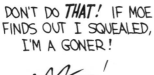

**DON'T DO *THAT!* IF MOE FINDS OUT I SQUEALED, I'M A GONER!**

**THIS KID CAN'T GET AWAY WITH STEALING, CALVIN. SOMEBODY'S GOT TO DO SOMETHING.**

**HERE'S A LIST OF WHAT I'M WEARING. SEE YOU AT THE MORGUE.**

Hey, Twinkie, here's the 25¢ I "borrowed" from you the other day.

Somebody ratted on me, and it's gonna be a dark day if I ever find out who!

I THINK I'LL USE THE QUARTER TO CALL MY INSURANCE AGENT.

WATTERSON

HI, DAD, IT'S ME!

CALVIN, IS THIS IMPORTANT? I'M VERY BUSY THIS MORNING.

I'LL MAKE IT FAST, DAD. CAN YOU PICK UP SOME TOPSOIL AND GRASS SEED ON YOUR WAY HOME?

OK, SURE. GOODBYE.

WATTERSON

RING RING

HELLO, CALVIN SPEAKING. I'D LIKE TO ORDER A LARGE ANCHOVY PIZZA.

WATTERSON

WHAT? I...??

OH, I'M SORRY. YOU MUST HAVE DIALED THE WRONG NUMBER. GOODBYE.

I TRY TO MAKE EVERYONE'S DAY A LITTLE MORE SURREAL.

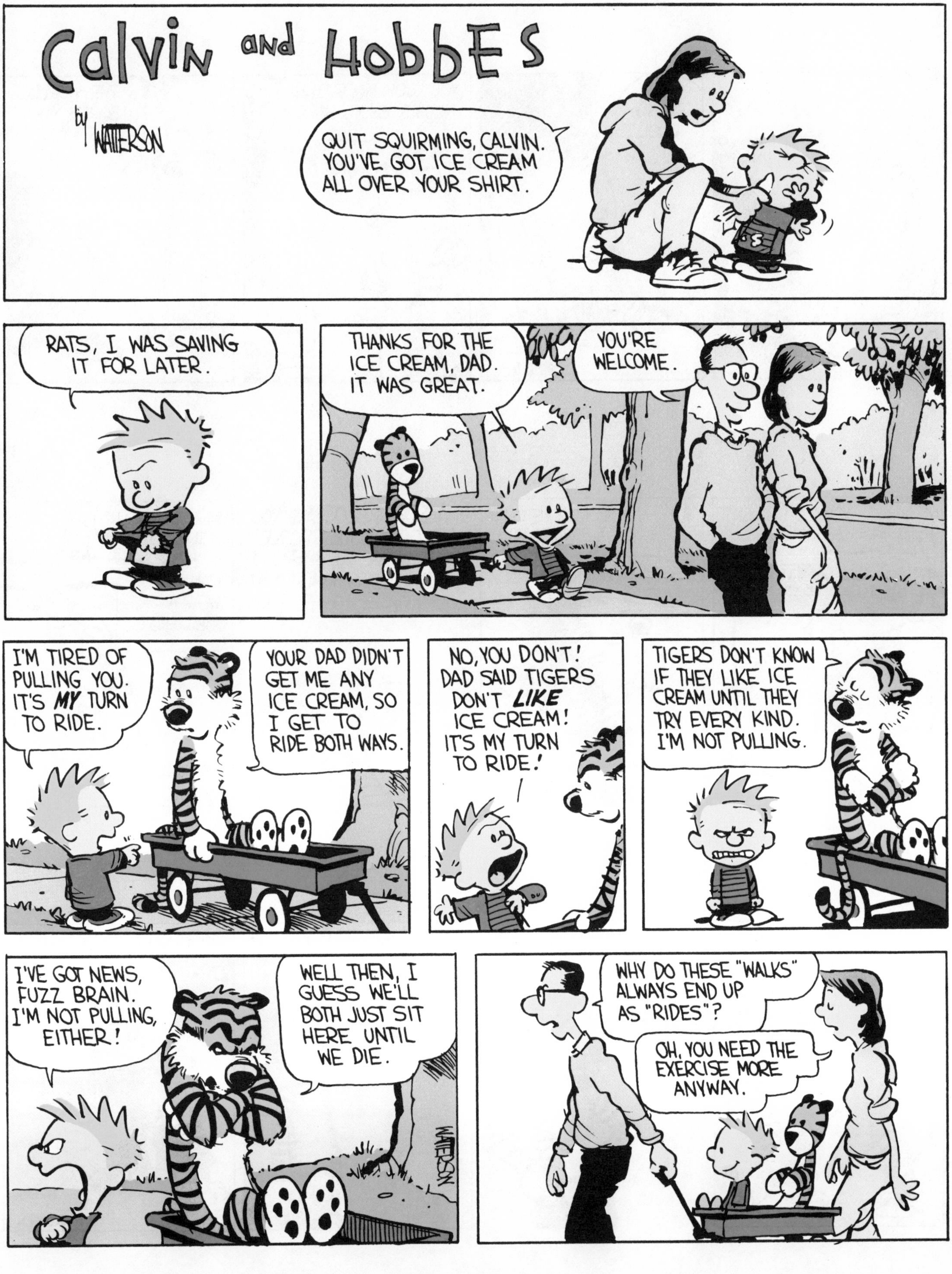
Calvin and HobbES
by WATTERSON
QUIT SQUIRMING, CALVIN. YOU'VE GOT ICE CREAM ALL OVER YOUR SHIRT.
RATS, I WAS SAVING IT FOR LATER.
THANKS FOR THE ICE CREAM, DAD. IT WAS GREAT.
YOU'RE WELCOME.
I'M TIRED OF PULLING YOU. IT'S *MY* TURN TO RIDE.
YOUR DAD DIDN'T GET ME ANY ICE CREAM, SO I GET TO RIDE BOTH WAYS.
NO, YOU DON'T! DAD SAID TIGERS DON'T *LIKE* ICE CREAM! IT'S MY TURN TO RIDE!
TIGERS DON'T KNOW IF THEY LIKE ICE CREAM UNTIL THEY TRY EVERY KIND. I'M NOT PULLING.
I'VE GOT NEWS, FUZZ BRAIN. I'M NOT PULLING, EITHER!
WELL THEN, I GUESS WE'LL BOTH JUST SIT HERE UNTIL WE DIE.
WATTERSON
WHY DO THESE "WALKS" ALWAYS END UP AS "RIDES"?
OH, YOU NEED THE EXERCISE MORE ANYWAY.

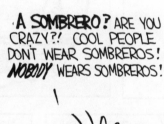

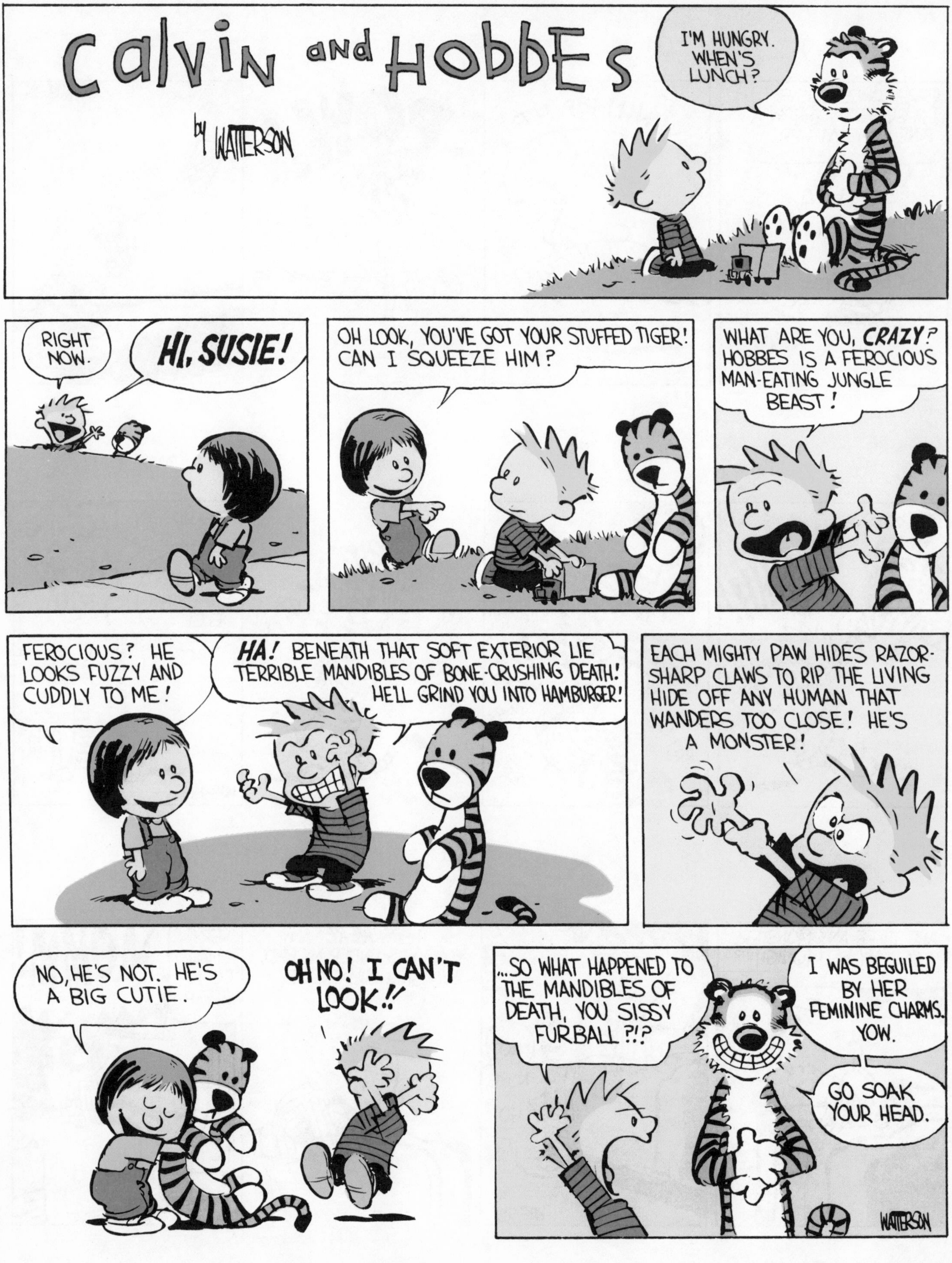
Calvin and HOBBES
by WATTERSON
I'M HUNGRY. WHEN'S LUNCH?
RIGHT NOW.
HI, SUSIE!
OH LOOK, YOU'VE GOT YOUR STUFFED TIGER! CAN I SQUEEZE HIM?
WHAT ARE YOU, CRAZY? HOBBES IS A FEROCIOUS MAN-EATING JUNGLE BEAST!
FEROCIOUS? HE LOOKS FUZZY AND CUDDLY TO ME!
HA! BENEATH THAT SOFT EXTERIOR LIE TERRIBLE MANDIBLES OF BONE-CRUSHING DEATH! HE'LL GRIND YOU INTO HAMBURGER!
EACH MIGHTY PAW HIDES RAZOR-SHARP CLAWS TO RIP THE LIVING HIDE OFF ANY HUMAN THAT WANDERS TOO CLOSE! HE'S A MONSTER!
NO, HE'S NOT. HE'S A BIG CUTIE.
OH NO! I CAN'T LOOK!!
...SO WHAT HAPPENED TO THE MANDIBLES OF DEATH, YOU SISSY FURBALL ?!?
I WAS BEGUILED BY HER FEMININE CHARMS. YOW.
GO SOAK YOUR HEAD.
WATTERSON

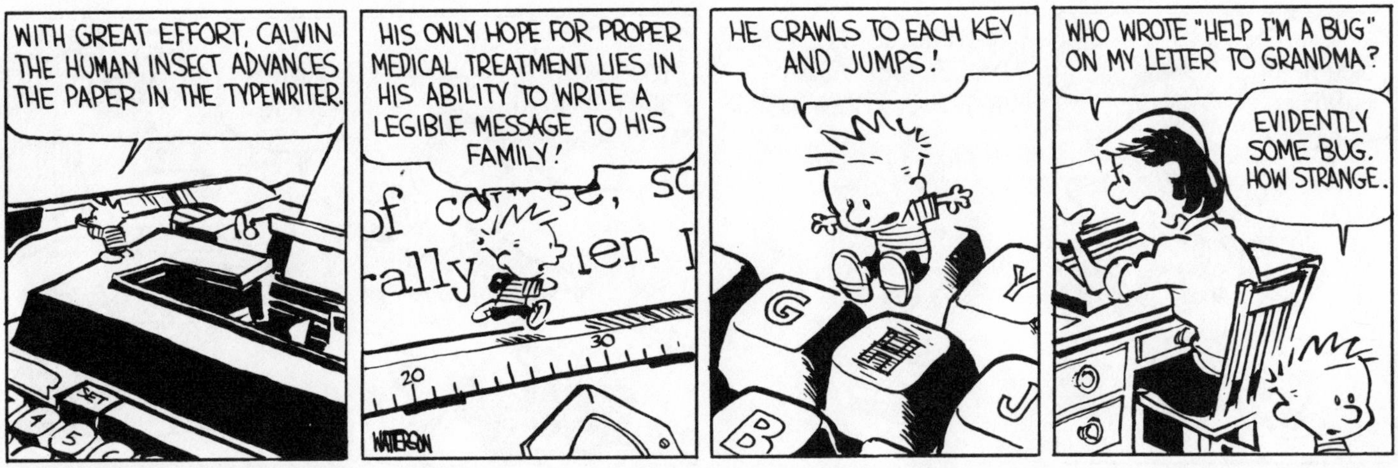
WITH GREAT EFFORT, CALVIN THE HUMAN INSECT ADVANCES THE PAPER IN THE TYPEWRITER.
HIS ONLY HOPE FOR PROPER MEDICAL TREATMENT LIES IN HIS ABILITY TO WRITE A LEGIBLE MESSAGE TO HIS FAMILY!
HE CRAWLS TO EACH KEY AND JUMPS!
WHO WROTE "HELP I'M A BUG" ON MY LETTER TO GRANDMA?
EVIDENTLY SOME BUG. HOW STRANGE.
WATTERSON

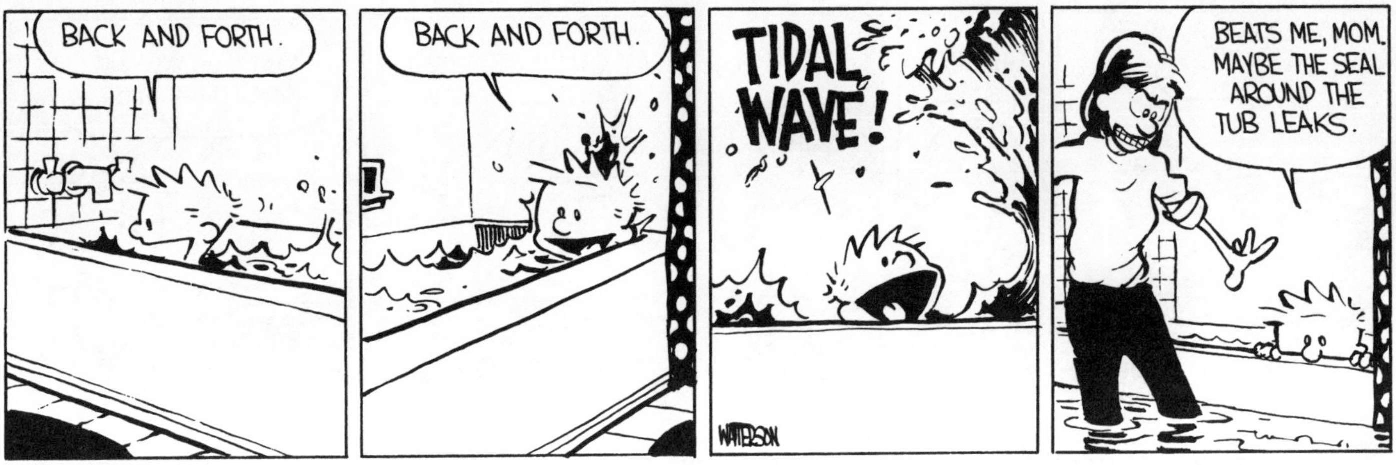
BACK AND FORTH.
BACK AND FORTH.
TIDAL WAVE!
BEATS ME, MOM. MAYBE THE SEAL AROUND THE TUB LEAKS.
WATTERSON

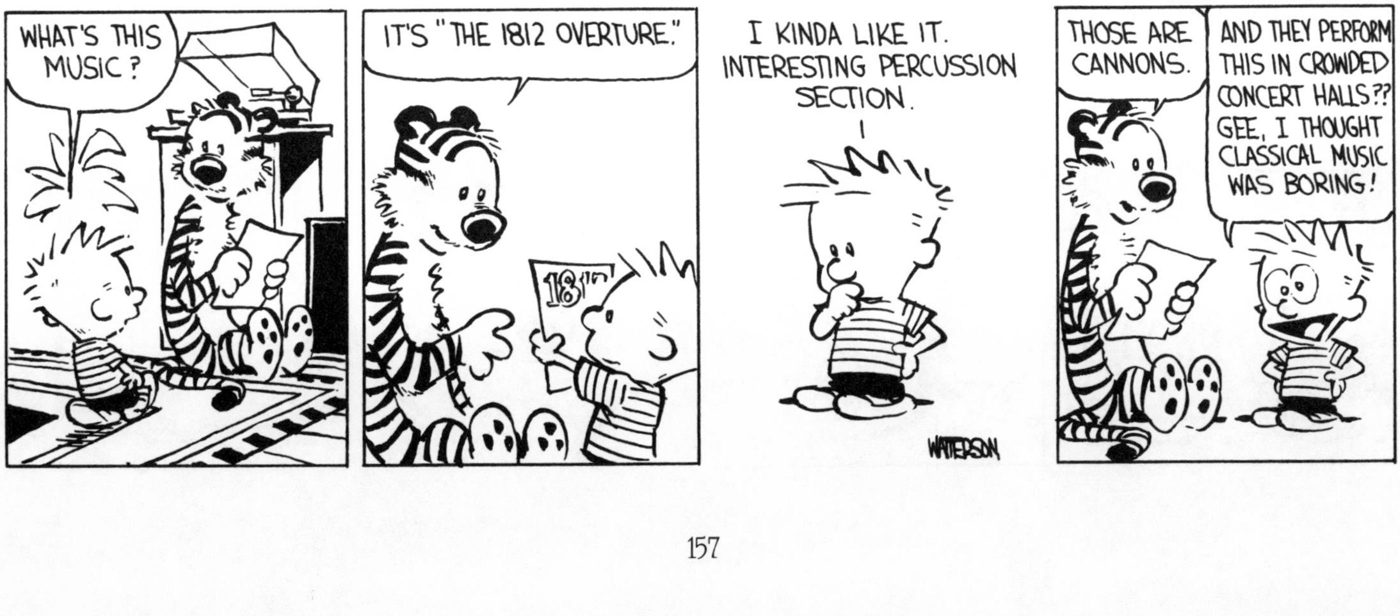
WHAT'S THIS MUSIC?
IT'S "THE 1812 OVERTURE."
I KINDA LIKE IT. INTERESTING PERCUSSION SECTION.
THOSE ARE CANNONS.
AND THEY PERFORM THIS IN CROWDED CONCERT HALLS?? GEE, I THOUGHT CLASSICAL MUSIC WAS BORING!
WATTERSON

# Calvin and Hobbes

by WATTERSON

**Calvin:** WERE THERE DINOSAURS WHEN YOU WERE A KID, DAD?

**Dad:** OH SURE! YOUR GRANDFATHER AND I USED TO PUT ON OUR LEOPARD SKINS AND HUNT BRONTOSAURUS FOR **ALL** THE CLAN RITUALS.

**Mom:** LISTEN, BUSTER, I THINK CALVIN'S GRADES ARE BAD ENOUGH **ALREADY**, DON'T YOU?

THE HORRIFYING TYRANNOSAURUS LUMBERS ACROSS THE PREHISTORIC VALLEY.

THE MIGHTY DINOSAUR IS A WALKING DEATH MACHINE!

ONLY ONE OTHER CREATURE DARES TO CHALLENGE THE TERRIBLE TYRANNOSAURUS!

...THE SAVAGE **SABER-TOOTHED TIGER!**

UNK GZZ...

GG *MMF* YOW GZZZ

MKN GBZZ..YOW....

WATTERSON

**Calvin:** WAKE UP!

THE MEEK TYRANNOSAURUS, VICTIM OF AN INNOCENT MISUNDERSTANDING, TEARS LIKE HECK ACROSS THE PREHISTORIC VALLEY..

TOMORROW WE'RE GOING TO DISCUSS "CURRENT EVENTS" IN SCHOOL.

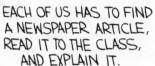

EACH OF US HAS TO FIND A NEWSPAPER ARTICLE, READ IT TO THE CLASS, AND EXPLAIN IT.

WHAT ARTICLE DID YOU CHOOSE?

THIS ONE.

"SPACE ALIEN WEDS TWO-HEADED ELVIS CLONE."

ACTUALLY, THERE'S NOT MUCH LEFT TO EXPLAIN.

LOOK WHAT YOU CAN DO WITH BIG SOCKS!

JUST PUT ONE OVER EACH EAR, AND ONE OVER YOUR NOSE...

AN ELEPHANT! HA HA! I WANT SOME SOCKS TOO!

IF I MISS THE BUS, IT'S GOING TO BE UNPLEASANT AROUND HERE!

CALVIN, HOW DID YOU BREAK THIS DISH?!

I WAS CARRYING TOO MUCH AND IT DROPPED.

YOUR PROBLEM IS YOU'VE GOT NO COMMON SENSE.

I'VE GOT **PLENTY** OF COMMON SENSE!

I JUST CHOOSE TO IGNORE IT.

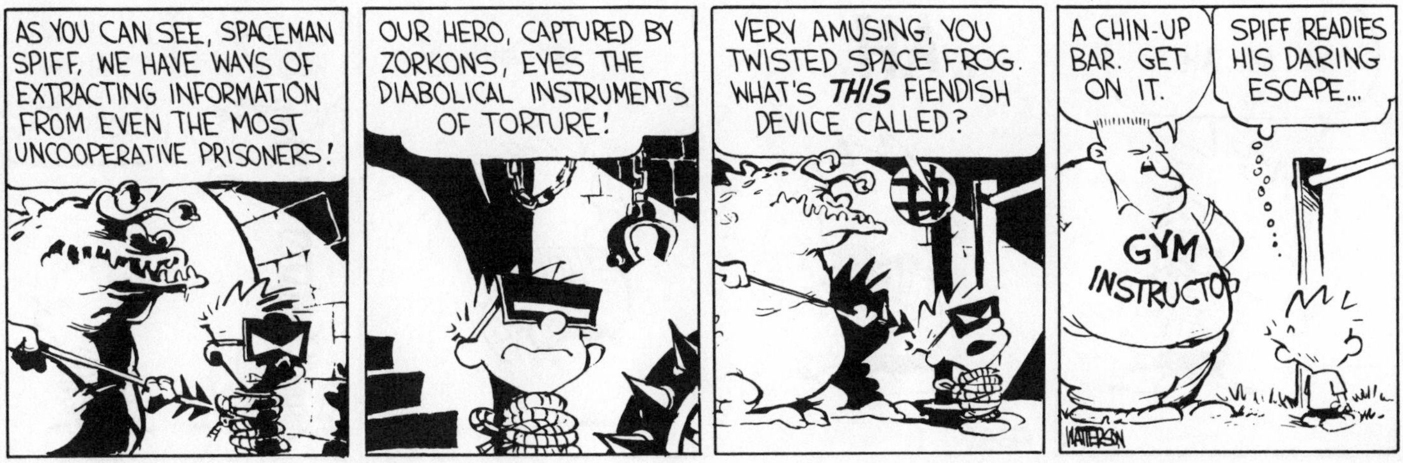
AS YOU CAN SEE, SPACEMAN SPIFF, WE HAVE WAYS OF EXTRACTING INFORMATION FROM EVEN THE MOST UNCOOPERATIVE PRISONERS!
OUR HERO, CAPTURED BY ZORKONS, EYES THE DIABOLICAL INSTRUMENTS OF TORTURE!
VERY AMUSING, YOU TWISTED SPACE FROG. WHAT'S THIS FIENDISH DEVICE CALLED?
A CHIN-UP BAR. GET ON IT.
SPIFF READIES HIS DARING ESCAPE...
GYM INSTRUCTOR
WATTERSON

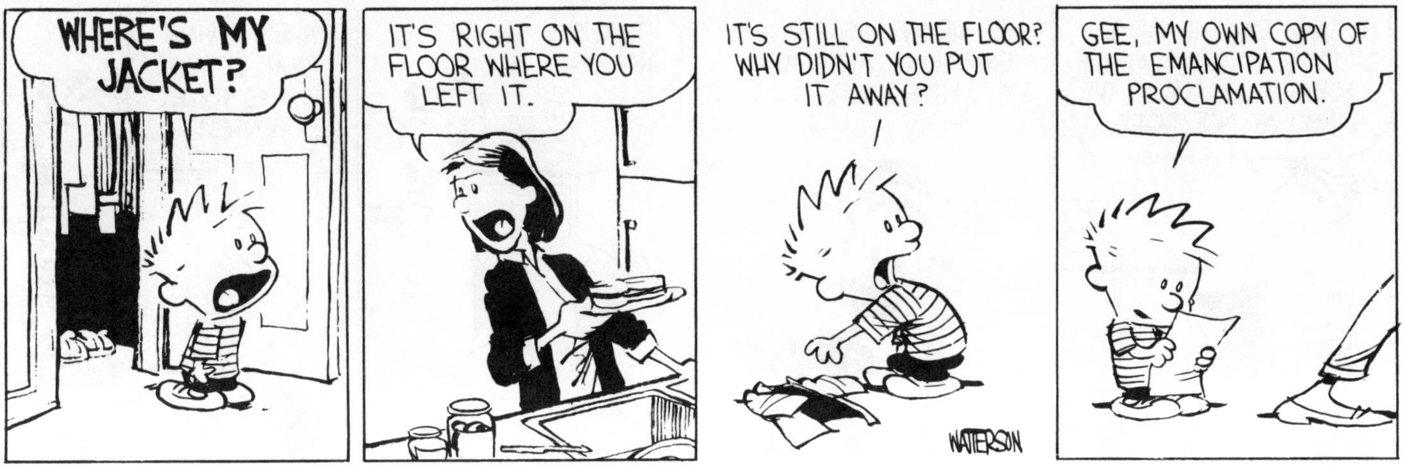
WHERE'S MY JACKET?
IT'S RIGHT ON THE FLOOR WHERE YOU LEFT IT.
IT'S STILL ON THE FLOOR? WHY DIDN'T YOU PUT IT AWAY?
GEE, MY OWN COPY OF THE EMANCIPATION PROCLAMATION.
WATTERSON

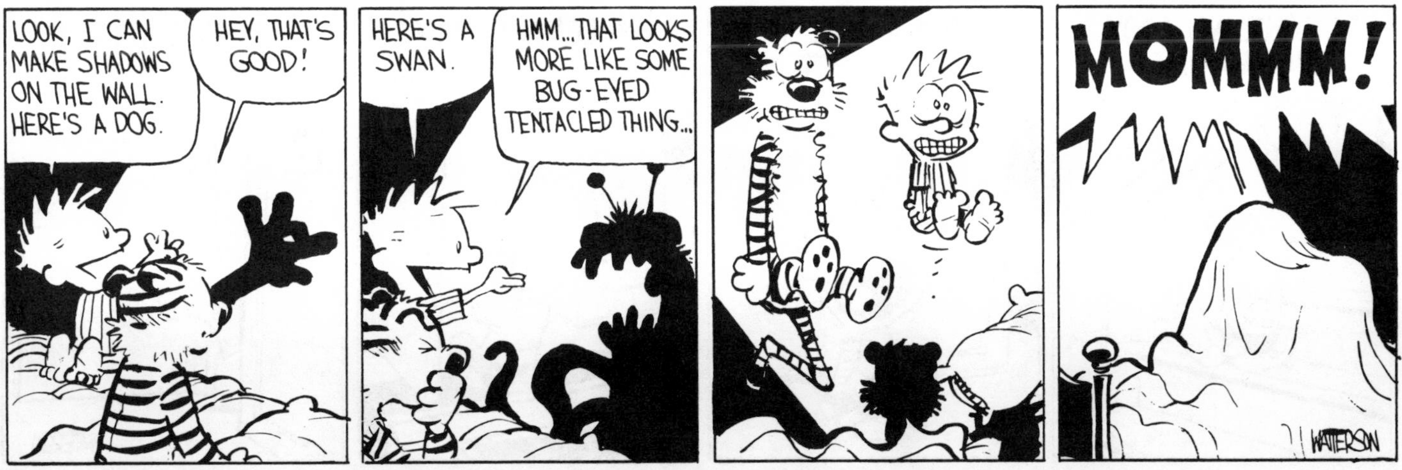
LOOK, I CAN MAKE SHADOWS ON THE WALL. HERE'S A DOG.
HEY, THAT'S GOOD!
HERE'S A SWAN.
HMM... THAT LOOKS MORE LIKE SOME BUG-EYED TENTACLED THING...
MOMMM!
WATTERSON

LOOK, MOM, I PUT ALL MY CLOTHES FOR TOMORROW ON THE STAIRS.

THEN IN THE MORNING, I'LL RUN OUT IN MY UNDERWEAR AND SLIDE DOWN AT TOP SPEED!

IF I AIM GOOD, I GO RIGHT INTO MY PANTS WHILE I'M PUTTING ON MY SHIRT, AND BY THE BOTTOM, I'M ALL DRESSED FOR SCHOOL!

AND IF YOU PUT MY CEREAL ON THE STAIRS TOO, I WON'T HAVE TO GET UP UNTIL 30 SECONDS BEFORE THE BUS COMES.

FORGET IT, CALVIN.

ACK   IGG

LOOK, MOM, I'VE GOT RABIES.

GO SPIT OUT YOUR TOOTHPASTE AND STOP BEING SILLY.

MAYBE DAD WILL FALL FOR IT IF I BITE HIM FIRST.

WHAT ARE YOU GOING TO DRESS UP AS FOR HALLOWEEN?

I DON'T KNOW YET. I CAN'T DECIDE.

WELL, THE IDEA IS TO BE THE SCARIEST THING YOU CAN THINK OF.

HMM...MAYBE I'LL JUST GO AS MYSELF!

I'M GOING AS A BARREL OF TOXIC WASTE!

WE'RE GOING TO CARVE A JACK-O'-LANTERN NOW.

SEE, WE'LL MAKE A FACE ON THIS PUMPKIN SO IT WILL LOOK LIKE A HEAD.

BUT FIRST WE HAVE TO OPEN UP THE TOP AND SCOOP OUT THE GLOP INSIDE.

OK, JACK, TIME FOR YOUR LOBOTOMY!!

HAND ME A BIG SPOON, WILL YOU, HOBBES?

UGH! NO ANESTHETIC EVEN.

WATTERSON

I THINK DAD LIKES HALLOWEEN AS MUCH AS WE DO.

IS HE TAKING US TRICK OR TREATING TONIGHT?

NO, MOM IS.

IS HE GOING TO STAY HOME AND GIVE OUT CANDY?

WATTERSON

NO, HE'S GOING TO SIT IN THE BUSHES WITH THE GARDEN HOSE AND DRENCH POTENTIAL T.P.ERS.

OOG, I FEEL AWFUL.

IF SOMEONE EVEN MENTIONS "MILK DUDS," I'M GONNA BARF.

WATTERSON

ANOTHER HALLOWEEN COME AND GONE.

IT'S ALWAYS SUCH A LETDOWN AFTER A HOLIDAY.

WE MIGHT AS WELL GO INTO TOWN AND LOOK AT THE CHRISTMAS DECORATIONS.

MOM'S NOT FEELING WELL, SO I'M MAKING HER A "GET WELL" CARD.

THAT'S THOUGHTFUL OF YOU.

SEE, ON THE FRONT IT SAYS, "GET WELL SOON."

AND ON THE INSIDE IT SAYS, "BECAUSE MY BED ISN'T MADE, MY CLOTHES NEED TO BE PUT AWAY, AND I'M HUNGRY."

"LOVE, CALVIN." WANT TO SIGN IT?

SURE. I'M HUNGRY TOO.

HI, MOM! SINCE YOU'RE SICK, I'M BRINGING YOU BREAKFAST IN BED!

I PREPARED EGGS, TOAST AND ORANGE JUICE FOR YOU ALL BY MYSELF!

HOW NICE!

THE EGGS KIND OF BURNED AND STUCK TO THE PAN, BUT YOU CAN PROBABLY CHIP THEM OUT WITH THIS CHISEL.

UM... WHERE IS THE TOAST AND ORANGE JUICE?

DAD SAID NOT TO TELL YOU ABOUT THAT TILL YOU'RE BETTER.

SINCE YOUR MOM'S SICK, I'LL BE MAKING DINNER TONIGHT.

*YOU* CAN COOK?

OF COURSE I CAN COOK.

AS YOU CAN SEE, I SURVIVED TWO YEARS OF MY OWN COOKING WHEN I HAD AN APARTMENT AFTER COLLEGE.

MOM SAYS YOU ATE FROZEN WAFFLES AND CANNED SOUP THREE MEALS A DAY.

YOUR MOM WASN'T THERE, SO SHE WOULDN'T KNOW. GET THE SYRUP OUT, WILL YOU?

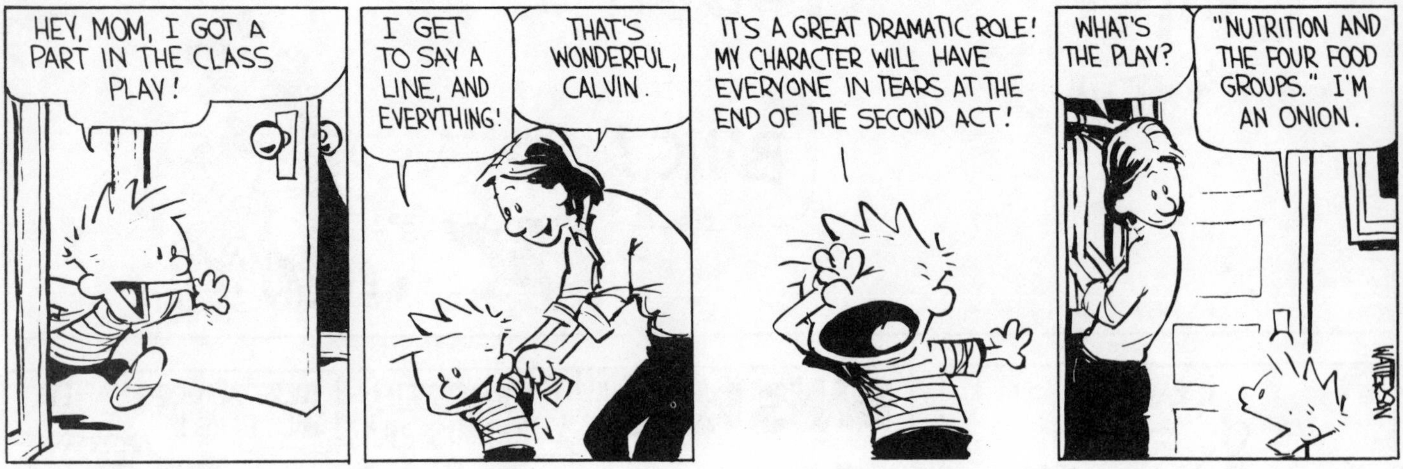
HEY, MOM, I GOT A PART IN THE CLASS PLAY!
I GET TO SAY A LINE, AND EVERYTHING!
THAT'S WONDERFUL, CALVIN.
IT'S A GREAT DRAMATIC ROLE! MY CHARACTER WILL HAVE EVERYONE IN TEARS AT THE END OF THE SECOND ACT!
WHAT'S THE PLAY?
"NUTRITION AND THE FOUR FOOD GROUPS." I'M AN ONION.

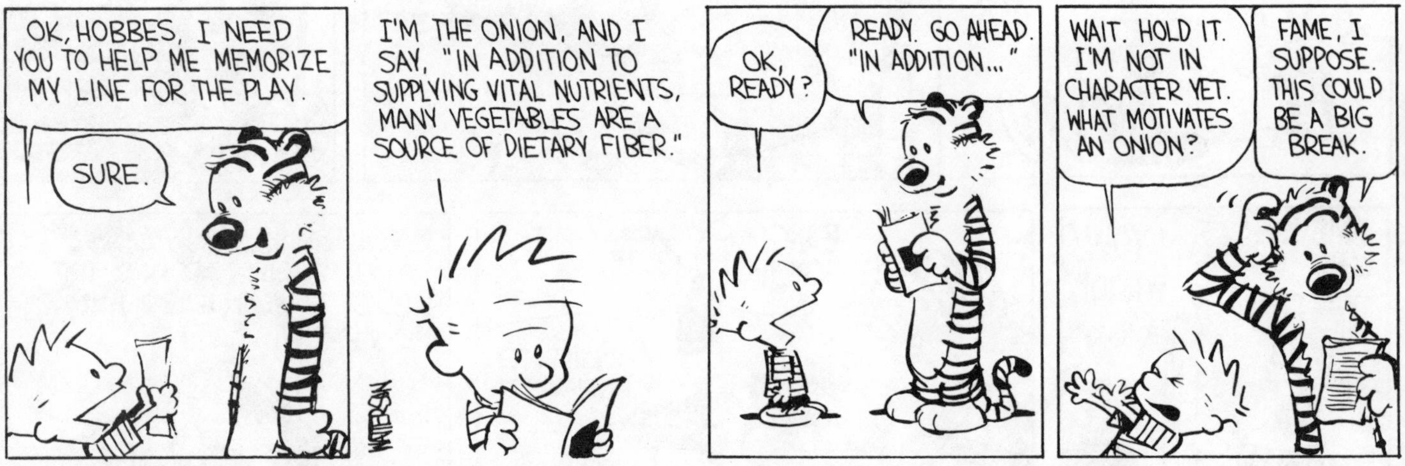
OK, HOBBES, I NEED YOU TO HELP ME MEMORIZE MY LINE FOR THE PLAY.
SURE.
I'M THE ONION, AND I SAY, "IN ADDITION TO SUPPLYING VITAL NUTRIENTS, MANY VEGETABLES ARE A SOURCE OF DIETARY FIBER."
OK, READY?
READY. GO AHEAD. "IN ADDITION..."
WAIT. HOLD IT. I'M NOT IN CHARACTER YET. WHAT MOTIVATES AN ONION?
FAME, I SUPPOSE. THIS COULD BE A BIG BREAK.

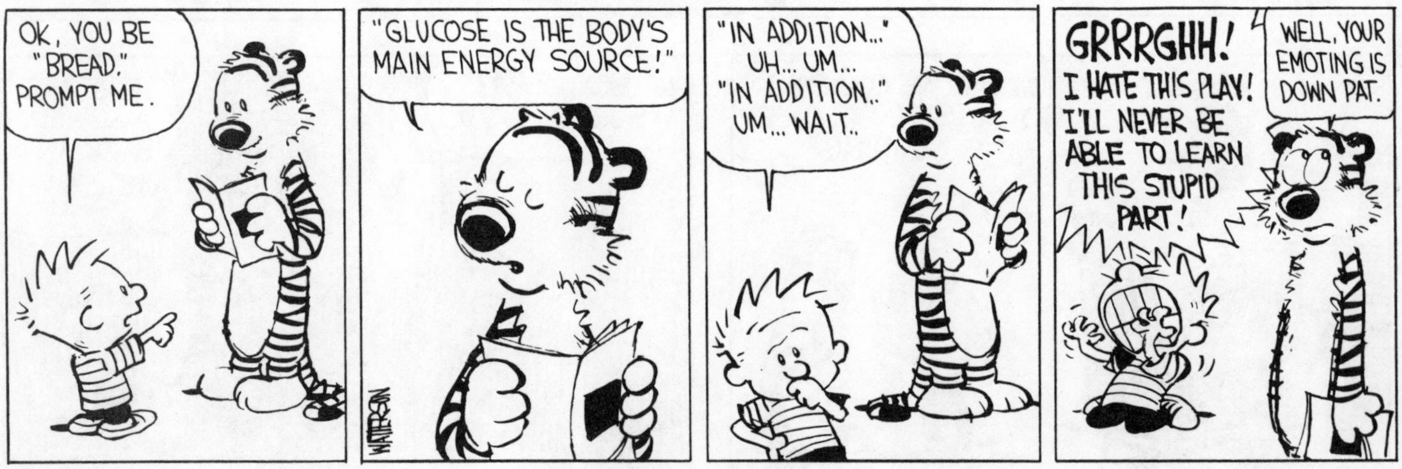
OK, YOU BE "BREAD." PROMPT ME.
"GLUCOSE IS THE BODY'S MAIN ENERGY SOURCE!"
"IN ADDITION..." UH... UM... "IN ADDITION.." UM... WAIT..
GRRRGHH! I HATE THIS PLAY! I'LL NEVER BE ABLE TO LEARN THIS STUPID PART!
WELL, YOUR EMOTING IS DOWN PAT.

I'VE GOT IT ALL FIGURED OUT, HOBBES. THIS PLAY WILL BE NO SWEAT.

YOU HAVE YOUR LINE ALL MEMORIZED?

NO, I THOUGHT I'D COME OUT, DO A LITTLE SOFT-SHOE, AND AD-LIB SOMETHING!

AD-LIB SOMETHING ABOUT DIETARY FIBER?

EITHER THAT, OR I'LL DO MY ONION IN MIME!

HOW'S MY ONION COSTUME COMING, MOM?

I'M STILL WORKING ON IT. I WISH YOUR CLASS WOULD DO SOMETHING A LITTLE LESS ELABORATE. I'M NOT MUCH OF A SEAMSTRESS.

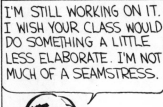

JUST BE GLAD I'M NOT RUSSY WHITE. *HE* HAS TO BE AN AMINO ACID.

MM... WHAT DO YOU THINK?

JABBA THE HUTT MEETS RUDOLF THE REINDEER. I DUNNO, MOM.

ARE YOU GOING TO COME TO MY PLAY, DAD? IT'S CALLED "NUTRITION AND THE FOUR FOOD GROUPS."

I'LL PROBABLY HAVE TO BE AT WORK, CALVIN.

BUT DAD, IT'LL BE GREAT DRAMA! I'M AN ONION!

WELL, WHY DON'T YOU SAY YOUR LINE FOR ME NOW?

OK! UM... ..LET'S SEE.. "IN ADDITION TO...".. UH... HOLD IT... UM..

25 KIDS IN FOOD SUITS, FORGETTING THEIR LINES. I'LL *DEFINITELY* BE AT WORK.

DEAR! CALVIN'S WORKED HARD.

OK, UH... " IN ADDITION.."..UH NO, WAIT.. UM...

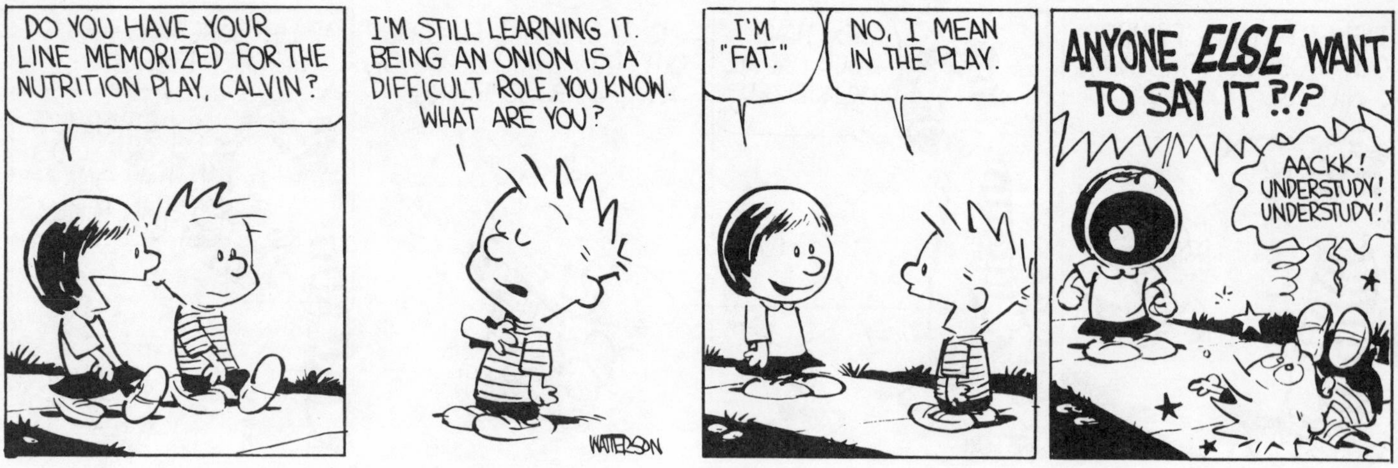
DO YOU HAVE YOUR LINE MEMORIZED FOR THE NUTRITION PLAY, CALVIN?
I'M STILL LEARNING IT. BEING AN ONION IS A DIFFICULT ROLE, YOU KNOW. WHAT ARE YOU?
WATTERSON
I'M "FAT."
NO, I MEAN IN THE PLAY.
ANYONE *ELSE* WANT TO SAY IT ?!?
AACKK! UNDERSTUDY! UNDERSTUDY!

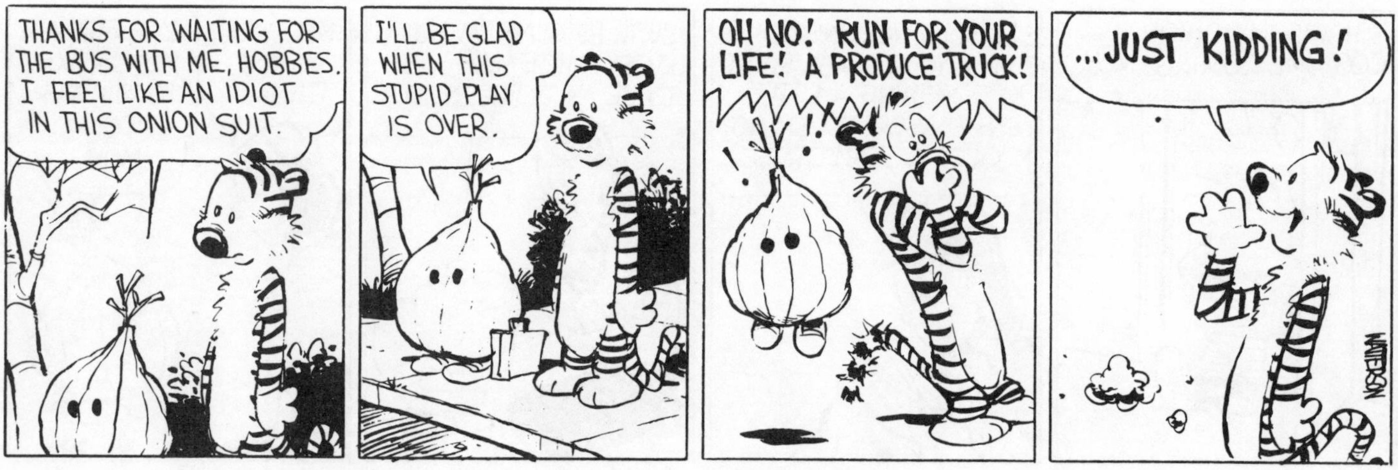
THANKS FOR WAITING FOR THE BUS WITH ME, HOBBES. I FEEL LIKE AN IDIOT IN THIS ONION SUIT.
I'LL BE GLAD WHEN THIS STUPID PLAY IS OVER.
OH NO! RUN FOR YOUR LIFE! A PRODUCE TRUCK!
...JUST KIDDING!
WATTERSON

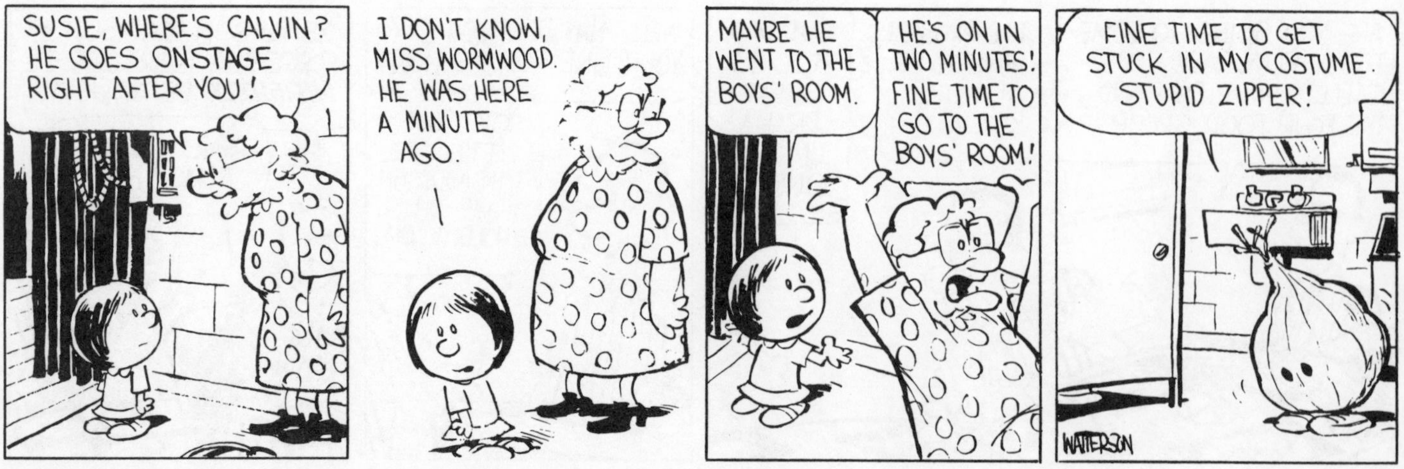
SUSIE, WHERE'S CALVIN? HE GOES ONSTAGE RIGHT AFTER YOU!
I DON'T KNOW, MISS WORMWOOD. HE WAS HERE A MINUTE AGO.
MAYBE HE WENT TO THE BOYS' ROOM.
HE'S ON IN TWO MINUTES! FINE TIME TO GO TO THE BOYS' ROOM!
FINE TIME TO GET STUCK IN MY COSTUME. STUPID ZIPPER!
WATTERSON

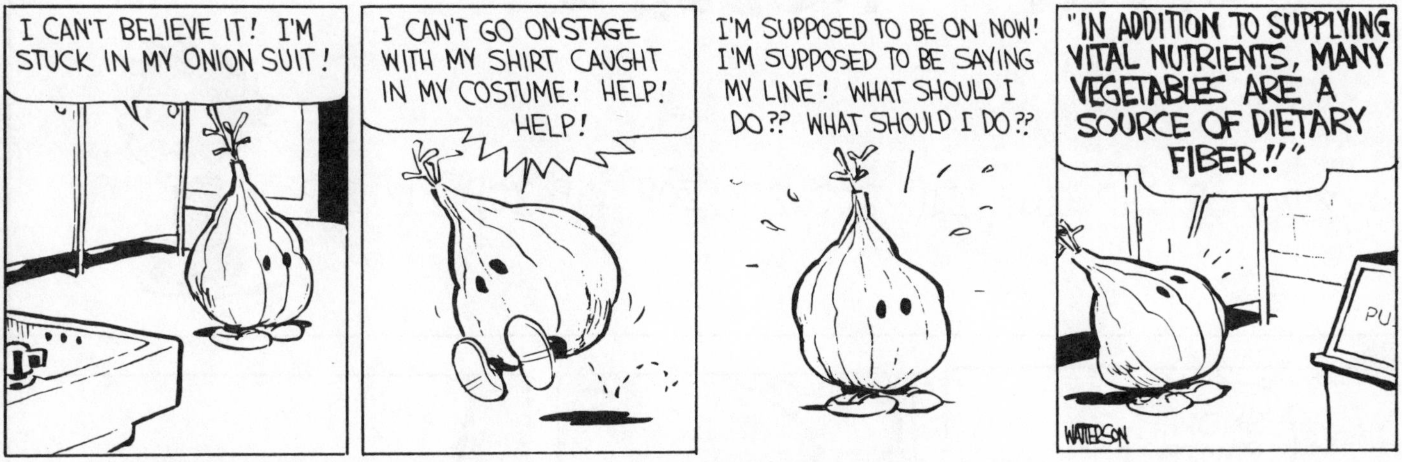
I CAN'T BELIEVE IT! I'M STUCK IN MY ONION SUIT!
I CAN'T GO ONSTAGE WITH MY SHIRT CAUGHT IN MY COSTUME! HELP! HELP!
I'M SUPPOSED TO BE ON NOW! I'M SUPPOSED TO BE SAYING MY LINE! WHAT SHOULD I DO?? WHAT SHOULD I DO??
"IN ADDITION TO SUPPLYING VITAL NUTRIENTS, MANY VEGETABLES ARE A SOURCE OF DIETARY FIBER!!"
WATTERSON

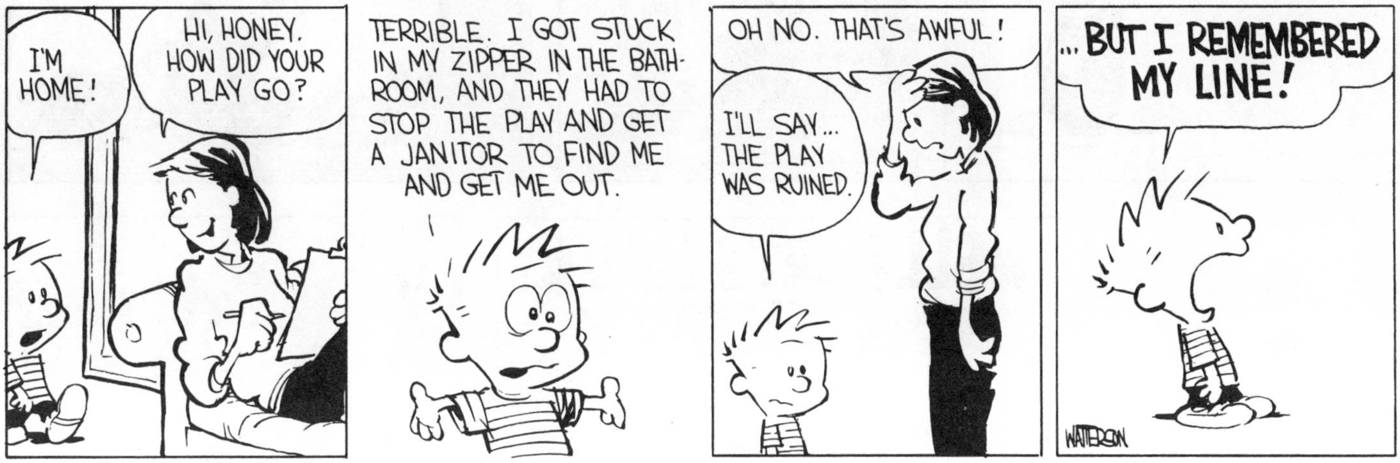
I'M HOME!
HI, HONEY. HOW DID YOUR PLAY GO?
TERRIBLE. I GOT STUCK IN MY ZIPPER IN THE BATHROOM, AND THEY HAD TO STOP THE PLAY AND GET A JANITOR TO FIND ME AND GET ME OUT.
OH NO. THAT'S AWFUL!
I'LL SAY... THE PLAY WAS RUINED.
...BUT I REMEMBERED MY LINE!
WATTERSON

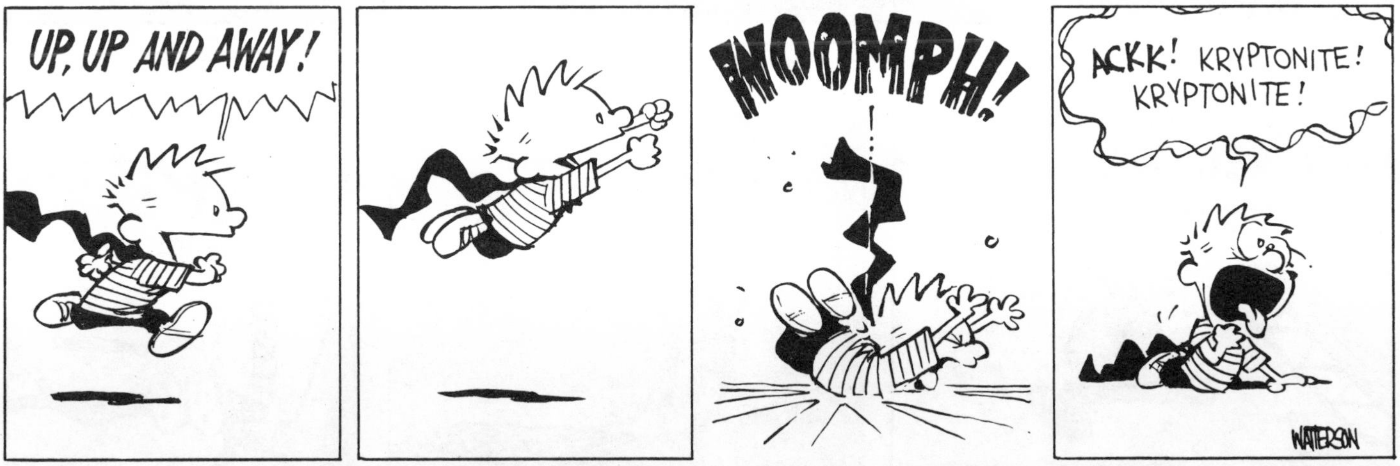
UP, UP AND AWAY!
WOOMPH!
ACKK! KRYPTONITE! KRYPTONITE!
WATTERSON

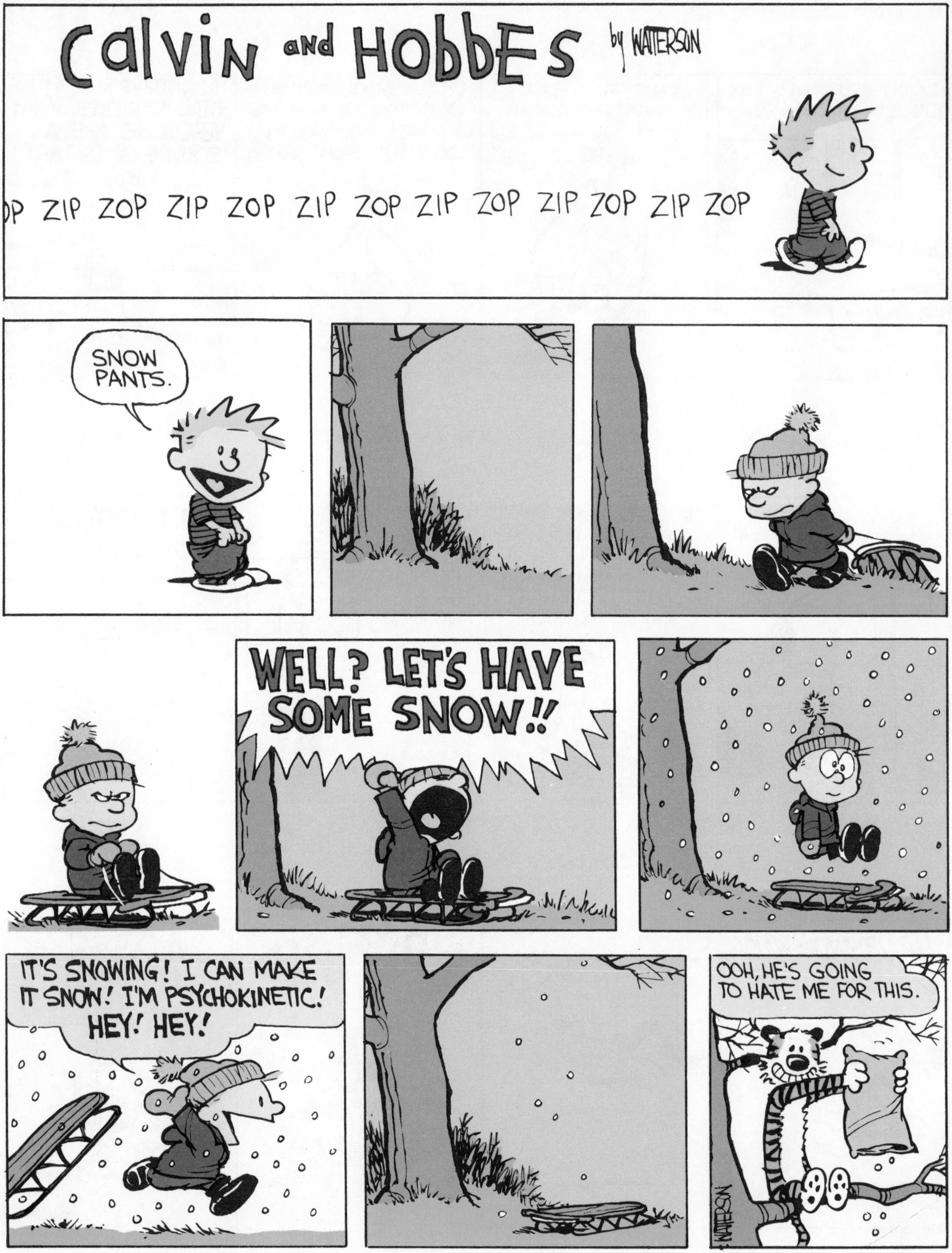
Calvin and HOBBES
by WATTERSON
ZOP ZIP ZOP ZIP ZOP ZIP ZOP ZIP ZOP ZIP ZOP ZIP ZOP
SNOW PANTS.
WELL? LET'S HAVE SOME SNOW!!
IT'S SNOWING! I CAN MAKE IT SNOW! I'M PSYCHOKINETIC! HEY! HEY!
OOH, HE'S GOING TO HATE ME FOR THIS.
WATTERSON

WANT TO TRADE SANDWICHES, CALVIN?

NO, I'VE GOT MY FAVORITE KIND. WHAT DID YOU BRING?

PEANUT BUTTER.

I HAVE PROCESSED MOUSE LOAF.

OH, GROSS. THAT'S NOT REALLY MOUSE LOAF. IT LOOKS LIKE EGG SALAD.

TASTE IT AND SEE. HERE, I THINK THIS IS A WHISKER. IT'S GOOD.

FORGET IT. I DON'T EVEN WANT MY *OWN* LUNCH ANY MORE.

YOU DON'T? WHAT KIND OF COOKIES ARE THOSE?

TRIP!

TA-DAAA !!

HOW DO THEY KNOW THE LOAD LIMIT ON BRIDGES, DAD?

LOAD LIMIT 10 TONS

THEY DRIVE BIGGER AND BIGGER TRUCKS OVER THE BRIDGE UNTIL IT BREAKS.

THEN THEY WEIGH THE LAST TRUCK AND REBUILD THE BRIDGE.

OH. I SHOULD'VE GUESSED.

DEAR, IF YOU DON'T KNOW THE ANSWER, JUST TELL HIM!

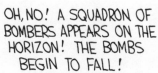

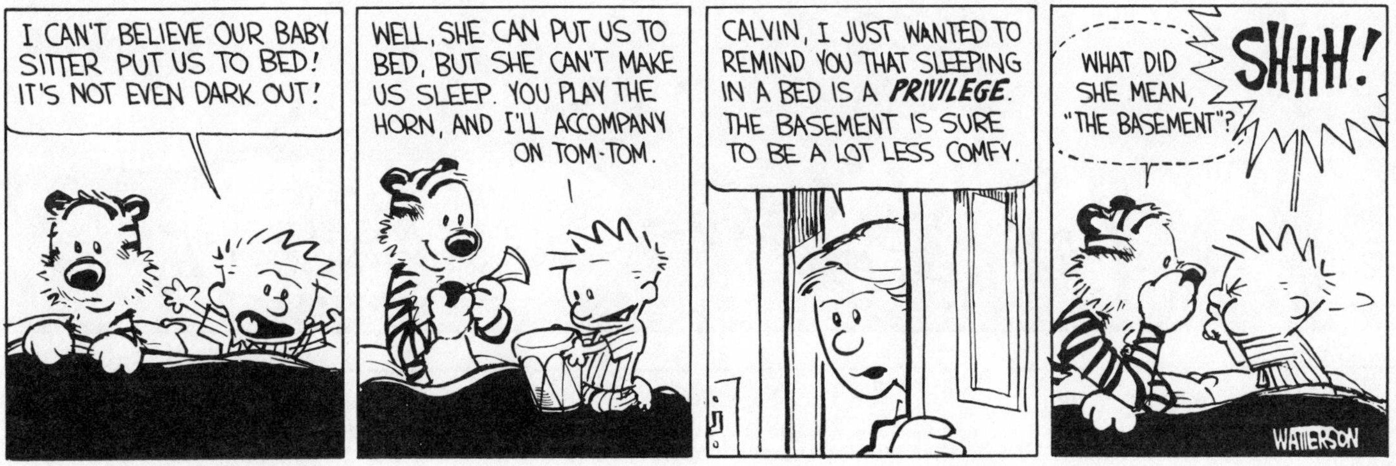
I CAN'T BELIEVE OUR BABY SITTER PUT US TO BED! IT'S NOT EVEN DARK OUT!
WELL, SHE CAN PUT US TO BED, BUT SHE CAN'T MAKE US SLEEP. YOU PLAY THE HORN, AND I'LL ACCOMPANY ON TOM-TOM.
CALVIN, I JUST WANTED TO REMIND YOU THAT SLEEPING IN A BED IS A PRIVILEGE. THE BASEMENT IS SURE TO BE A LOT LESS COMFY.
WHAT DID SHE MEAN, "THE BASEMENT"?
SHHH!
WATTERSON

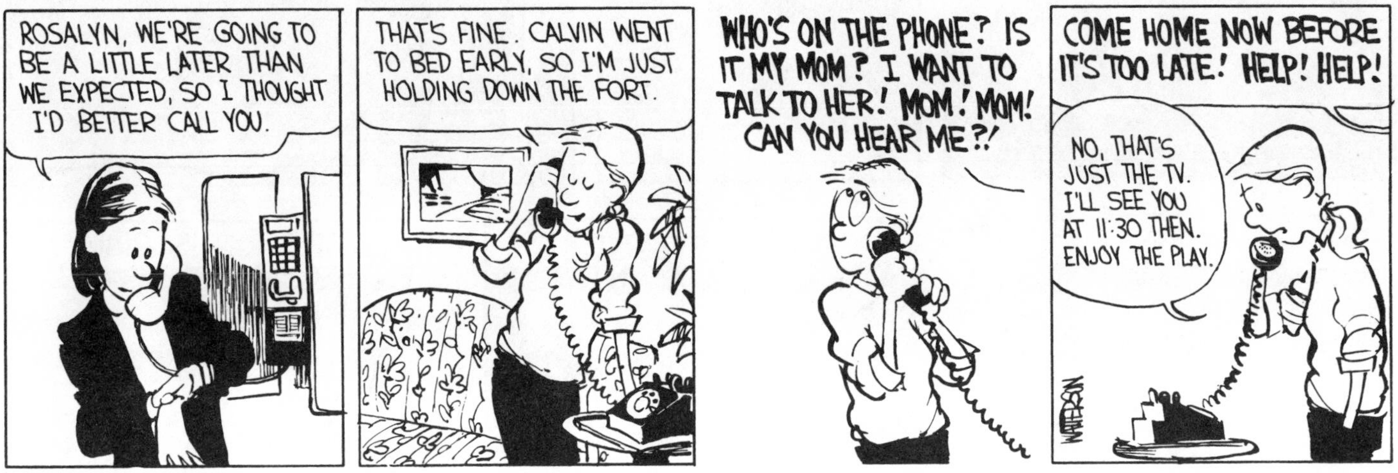
ROSALYN, WE'RE GOING TO BE A LITTLE LATER THAN WE EXPECTED, SO I THOUGHT I'D BETTER CALL YOU.
THAT'S FINE. CALVIN WENT TO BED EARLY, SO I'M JUST HOLDING DOWN THE FORT.
WHO'S ON THE PHONE? IS IT MY MOM? I WANT TO TALK TO HER! MOM! MOM! CAN YOU HEAR ME?!
COME HOME NOW BEFORE IT'S TOO LATE! HELP! HELP!
NO, THAT'S JUST THE TV. I'LL SEE YOU AT 11:30 THEN. ENJOY THE PLAY.
WATTERSON

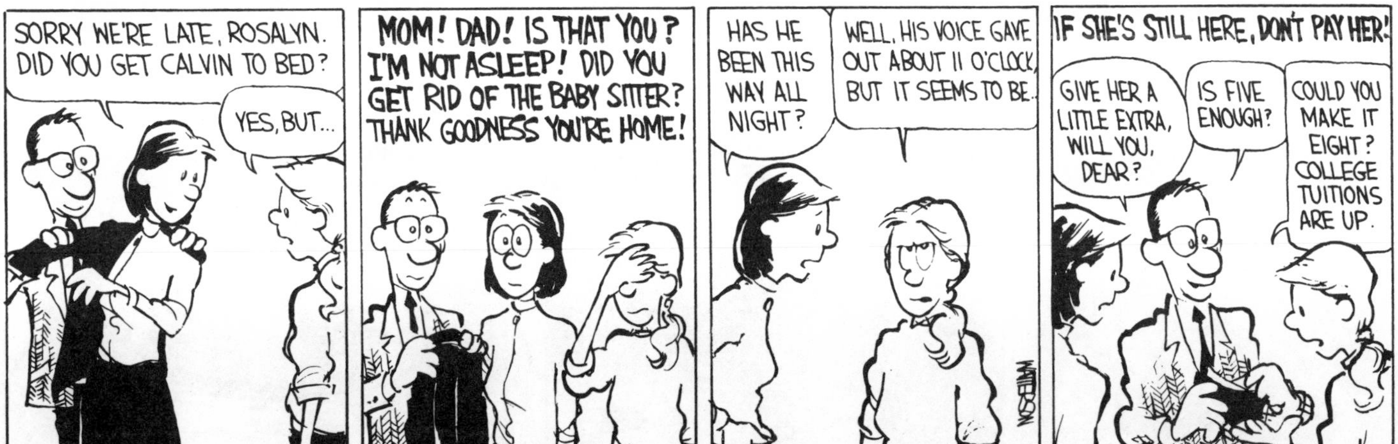
SORRY WE'RE LATE, ROSALYN. DID YOU GET CALVIN TO BED?
YES, BUT...
MOM! DAD! IS THAT YOU? I'M NOT ASLEEP! DID YOU GET RID OF THE BABY SITTER? THANK GOODNESS YOU'RE HOME!
HAS HE BEEN THIS WAY ALL NIGHT?
WELL, HIS VOICE GAVE OUT ABOUT 11 O'CLOCK, BUT IT SEEMS TO BE...
WATTERSON
IF SHE'S STILL HERE, DON'T PAY HER!
GIVE HER A LITTLE EXTRA, WILL YOU, DEAR?
IS FIVE ENOUGH?
COULD YOU MAKE IT EIGHT? COLLEGE TUITIONS ARE UP.

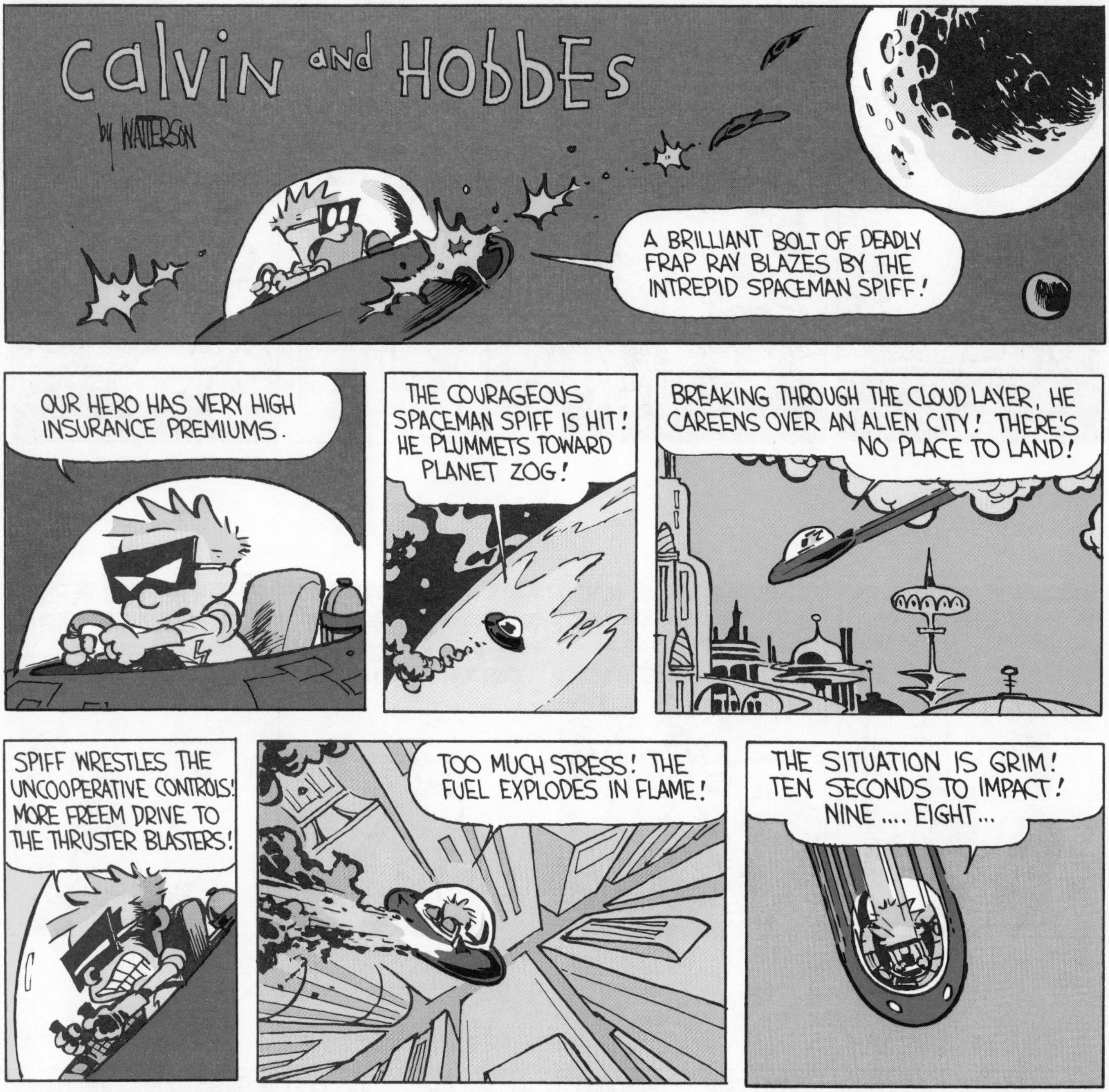
Calvin and HOBBES
by WATTERSON
A BRILLIANT BOLT OF DEADLY FRAP RAY BLAZES BY THE INTREPID SPACEMAN SPIFF!
OUR HERO HAS VERY HIGH INSURANCE PREMIUMS.
THE COURAGEOUS SPACEMAN SPIFF IS HIT! HE PLUMMETS TOWARD PLANET ZOG!
BREAKING THROUGH THE CLOUD LAYER, HE CAREENS OVER AN ALIEN CITY! THERE'S NO PLACE TO LAND!
SPIFF WRESTLES THE UNCOOPERATIVE CONTROLS! MORE FREEM DRIVE TO THE THRUSTER BLASTERS!
TOO MUCH STRESS! THE FUEL EXPLODES IN FLAME!
THE SITUATION IS GRIM! TEN SECONDS TO IMPACT! NINE .... EIGHT...
WELL, CALVIN??
SEVEN!
VERY GOOD, CALVIN. TEN MINUS THREE EQUALS SEVEN. I DIDN'T THINK YOU WERE PAYING ATTENTION. THAT QUESTION WAS WORTH THREE POINTS.
OUR HERO MIRACULOUSLY MAKES A THREE-POINT LANDING. SPIFF SAVES THE DAY AGAIN!
WATTERSON

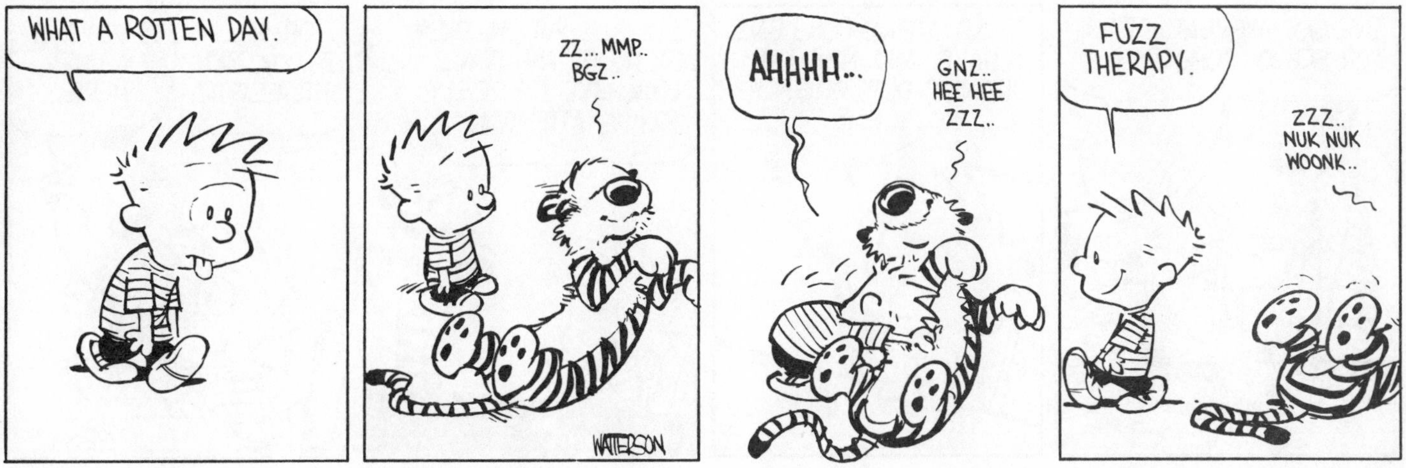
WHAT A ROTTEN DAY.
ZZ... MMP.. BGZ..
AHHHH...
GNZ.. HEE HEE ZZZ..
FUZZ THERAPY.
ZZZ.. NUK NUK WOONK..
WATTERSON

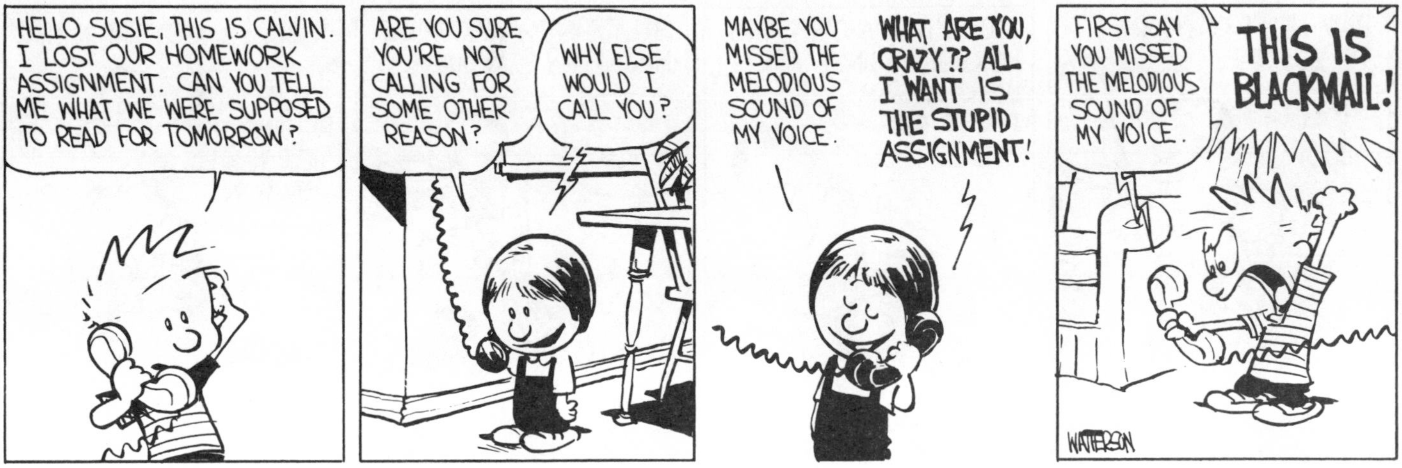
HELLO SUSIE, THIS IS CALVIN. I LOST OUR HOMEWORK ASSIGNMENT. CAN YOU TELL ME WHAT WE WERE SUPPOSED TO READ FOR TOMORROW?
ARE YOU SURE YOU'RE NOT CALLING FOR SOME OTHER REASON?
WHY ELSE WOULD I CALL YOU?
MAYBE YOU MISSED THE MELODIOUS SOUND OF MY VOICE.
WHAT ARE YOU, CRAZY?? ALL I WANT IS THE STUPID ASSIGNMENT!
FIRST SAY YOU MISSED THE MELODIOUS SOUND OF MY VOICE.
THIS IS BLACKMAIL!
WATTERSON

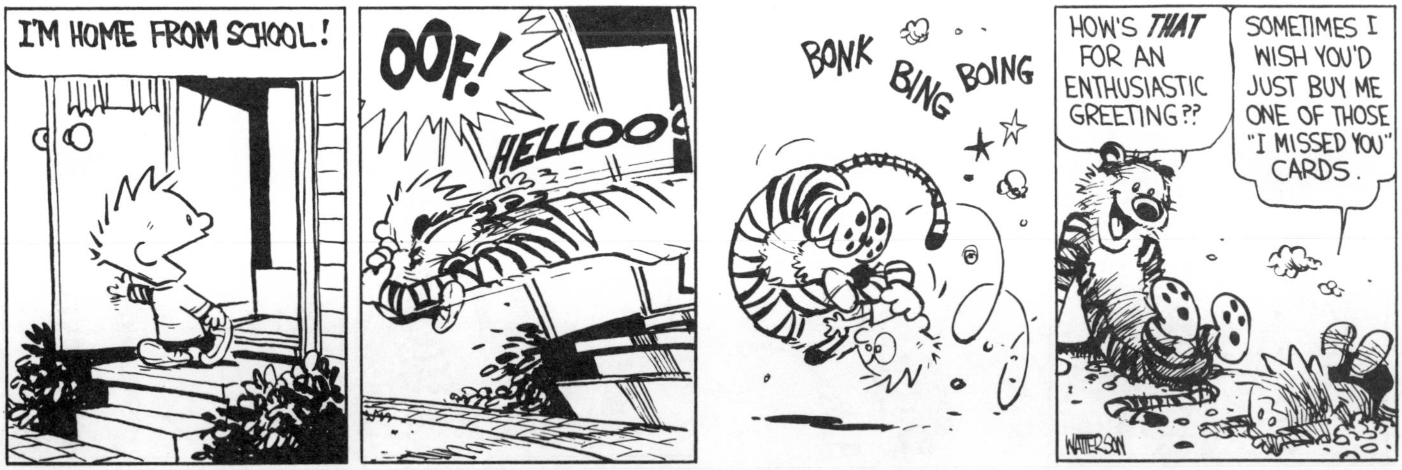
I'M HOME FROM SCHOOL!
OOF!
HELLOO
BONK
BING
BOING
HOW'S *THAT* FOR AN ENTHUSIASTIC GREETING??
SOMETIMES I WISH YOU'D JUST BUY ME ONE OF THOSE "I MISSED YOU" CARDS.
WATTERSON

**Panel 1:** I'VE GOT A GREAT IDEA FOR SCHOOL TOMORROW.

**Panel 2:** I CUT A PING-PONG BALL IN HALF, AND NOW I'M DRAWING DOTS ON EACH END.

**Panel 3:** I'LL JUST PUT ONE OVER EACH EYE, AND IT WILL LOOK LIKE I'M REALLY PAYING ATTENTION.

**Panel 4:** ... OR WILL I LOOK *TOO* INTERESTED?

I DOUBT IT. I'M OVER HERE.

**Panel 5:** BAD NEWS ON YOUR POLLS, DAD.

**Panel 6:** YOU SLIPPED ANOTHER TWO NOTCHES. THINGS ARE LOOKING GRIM FOR FUTURE OFFICE.

IS THAT SO?

**Panel 7:** ANY IDEAS ON WHAT WOULD IMPROVE MY STANDINGS?

I NEED A VCR.

**Panel 8:** RIGHT. I'LL KEEP THAT IN MIND.

I HOPE YOU'RE READING THE "HELP WANTED" SECTION.

**Panel 9:** LOOK, I GOT A LETTER I'M SUPPOSED TO COPY AND SEND TO 20 PEOPLE FOR GOOD LUCK.

IT'S A CHAIN LETTER.

**Panel 10:** IT SAYS, "A MAN IN DENVER MADE 20 COPIES AND THE NEXT DAY HE GOT A RAISE. A MAN IN SEATTLE BROKE THE CHAIN AND HE WENT BALD."

**Panel 11:** HA! YOU BELIEVE THAT? THESE LETTERS ARE FOR SUPERSTITIOUS NINCOMPOOPS. THROW IT AWAY.

**Panel 12:** "... AND A DUMB KID LIKE YOU LISTENED TO A FRIEND AND GOT RUN OVER BY A CEMENT MIXER."

# Calvin and Hobbes

by WATTERSON

I'M READY FOR BED, DAD. WHAT'S TONIGHT'S STORY GOING TO BE?

HERE'S ONE. "READINGS ON DIALECTICAL METAPHYSICS." YOU'LL LOVE IT.

FORGET IT, DAD. YOU CAN'T GET ME TO DROP OFF *THAT* EASY.

WILL YOU READ US *THIS* STORY? HOBBES WROTE IT HIMSELF.

HOBBES WROTE IT, HUH?

"GOLDILOCKS AND THE THREE TIGERS."

OH BOY, THIS IS GONNA BE GREAT!

"ONCE UPON A TIME THERE LIVED A YOUNG GIRL NAMED GOLDILOCKS. SHE WENT INTO THE FOREST AND SAW A COTTAGE. NO ONE WAS HOME SO SHE WENT IN."

"INSIDE SHE SAW THREE BOWLS OF PORRIDGE. A BIG BOWL, A MEDIUM BOWL, AND A SMALL BOWL. SHE WAS JUST ABOUT TO TASTE THE PORRIDGE WHEN THE THREE TIGERS CAME HOME."

"THEY QUICKLY DIVIDED GOLDILOCKS INTO BIG, MEDIUM, AND SMALL PIECES AND DUNKED THEM IN THE PORRIDGE THAT..."

CALVIN, I'M NOT GOING TO FINISH THIS! THIS IS DISGUSTING!!

I DON'T KNOW WHY I LET YOU TALK ME INTO THIS. *GOOD NIGHT!*

CLICK

HE DIDN'T EVEN LOOK AT OUR ILLUSTRATIONS.

NOW I'M ALL HUNGRY.

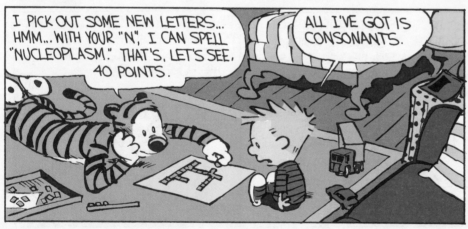

CALVIN HAS MYSTERIOUSLY SHRUNK TO THE SIZE OF AN INSECT!

HIS ONLY HOPE IS TO CALL FOR HELP! PUSHING WITH ALL HIS MIGHT, CALVIN DIALS THE GIGANTIC TELEPHONE!

IT'S RINGING! HE RUNS TO THE MOUTHPIECE! WILL ANYONE BE ABLE TO HEAR HIM??

BZZ BZ! BZZZZ! BZZ BZZ! BZZZ BZ!

CALVIN, THIS HAD BETTER NOT BE YOU.

FWOOSHHH

GREETINGS, EARTH FEMALE. DO NOT BE ALARMED.

OUR PLANET IS DYING. WE NEED COOKIES TO SURVIVE. DO NOT TRY TO RESIST OR YOU WILL BE DESTROYED.

WE'LL SEE ABOUT THAT. GET BACK HERE.

WHY DO I HAVE TO GO TO BED NOW? I NEVER GET TO DO WHAT I WANT!

IF I GROW UP TO BE SOME SORT OF PSYCHOPATH BECAUSE OF THIS, YOU'LL ALL BE SORRY!!

NOBODY EVER BECAME A PSYCHOPATH BECAUSE HE HAD TO GO TO BED AT A REASONABLE HOUR.

YEAH, BUT YOU WON'T LET ME CHEW TOBACCO EITHER! YOU NEVER KNOW WHAT MIGHT PUSH ME OVER THE BRINK!

GO TO BED, CALVIN.

OH BOY, YOU GOT SOME CLAY.

I'M MAKING MOM AND DAD A CHRISTMAS PRESENT.

WHAT ARE YOU MAKING?

AN ASHTRAY.

YOUR PARENTS DON'T SMOKE, OF COURSE...

OK, MICHELANGELO, YOU SCULPT SOMETHING!

A HOMEMADE GIFT SAYS MORE THAN A STORE-BOUGHT GIFT.

IT SAYS YOU CARE ENOUGH TO INVEST YOUR TIME AND SKILL IN IT.

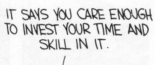

IT SAYS THIS IS A PERSONAL GIFT, NOT A GENERIC ONE.

IT SAYS YOU NEED A BIGGER ALLOWANCE.

THIS ARTICLE SAYS THAT MANY PEOPLE FIND CHRISTMAS THE MOST STRESSFUL TIME OF YEAR.

I BELIEVE IT. THIS SEASON SURE FILLS *ME* WITH STRESS.

REALLY? HOW COME?

I HATE BEING GOOD.

PSST! ARE YOU AWAKE?

IS IT CHRISTMAS? IT IS! IT IS!

LET'S GO WAKE MOM AND DAD AND OPEN ALL OUR LOOT!

SINCE IT'S CHRISTMAS, MAYBE WE SHOULD LET THEM SLEEP IN A LITTLE.

THAT'S LONG ENOUGH! WAKE UP! WAKE UP! IT'S CHRISTMAS!!

QUARTER TO 6. HE LET US SLEEP IN THIS YEAR.

OMIGOSH! THIS LIBRARY BOOK WAS DUE TWO DAYS AGO!

WHAT WILL THEY DO? ARE THEY GOING TO INTERROGATE ME AND BEAT ME UP?! ARE THEY GOING TO BREAK MY KNEES?? WILL I HAVE TO SIGN SOME CONFESSION???

THEY'LL FINE YOU TEN CENTS. NOW GO RETURN IT.

THE WAY SOME OF THOSE LIBRARIANS LOOK AT YOU, I NATURALLY ASSUMED THE CONSEQUENCES WOULD BE MORE DIRE.

HEY DAD, I HAVE A QUESTION.

SURE, CALVIN. WHAT DO YOU WANT TO KNOW?

IF YOU PLUGGED UP YOUR NOSE AND MOUTH RIGHT BEFORE YOU SNEEZED...

...WOULD THE SNEEZE GO OUT YOUR EARS, OR WOULD YOUR HEAD EXPLODE?

I WAS KIND OF HOPING YOU HAD A MATH PROBLEM OR SOMETHING.

...EITHER WAY, I'M SCARED TO TRY IT.

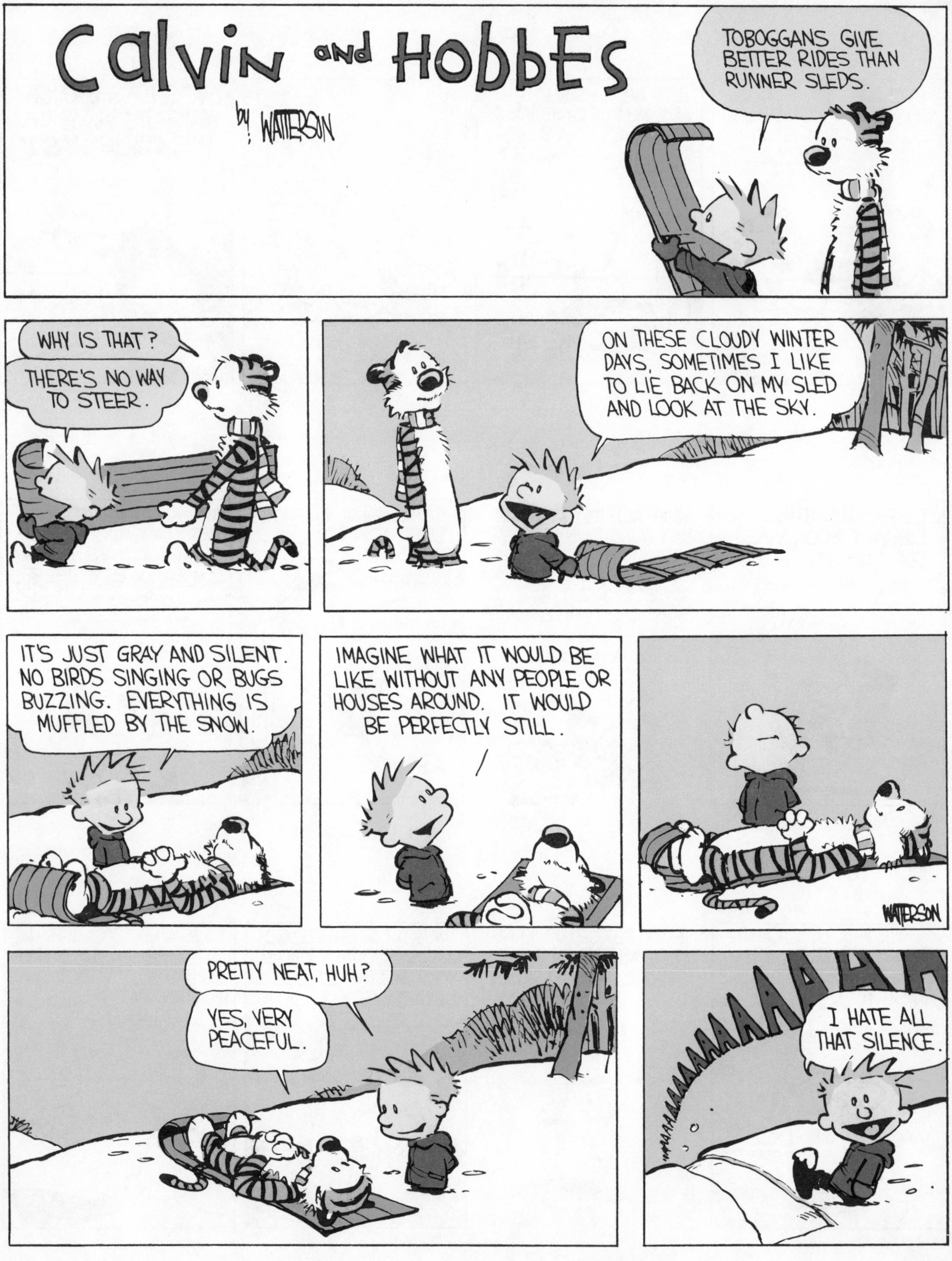
Calvin and HOBBES
by WATTERSON
TOBOGGANS GIVE BETTER RIDES THAN RUNNER SLEDS.
WHY IS THAT?
THERE'S NO WAY TO STEER.
ON THESE CLOUDY WINTER DAYS, SOMETIMES I LIKE TO LIE BACK ON MY SLED AND LOOK AT THE SKY.
IT'S JUST GRAY AND SILENT. NO BIRDS SINGING OR BUGS BUZZING. EVERYTHING IS MUFFLED BY THE SNOW.
IMAGINE WHAT IT WOULD BE LIKE WITHOUT ANY PEOPLE OR HOUSES AROUND. IT WOULD BE PERFECTLY STILL.
WATTERSON
PRETTY NEAT, HUH?
YES, VERY PEACEFUL.
I HATE ALL THAT SILENCE.

BEHOLD THE DREADED TOBOGGAN: SUICIDE SLED.

ITS UNIQUE DESIGN SENDS A BLINDING SPRAY OF SNOW ON ITS PASSENGERS AT THE SLIGHTEST BUMP. NOTE, TOO, THE LACK OF ANY STEERING MECHANISM.

YES, THIS SLED IS TRULY A HAZARD TO LIFE AND LIMB.

WHEEE OOMPH! EEEEE

BOY, IS IT COLD! CAN'T WE TURN THE HEAT UP?

HEAT IS EXPENSIVE, CALVIN. JUST PUT ON A SWEATER.

LOOK, THE THERMOSTAT GOES ALL THE WAY UP TO 90 DEGREES! WE COULD BE SITTING AROUND IN OUR SHORTS!

LEAVE THE THERMOSTAT ALONE, CALVIN.

I CAN ALMOST SEE MY BREATH. I'LL JUST CRANK IT UP TO 75, OK?

I SAID DON'T TOUCH IT!

GEE, MY HANDS ARE SO NUMB, I CAN'T MOVE THE SWITCH. GUESS I'LL PUT ON A SWEATER.

OOH, YOU LOOK COLD, CALVIN! THERE'S A FIRE MADE. WHY DON'T YOU GO WARM UP?

OH BOY!

NOTHING BEATS SITTING BY A ROARING FIRE AFTER YOU'VE BEEN OUT IN THE COLD.

OF COURSE, SOME PEOPLE SAY WHY BOTHER GOING OUTSIDE FIRST?

CALVIN, I HOPE YOU TOOK YOUR BOOTS OFF BEFORE YOU WALKED ACROSS THE FLOOR.

OF COURSE I DID! YOU DON'T NEED TO TELL ME ALL THE TIME!

WATTERSON

WATTERSON

GIVEN ANY MORE THOUGHT TO THAT BACKYARD SKI LIFT PROPOSAL OF MINE?

OH, YES. LOTS.

1-2

HOBBES IS ALWAYS A LITTLE LOOPY WHEN HE COMES OUT OF THE DRYER.

WATTERSON

— WHIFFFFF...

WHIFF — WHIFF — WHIFF — WHIFF — WHIFF — GALOSH

FOR ALL THAT PREPARATION, YOU SURE ARE A LOUSY SHOT!

GO AHEAD DOWN. YOU'LL MISS ALL THOSE TREES.

YOU CAN DO IT. YOU'LL STOP BEFORE YOU GO OVER THAT LEDGE AT THE BOTTOM.

YOU WON'T GO INTO THAT POND. BESIDES, THE ICE IS PROBABLY REAL THICK ANYWAY. GO AHEAD DOWN.

MY BRAIN IS TRYING TO KILL ME.

GALOSH GALOSH GALOSH

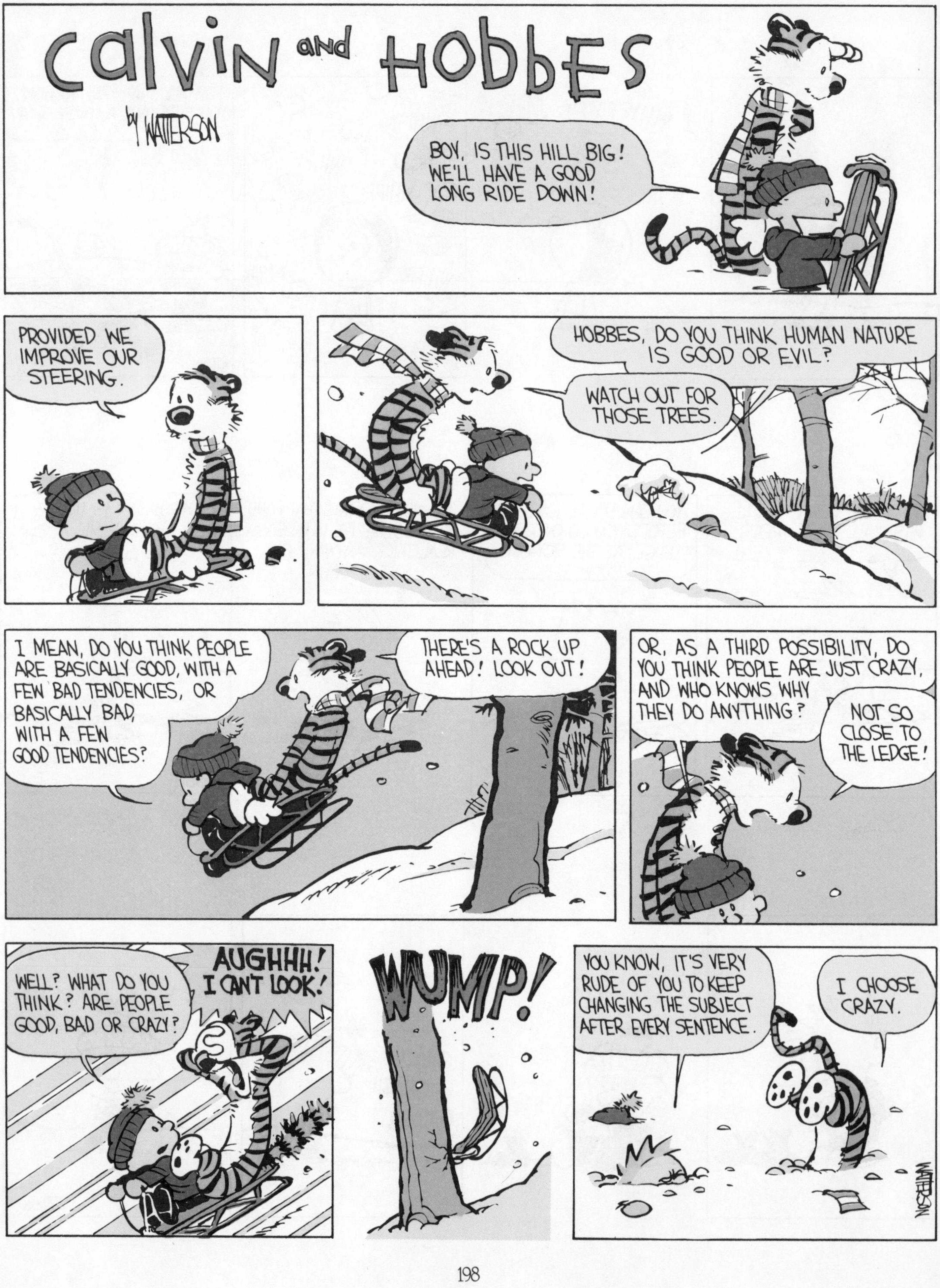
Calvin and HOBBES
by WATTERSON
BOY, IS THIS HILL BIG! WE'LL HAVE A GOOD LONG RIDE DOWN!
PROVIDED WE IMPROVE OUR STEERING.
HOBBES, DO YOU THINK HUMAN NATURE IS GOOD OR EVIL?
WATCH OUT FOR THOSE TREES.
I MEAN, DO YOU THINK PEOPLE ARE BASICALLY GOOD, WITH A FEW BAD TENDENCIES, OR BASICALLY BAD, WITH A FEW GOOD TENDENCIES?
THERE'S A ROCK UP AHEAD! LOOK OUT!
OR, AS A THIRD POSSIBILITY, DO YOU THINK PEOPLE ARE JUST CRAZY, AND WHO KNOWS WHY THEY DO ANYTHING?
NOT SO CLOSE TO THE LEDGE!
WELL? WHAT DO YOU THINK? ARE PEOPLE GOOD, BAD OR CRAZY?
AUGHHH! I CAN'T LOOK!
WUMP!
YOU KNOW, IT'S VERY RUDE OF YOU TO KEEP CHANGING THE SUBJECT AFTER EVERY SENTENCE.
I CHOOSE CRAZY.
WATTERSON

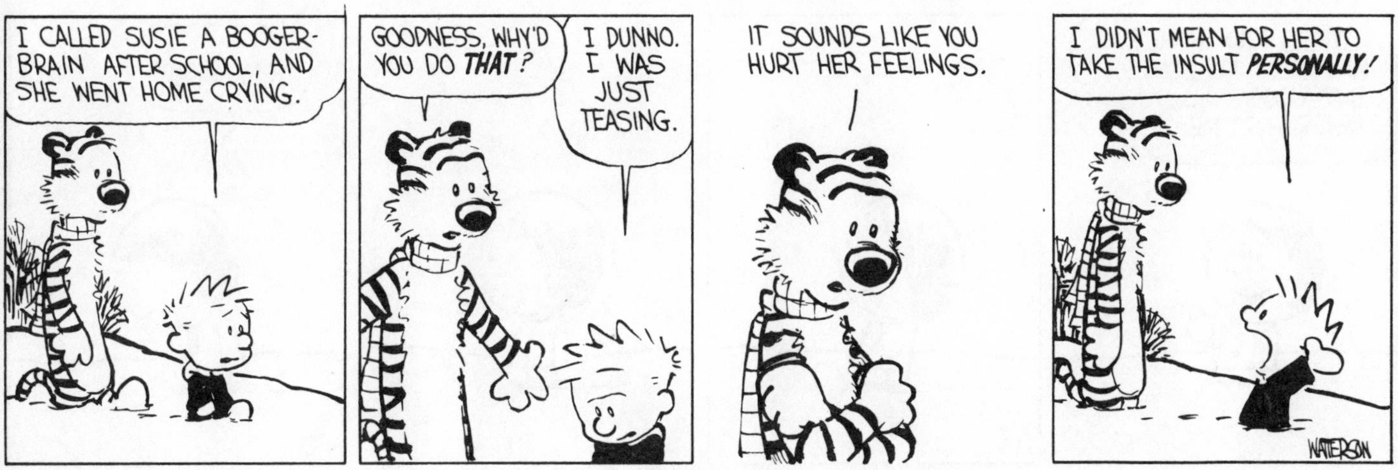
I CALLED SUSIE A BOOGER-BRAIN AFTER SCHOOL, AND SHE WENT HOME CRYING.
GOODNESS, WHY'D YOU DO *THAT*?
I DUNNO. I WAS JUST TEASING.
IT SOUNDS LIKE YOU HURT HER FEELINGS.
I DIDN'T MEAN FOR HER TO TAKE THE INSULT *PERSONALLY*!
WATTERSON

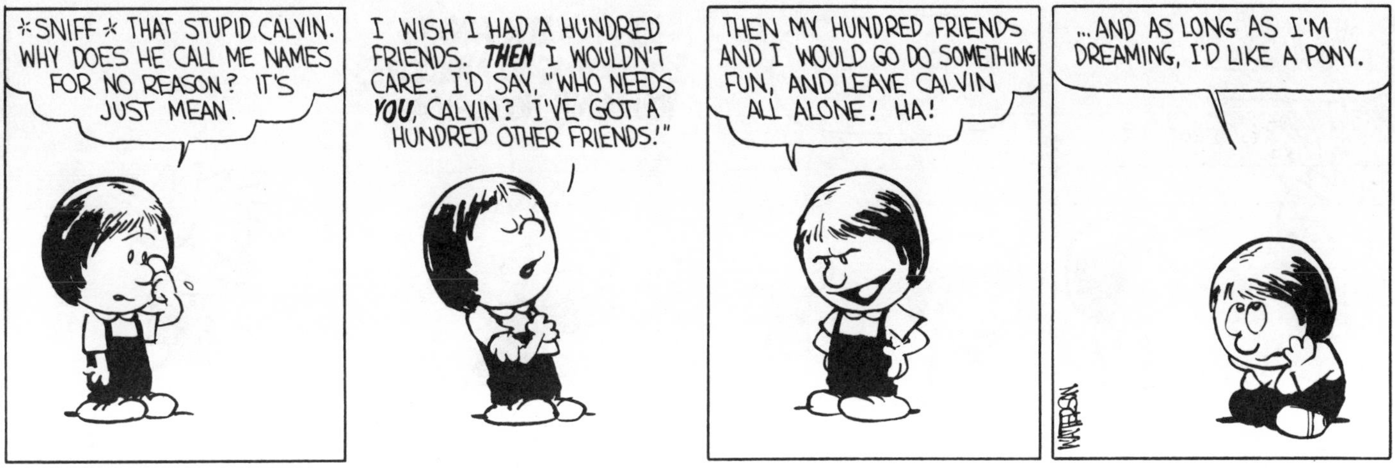
*SNIFF* THAT STUPID CALVIN. WHY DOES HE CALL ME NAMES FOR NO REASON? IT'S JUST MEAN.
I WISH I HAD A HUNDRED FRIENDS. *THEN* I WOULDN'T CARE. I'D SAY, "WHO NEEDS *YOU*, CALVIN? I'VE GOT A HUNDRED OTHER FRIENDS!"
THEN MY HUNDRED FRIENDS AND I WOULD GO DO SOMETHING FUN, AND LEAVE CALVIN ALL ALONE! HA!
...AND AS LONG AS I'M DREAMING, I'D LIKE A PONY.
WATTERSON

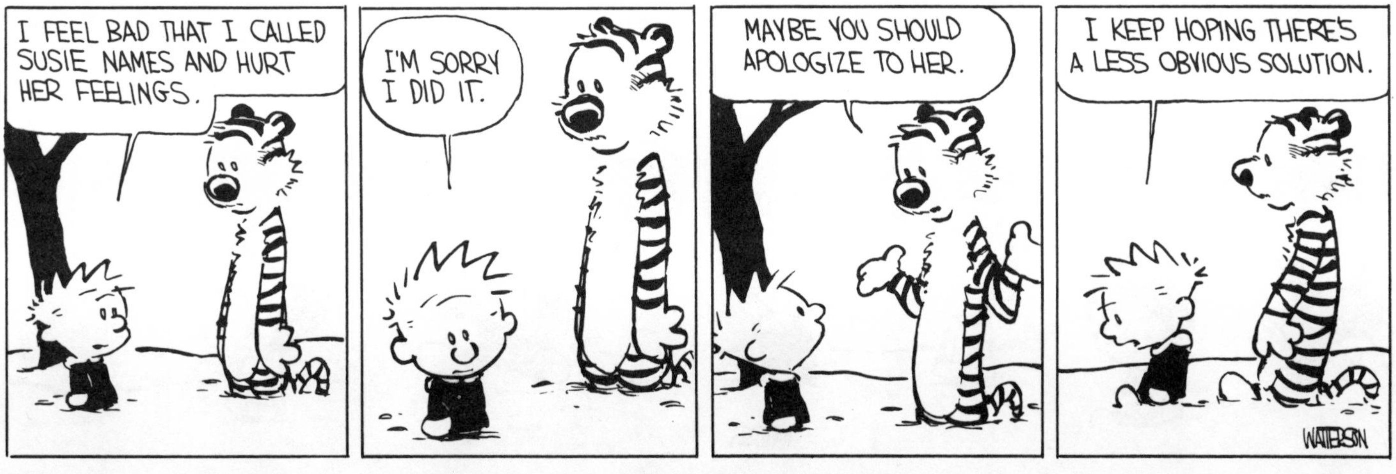
I FEEL BAD THAT I CALLED SUSIE NAMES AND HURT HER FEELINGS.
I'M SORRY I DID IT.
MAYBE YOU SHOULD APOLOGIZE TO HER.
I KEEP HOPING THERE'S A LESS OBVIOUS SOLUTION.
WATTERSON

"STICKS AND STONES MAY BREAK MY BONES, BUT WORDS WILL NEVER HURT ME."

YEAH, RIGHT.

UM... HI, SUSIE.. I... UH... WELL...

GET LOST, CALVIN. YOU'RE MEAN.

DON'T WALK AWAY! I'M TRYING TO APOLOGIZE, YOU DUMB NOODLELOAF!

SLAP

SUSIE, I'M SORRY I CALLED YOU NAMES. I DIDN'T MEAN TO HURT YOUR FEELINGS.

WELL, YOU DID HURT MY FEELINGS, BUT I ACCEPT YOUR APOLOGY. THANK YOU.

OH BOY, THANK GOODNESS I GOT THAT OVER WITH!

...ON SECOND THOUGHT, LET'S SEE YOU GROVEL A LITTLE BIT!

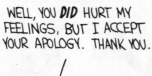

201

HEY, HOBBES, YOU GOT A LETTER.

A LETTER? FOR ME? WOW. I NEVER GET LETTERS!

WHAT FUN! A LETTER FOR ME! I WONDER WHO SENT IT? I WONDER WHAT IT SAYS? WHAT COULD THIS POSSIBLY BE?

OPEN IT AND FIND OUT, YOU LUNATIC!

DON'T GET HUFFY. I WANT TO SAVOR THIS.

WELL? WELL? WHAT'D YOU GET?

IT LOOKS LIKE AN INVITATION.

AN INVITATION? WHO'D INVITE YOU ANYWHERE?

A LOT OF PEOPLE, THAT'S WHO, BUSTER.

THERE'S OBVIOUSLY BEEN SOME MISTAKE. NOBODY INVITES A TIGER ANYWHERE. YOU CAN'T GET THE INSURANCE.

WELL SOMEBODY IS INVITING ME SOMEWHERE. I GOT AN INVITATION.

WHO? WHAT'S IT SAY?? READ IT ALREADY!!

PROBABLY SOME BIG STATE DINNER. I HOPE I CAN FIND MY CUMMERBUND.

SO WHAT DOES THE INVITATION SAY, YOU DUMB HAIRBALL?

CALL ME NAMES, WILL YOU? I'LL READ IT WHEN I'M GOOD AND READY.

AARGGHH! OOOOHH! MPF! GGH! RRGGHGHMFMPF!

OK, NOW I'M READY...AHEM..

"DEAR"

"HOBBES"

FASTER!

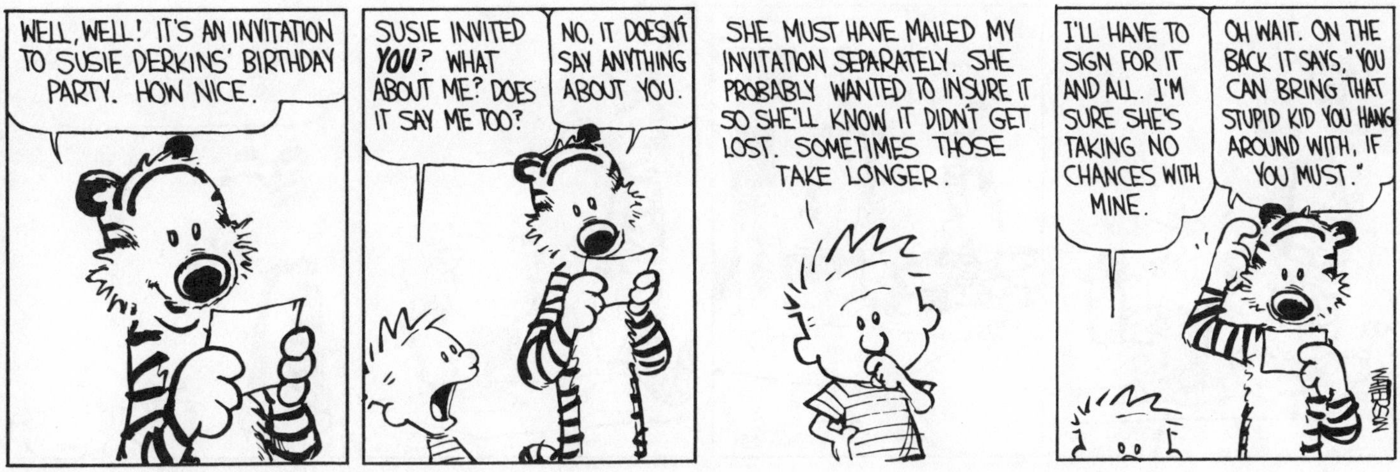
WELL, WELL! IT'S AN INVITATION TO SUSIE DERKINS' BIRTHDAY PARTY. HOW NICE.
SUSIE INVITED *YOU*? WHAT ABOUT ME? DOES IT SAY ME TOO?
NO, IT DOESN'T SAY ANYTHING ABOUT YOU.
SHE MUST HAVE MAILED MY INVITATION SEPARATELY. SHE PROBABLY WANTED TO INSURE IT SO SHE'LL KNOW IT DIDN'T GET LOST. SOMETIMES THOSE TAKE LONGER.
I'LL HAVE TO SIGN FOR IT AND ALL. I'M SURE SHE'S TAKING NO CHANCES WITH MINE.
OH WAIT. ON THE BACK IT SAYS, "YOU CAN BRING THAT STUPID KID YOU HANG AROUND WITH, IF YOU MUST."
WATTERSON

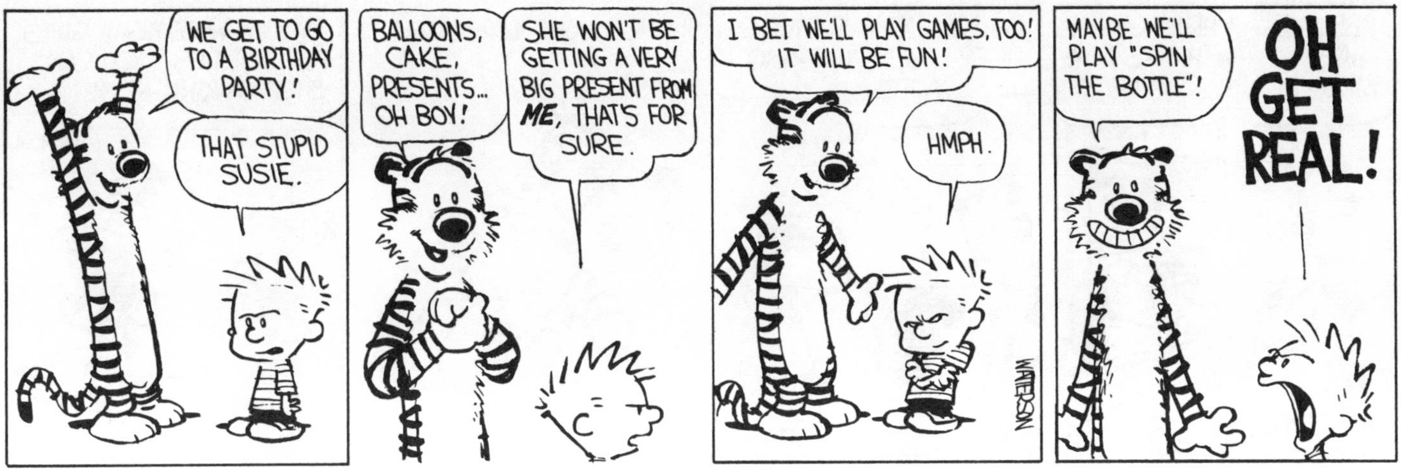
WE GET TO GO TO A BIRTHDAY PARTY!
THAT STUPID SUSIE.
BALLOONS, CAKE, PRESENTS... OH BOY!
SHE WON'T BE GETTING A VERY BIG PRESENT FROM *ME*, THAT'S FOR SURE.
I BET WE'LL PLAY GAMES, TOO! IT WILL BE FUN!
HMPH.
WATTERSON
MAYBE WE'LL PLAY "SPIN THE BOTTLE"!
OH GET REAL!

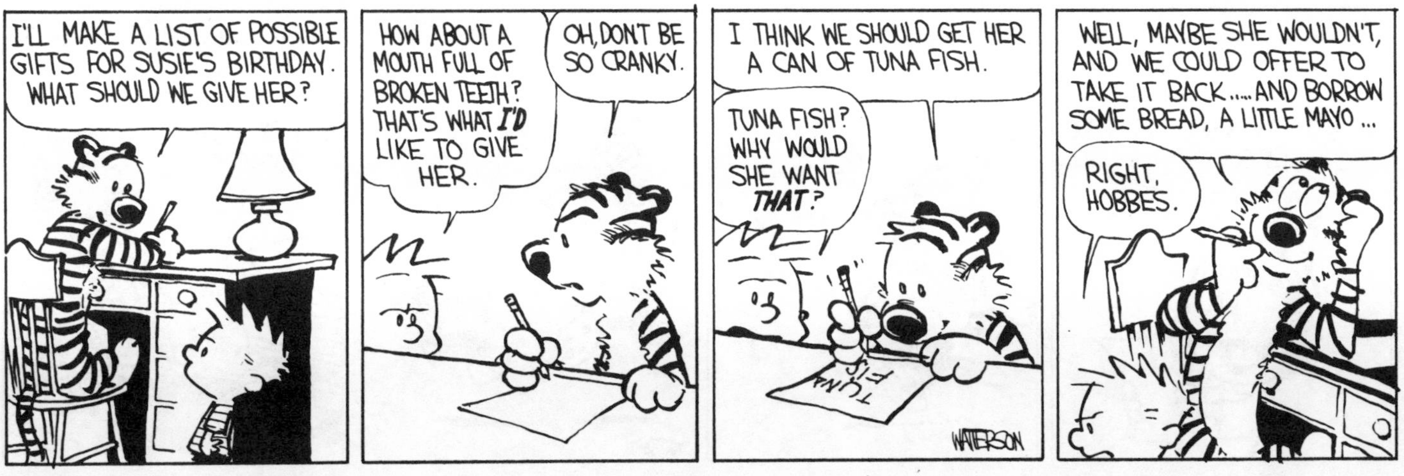
I'LL MAKE A LIST OF POSSIBLE GIFTS FOR SUSIE'S BIRTHDAY. WHAT SHOULD WE GIVE HER?
HOW ABOUT A MOUTH FULL OF BROKEN TEETH? THAT'S WHAT *I'D* LIKE TO GIVE HER.
OH, DON'T BE SO CRANKY.
I THINK WE SHOULD GET HER A CAN OF TUNA FISH.
TUNA FISH? WHY WOULD SHE WANT *THAT*?
TUNA FISH
WATTERSON
WELL, MAYBE SHE WOULDN'T, AND WE COULD OFFER TO TAKE IT BACK..... AND BORROW SOME BREAD, A LITTLE MAYO ...
RIGHT, HOBBES.

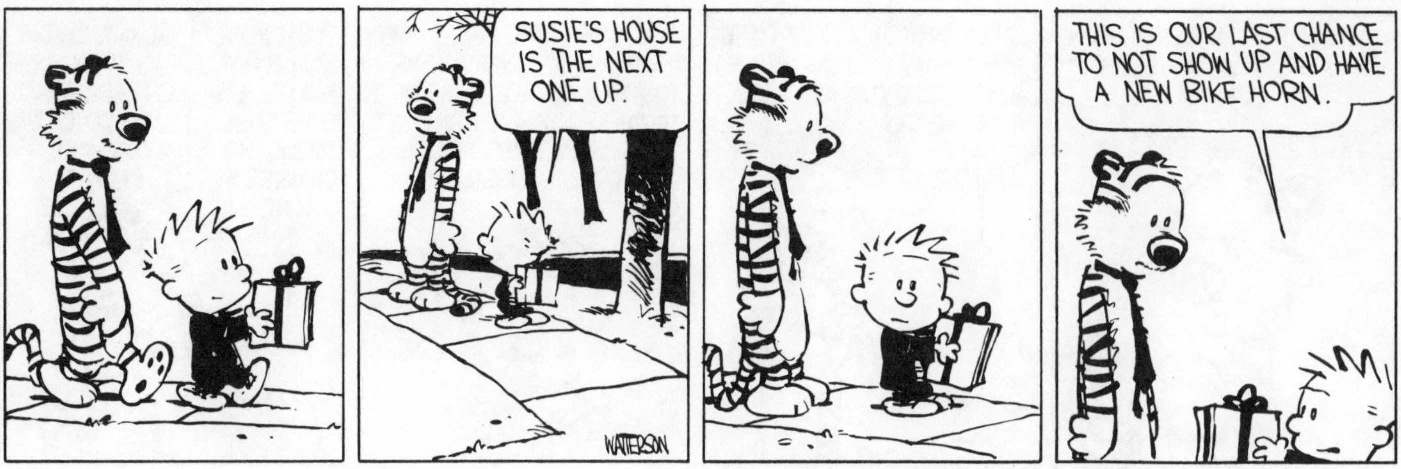
SUSIE'S HOUSE IS THE NEXT ONE UP.
WATTERSON
THIS IS OUR LAST CHANCE TO NOT SHOW UP AND HAVE A NEW BIKE HORN.

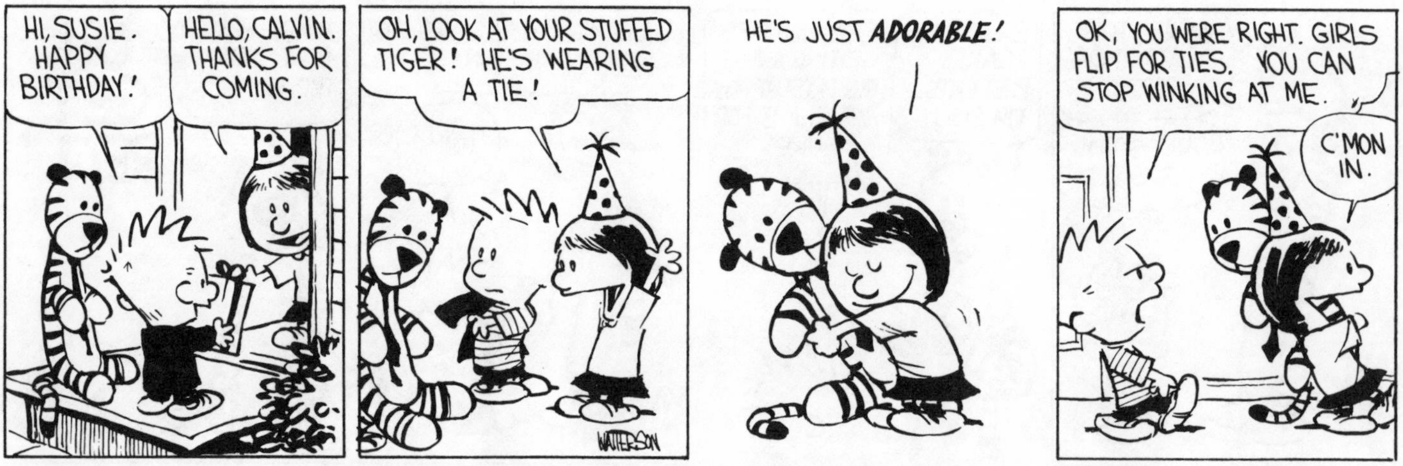
HI, SUSIE. HAPPY BIRTHDAY!
HELLO, CALVIN. THANKS FOR COMING.
OH, LOOK AT YOUR STUFFED TIGER! HE'S WEARING A TIE!
WATTERSON
HE'S JUST ADORABLE!
OK, YOU WERE RIGHT. GIRLS FLIP FOR TIES. YOU CAN STOP WINKING AT ME.
C'MON IN.

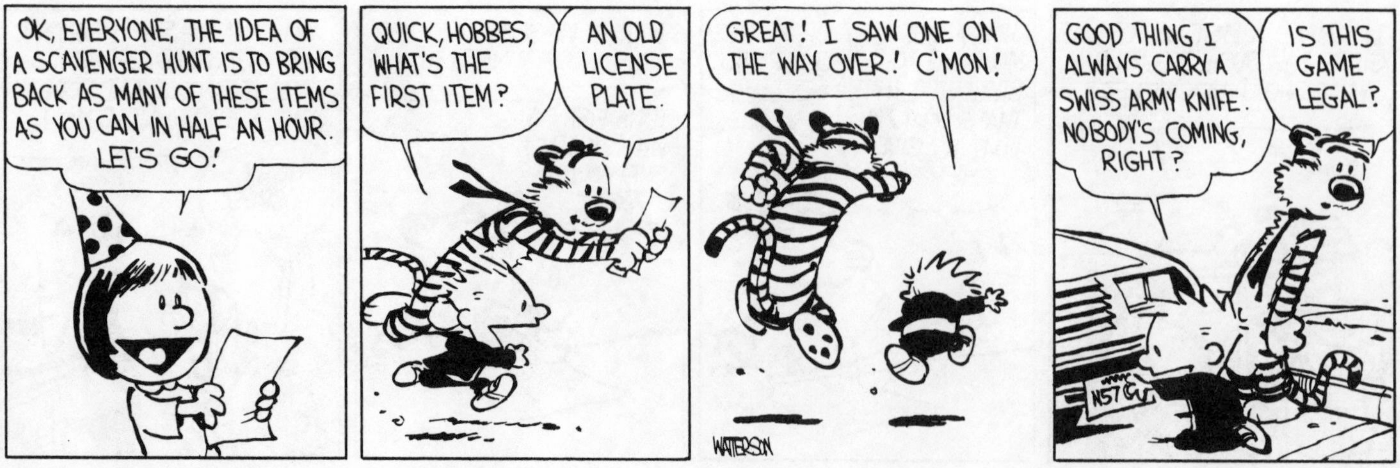
OK, EVERYONE, THE IDEA OF A SCAVENGER HUNT IS TO BRING BACK AS MANY OF THESE ITEMS AS YOU CAN IN HALF AN HOUR. LET'S GO!
QUICK, HOBBES, WHAT'S THE FIRST ITEM?
AN OLD LICENSE PLATE.
GREAT! I SAW ONE ON THE WAY OVER! C'MON!
WATTERSON
GOOD THING I ALWAYS CARRY A SWISS ARMY KNIFE. NOBODY'S COMING, RIGHT?
IS THIS GAME LEGAL?

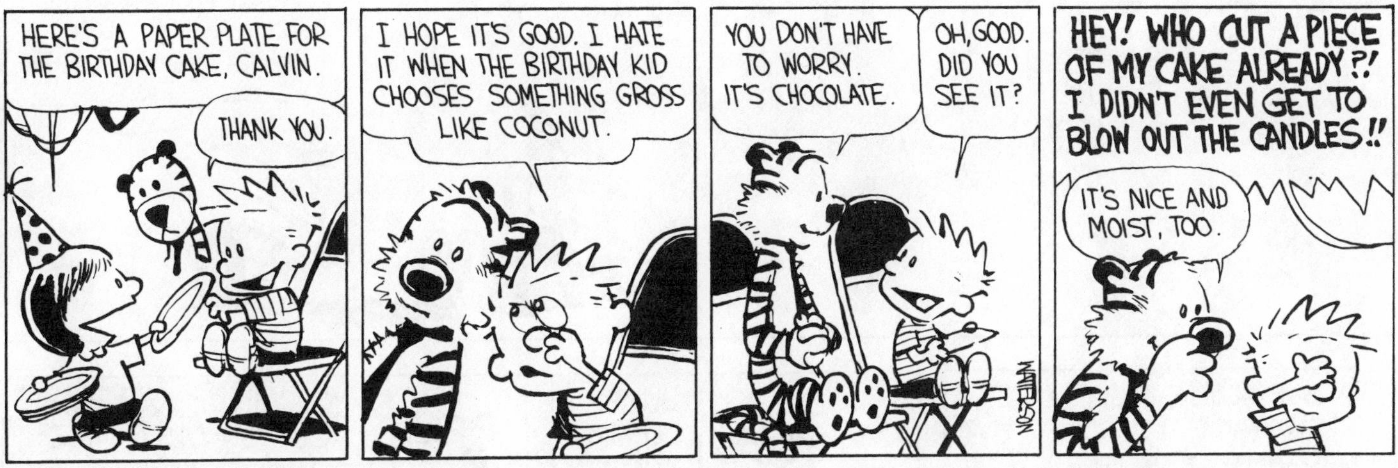
HERE'S A PAPER PLATE FOR THE BIRTHDAY CAKE, CALVIN.
THANK YOU.
I HOPE IT'S GOOD. I HATE IT WHEN THE BIRTHDAY KID CHOOSES SOMETHING GROSS LIKE COCONUT.
YOU DON'T HAVE TO WORRY. IT'S CHOCOLATE.
OH, GOOD. DID YOU SEE IT?
HEY! WHO CUT A PIECE OF MY CAKE ALREADY?! I DIDN'T EVEN GET TO BLOW OUT THE CANDLES!!
IT'S NICE AND MOIST, TOO.

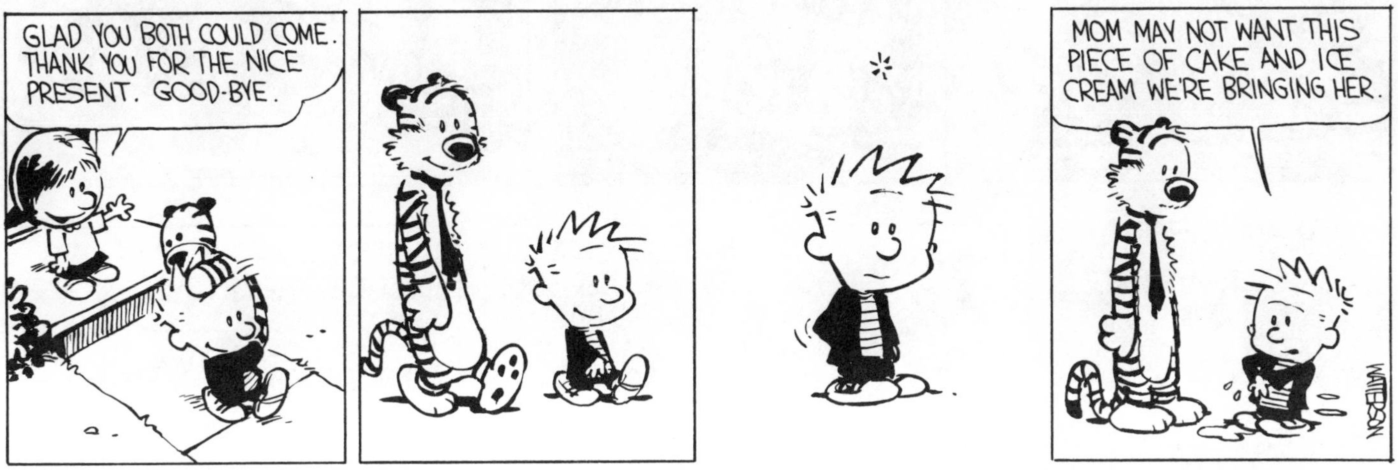
GLAD YOU BOTH COULD COME. THANK YOU FOR THE NICE PRESENT. GOOD-BYE.
MOM MAY NOT WANT THIS PIECE OF CAKE AND ICE CREAM WE'RE BRINGING HER.

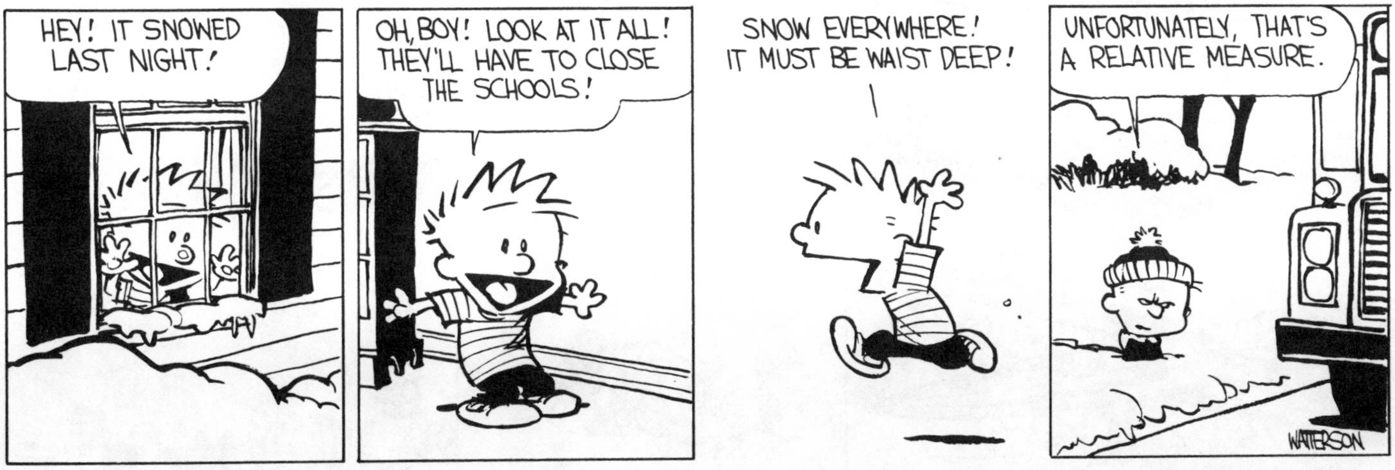
HEY! IT SNOWED LAST NIGHT!
OH, BOY! LOOK AT IT ALL! THEY'LL HAVE TO CLOSE THE SCHOOLS!
SNOW EVERYWHERE! IT MUST BE WAIST DEEP!
UNFORTUNATELY, THAT'S A RELATIVE MEASURE.
WATTERSON

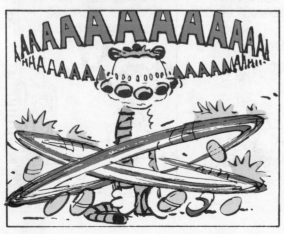

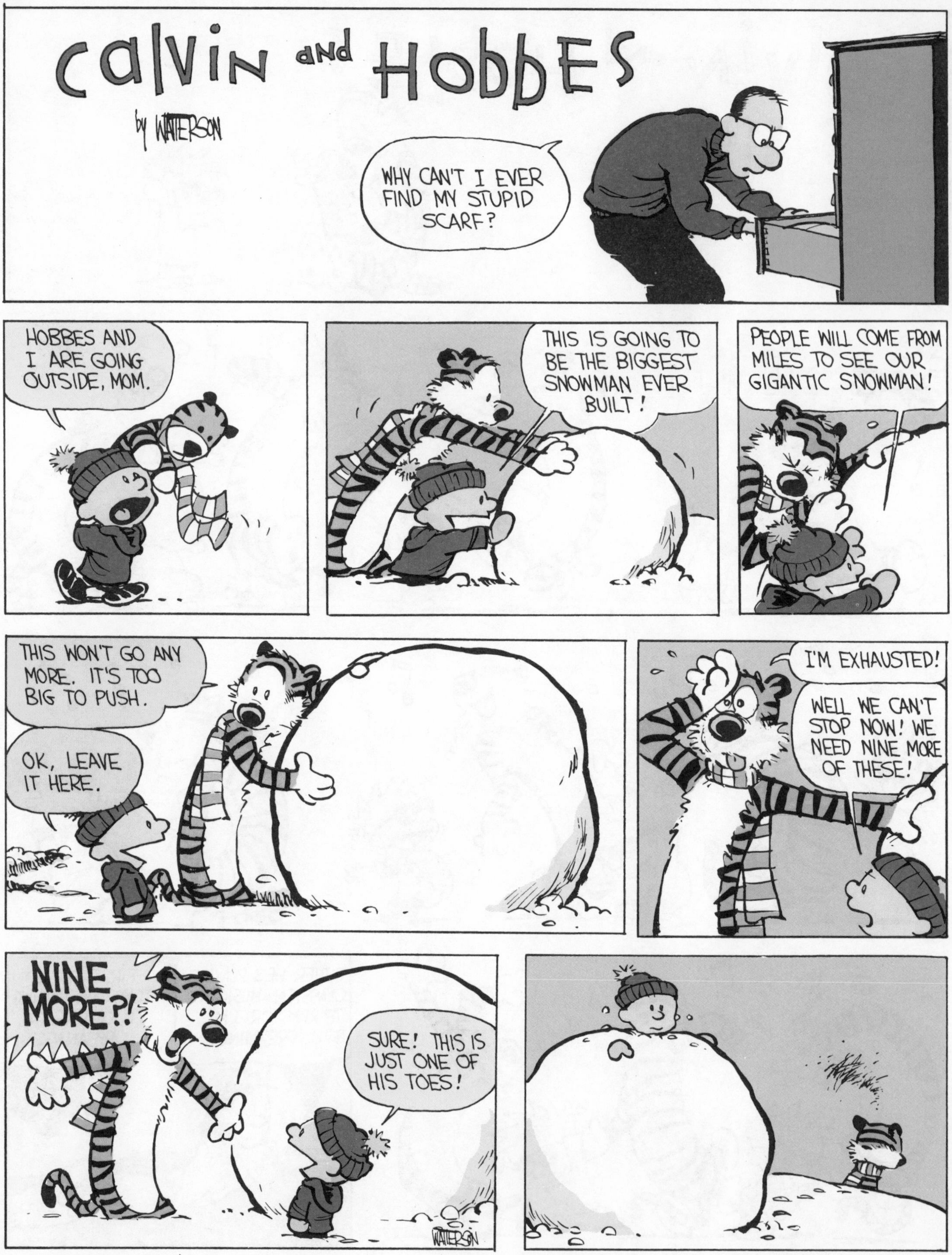
Calvin and HOBBES
by WATTERSON
WHY CAN'T I EVER FIND MY STUPID SCARF?
HOBBES AND I ARE GOING OUTSIDE, MOM.
THIS IS GOING TO BE THE BIGGEST SNOWMAN EVER BUILT!
PEOPLE WILL COME FROM MILES TO SEE OUR GIGANTIC SNOWMAN!
THIS WON'T GO ANY MORE. IT'S TOO BIG TO PUSH.
OK, LEAVE IT HERE.
I'M EXHAUSTED!
WELL WE CAN'T STOP NOW! WE NEED NINE MORE OF THESE!
NINE MORE?!
SURE! THIS IS JUST ONE OF HIS TOES!
WATTERSON

WHERE DO WE KEEP ALL OUR CHAINSAWS, MOM?

WE DON'T HAVE ANY CHAINSAWS, CALVIN.

WE DON'T? NOT ANY?

NOPE.

HOW AM I EVER GOING TO LEARN HOW TO JUGGLE?

THE GIANT AMOEBA SLIDES ALONG THE KITCHEN FLOOR.

EXTENDING A CYTOPLASMIC PSEUDOPOD, THE PROTOZOAN ENGULFS A PACKAGE OF OATMEAL COOKIES.

CRUNCH CRUNCH

NICE TRY. PUT THEM BACK.

THE MAJESTIC EAGLE CIRCLES SLOWLY IN THE CLOUDS.

WITH EYES SO SHARP HE CAN SPOT MOVEMENT A MILE BELOW, HE SIGHTS HIS PREY AND DIVES!

REACHING SPEEDS OF MORE THAN 100 MPH, HIS UNWARY PRIZE WILL NEVER KNOW WHAT HIT IT!

WAKE UP, DAD! IT'S SATURDAY!

ZZ... WHA?

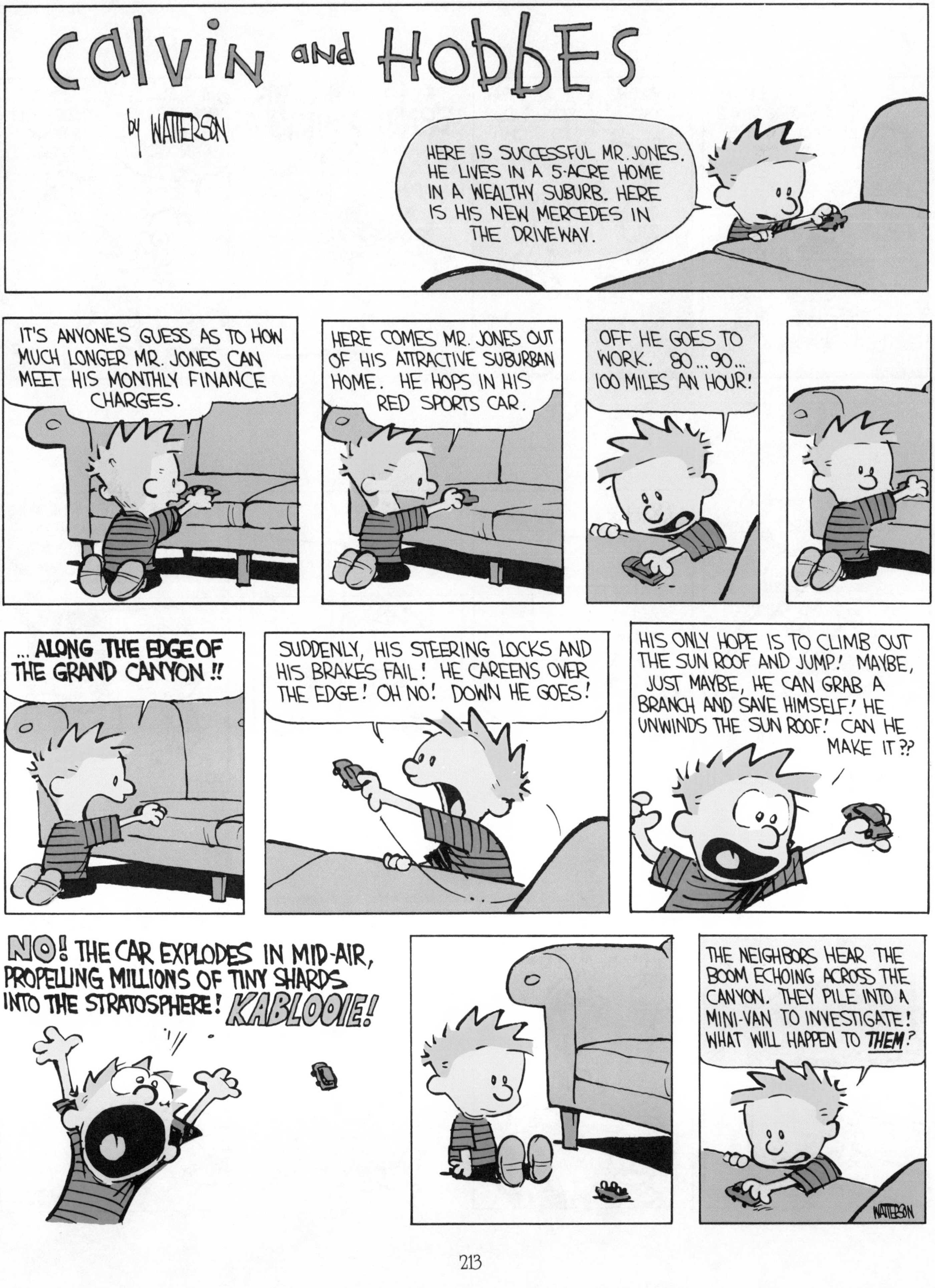
Calvin and HOBBES
by WATTERSON
HERE IS SUCCESSFUL MR. JONES. HE LIVES IN A 5-ACRE HOME IN A WEALTHY SUBURB. HERE IS HIS NEW MERCEDES IN THE DRIVEWAY.
IT'S ANYONE'S GUESS AS TO HOW MUCH LONGER MR. JONES CAN MEET HIS MONTHLY FINANCE CHARGES.
HERE COMES MR. JONES OUT OF HIS ATTRACTIVE SUBURBAN HOME. HE HOPS IN HIS RED SPORTS CAR.
OFF HE GOES TO WORK. 80... 90... 100 MILES AN HOUR!
... ALONG THE EDGE OF THE GRAND CANYON !!
SUDDENLY, HIS STEERING LOCKS AND HIS BRAKES FAIL! HE CAREENS OVER THE EDGE! OH NO! DOWN HE GOES!
HIS ONLY HOPE IS TO CLIMB OUT THE SUN ROOF AND JUMP! MAYBE, JUST MAYBE, HE CAN GRAB A BRANCH AND SAVE HIMSELF! HE UNWINDS THE SUN ROOF! CAN HE MAKE IT??
NO! THE CAR EXPLODES IN MID-AIR, PROPELLING MILLIONS OF TINY SHARDS INTO THE STRATOSPHERE! KABLOOIE!
THE NEIGHBORS HEAR THE BOOM ECHOING ACROSS THE CANYON. THEY PILE INTO A MINI-VAN TO INVESTIGATE! WHAT WILL HAPPEN TO THEM?
WATTERSON

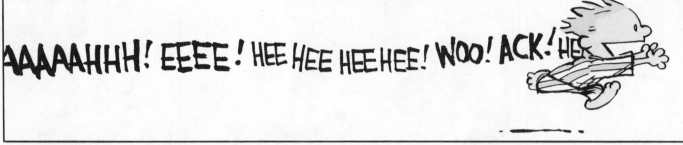

**Calvin:** OH, MOM, I NEED SOME CRISCO FOR SCHOOL TODAY!

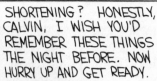

**Mom:** SHORTENING? HONESTLY, CALVIN, I WISH YOU'D REMEMBER THESE THINGS THE NIGHT BEFORE. NOW HURRY UP AND GET READY.

**Calvin:** RIGHT.

**Calvin:** HERE'S THE CRISCO BACK. THANKS.

**Mom:** YOU PUT IT IN YOUR *HAIR??*

**Mom:** GET BACK HERE! YOU'RE NOT GOING TO SCHOOL LIKE *THAT!*

**Calvin:** AW C'MON, MOM! IT'S CLASS PICTURE DAY!

---

**Hobbes:** WHAT'S WITH YOUR HAIR?

**Calvin:** I TOLD MOM I'M GETTING MY SCHOOL PICTURE TAKEN TODAY, AND SHE MADE ME COMB OUT THE CRISCO I PUT IN MY HAIR. NOW I LOOK LIKE A MORON.

**Hobbes:** THAT'S TRUE. YOU DO.

**Calvin:** WELL DON'T JUST STAND THERE! THINK OF SOMETHING! WHAT CAN I DO?

**Hobbes:** THERE. MUCH BETTER!

**Calvin:** WHAT'D YOU DO? IS IT COOL? IS IT NEW WAVE? GEE, I WISH I HAD A MIRROR.

---

**Calvin:** THE BUS IS GOING TO BE HERE ANY MINUTE. YOU'RE SURE YOU FIXED MY HAIR SO IT LOOKS OK?

**Hobbes:** IT LOOKS GREAT. TRY NOT TO MUSS IT UP.

**Calvin:** YOU'RE NOT KIDDING ME, ARE YOU? THIS REALLY LOOKS GOOD?

**Hobbes:** TRUST ME. YOU LOOK LIKE ... LIKE ...

**Hobbes:** ..."ASTRO BOY."

**Calvin:** ALL RIGHT! I CAN'T *WAIT* TO GET MY PICTURE TAKEN *NOW!*

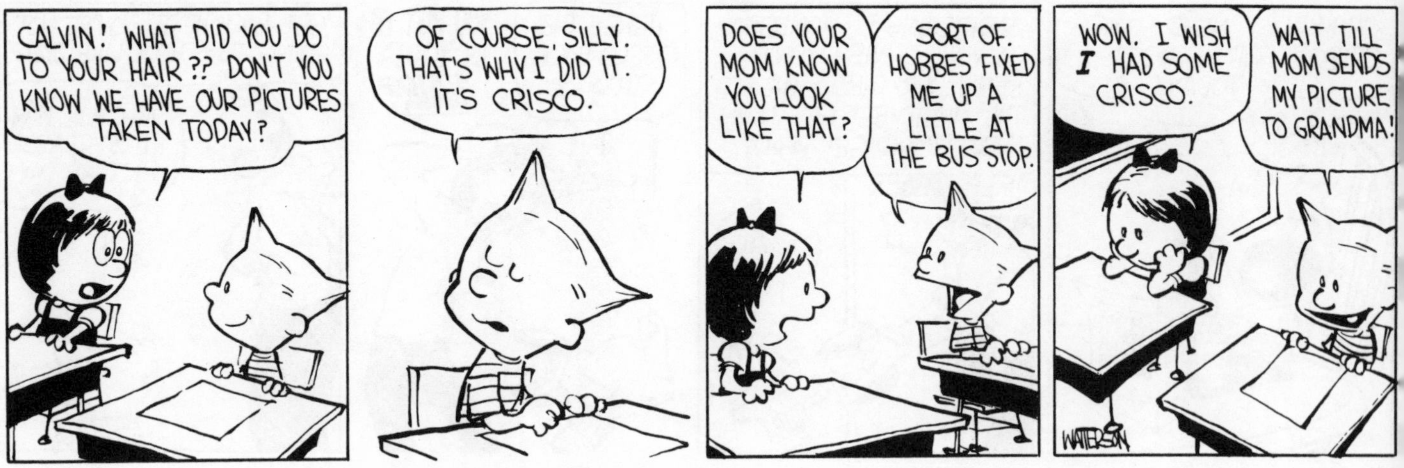
CALVIN! WHAT DID YOU DO TO YOUR HAIR?? DON'T YOU KNOW WE HAVE OUR PICTURES TAKEN TODAY?
OF COURSE, SILLY. THAT'S WHY I DID IT. IT'S CRISCO.
DOES YOUR MOM KNOW YOU LOOK LIKE THAT?
SORT OF. HOBBES FIXED ME UP A LITTLE AT THE BUS STOP.
WOW. I WISH I HAD SOME CRISCO.
WAIT TILL MOM SENDS MY PICTURE TO GRANDMA!
WATTERSON

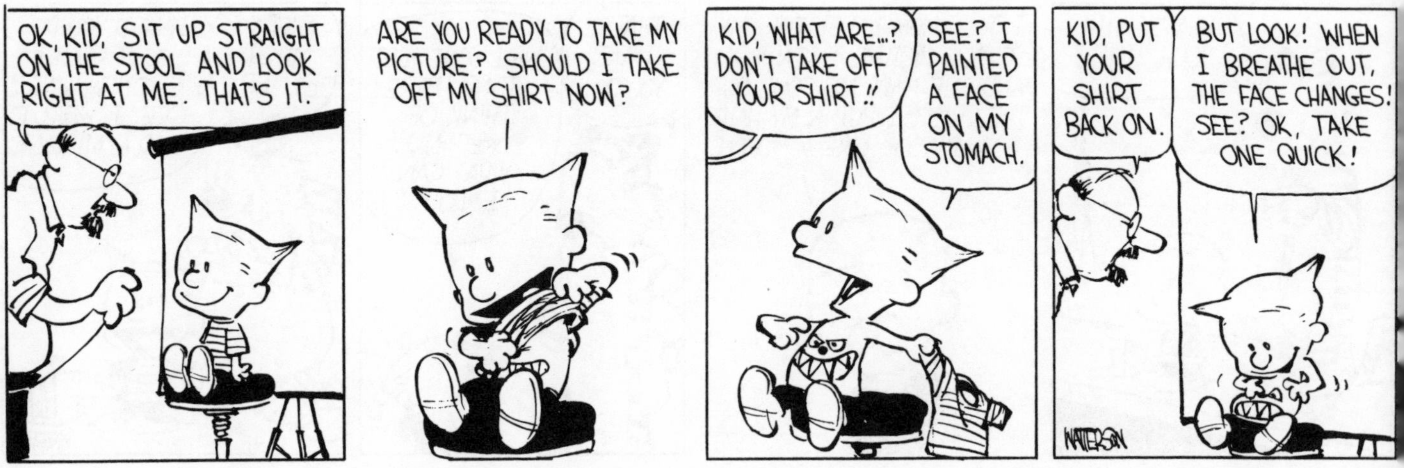
OK, KID, SIT UP STRAIGHT ON THE STOOL AND LOOK RIGHT AT ME. THAT'S IT.
ARE YOU READY TO TAKE MY PICTURE? SHOULD I TAKE OFF MY SHIRT NOW?
KID, WHAT ARE...? DON'T TAKE OFF YOUR SHIRT!!
SEE? I PAINTED A FACE ON MY STOMACH.
KID, PUT YOUR SHIRT BACK ON.
BUT LOOK! WHEN I BREATHE OUT, THE FACE CHANGES! SEE? OK, TAKE ONE QUICK!
WATTERSON

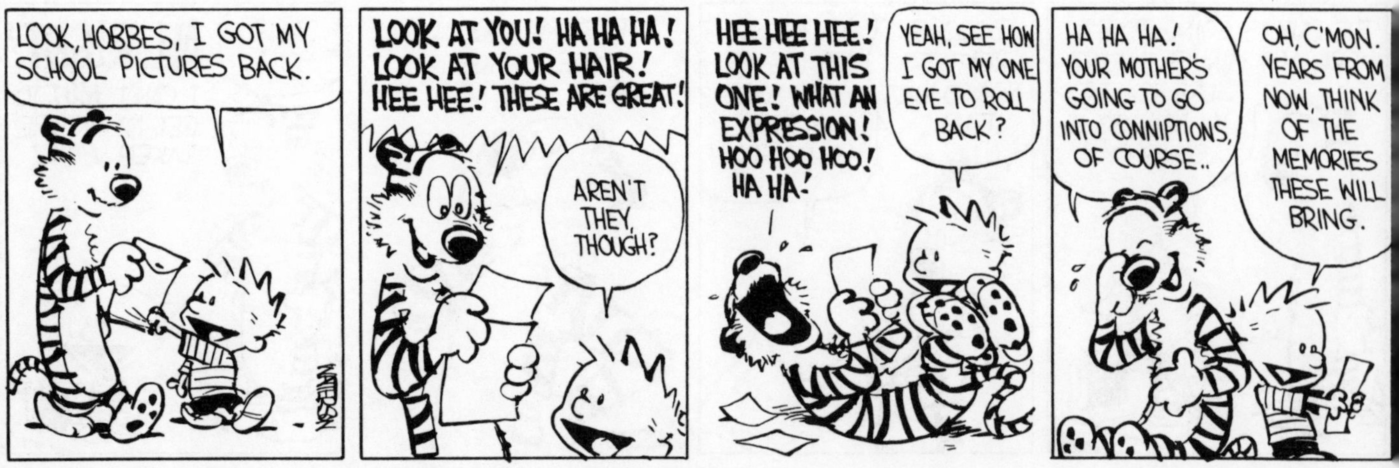
LOOK, HOBBES, I GOT MY SCHOOL PICTURES BACK.
WATTERSON
LOOK AT YOU! HA HA HA! LOOK AT YOUR HAIR! HEE HEE! THESE ARE GREAT!
AREN'T THEY, THOUGH?
HEE HEE HEE! LOOK AT THIS ONE! WHAT AN EXPRESSION! HOO HOO HOO! HA HA!
YEAH, SEE HOW I GOT MY ONE EYE TO ROLL BACK?
HA HA HA! YOUR MOTHER'S GOING TO GO INTO CONNIPTIONS, OF COURSE..
OH, C'MON. YEARS FROM NOW, THINK OF THE MEMORIES THESE WILL BRING.

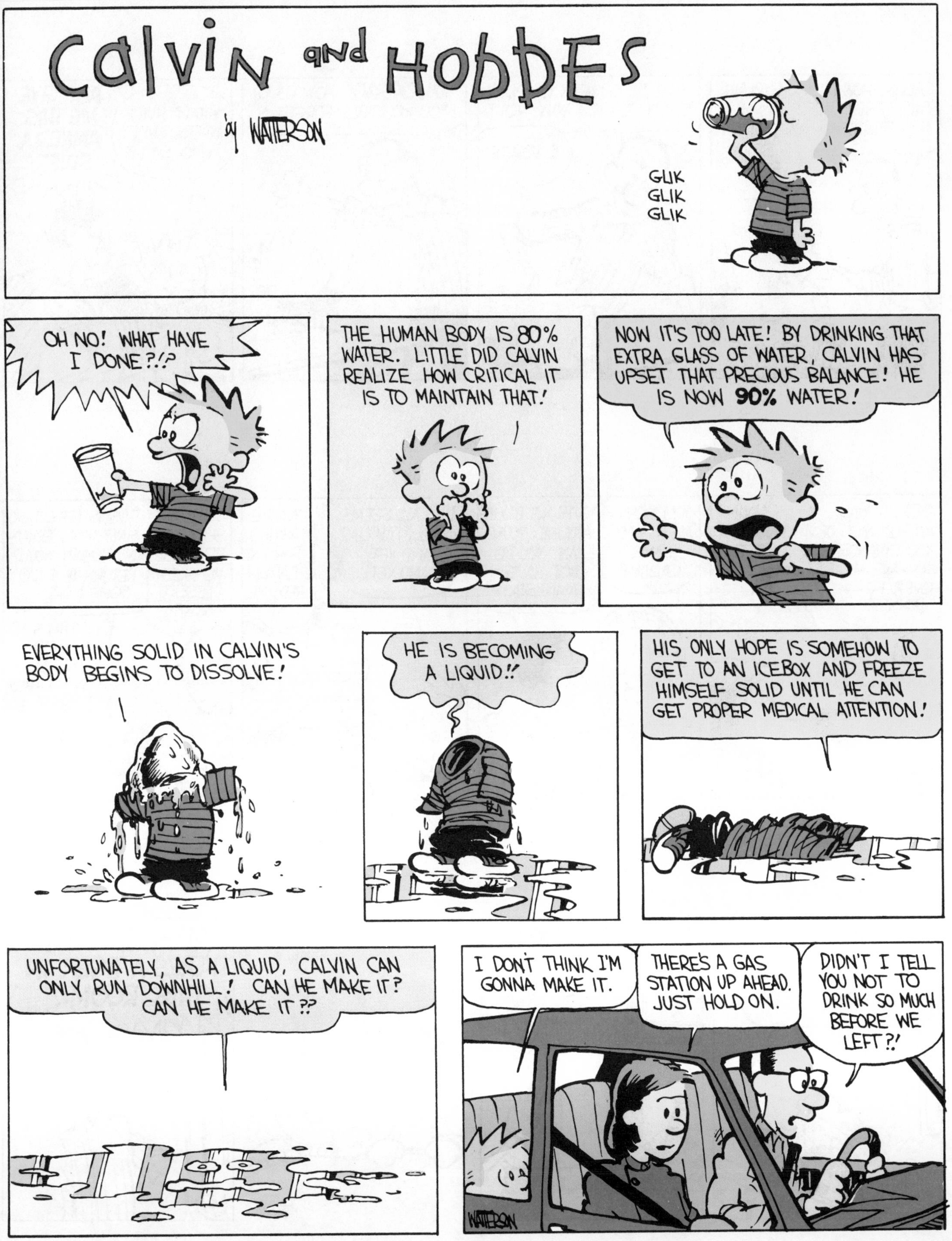
Calvin and HOBBES
by WATTERSON
GLIK GLIK GLIK
OH NO! WHAT HAVE I DONE?!?
THE HUMAN BODY IS 80% WATER. LITTLE DID CALVIN REALIZE HOW CRITICAL IT IS TO MAINTAIN THAT!
NOW IT'S TOO LATE! BY DRINKING THAT EXTRA GLASS OF WATER, CALVIN HAS UPSET THAT PRECIOUS BALANCE! HE IS NOW 90% WATER!
EVERYTHING SOLID IN CALVIN'S BODY BEGINS TO DISSOLVE!
HE IS BECOMING A LIQUID!!
HIS ONLY HOPE IS SOMEHOW TO GET TO AN ICEBOX AND FREEZE HIMSELF SOLID UNTIL HE CAN GET PROPER MEDICAL ATTENTION!
UNFORTUNATELY, AS A LIQUID, CALVIN CAN ONLY RUN DOWNHILL! CAN HE MAKE IT? CAN HE MAKE IT??
I DON'T THINK I'M GONNA MAKE IT.
THERE'S A GAS STATION UP AHEAD. JUST HOLD ON.
DIDN'T I TELL YOU NOT TO DRINK SO MUCH BEFORE WE LEFT?!
WATTERSON

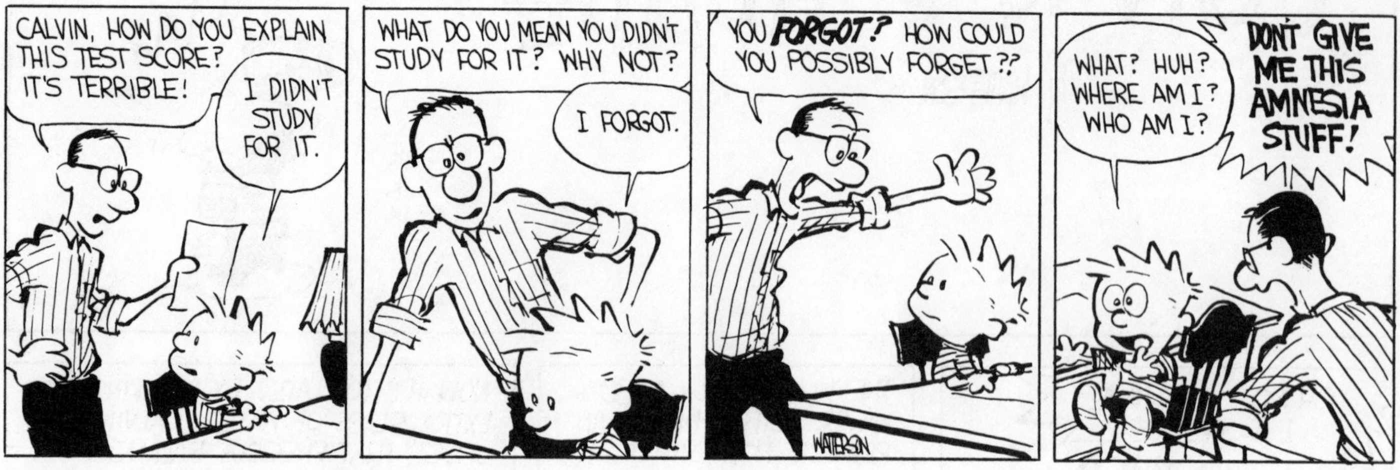
CALVIN, HOW DO YOU EXPLAIN THIS TEST SCORE? IT'S TERRIBLE!
I DIDN'T STUDY FOR IT.
WHAT DO YOU MEAN YOU DIDN'T STUDY FOR IT? WHY NOT?
I FORGOT.
YOU FORGOT? HOW COULD YOU POSSIBLY FORGET??
WATTERSON
WHAT? HUH? WHERE AM I? WHO AM I?
DON'T GIVE ME THIS AMNESIA STUFF!

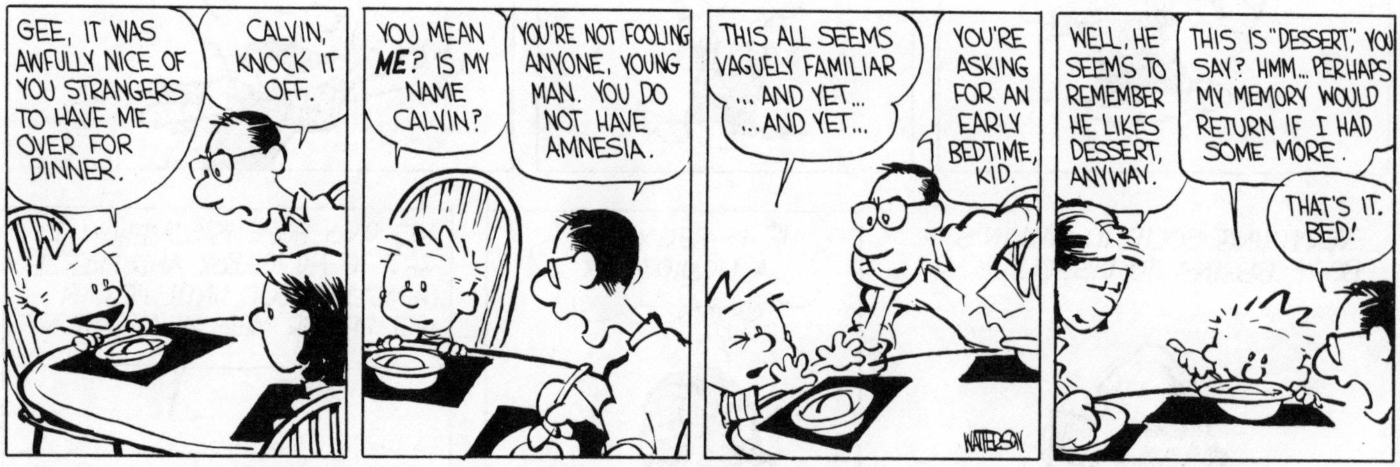
GEE, IT WAS AWFULLY NICE OF YOU STRANGERS TO HAVE ME OVER FOR DINNER.
CALVIN, KNOCK IT OFF.
YOU MEAN ME? IS MY NAME CALVIN?
YOU'RE NOT FOOLING ANYONE, YOUNG MAN. YOU DO NOT HAVE AMNESIA.
THIS ALL SEEMS VAGUELY FAMILIAR ... AND YET... ...AND YET...
YOU'RE ASKING FOR AN EARLY BEDTIME, KID.
WATTERSON
WELL, HE SEEMS TO REMEMBER HE LIKES DESSERT, ANYWAY.
THIS IS "DESSERT," YOU SAY? HMM... PERHAPS MY MEMORY WOULD RETURN IF I HAD SOME MORE.
THAT'S IT. BED!

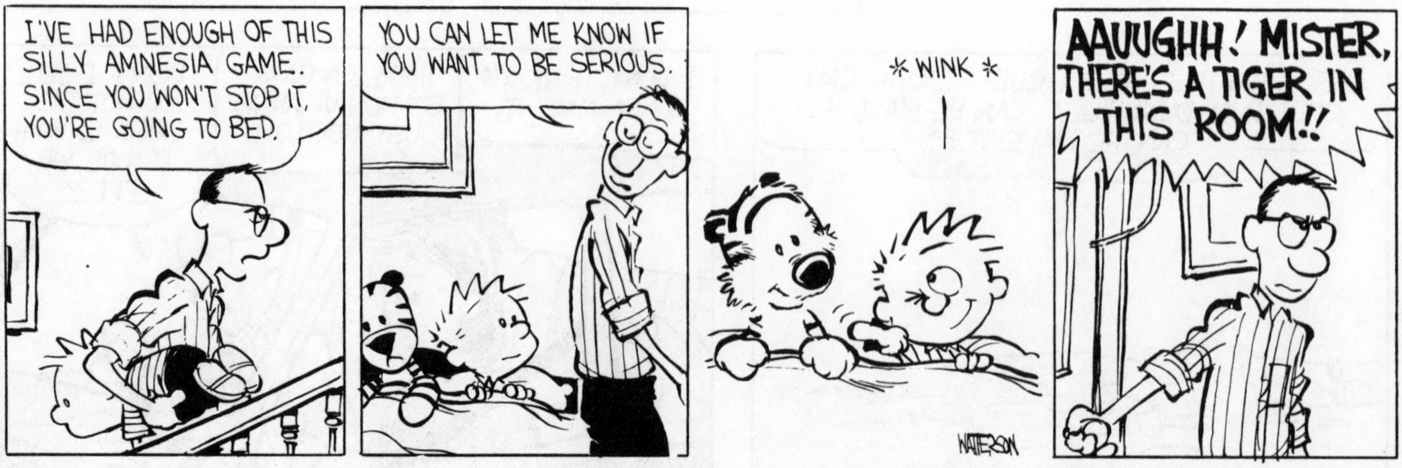
I'VE HAD ENOUGH OF THIS SILLY AMNESIA GAME. SINCE YOU WON'T STOP IT, YOU'RE GOING TO BED.
YOU CAN LET ME KNOW IF YOU WANT TO BE SERIOUS.
* WINK *
WATTERSON
AAUUGHH! MISTER, THERE'S A TIGER IN THIS ROOM!!

# Calvin and Hobbes

by WATTERSON

I'M HOME!

AUUGH! YAAAA

I THOUGHT THAT AFTER SEVEN BORING HOURS AT SCHOOL, YOU MIGHT APPRECIATE ONE MOMENT OF PURE, ABJECT TERROR.

LET ME UP TO GET MY BAT AND I'LL THANK YOU.

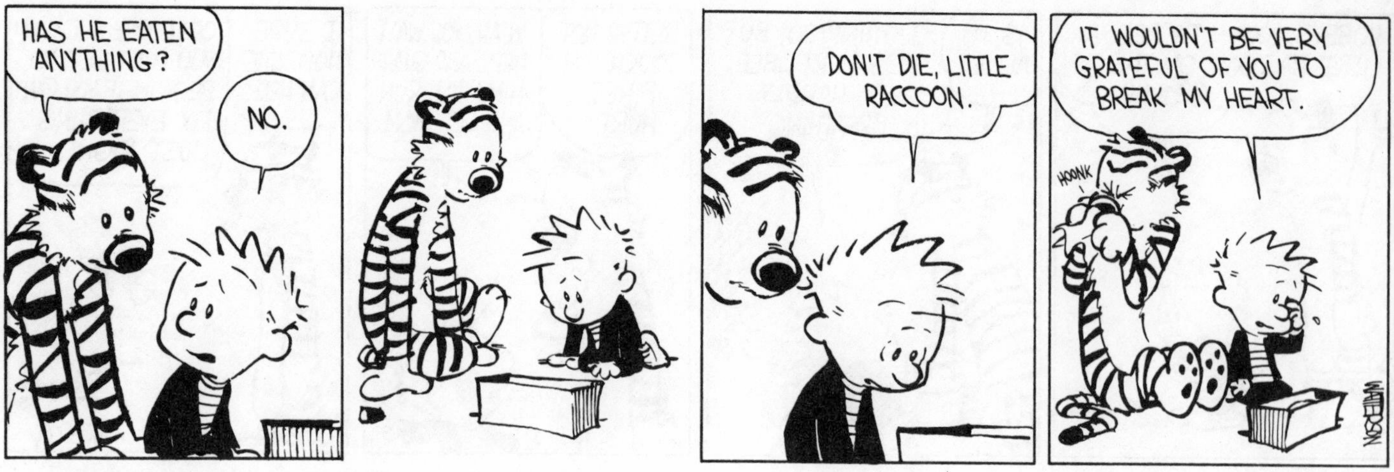
HAS HE EATEN ANYTHING?
NO.
DON'T DIE, LITTLE RACCOON.
IT WOULDN'T BE VERY GRATEFUL OF YOU TO BREAK MY HEART.
HOONK

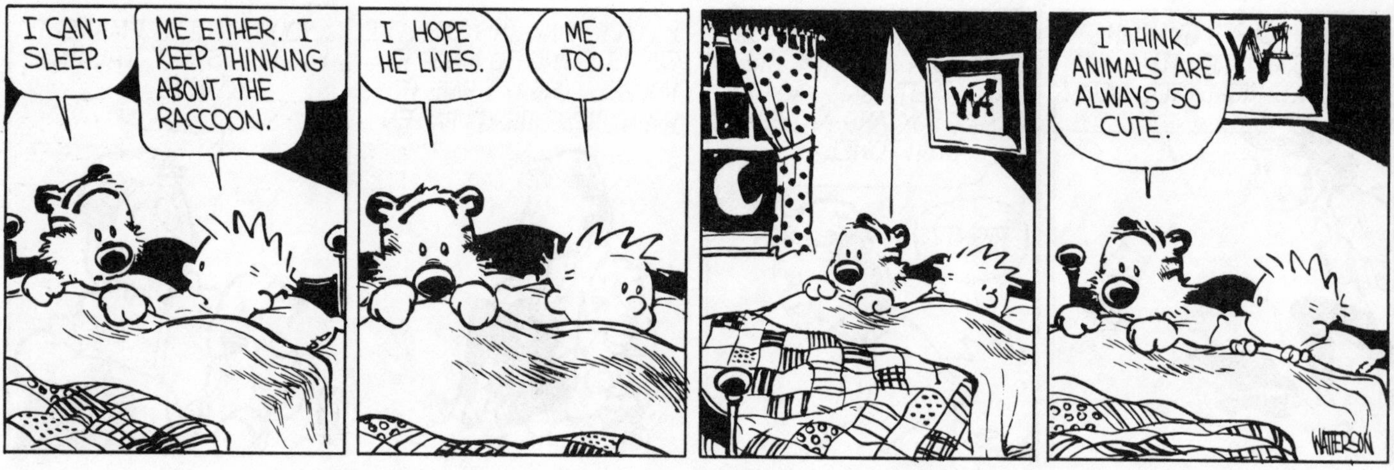
I CAN'T SLEEP.
ME EITHER. I KEEP THINKING ABOUT THE RACCOON.
I HOPE HE LIVES.
ME TOO.
I THINK ANIMALS ARE ALWAYS SO CUTE.

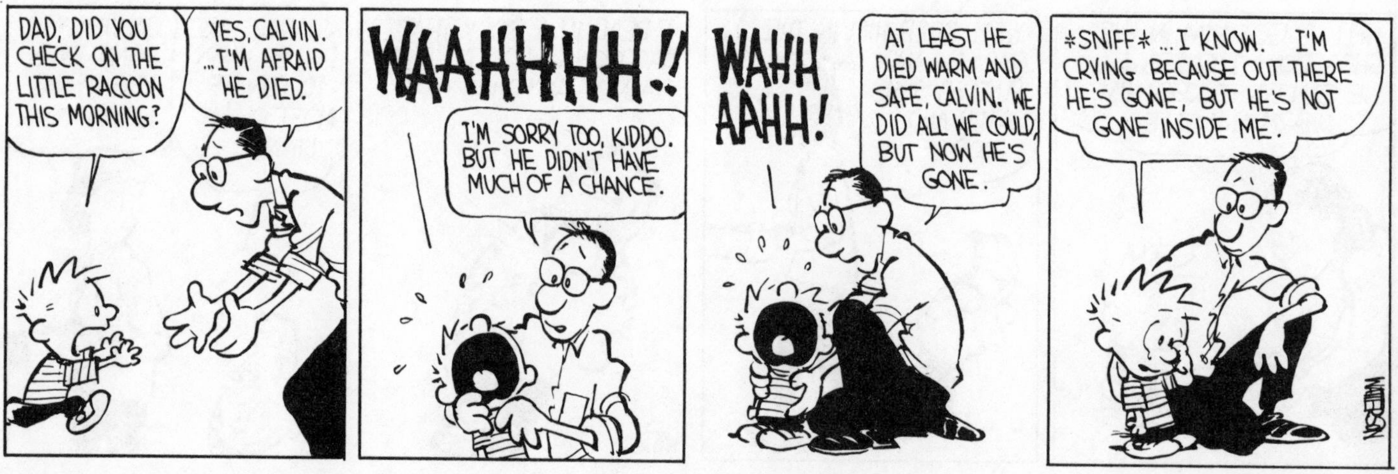
DAD, DID YOU CHECK ON THE LITTLE RACCOON THIS MORNING?
YES, CALVIN. ...I'M AFRAID HE DIED.
WAAHHHH!!
I'M SORRY TOO, KIDDO. BUT HE DIDN'T HAVE MUCH OF A CHANCE.
WAHH AAHH!
AT LEAST HE DIED WARM AND SAFE, CALVIN. WE DID ALL WE COULD, BUT NOW HE'S GONE.
*SNIFF* ...I KNOW. I'M CRYING BECAUSE OUT THERE HE'S GONE, BUT HE'S NOT GONE INSIDE ME.

THIS IS WHERE DAD BURIED THE LITTLE RACCOON.

I DIDN'T EVEN KNOW HE EXISTED A FEW DAYS AGO AND NOW HE'S GONE FOREVER. IT'S LIKE I FOUND HIM FOR NO REASON. I HAD TO SAY GOOD-BYE AS SOON AS I SAID HELLO.

STILL... IN A SAD, AWFUL, TERRIBLE WAY, I'M HAPPY I MET HIM.

*SNIFF*

WHAT A STUPID WORLD.

YOU KNOW, HOBBES, I CAN'T FIGURE OUT THIS DEATH STUFF.

WHY DID THAT LITTLE RACCOON HAVE TO DIE? HE DIDN'T DO ANYTHING WRONG.

HE WAS JUST LITTLE! WHAT'S THE POINT OF PUTTING HIM HERE AND TAKING HIM BACK SO SOON?!?

IT'S EITHER MEAN OR IT'S ARBITRARY, AND EITHER WAY I'VE GOT THE HEEBIE-JEEBIES.

WHY IS IT ALWAYS NIGHT WHEN WE TALK ABOUT THESE THINGS?

MOM SAYS DEATH IS AS NATURAL AS BIRTH, AND IT'S ALL PART OF THE LIFE CYCLE.

SHE SAYS WE DON'T REALLY UNDERSTAND IT, BUT THERE ARE MANY THINGS WE DON'T UNDERSTAND, AND WE JUST HAVE TO DO THE BEST WE CAN WITH THE KNOWLEDGE WE HAVE.

I GUESS THAT MAKES SENSE.

...BUT DON'T *YOU* GO ANYWHERE.

DON'T WORRY.

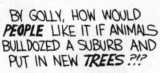

227

# CalVin and HobbES

by WATTERSON

KABLOOIE!

OOOOH, YOU'VE TWICKED ME FOR THE WAST TIME, WABBIT!

---

HA HA HA! BOY, I WISH *I* HAD SOME DYNAMITE!

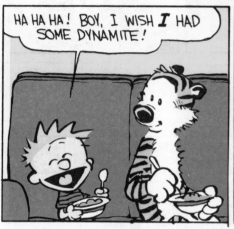

BOY, I LOVE WEEKENDS! WHAT BETTER WAY TO SPEND ONE'S FREEDOM THAN EATING CHOCOLATE CEREAL AND WATCHING CARTOONS!

MM... I BEG TO DIFFER ON THE CEREAL PART.

CALVIN, YOU'VE BEEN SITTING IN FRONT OF THAT STUPID TV ALL MORNING! IT'S A BEAUTIFUL DAY! YOU SHOULD BE OUTSIDE!

---

IT'S GOING TO BE A GRIM DAY WHEN THE WORLD IS RUN BY A GENERATION THAT DOESN'T KNOW ANYTHING BUT WHAT IT'S SEEN ON TV!

click

HEY!

HOW CAN YOU SIT INSIDE ALL DAY? GO ON! OUT! OUT!

KIDS ARE SUPPOSED TO RUN AROUND IN THE FRESH AIR! HAVE SOME FUN! GET SOME EXERCISE!

WATTERSON

---

SLAM!

WELL, I GUESS THAT'S THAT. COME ON.

HI, SUSIE, ARE YOU WATCHING TV? CAN WE COME IN?

SURE, HURRY UP! IT'S A COMMERCIAL.

229

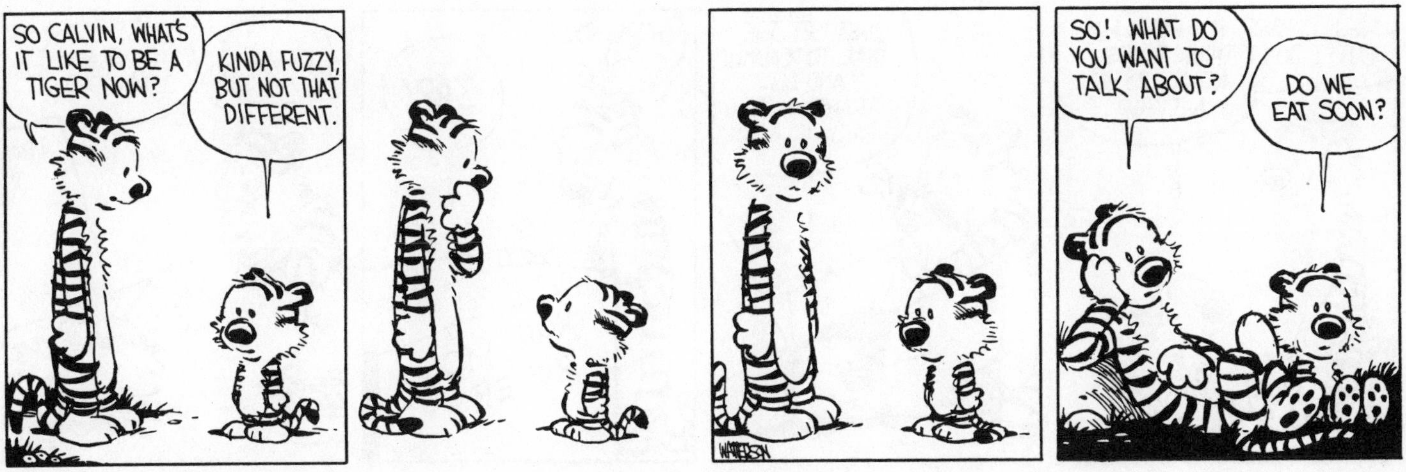
SO CALVIN, WHAT'S IT LIKE TO BE A TIGER NOW?
KINDA FUZZY, BUT NOT THAT DIFFERENT.
SO! WHAT DO YOU WANT TO TALK ABOUT?
DO WE EAT SOON?
WATTERSON

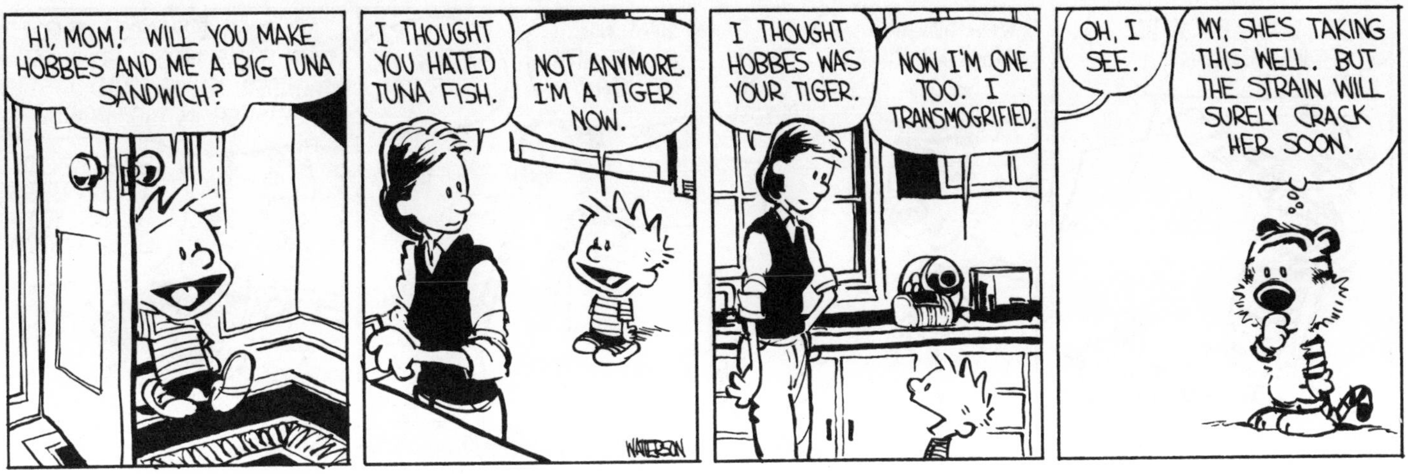
HI, MOM! WILL YOU MAKE HOBBES AND ME A BIG TUNA SANDWICH?
I THOUGHT YOU HATED TUNA FISH.
NOT ANYMORE. I'M A TIGER NOW.
WATTERSON
I THOUGHT HOBBES WAS YOUR TIGER.
NOW I'M ONE TOO. I TRANSMOGRIFIED.
OH, I SEE.
MY, SHE'S TAKING THIS WELL. BUT THE STRAIN WILL SURELY CRACK HER SOON.

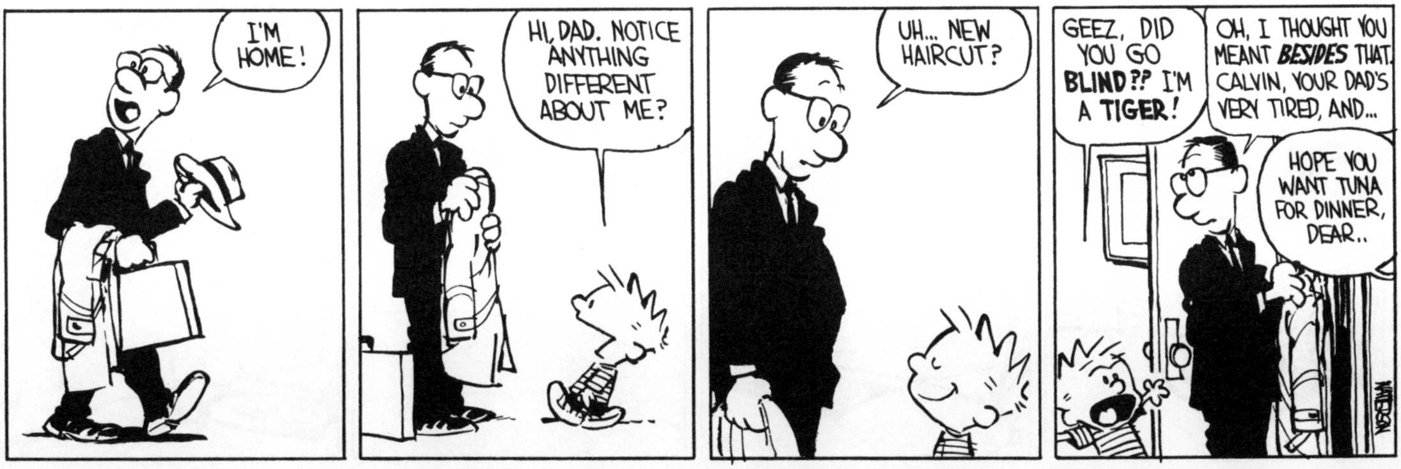
I'M HOME!
HI, DAD. NOTICE ANYTHING DIFFERENT ABOUT ME?
UH... NEW HAIRCUT?
GEEZ, DID YOU GO **BLIND**?? I'M A **TIGER**!
OH, I THOUGHT YOU MEANT ***BESIDES*** THAT. CALVIN, YOUR DAD'S VERY TIRED, AND...
HOPE YOU WANT TUNA FOR DINNER, DEAR..
WATTERSON

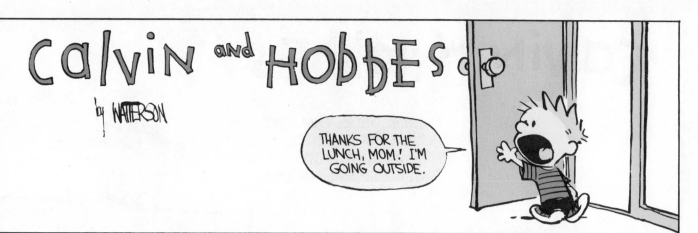

# CalViN aNd HobbES

by WATTERSON

Look, Jane. See Spot.
See Spot run.
Run, Spot, run.
Jane sees Spot run.

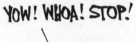
WAY TO GO, JANE!

BOY, I HATE HOMEWORK.

YAHH! WHOOP! HEY!

YOW! WHOA! STOP! GALOOP GALOOP

AAAUGHH!!

GAACKK! HELP! HELP!

WHAP!!

BONK! BONK!

WHAT ON EARTH ARE YOU *DOING?* WHERE'S YOUR HOMEWORK?

I COULDN'T CONCENTRATE.

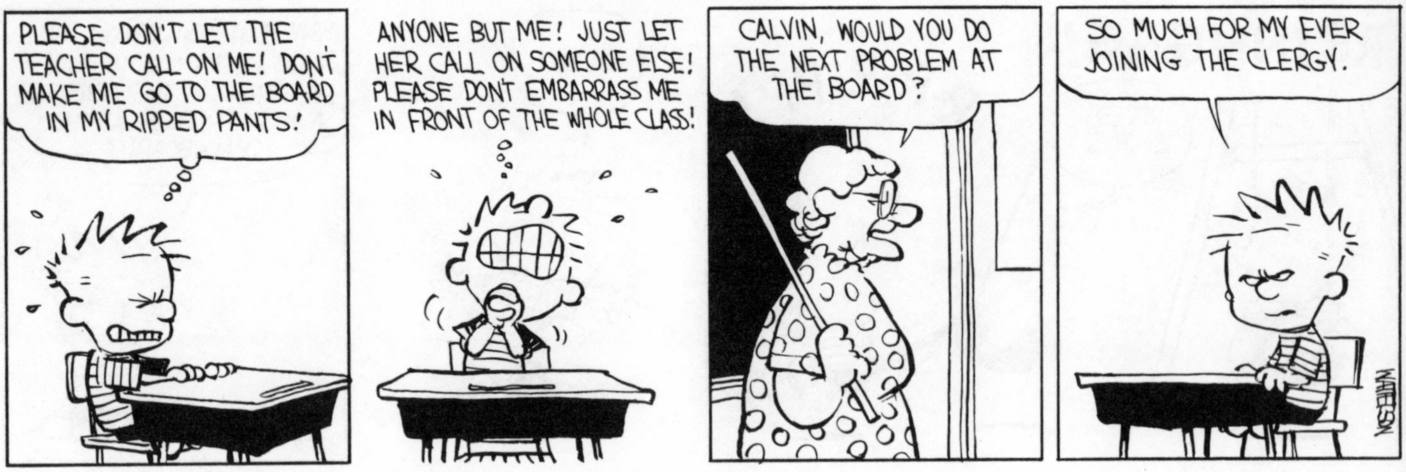
PLEASE DON'T LET THE TEACHER CALL ON ME! DON'T MAKE ME GO TO THE BOARD IN MY RIPPED PANTS!
ANYONE BUT ME! JUST LET HER CALL ON SOMEONE ELSE! PLEASE DON'T EMBARRASS ME IN FRONT OF THE WHOLE CLASS!
CALVIN, WOULD YOU DO THE NEXT PROBLEM AT THE BOARD?
SO MUCH FOR MY EVER JOINING THE CLERGY.

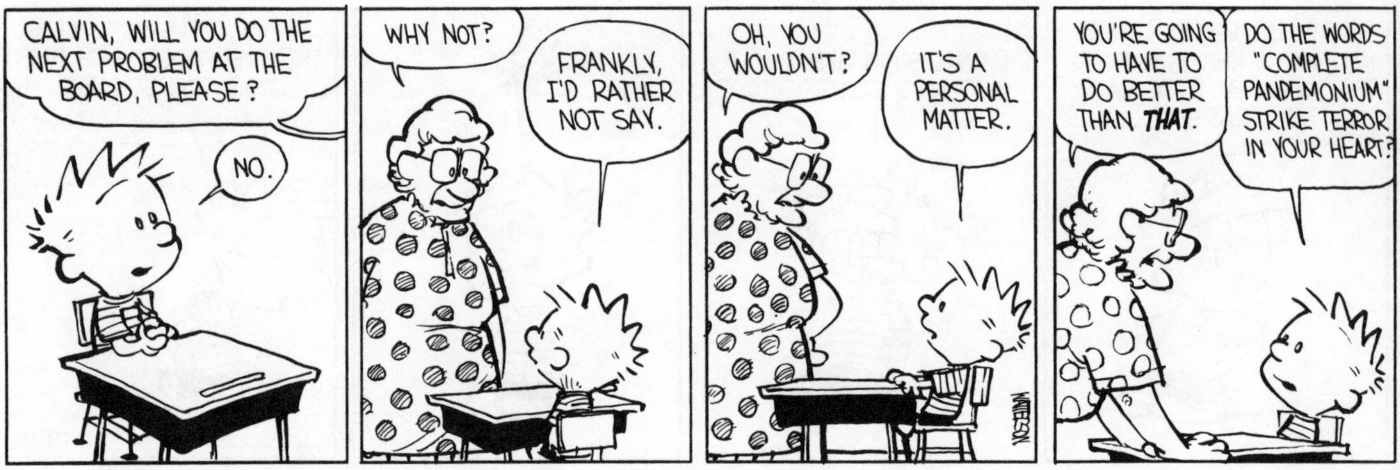
CALVIN, WILL YOU DO THE NEXT PROBLEM AT THE BOARD, PLEASE?
NO.
WHY NOT?
FRANKLY, I'D RATHER NOT SAY.
OH, YOU WOULDN'T?
IT'S A PERSONAL MATTER.
YOU'RE GOING TO HAVE TO DO BETTER THAN ***THAT***.
DO THE WORDS "COMPLETE PANDEMONIUM" STRIKE TERROR IN YOUR HEART?

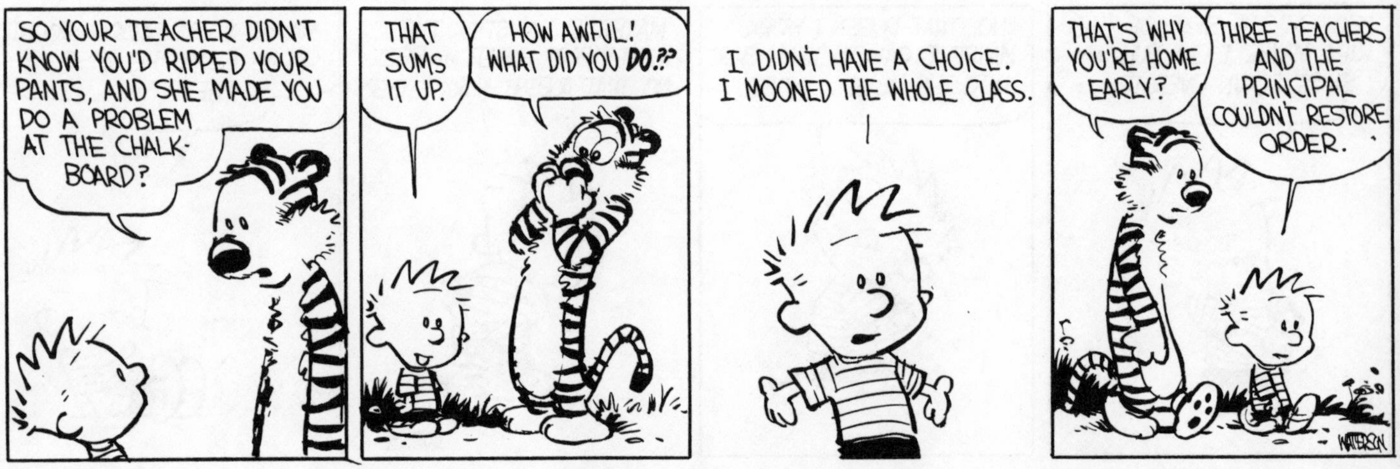
SO YOUR TEACHER DIDN'T KNOW YOU'D RIPPED YOUR PANTS, AND SHE MADE YOU DO A PROBLEM AT THE CHALKBOARD?
THAT SUMS IT UP.
HOW AWFUL! WHAT DID YOU ***DO?!?***
I DIDN'T HAVE A CHOICE. I MOONED THE WHOLE CLASS.
THAT'S WHY YOU'RE HOME EARLY?
THREE TEACHERS AND THE PRINCIPAL COULDN'T RESTORE ORDER.

238

Mr. Jones lives 50 miles away from you. You both leave home at 5:00 and drive toward each other.

Mr. Jones travels at 35 mph., and you drive at 40 mph. At what time will you pass Mr. Jones on the road?

GIVEN THE TRAFFIC AROUND HERE at 5:00, WHO KNOWS?

I ALWAYS CATCH THESE TRICK QUESTIONS.

I'VE GOT A SCHEME TO GET US SOME MONEY.

OH BOY.

SEE? I SNEAKED ALL THESE KERNELS OF CORN OFF MY DINNER PLATE TONIGHT.

HOW IS THAT GOING TO GET US MONEY?

EASY. I JUST STICK THEM UNDER MY PILLOW.

WITH ANY LUCK, THE TOOTH FAIRY WON'T KNOW THEY'RE FAKES UNTIL IT'S TOO LATE!

DAD, HOW DO PEOPLE MAKE BABIES?

MOST PEOPLE JUST GO TO SEARS, BUY THE KIT, AND FOLLOW THE ASSEMBLY INSTRUCTIONS.

I CAME FROM SEARS??

NO, YOU WERE A BLUE LIGHT SPECIAL AT K MART. ALMOST AS GOOD, AND A LOT CHEAPER.

AAUU GHHH!

DEAR, WHAT ARE YOU TELLING CALVIN NOW?!

HOW COME YOU DON'T PUT ON ANY PAJAMAS?

FACT IS, I NEVER TAKE 'EM OFF!

DID YOU WASH YOUR FACE AND BRUSH YOUR TEETH?

YEP! WE BOTH DID!

OK THEN, GOOD NIGHT.

GOOD NIGHT.

MOVE OVER, WILL YA?

I'M ALREADY OVER! *YOU* SHOULD BE OVER *THERE*!

QUIT PUSHING, FUZZ-FOR-BRAINS! YOU'RE ON *MY* SIDE!

CALL ME NAMES, WILL YOU?!

YEAH!

WHUMPP!

YAAAAH! AAAAH! OH NO!

OK! OK! YOU WIN!

PHOO... I WISH YOU HAD BRUSHED YOUR TEETH!

YECCH... I WISH YOU HAD WASHED YOUR FACE!

I'VE GOT TO GIVE A 5-MINUTE ORAL REPORT IN SCHOOL ON THURSDAY.

WE'RE SUPPOSED TO RESEARCH OUR SUBJECT, WRITE IT UP, AND PRESENT IT TO THE CLASS WITH A VISUAL AID.

THAT'S A BIG ASSIGNMENT.

I'LL SAY. I HATE MY TEACHER.

SHE KNOWS WE'LL ALL DO IT ON THE LAST EVENING, BUT SHE GAVE US THREE DAYS TO WORRY ABOUT IT.

WHAT'S THE SUBJECT OF YOUR REPORT?

THE BRAIN.

WHAT DO YOU KNOW ABOUT BRAINS?

WELL, I SAW THIS MOVIE WHERE THEY KEPT THIS GUY'S BRAIN ALIVE IN A TANK OF WATER.

THEN A POWER SURGE MUTATED THE BRAIN, AND IT CRAWLED OUT AND TERRORIZED THE POPULACE.

THAT'S INFORMATIVE.

UNFORTUNATELY FOR MY REPORT, MOM CAUGHT ME, AND I DIDN'T GET TO SEE HOW IT ENDED.

I'VE GOT TO GIVE MY REPORT ON "THE BRAIN" AT SCHOOL TODAY.

SEE MY VISUAL AID? I COOKED SOME NOODLES AND PUT THEM IN A PAPER BAG. DOESN'T THAT LOOK LIKE BRAINS?

UGH.

WELL, I GUESS I'M ALL SET.

DID YOU WRITE YOUR REPORT YET?

NAH. I BORROWED MOM'S POCKET DICTIONARY. I'LL DO IT ON THE BUS.

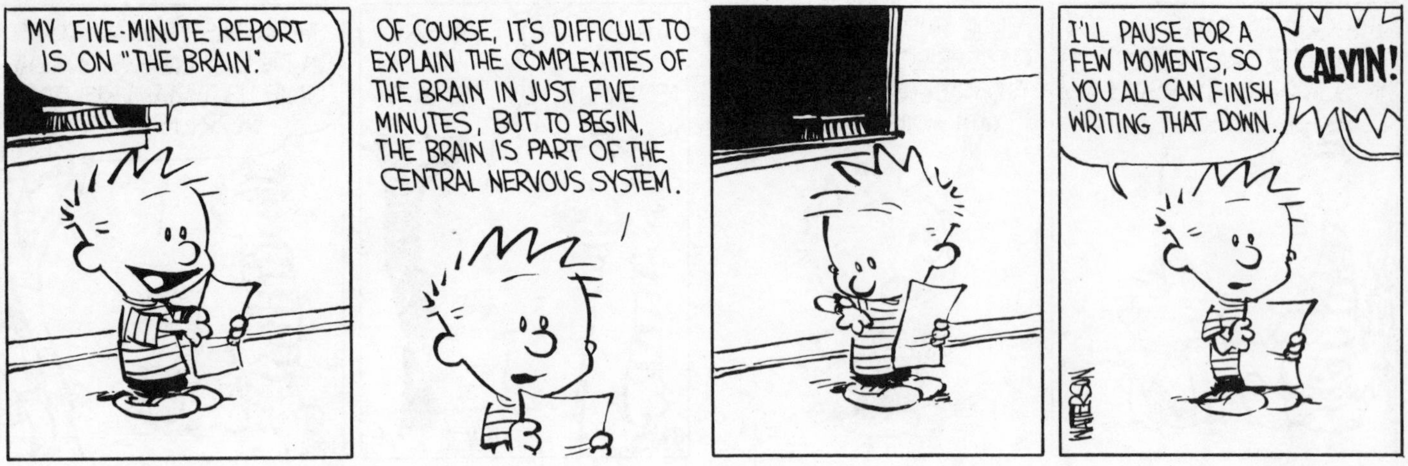
MY FIVE-MINUTE REPORT IS ON "THE BRAIN."
OF COURSE, IT'S DIFFICULT TO EXPLAIN THE COMPLEXITIES OF THE BRAIN IN JUST FIVE MINUTES, BUT TO BEGIN, THE BRAIN IS PART OF THE CENTRAL NERVOUS SYSTEM.
I'LL PAUSE FOR A FEW MOMENTS, SO YOU ALL CAN FINISH WRITING THAT DOWN.
CALVIN!

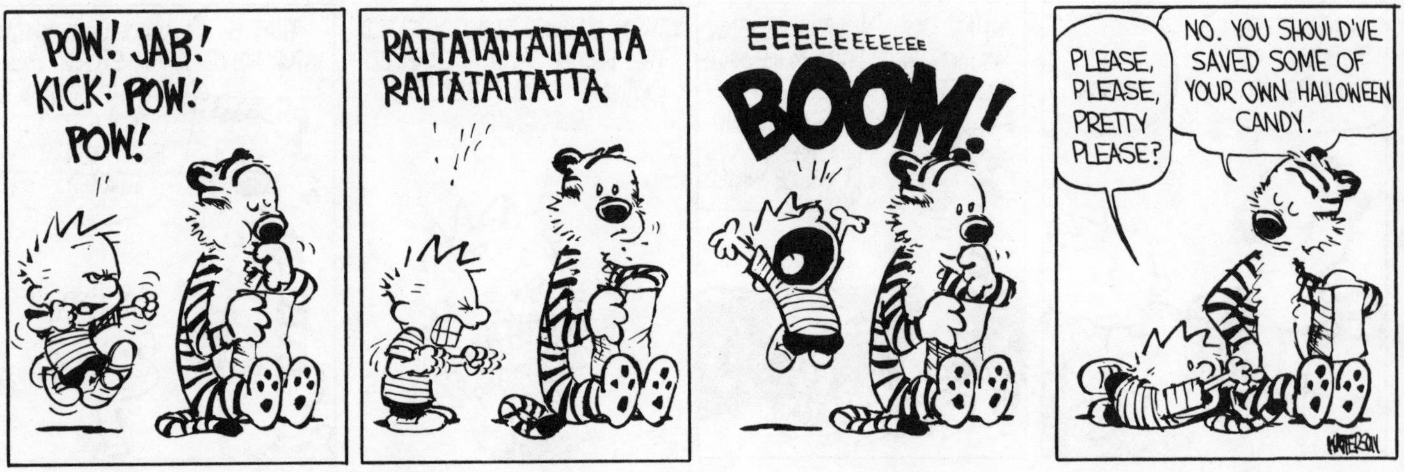
POW! JAB! KICK! POW! POW!
RATTATATTATTATTA RATTATATTATTA
EEEEEEEEEEE
BOOM!
PLEASE, PLEASE, PRETTY PLEASE?
NO. YOU SHOULD'VE SAVED SOME OF YOUR OWN HALLOWEEN CANDY.

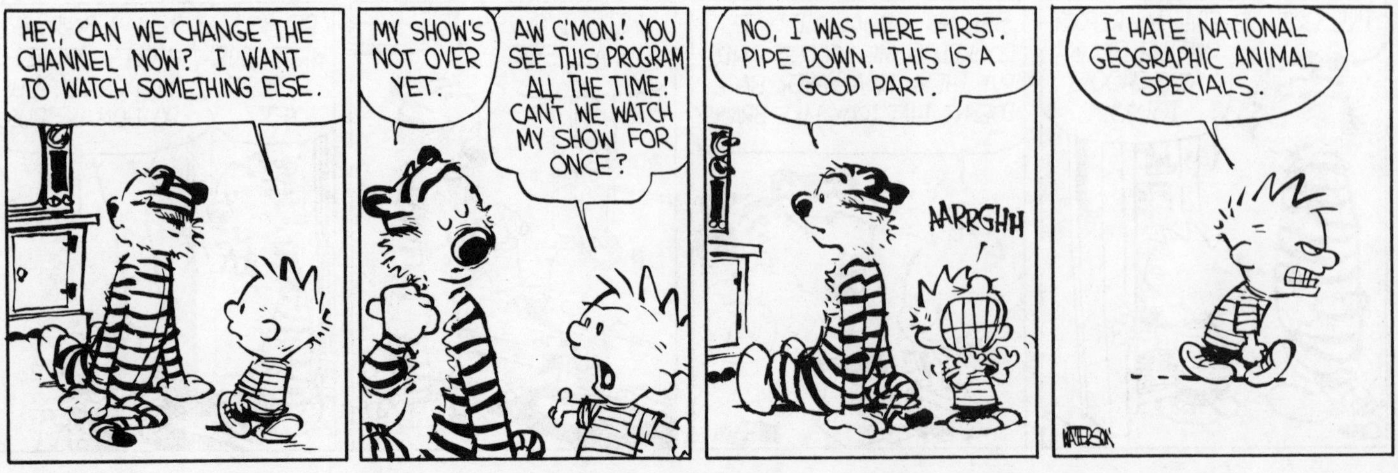
HEY, CAN WE CHANGE THE CHANNEL NOW? I WANT TO WATCH SOMETHING ELSE.
MY SHOW'S NOT OVER YET.
AW C'MON! YOU SEE THIS PROGRAM ALL THE TIME! CAN'T WE WATCH MY SHOW FOR ONCE?
NO, I WAS HERE FIRST. PIPE DOWN. THIS IS A GOOD PART.
AARRGHH
I HATE NATIONAL GEOGRAPHIC ANIMAL SPECIALS.

# Calvin and Hobbes

by WATTERSON

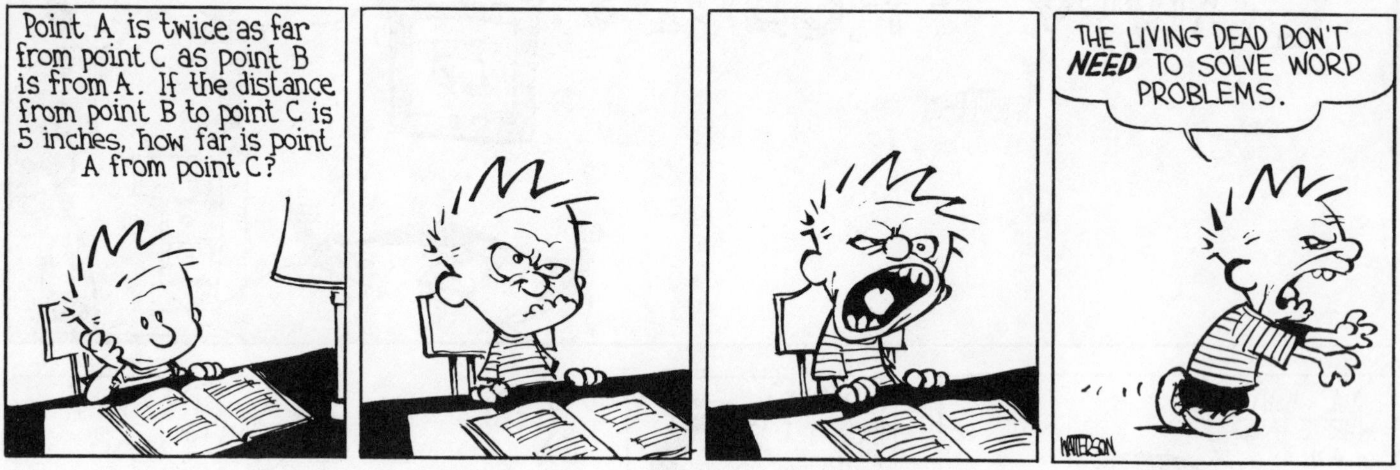
Point A is twice as far from point C as point B is from A. If the distance from point B to point C is 5 inches, how far is point A from point C?
THE LIVING DEAD DON'T **NEED** TO SOLVE WORD PROBLEMS.

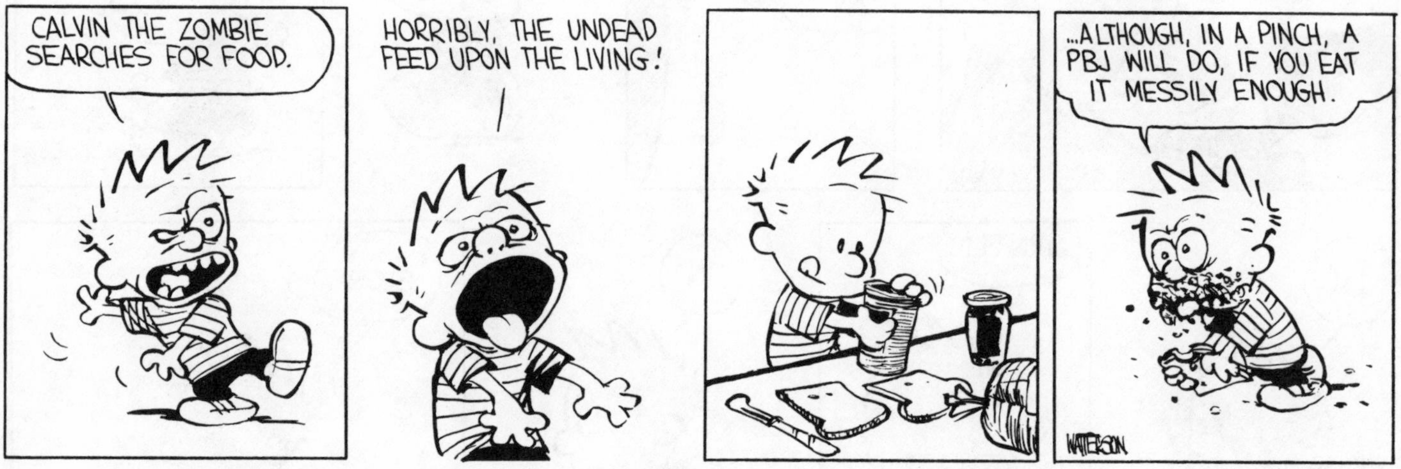
CALVIN THE ZOMBIE SEARCHES FOR FOOD.
HORRIBLY, THE UNDEAD FEED UPON THE LIVING!
...ALTHOUGH, IN A PINCH, A PBJ WILL DO, IF YOU EAT IT MESSILY ENOUGH.

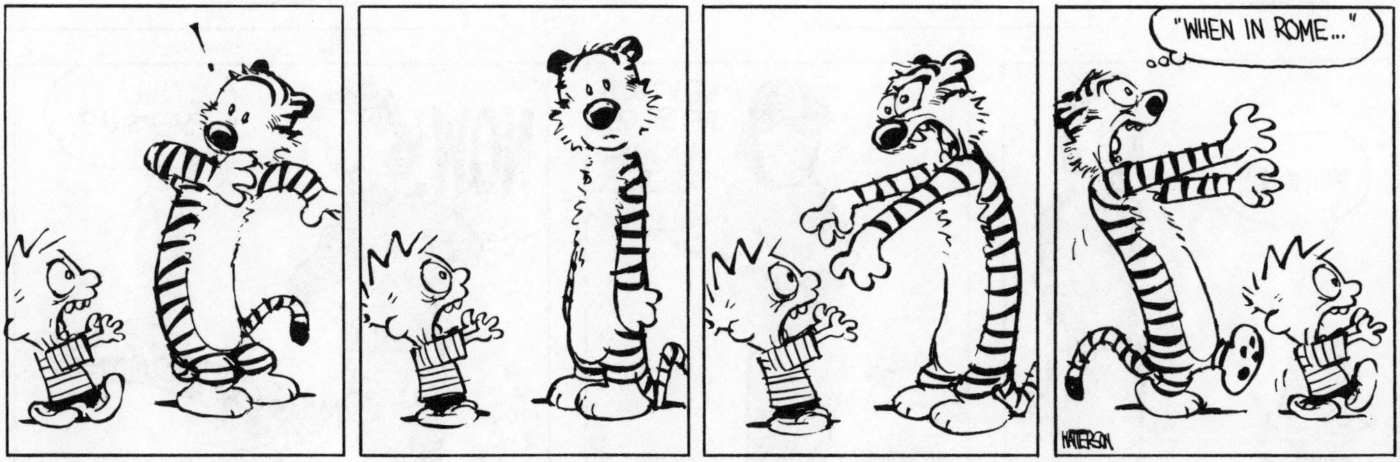
!
"WHEN IN ROME..."

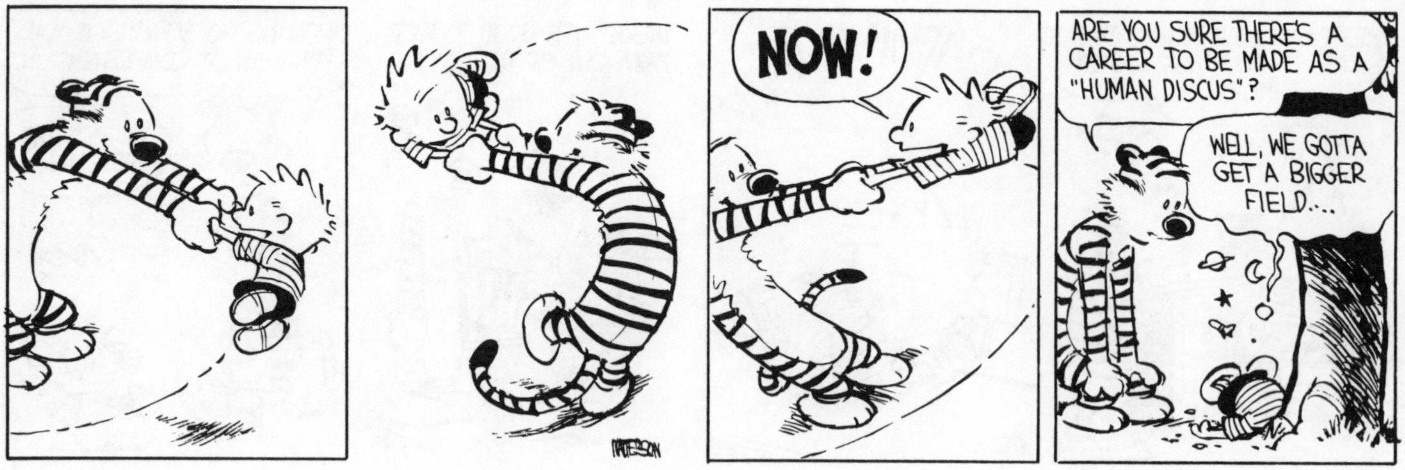
NOW!
ARE YOU SURE THERE'S A CAREER TO BE MADE AS A "HUMAN DISCUS"?
WELL, WE GOTTA GET A BIGGER FIELD...
WATTERSON

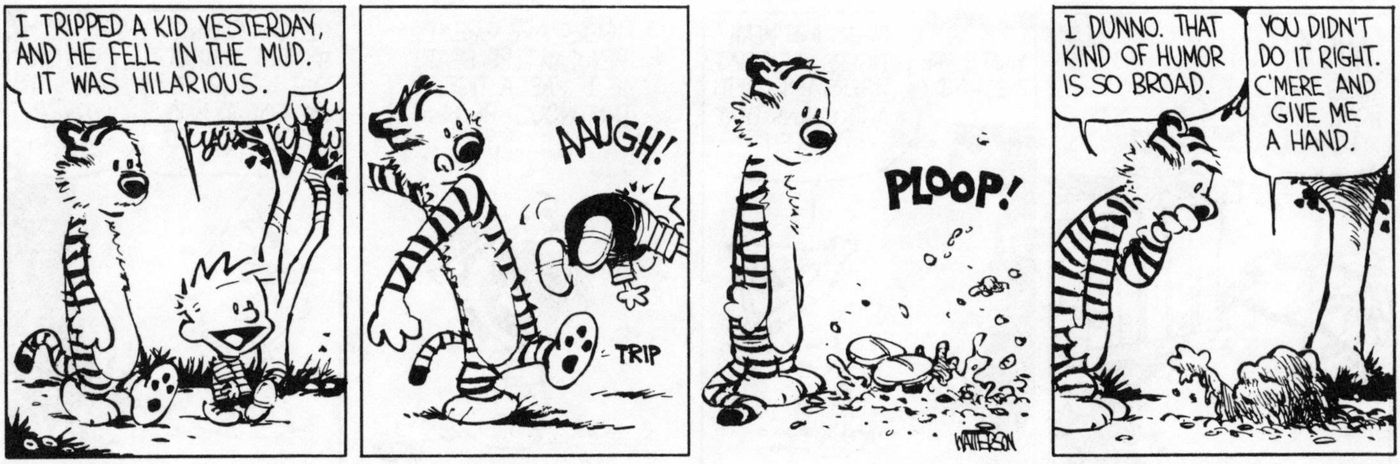
I TRIPPED A KID YESTERDAY, AND HE FELL IN THE MUD. IT WAS HILARIOUS.
AAUGH!
TRIP
PLOOP!
WATTERSON
I DUNNO. THAT KIND OF HUMOR IS SO BROAD.
YOU DIDN'T DO IT RIGHT. C'MERE AND GIVE ME A HAND.

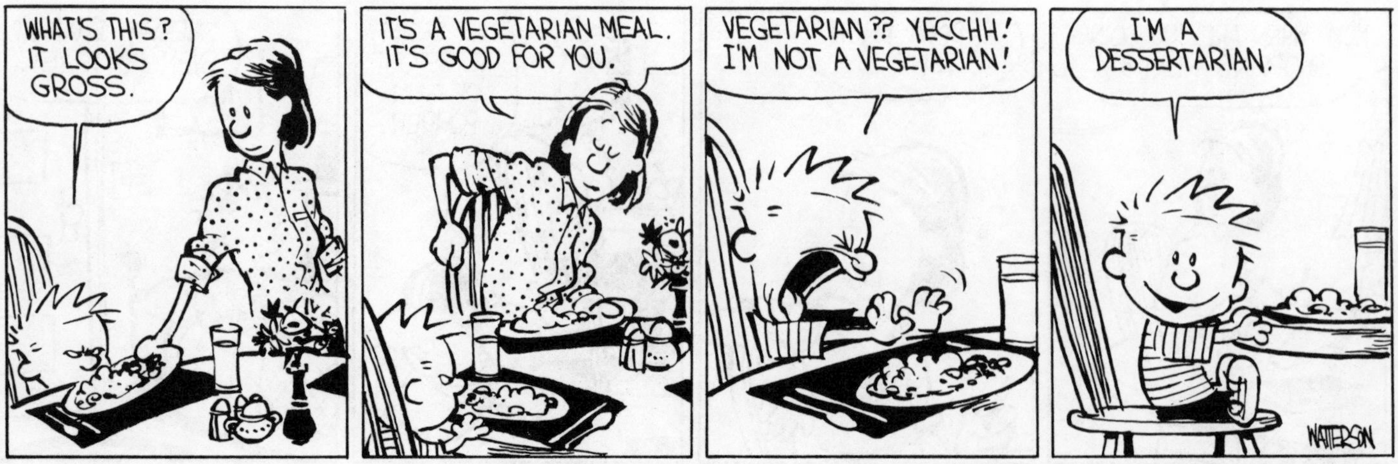
WHAT'S THIS? IT LOOKS GROSS.
IT'S A VEGETARIAN MEAL. IT'S GOOD FOR YOU.
VEGETARIAN?? YECCHH! I'M NOT A VEGETARIAN!
I'M A DESSERTARIAN.
WATTERSON

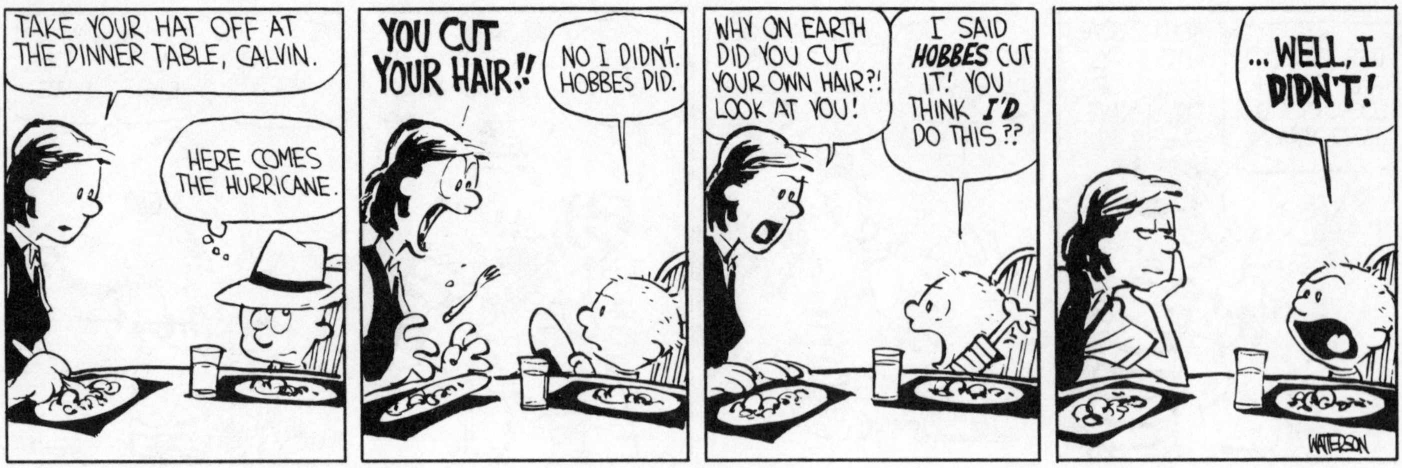
TAKE YOUR HAT OFF AT THE DINNER TABLE, CALVIN.
HERE COMES THE HURRICANE.
YOU CUT YOUR HAIR!!
NO I DIDN'T. HOBBES DID.
WHY ON EARTH DID YOU CUT YOUR OWN HAIR?! LOOK AT YOU!
I SAID HOBBES CUT IT! YOU THINK I'D DO THIS??
...WELL, I DIDN'T!

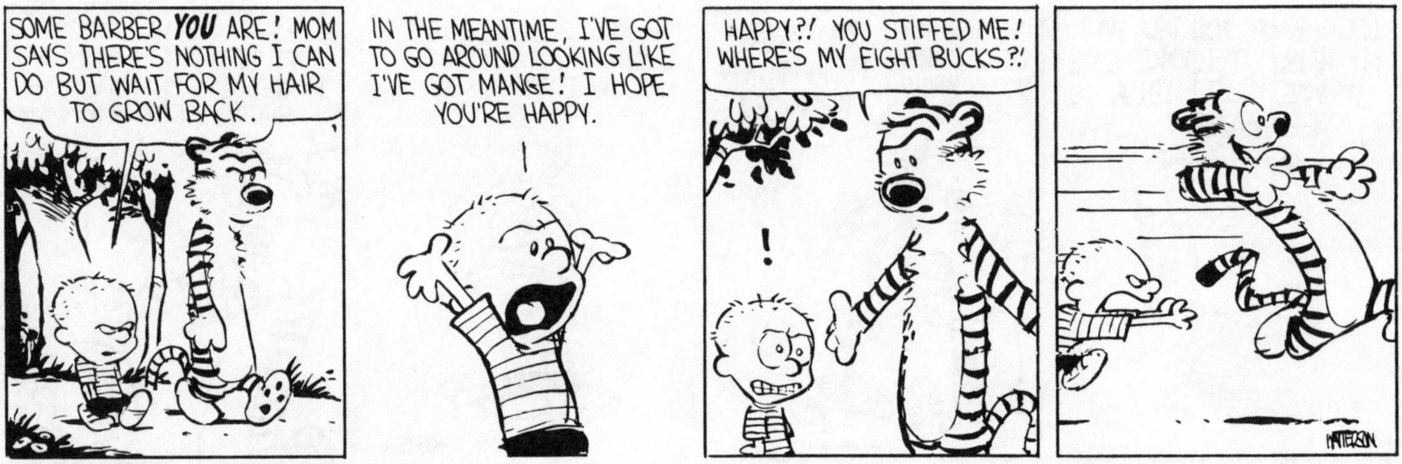
SOME BARBER YOU ARE! MOM SAYS THERE'S NOTHING I CAN DO BUT WAIT FOR MY HAIR TO GROW BACK.
IN THE MEANTIME, I'VE GOT TO GO AROUND LOOKING LIKE I'VE GOT MANGE! I HOPE YOU'RE HAPPY.
HAPPY?! YOU STIFFED ME! WHERE'S MY EIGHT BUCKS?!
!

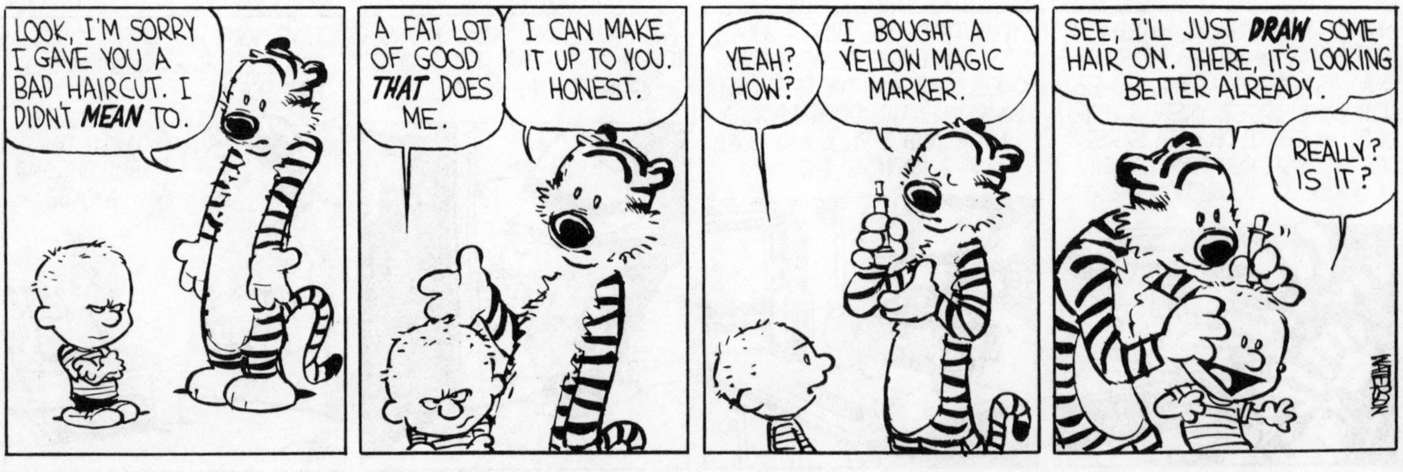
LOOK, I'M SORRY I GAVE YOU A BAD HAIRCUT. I DIDN'T MEAN TO.
A FAT LOT OF GOOD THAT DOES ME.
I CAN MAKE IT UP TO YOU. HONEST.
YEAH? HOW?
I BOUGHT A YELLOW MAGIC MARKER.
SEE, I'LL JUST DRAW SOME HAIR ON. THERE, IT'S LOOKING BETTER ALREADY.
REALLY? IS IT?

WELL, YOUR HAIR DOESN'T STICK UP THE WAY IT USED TO, BUT AT LEAST YOUR HEAD'S YELLOW AGAIN.

THANKS, HOBBES. YOU'RE A REAL LIFE SAVER. I'M SORRY I GOT SO MAD AT YOU.

NONSENSE. NO HARM DONE.

BOY, WAIT TILL I SHOW MOM!

UH OH. DOES IT COME OFF?

FROM NOW ON, JUST KEEP YOUR BRAINY IDEAS TO YOURSELF, OK?

calvin

calvin the GENIUS

calvin the SUPER GENIUS

THIS IS HOW YOU SIGN YOUR REPORTS?

IT KIND OF INCLINES YOU TO READ IT MORE CHARITABLY, DON'T YOU THINK?

CLINK CLINK

MY ICED TEA IS A FAILURE.

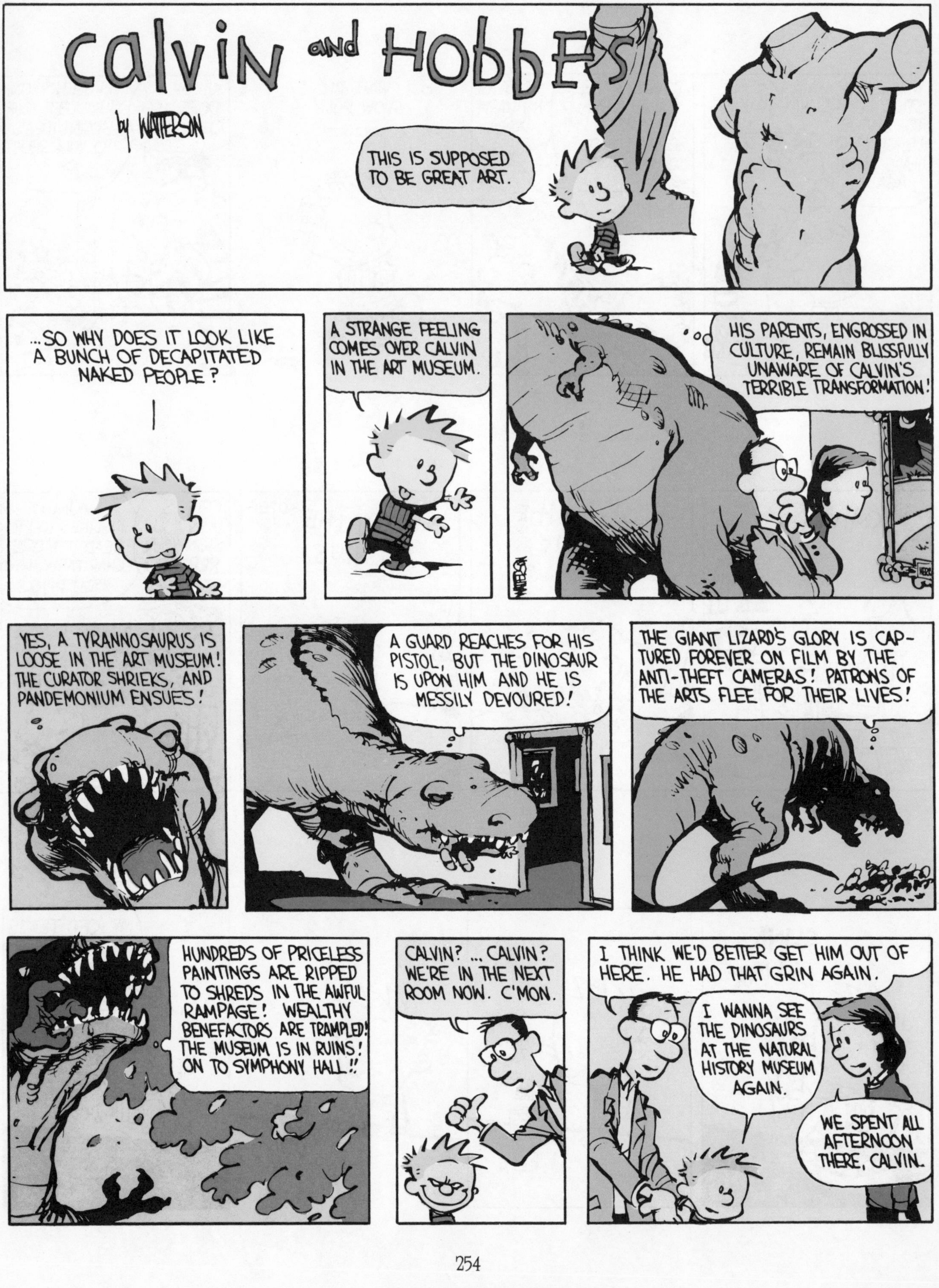

Calvin and HOBBES
by WATTERSON
THIS IS SUPPOSED TO BE GREAT ART.
...SO WHY DOES IT LOOK LIKE A BUNCH OF DECAPITATED NAKED PEOPLE?
A STRANGE FEELING COMES OVER CALVIN IN THE ART MUSEUM.
HIS PARENTS, ENGROSSED IN CULTURE, REMAIN BLISSFULLY UNAWARE OF CALVIN'S TERRIBLE TRANSFORMATION!
YES, A TYRANNOSAURUS IS LOOSE IN THE ART MUSEUM! THE CURATOR SHRIEKS, AND PANDEMONIUM ENSUES!
A GUARD REACHES FOR HIS PISTOL, BUT THE DINOSAUR IS UPON HIM AND HE IS MESSILY DEVOURED!
THE GIANT LIZARD'S GLORY IS CAPTURED FOREVER ON FILM BY THE ANTI-THEFT CAMERAS! PATRONS OF THE ARTS FLEE FOR THEIR LIVES!
HUNDREDS OF PRICELESS PAINTINGS ARE RIPPED TO SHREDS IN THE AWFUL RAMPAGE! WEALTHY BENEFACTORS ARE TRAMPLED! THE MUSEUM IS IN RUINS! ON TO SYMPHONY HALL!!
CALVIN? ... CALVIN? WE'RE IN THE NEXT ROOM NOW. C'MON.
I THINK WE'D BETTER GET HIM OUT OF HERE. HE HAD THAT GRIN AGAIN.
I WANNA SEE THE DINOSAURS AT THE NATURAL HISTORY MUSEUM AGAIN.
WE SPENT ALL AFTERNOON THERE, CALVIN.

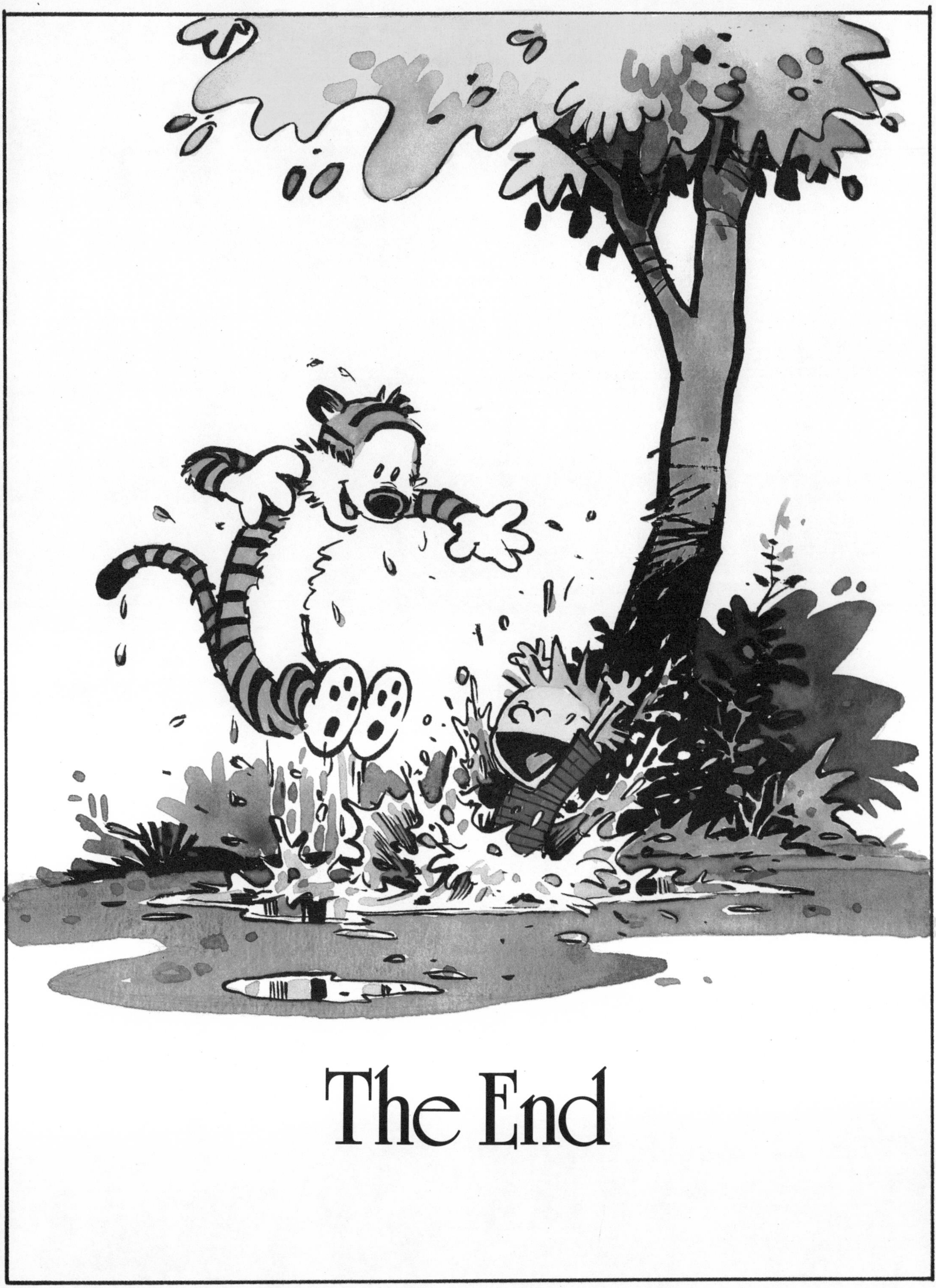

# The End